Spiritual Titanism

SUNY Series in
Constructive Postmodern Thought
David Ray Giffin, editor

David Ray Griffin, editor, *The Reenchantment of Science: Postmodern Proposals*
David Ray Giffin, editor, *Spirituality and Society: Postmodern Visions*
David Ray Giffin, *God and Religion in the Postmodern World: Essays in Postmodern Theology*
David Ray Giffin, William A. Beardslee, and Joe Holland, *Varieties of Postmodern Theology*
David Ray Giffin and Huston Smith, *Primordial Truth and Postmodern Theology*
David Ray Giffin, editor, *Sacred Interconnections: Postmodern Spirituality, Political Economy, and Art*
Robert Inchausti, *The Ignorant Perfection of Ordinary People*
David W. Orr, *Ecological Literacy: Education and the Transition to a Postmodern World*
David Ray Griffin, John B. Cobb Jr., Marcus P. Ford, Pete A. Y. Gunter, and Peter Ochs, *Founders of Constructive Postmodern Philosophy: Peirce, James, Bergson, Whitehead, and E. A. Hartshorne*
David Ray Griffin and Richard A. Falk, editors, *Postmodern Politics for a Planet in Crisis: Policy, Process, and Presidential Vision*
Steve Odin, *The Social Self in Zen and American Pragmatism*
Frederick Ferré, *Being and Value: Toward a Constructive Postmodern Metaphysics*
Frederick Ferré, *Knowing and Value: Toward a Constructive Postmodern Epistemology*
Sandra B. Lubarsky and David Ray Griffin, editors, *Jewish Theology and Process Thought*
David Ray Griffin, *Parapsychology, Philosophy, and Spirituality: A Postmodern Exploration*
Jay Earley, *Transforming Human Culture: Social Evolution and the Planetary Crisis*
Daniel A. Dombrowski, *Kazantzakis and God*
E. M. Adams, *A Society Fit for Human Beings*
Jerry H. Gill, *The Tacit Mode: Michael Polanyi's Postmodern Philosophy*

SPIRITUAL TITANISM

Indian, Chinese, and Western Perspectives

Nicholas F. Gier

State University of New York Press

Published by
State University of New York Press, Albany

Printed in the United States of America

For information, address State University of New York Press, State University Plaza, Albany, N.Y., 12246

Production by Diane Ganeles
Marketing by Fran Keneston

Library of Congress Cataloging-in-Publication Data

Gier, Nicholas F., 1944–
Spiritual titanism : Indian, Chinese, and Western perspectives / Nicholas F. Gier.
p. cm. — (SUNY series in constructive postmodern thought)
Includes bibliographical references and index.
ISBN 0–7914–4527–5 (hardcover : alk. paper) —
ISBN 0–7914–4528–3 (pbk. : alk. paper)
1. Religion—Philosophy. 2. Superman (Philosophical concept) 3. Philosophy, Comparative. 4. Religions. 5. Hinduism—Philosophy. I. Title. II. Series

BL51.G625 2000
291.2'13—dc21 99-038494

10 9 8 7 6 5 4 3 2 1

To my father and mother
In loving memory

The majestic aloofness of the perfected, balanced, absolutely self-contained figure of the [Jaina] saint becomes emphasized in its triumphant isolation. The image of the released one seems to be neither animate nor inanimate, but pervaded by a strange and timeless calm. It is human in shape and feature, yet as inhuman as an icicle; . . . [the saint] stands supernally motionless, absolutely unconcerned about the worshipping, jubilant crowds that throng around his feet.

Heinrich Zimmer, *Philosophies of India*

Contents

Preface

> What matters most for India is not so much the salvation of the personality as the acquisition of absolute freedom.
>
> —Mircea Eliade[1]

> In the millennium to come we are meant to become Gods on other planets. This is the great potential of our Divinity.
>
> —Gopi Krishna[2]

> The whole ascetic tradition . . . springs from that most polluted of all sources, the Satanic sin of pride, the desire to be "like gods." We are not gods, we are social irrational animals, designed to become rational, social animals. . . .
>
> —R. C. Zaehner[3]

The idea for this book arose out of an insight I had about the use of the term *humanism* by the Religious Right. The typical conservative Christian describes a humanist as one who attempts to move God aside and to take God's place. For such a Christian, humanism is Titanism, a worldview in which human beings take on divine attributes and divine prerogatives. (The Religious Right is especially keen on maintaining God's right to set the laws of human conduct.) As I show in chapter 1, some existentialists express a form of Titanism, but the Religious Right's blanket condemnation does a gross injustice to more moderate forms of humanism, which include Christian humanists as diverse as Aquinas, Erasmus, the American Founding Fathers, and C. S. Lewis.[4] Over the twenty-five years that I have taught Indian philosophy and religion, I have been struck by the number of texts that contain a form of spiritual Titanism, in many ways more extreme than Western Titanism. Whereas the latter humanist rarely, if ever, claims that humans have divine attributes, this *is* the basic view of human nature in Jainism, Sāṃkhya, Yoga, and later Hindu texts.

The spiritual Titanism of India as been obscured by what some have called affirmative Orientalism, a response to the "negative Orientalism" that arose out of the first Western encounters with Indian culture. Negative Orientalism viewed the Indian as an uncivilized, irrational, superstitious, lazy, cowardly, and effeminate man. Edward Said has defined Orientalism as a "Western style of dominating, restructuring, and having authority over the Orient."[5] He sees it as a form of cultural and political Titanism, an expression of the will to power over Asia. Orientalism promoted an invisible combination of cultural and technological knowledge as power. It is, according to Said, a "political doctrine willed over the Orient because the Orient was weaker than the West, which elided the Orient's difference with its weakness."[6] The Orient then became an idea, a representation, an alien Other.

While granting the technological advantage of Western culture, Anne Besant and the theosophists promoted affirmative Orientalism, a view that proclaimed the spiritual superiority of Indian civilization and the nobility of its commitment to the virtues of passivity, nonviolence, and compassion. (Ironically, Gandhi learned to appreciate the value of his own Indian tradition from his association with theosophists in London.) Affirmative Orientalism is still very strong today and Indian philosophy and religion are still viewed by many as the answer to the ills and deficiencies of modern society. A great many Indian scholars, far more sophisticated than Besant, remain committed to the view that their own monistic metaphysics is the proper response to the anthropocentric philosophies of the West.[7] This book will remind readers that some Indian philosophies are dualistic (even Manichean) and that some are even more human-centered than Western humanism.

I submit that affirmative Orientalism is just as guilty of making the Indian an alien Other, even though this Other is dressed in attractive soteriological garb. Both forms of Orientalism cover up the roots of our common humanity and the view that the human mind, even though profoundly affected by culture, is capable of experiencing the world and conceiving of philosophical problems in very similar ways. In his classic work *Mysticism East and West*, Rudolph Otto showed that the basic idea of the union of human soul with the divine was common to Christianity and Hinduism. (The fact that Christian mystics find themselves at the margins of society rather than at the center, where their Asian counterparts sit, is simply a cultural variation.) More popular (and less accurate) works such as Aldous Huxley's *Perennial Philosophy* have given the false impression that mysticism is the Asian philosophy par excellence. More egregious yet, some have claimed that Asian mysticism anticipates the theories of contemporary physics. Such views overlook the fact that the original philosophies of India—Jainism and Sāṃkhya—assert the radical autonomy of the individual rather than its dissolution into a divine One. Just as the Western mind is capable of mystical thought, so is the Asian mind equally able to think of human beings as individual and isolated as well. We will find that the isolated *jīva* and *puruṣa* souls of Jainism and Sāṃkhya are the main sources of Indian Titanism. In answer to Kipling's famous line "Never the twain shall meet," one could say that East and West did "meet" centuries ago just as they are meeting again today. Goethe said it best: "He who knows himself and others will also recognize that East and West cannot be set apart."[8]

The idea of an Indian Titanism has upset some practitioners of yoga and advocates of other spiritual disciplines. They represent a common view that Asian spirituality is the only answer to Western individualism and technological Titanism. Let me just say for the record that I, too, practice yoga (every day if my schedule allows); and that I have found it to be not only a solution to a lower back problem, but also a recipe for general physical, mental, and emotional well-being. Even here, however, there is surprising confirmation of my thesis in the mantra that I use for my daily meditation. I learned yoga twenty-five years ago from the Ananda Margis. The mantra they gave me was *babanam kaivalyam*, which they translated as "in the name of the father, liberate me." I did not interpret this in terms of the personal theism in which I was raised; rather, I conceived it as Gandhi himself has explained prayer: a petition by the ego self to the Higher Self.[9] But the total inwardness of this meditative state is much more intensified now that I know that the literal meaning of *kaivalya* is being totally isolated, alone, and independent. Is there a basic tendency in human beings, at least in male human beings, to escape nature and the body by Titanistic declarations of autonomy—whether through external domination through technology and politics or by journeys of inward spiritual conquest? I address the issue of gender dynamics in chapter 6—The Yogi and the Goddess—where the goddess religion is offered as a counter to spiritual Titanism.

The fact that I can find personal satisfaction in a discipline whose philosophical foundations I find unsatisfactory has forced me to reconsider the thesis that certain theories of the self—for instance, seeing the self as isolated and self-contained—will necessarily lead to certain practices. Disconfirmation of this thesis is especially strong and dramatic in Jainism, where the goal of the Jaina saint is complete separation from the body and isolation from nature. Not expected by my thesis, however, is the fact that contemporary Jainas are at the forefront of India's environmental movement. Although as a philosopher I am thwarted in my belief that practice ought to follow theory, I rejoice in the fact that, even though they are conceptually handicapped by a Manichean dualism and by an extreme individualism and anthropocentrism, the Jainas can nevertheless be great champions of nonviolence and ecological concern. By the same token I also acknowledge that the Chinese, even though their cosmology of balance and harmony should have helped them, were no more sensitive to their environment than Westerners and had less positive views of nature. Neither were they kinder to their women, although contemporary feminists should celebrate the relational self that one finds in Confucianism.

The discovery that we tend to make both other people and other cultures into the "Other" is the greatest contribution of postmodern thought. An important achievement of modernism, at least initially, was its axiom—exemplified by Descartes's search for clear and distinct ideas—that truth lies in making distinctions and in reducing to simples. A whole set of dualistic distinctions—between fact and value, object and subject, public and private, science and faith, politics and religion, and theory and practice—are the great conceptual landmarks of modernism. (As I will demonstrate in chap. 2, both modernism and its postmodern critique were already nascent in "axial" thinkers in Asia and Europe and that Titanism can be seen as the most negative form of modernism.) More and more, however, these modernist distinctions have been found to be, arguably, the cause of institutionalized racism (a modernist invention),[10] militarism, social disintegration, and environmental degradation. Rather than making the elimination of all otherness the goal—achieved in either a premodern dissolution into the One or an equally amorphous dissipation in Derridean *différance*—I have chosen the constructive postmodernist approach promoted in this SUNY Press series.

The constructive postmodern framework I choose is broader than the one found in the book *Founders of Constructive Postmodern Philosophy: Peirce, James, Bergson, Whitehead, and Hartshorne.*

The common ground is there: major Asian philosophers reject a mechanistic worldview; many are panexperientialists; some propose nonsensuous forms of perception; most preserve the laws of logic. However, only Buddhism and Chinese philosophy reject substance metaphysics and only the Buddha of the Pāli scriptures is arguably a radical empiricist like James. The strongest expressions of pansubjectivism are found in Vedānta and Jainism—*ātman* and *jīva* reside in everything—but we will discover that the former is primarily a premodern philosophy while the Jaina's autonomous self and dualism foreshadow modernism. Therefore, only Buddhism and Confucianism truly anticipate constructive postmodern philosophy. The focus of the book will be the reconstructed self of Buddhism and the naturally social self of Confucianism. I say "naturally" because the Chinese did not ever have a substantial self such as *ātman* to react against, so the self did not have to be reconstructed. With this focus on a social, relational self I choose to embrace the "dialogical" existentialists (defined in chap. 1) as constructive postmodern philosophers.

I offer a broader view of constructive postmodern philosophy in yet another sense. I include Heidegger, Merleau-Ponty, and Wittgenstein in this movement because I believe that they have been mistakenly viewed as panlinguists and as deconstructive postmodernists.[11] In other works I have demonstrated that Wittgenstein's language-games are derived from forms of life (*Lebensformen*), forms of human behavior that have both cultural and biological roots.[12] While Heidegger never refers to a biological basis for his "existentials," I have proposed a parallel between Heidegger's ways of being-in-the-world and Wittgenstein's *Lebensformen*.[13] We can, therefore, speak of a common humanity (an idea deconstructed in French postmodernism) that makes communication across cultures possible. (It is found in Wittgenstein's bedrock on which "our spade turns," a foundation that makes Hans-Georg Gadamer's *Horizontsverschmelzung* possible.) This means that when we read about the yogi's desire for complete independence, we can be confident that this is essentially the same desire that some Westerners feel in their own misdirected yearnings for complete and total freedom. To avoid the temptations of spiritual Titanism we should follow the model of the Chinese sage, who, instead of independence seeks integration, in place of autonomy chooses sociality, and rather than the conquest of nature, as the *Analects* tell us, finds "joy in water [and] . . . joy in mountains."[14]

N. F. G., Bangalore

Acknowledgments

This project began in the early 1980s and in 1984 I had occasion to speak with Wendy Doniger about the anthropomorphism of the Puruṣa hymn and her encouragement on the first draft of chapter 5 and frequent consultations on specific textual and linguistic matters were greatly appreciated. Doniger's thorough scholarship and creative insights have been a great inspiration to me.

I wish to thank the University of Idaho for granting me a sabbatical leave in 1992–93 to study in India, China, and Japan. During the summer of 1992 the Department of Philosophy at the Chinese University of Hong Kong was kind enough to provide me with library privileges to research chapter 9. I am grateful to Chen Lai of Beijing University and Tang Yi of Beijing's Institute of World Religions for helping me with Mencius's use of the word *shen* as discussed in chapter 9. I also thank Father Thomas Manninezhath for inviting me to Dharmaram College, Bangalore, India, where in the fall of 1992 I was a visiting scholar. In the winter and spring of 1993 Doshisha University, Otani University, and the NCC Center for the Study of Japanese Religion in Kyoto and the Nanzan Institute of Religion and Culture in Nagoya kindly allowed me to use their excellent libraries.

While on leave in 1995 I was the guest of the Department of Studies in Religion at the University of Queensland, where I consulted with their Asian specialists—N. Ross Reat and Rod Bucknell—and was given access to their superb library. The last part of 1995 was spent in Bangalore where I worked in the library of United Theological College. I am very grateful to the people in Brisbane and Bangalore who aided me in my research.

P. S. Jaini of the University of California at Berkeley was particularly helpful in making comments on a draft of chapter 4. Graham Parkes of the University of Hawaii gave me encouragement in my Nietzsche research. I owe a great deal to P. J. Ivanhoe of the University of Michigan, who read the last three chapters thoroughly and who offered insightful suggestions. He and Paul Kjellberg of Whittier College are responsible for my new passion for Zhuangzi. I was inspired by Jeffrey Kripal's brilliant book on Ramakrishna and was grateful for his comments on chapter 7. Cynthia Humes of Claremont McKenna College read the first draft of chapter 6 and offered essential corrections and criticisms. I am also grateful to two anonymous reviewers of this chapter for the challenge to learn more about the relationship between *tejas* and *śakti*. The chapter is immeasurably improved because of their criticisms. I also thank Arthur Herman of the University of Wisconsin at Stevens Point for constructive comments on a draft of chapter 5. Edward Machle of the University of Colorado wrote extensive comments on a draft of chapter 10. His new translation of Xunzi was essential for my construction of a Chinese answer to spiritual Titanism. Finally, Michael Myer, my counterpart across the state line at Washington State University, read and commented on drafts of chapters 5 and 6.

At the University of Idaho I would like to thank my department chair Kathyrn George for her support and encouragement; Michael O'Rourke for his good comments on chapter 11; Cecilia Luschnig for checking my understanding of Greek mythology; the Eta Sigma Phi honorary for inviting me to present the contents of chapter 3; and the research council for their financial support on this project.

Three student assistants have been invaluable. Nicholas Merrill proofread the manuscript with amazing thoroughness; I bowed to his superior phrasing on most occasions. (He helped me break a bad habit of overusing the semicolon.) As my research assistant, Shelly Hill located dozens of articles and books in various libraries, but unfortunately we never did locate that great quotation from Mircea Eliade. Finally, Jennifer Eggleston did an excellent job of compiling the bibliography.

I wish to thank the International Religious Foundation for permission to reprint a revised version of "Titanism: Radical Humanism—East and West" from *Dialogue & Alliance* 1: 3 (Fall 1987), pp. 53–69; the International Institute of Hindu Studies for permission to reprint revised version of "The Yogi and the Goddess" from the *International Journal of Hindu Studies* 1: 2 (August 1997), pp. 265–87; the *International Philosophical Quarterly* for permission to reprint parts of "Ahimsa, the Self, and Postmodernism" 35: 1 (March 1995), pp. 71–86; *Philosophy East & West* (© University of Hawaii Press) for permission to reprint a revised version of "Hindu Titanism" 45: 1 (January 1995), pp. 73–96; *Asian Philosophy* for permission to reprint a revised version of "On the Deification of Confucius" 1: 3 (1993), pp. 43–54; *The Scottish Journal of Religious Studies* for permission to reprint a revised version of "Jaina Superhumanism and

Gnostic Titanism" 17: 2 (Autumn 1996), pp. 139–58; *The Journal of Chinese Philosophy* for permission to reprint a revised version of "Xunzi and the Confucian Answer to Titanism" 22: 2 (June 1995), pp. 129–51; and W. W. Norton for permission to reprint a long passage from Dostoevsky's *Crime and Punishment*.

Walks with Katja, my golden retriever, offered refreshing breaks from writing and research. Ellora the Cat, named after the magnificent cave temples outside of Aurangabad, also relieved my writing stress. Ellie stretched out her beautiful body on my desk and added a touch of feline grace to the otherwise heavy atmosphere. With Ellie's "mom" Gail Adele I have shared the wonders of India and have discovered the joys of its exquisite cuisine. Gail has been an essential support for both my work and my life.

Introduction to SUNY Series in Constructive Postmodern Thought*

The rapid spread of the term *postmodern* in recent years witnesses to a growing dissatisfaction with modernity and to an increasing sense that the modern age not only had a beginning but can have an end as well. Whereas the word *modern* was almost always used until quite recently as a word of praise and as a synonym for *contemporary*, a growing sense is now evidenced that we can and should leave modernity behind—in fact, that we must if we are to avoid destroying ourselves and most of the life on our planet.

Modernity, rather than being regarded as the norm for human society toward which all history has been aiming and into which all societies should be ushered—forcibly if necessary—is instead increasingly seen as an aberration. A new respect for the wisdom of traditional societies is growing as we realize that they have endured for thousands of years and that, by contrast, the existence of modern civilization for even another century seems doubtful. Likewise, *modernism* as a worldview is less and less seen as the Final Truth, in comparison with which all divergent worldviews are automatically regarded as "superstitious." The modern worldview is increasingly relativized to the status of one among many, useful for some purposes, inadequate for others.

Although there have been antimodern movements before, beginning perhaps near the outset of the nineteenth century with the Romanticists and the Luddites, the rapidity with which the term *postmodern* has become widespread in our time suggests that the antimodern sentiment is more extensive and intense than before, and also that it includes the sense that modernity can be successfully overcome only by going beyond it, not by attempting to return to a premodern form of existence. Insofar as a common element is found

---

*The present version of this introduction is slightly different from the first version, which was contained in the volumes that appeared prior to 2000. My thanks to Catherine Keller and Edward Carlos Munn for helpful suggestions.

in the various ways in which the term is used, *postmodernism* refers to a diffuse sentiment rather than to any common set of doctrines—the sentiment that humanity can and must go beyond the modern.

Beyond connoting this sentiment, the term *postmodern* is used in a confusing variety of ways, some of them contradictory to others. In artistic and literary circles, for example, postmodernism shares in this general sentiment but also involves a specific reaction against "modernism" in the narrow sense of a movement in artistic-literary circles in the late nineteenth and early twentieth centuries. Postmodern architecture is very different from postmodern literary criticism. In some circles, the term *postmodern* is used in reference to that potpourri of ideas and systems sometimes called *new age metaphysics,* although many of these ideas and systems are more premodern than postmodern. Even in philosophical and theological circles, the term *postmodern* refers to two quite different positions, one of which is reflected in this series. Each position seeks to transcend both *modernism*, in the sense of the worldview that has developed out of the seventeenth-century Galilean-Cartesian-Baconian-Newtonian science, and *modernity,* in the sense of the world order that both conditioned and was conditioned by this worldview. But the two positions seek to transcend the modern in different ways.

Closely related to literary-artistic postmodernism is a philosophical postmodernism inspired variously by physicalism, Ludwig Wittgenstein, Martin Heidegger, a cluster of French thinkers—including Jacques Derrida, Michel Foucault, Gilles Deleuze, and Julia Kristeva—and certain features of American pragmatism.* By the use of terms that arise out of particular segments of this movement, it can be called *deconstructive, relativistic,* or *eliminative* postmodernism. It overcomes the modern worldview through an antiworld-

*The fact that the thinkers and movements named here are said to have inspired the deconstructive type of postmodernism should not be taken, of course, to imply that they have nothing in common with constructive postmodernists. For example, Wittgenstein, Heidegger, Derrida, and Deleuze share many points and concerns with Alfred North Whitehead, the chief inspiration behind the present series. Furthermore, the actual positions of the founders of pragmatism, especially William James and Charles Peirce, are much closer to Whitehead's philosophical position—see the volume in this series entitled *The Founders of Constructive Postmodern Philosophy: Peirce, James, Bergson, Whitehead, and Hartshorne*—than they are to Richard Rorty's so-called neopragmatism, which reflects many ideas from Rorty's explicitly physicalistic period.

view, deconstructing or even entirely eliminating various concepts that have generally been thought necessary for a worldview, such as self, purpose, meaning, a real world, givenness, reason, truth as correspondence, universally valid norms, and divinity. While motivated by ethical and emancipatory concerns, this type of postmodern thought tends to issue in relativism. Indeed, it seems to many thinkers to imply nihilism.* It could, paradoxically, also be called *ultramodernism,* in that its eliminations result from carrying certain modern premises—such as the sensationist doctrine of perception, the mechanistic doctrine of nature, and the resulting denial of divine presence in the world—to their logical conclusions. Some critics see its deconstructions or eliminations as leading to self-referential inconsistencies, such as "performative self-contradictions" between what is said and what is presupposed in the saying.

The postmodernism of this series can, by contrast, be called *revisionary, constructive,* or—perhaps best—*reconstructive.* It seeks to overcome the modern worldview not by eliminating the possibility of worldviews (or "metanarratives") as such, but by constructing a postmodern worldview through a revision of modern premises and traditional concepts in the light of inescapable presuppositions of our various modes of practice. That is, it agrees with deconstructive postmodernists that a massive deconstruction of many received concepts is needed. But its deconstructive moment, carried out for the sake of the presuppositions of practice, does not result in self-referential inconsistency. It also is not so totalizing as to prevent *re*construction. The reconstruction carried out by this type of postmodernism involves a new unity of scientific, ethical, aesthetic, and religious intuitions (whereas post-structuralists tend to reject all such unitive projects as "totalizing modern metanarratives"). While critical of many ideas often associated with modern science, it rejects not science as such but only that *scientism* in which the data of the modern

*Peter Dews says that, although Derrida's early work was "driven by profound ethical impulses," its insistence that no concepts were immune to deconstruction "drove its own ethical presuppositions into a penumbra of inarticulacy" (*The Limits of Disenchantment: Essays on Contemporary European Culture* [London: New York: Verso, 1995], 5). In his more recent thought, Derrida has declared an "emancipatory promise" and an "idea of justice" to be "irreducible to any deconstruction." Although the "ethical turn" in deconstruction implies its pulling back from a completely disenchanted universe, it also, Dews points out (6–7), implies the need to renounce "the unconditionality of its own earlier dismantling of the unconditional."

natural sciences alone are allowed to contribute to the construction of our public worldview.

The reconstructive activity of this type of postmodern thought is not limited to a revised worldview. It is equally concerned with a postmodern *world* that will both support and be supported by the new worldview. A postmodern world will involve postmodern persons, with a postmodern spirituality, on the one hand, and a postmodern society, ultimately a postmodern global order, on the other. Going beyond the modern world will involve transcending its individualism, anthropocentrism, patiarchy, economism, consumerism, nationalism, and militarism. Reconstructive postmodern thought provides support for the ethnic, ecological, feminist, peace, and other emancipatory movements of our time, while stressing that the inclusive emancipation must be from the destructive features of modernity itself. However, the term *postmodern,* by contrast with *premodern*, is here meant to emphasize that the modern world has produced unparalleled advances, as Critical Theorists have emphasized, which must not be devalued in a general revulsion against modernity's negative features.

From the point of view of deconstructive postmodernists, this reconstructive postmodernism will seem hopelessly wedded to outdated concepts, because it wishes to salvage a positive meaning not only for the notions of selfhood, historical meaning, reason, and truth as correspondence, which were central to modernity, but also for notions of divinity, cosmic meaning, and an enchanted nature, which were central to premodern modes of thought. From the point of view of its advocates, however, this revisionary postmodernism is not only more adequate to our experience but also more genuinely postmodern. It does not simply carry the premises of modernity through to their logical conclusions, but criticizes and revises those premises. By virtue of its return to organicism and its acceptance of nonsensory perception, it opens itself to the recovery of truths and values from various forms of premodern thought and practice that had been dogmatically rejected, or at least restricted to "practice," by modern thought. This reconstructive postmodernism involves a creative synthesis of modern and premodern truths and values.

This series does not seek to create a movement so much as to help shape and support an already existing movement convinced that modernity can and must be transcended. But in light of the fact that those antimodern movements that arose in the past failed to deflect or even retard the onslaught of modernity, what reasons are there for expecting the current movement to be more successful?

First, the previous antimodern movements were primarily calls to return to a premodern form of life and thought rather than calls to advance, and the human spirit does not rally to calls to turn back. Second, the previous antimodern movements either rejected modern science, reduced it to a description of mere appearances, or assumed its adequacy in principle. They could, therefore, base their calls only on the negative social and spiritual effects of modernity. The current movement draws on natural science itself as a witness against the adequacy of the modern worldview. In the third place, the present movement has even more evidence than did previous movements of the ways in which modernity and its worldview are socially and spiritually destructive. The fourth and probably most decisive difference is that the present movement is based on the awareness that *the continuation of modernity threatens the very survival of life on our planet*. This awareness, combined with the growing knowledge of the interdependence of the modern worldview with modernity's militarism, nuclearism, patiarchy, global apartheid, and ecological devastation, is providing an unprecedented impetus for people to see the evidence for a postmodern worldview and to envisage postmodern ways of relating to each other, the rest of nature, and the cosmos as a whole. For these reasons, the failure of the previous antimodern movements says little about the possible success of the current movement.

Advocates of this movement do not hold the naively utopian belief that the success of this movement would bring about a global society of universal and lasting peace, harmony and happiness, in which all spiritual problems, social conflicts, ecological destruction, and hard choices would vanish. There is, after all, surely a deep truth in the testimony of the world's religions to the presence of a transcultural proclivity to evil deep within the human heart, which no new paradigm, combined with a new economic order, new childrearing practices, or any other social arrangements, will suddenly eliminate. Furthermore, it has correctly been said that "life is robbery": a strong element of competition is inherent within finite existence, which no social-political-economic-ecological order can overcome. These two truths, especially when contemplated together, should caution us against unrealistic hopes.

No such appeal to "universal constants," however, should reconcile us to the present order, as if it were thereby uniquely legitimated. The human proclivity to evil in general, and to conflictual competition and ecological destruction in particular, can be greatly exacerbated or greatly mitigated by a world order and its worldview. Modernity exacerbates it about as much as imaginable. We can therefore envision, without being naively utopian, a far better world order, with a far less dangerous trajectory, than the one we now have.

This series, making no pretense of neutrality, is dedicated to the success of this movement toward a postmodern world.

David Ray Griffin
Series Editor

Introduction

Indian philosophy *does* in fact elevate power, control or freedom to a supereminent position . . . the ultimate value. . . is not morality but freedom . . . complete control over one's environment—something which includes self-control but also includes control of others and even control of the physical sources of power in the universe.

—Karl H. Potter[1]

The great spiritual adventure of the "Crossing-Maker" [the Jaina Tīrthaṇkara], a stepping place to the superhuman sphere. That sphere, moreover, is not only superhuman but even superdivine—beyond the gods, their heavens . . . and their cosmic powers.

—Heinrich Zimmer[2]

Nuclear weapons remain the most serious danger for mankind and the most serious insult to God.

—George Kennan[3]

Introduction

It is truly ironic that the most famous gods of the world's religions—Gautama, Kṛṣṇa, and Jesus—began their religious careers as human beings. In his sermons Gautama Buddha made it clear that he had come only to teach the Dharma and that his disciples were not to worship him as a god or a savior. Although a few commentators choose to read divine attributes into the earliest reference, the *Chāndogya Upaniṣad* describes Kṛṣṇa as a man, the son of Vasudeva and Devakī.[4] The Jesus of the Synoptic Gospels speaks of himself as a good Jew would, making a clear distinction between himself and God. Once he rebuked those who called him good, for "no one is good but God alone."[5] An early and widespread Christology was "adoptionism," the view that Jesus was just a human being, approved and adopted by God at his baptism.

It is doubly ironic that Kṛṣṇa and Gautama actually became higher than the Vedic gods: the Buddha is called "God beyond the gods" (*devatīdeva*) and Kṛṣṇa becomes the highest expression of divinity, surpassing even Brahman itself. Already in some Upaniṣads the divine person (*puruṣa*) exceeds everything, including Brahman, and Kṛṣṇa is the culmination of this Vedic personalism. In some Christian sects, God the Father seems almost totally displaced by the worship of Jesus. (During the Protestant Reformation this heresy was called *Jesuologie* and some mainstream Protestants considered it a form of atheism.) At the World Congress of Religions in 1893, Swami Vivekananda defended the atheism of Buddhism and Jainism by arguing that it is perfectly legitimate "to evolve God out of man." He then presented what appears to be the "Buddhology" equivalent of *Jesuologie*: "They have not seen the Father, but they have seen the Son."[6] We shall see shortly how Vivekananda's Vedāntist assumptions lead to an alternative interpretation of this passage.

The Titans: Superhuman and Superdivine

Heinrich Zimmer has called the preemption of divine prerogatives and confusion of human and divine attributes the "heresy of Titanism,"[7] and it could be that the deification of Gautama, Kṛṣṇa, Mahāvīra, Jesus, and other religious figures may constitute a form of spiritual Titanism. Zimmer observes that Titans are not only superhuman, but they, as we have just seen, are superdivine; and as such, they are involved in a supergodly task. Even the gods accrue karma, so the human savior will also become the redeemer of the gods. To my knowledge, no one has ever worked out the details of Zimmer's thesis with regard to Indian forms of Titanism. Standing in the shadow of a giant in his own right, I presume to take up that task in this book.

Titanism is an extreme form of humanism that does not recognize that there are limits to what humans can become and what they should do. (Hesiod related, incorrectly as it turns out, the meaning of "Titan" to two words—*titaínein* (to stretch, to strive, or to exert) and *tísis* (retribution)—i.e., punishment for their overexertion.)[8] The Greek Titans were known for their boundless pride (*hubris*) and for their violence (*atasthalíē*). Titanism is humanism gone berserk; it is anthropocentricism and anthropomorphism taken to their limits. The Titan insists that human experience is the norm. Titans deliberately reverse the positions of humanity and divinity; they take over divine prerogatives, and as a result of their hubris, they lose sight of their proper place in the universe. This book will define a deity as any being who is omniscient, omnipotent, infinite, and omnipresent. We maintain that a human being is a spiritual Titan by claiming any or all of these attributes. Even if there is no God, humans obviously delude themselves if they believe that they can become divine in the sense of these attributes.

Following Zimmer's lead, we will identify five types of Indian Titanism. The first is Asura Titanism, discussed in chapter 3, in which the *asuras* (demons, antigods, or Titans) constantly battle the Hindu gods. The second is Brahmin Titanism, in which the priests take over the divine power of the sacrifice. The third is Gnostic Titanism, in which humans contend that they have perfect knowledge. The fourth is Yoga Titanism, in which yogis claim to have divine powers by the practice of austerities. (Gnostic and Yoga Titanism are intimately linked in Jainism, where yogic discipline leads to absolute knowledge. But they are separate in Sāṃkhya-Yoga, where the practice leads to spiritual liberation but knowledge without content, and in Purānic mythology where the practice of austerities leads to great power not knowledge.) Finally, there is Bhakti Titanism, in which humans such as Kṛṣṇa are bestowed with powers of universal redemption. The common thread throughout these five forms of Titanism is a determined attempt to acquire and to monopolize total power.

Except for the violent *asura-deva* conflict, Indian Titanism has expressed itself almost exclusively in an internal, spiritual way; therefore, one can say that it is a rather benign form of extreme humanism. By contrast, the expressions of Western Titanism are primarily external, and with the aid of technology, a Titanistic spirit can be said to inspire militarism, environmental pollution and degradation, and the possible misuse of genetic engineering. If left unchecked, Titanism might destroy or radically change life as we know it on earth. Even though it is technological Titanism that poses the real threat, it is essential to show that Indian Titans share some of the same views as their Western counterparts, namely, anthropocentrism and autonomous selfhood. Some Indian views of self—

particularly the Sāṃkhya-Yoga and Jainism—express a view of human autonomy just as extreme as existentialism. Therefore, early Indian and Western philosophy share a basic conceptual bond that has been rarely discerned or mentioned.

The term *Titan* comes from a race of older gods, who, under the leadership of Prometheus, contended with Zeus and with the other Olympian deities for the control of the universe. Western humanists have generally viewed the Promethean revolt not only as a necessary transgression but as a good one. Byron claimed that Prometheus' only "crime" was that he liberated humanity:

> Thy Godlike crime was to be kind,
> to render with thy precepts less
> the sum of human wretchedness
> And strengthen Man with his own mind.[9]

In his preface to *Prometheus Unbound* Percy Bysshe Shelly claimed that "Prometheus is . . . the highest perfection of moral and intellectual nature, impelled by the purest and the truest motives of the best and noblest ends."[10] Mary Shelly described her husband as a spiritual Titan: he thought that "man could be so perfectionized as to be able to expel evil from his own nature, and from the greater part of the creation. . . ."[11]

Goethe's poem "Prometheus" is remarkable both in terms of the liberties he takes with the myth and the insights that he nonetheless offers for this study. First, Goethe makes the Greek gods just as dependent on the sacrifice as the Vedic gods:

> I know of nothing more wretched
> Under the sun than you gods!
> Meagerly you nourish
> Your majesty
> On dues of sacrifice
> And breath of prayers
> And would suffer want
> But for children and beggars,
> Poor hopeful fools.[12]

Goethe allows Zeus to have his heaven and to play his games there, but Prometheus has given earth to humanity and to them alone. Zeus can only envy humans, and they, in turn can only pity the gods. As Lord of the Earth, as Protoanthropos, Prometheus proclaims:

Here I sit, forming men
In my image,
A race to resemble me:
To suffer, to weep,
To enjoy, to be glad—
and never to heed you,
like me!
to have no regard for you.[13]

In fragments of a play Goethe wrote on Prometheus, Epimetheus urges his brother to take Zeus' offer to reside on Mt. Olympus. Asserting the stubborn independence that the Greek writers gave him, Prometheus' answer anticipates Milton's Satan: it is far preferable to rule on earth rather than to serve in heaven. Staying on earth the Titan possesses a power that even the gods do not have, the power to create a living world:

Here is my world, my all!
Here I know who I am!
Here—all my wishes
Embodied in these figures,
My spirit split a thousand ways
Yet whole in my beloved children.[14]

The hymns of the Ṛgveda were not yet known to Europeans, but Goethe had created an image very similar to the Puruṣa hymn, a thousand-headed cosmic man who forms the very body and contents of the universe. But unlike this Vedic hymn, which only hints at the necessity of a corollary feminine power in the word *virāj*, Goethe follows one version of the Greek myth that has Athene actively aiding Prometheus in his earthly creations. Unlike the great Indian yogis, Prometheus realizes that "you [Minerva = Athene] are to my spirit as it is to itself" and that his creative powers grow in her presence, which are "the sources of all life."[15] We will discover that this joining of *animus* and *anima* is one significant difference between Prometheanism and the spiritual Titanism of India.

There are too many parallels, however, between Satan and Prometheus for most Christians to be completely comfortable with Prometheus as a model for human action. Elizabeth Barrett Browning, however, saw more contrasts than similarities:

> Satan suffered from his ambition; Prometheus from his humanity: Satan for himself; Prometheus for mankind: Satan

> dared peril which he had not weighed; Prometheus devoted himself to sorrows which he had foreknown. . . . The Satan of Milton and the Prometheus of Aeschylus stand upon ground as unequal as do the sublime of sin and the sublime of virtue.[16]

Some of the early Church fathers actually agreed with Browning, and they saw Prometheus as one who, like Job, prefigures Christ. Some of them noted the parallel in the creation of humanity out of clay and their descent into Hell, and Tertullian was willing to grant a mythical foreshadowing of the Passion of Christ in "the stories of the sacrifices of the Taurians . . . the torments of the Caucasus."[17] Simone Weil's view of Prometheus represents a twentieth-century extension of Tertullian's view: "The story of Prometheus is like the refraction into eternity of the Passion of Christ. Prometheus is the Lamb slain from the foundation of the world."[18] In chapter 3 I will analyze mitigating factors in the Prometheus myth that lead me to distinguish between Prometheanism and Titanism.

Even though I have chosen to give the term *Titanism* a negative connotation, I do not wish to give the impression that more knowledge or even new technology is undesirable; and I certainly do not mean to imply that we do not need heroes or saints. It is sometimes said that our heroes are "larger than life," or alternatively it is said that "we stand on the shoulders of giants" in relation to them. I contend that these images represent a distortion of how heroes are actually made. These ideas are also most likely responsible for the mistaken view, expressed for example in Hobbes's monarch or in Raskalnikov's Napoleon, that some people are beyond our ken and above the law. Therefore, I believe that we require a new vision of human nature, one that breaks with both the autonomous self and the yogic self, which is exhorted to be totally independent from others and separate from an unredeemable nature.

Humanism arose during the so-called axial period, and it is commonly observed that while the Greeks generally responded to the discovery of human individuality by externalizing their new desires in a positive way, the Indians turned inward in an attempt to reconcile anxieties caused by an increased awareness of the self-world split. But even in their world-denying practices, many Indian thinkers have remained very much attached to the human form. They have made it the prototype for the shape and origin of the universe (some Jainas are most explicit on this point); they have made it the locus of all spiritual liberation—to be saved the gods must eventually have a human incarnation. Even if this anthropocentric and anthropomorphic cosmos is not taken literally, the image itself is sufficient to indicate a distorted view of human beings and of their relation to the world. Not only are the gods supplanted, but nature in general is denigrated in status and value. This becomes an especially serious problem when human beings develop technological means to control and to alter nature.

One might say that as there is no ontological difference between deity and humanity in Indian thought, there can be no Indian Titanism. A. L. Basham once said that "divinity was cheap in ancient India,"[19] but this may represent only one Indian tradition. If Mary Boyce is right about a much earlier date for Zoroaster and for his transcendent Creator Ahura Mazda, and if she is correct about an original Indo-Iranian moral tritheism of Varuṇa, Mitra, and Ahura, then Zoroaster's predecessors and the original Indo-Aryans may well have shared the same views of transcendent deity.[20] (In chapter 1 we will call this the Hebraic principle, but for general comparative purposes, it could be called the Indo-Iranian theistic principle.) This original Aryan theology is best preserved in the hymns to Varuṇa, the most moral but also the most distant and transcendent of the Vedic gods. This high theism is undermined in the hymns to the amoral Indra, who is close and intimate—especially with the warriors he exhorts to battle. Such a weak theism may well have been conducive to the various forms of spiritual Titanism, while the strong theism of the Abrahamic religions inhibited its development. With the spread of science and secular culture, extreme humanism found an alternative expression in technological Titanism.

If deity is so cheap in ancient India, then one cannot understand, from the Vedas to the Purāṇas, the fierce resistance the gods display in defending their prerogatives nor the outrage that occurs when humans—like Vena and Divodāsa—make claim to them. In the *Jaiminīya Brāhmaṇa* the gods are so protective of their advantages that they deliberately made humans evil so they would be unable to go to heaven.[21] In her analysis of sexual encounters between the gods and humans, Wendy Doniger argues that the Vedic separation of gods and humans, not Vedāntist monism, prevails even in the Purāṇas.[22] The sage Vyāsa knows the rule: "By rituals one reaches the world of the gods; and the gods do not wish that mortals should live on high."[23] One would think that the famous story of Naciketas would have finally overcome any residue of Vedic mortalism, but it is found in many passages. Adi, son of Andhaka, does *tapas* and asks Brahmā for immortality, but the creator-god answers that "No living creature can exist without death."[24] The great *asura* Mahiṣa makes the same request, but Brahmā states that "birth must be followed by death, and death must be followed by birth; this is the eternal law of nature."[25] Even the Vedāntist who unequivocally affirms an eternal human essence realizes that this truth is expressed in a very particular way. They know the difference between the Upaniṣadic truth "I am Brahman (as Ātman)" and the untruth and blasphemy of "I am Īśvara," namely, the creator of the universe.[26] The first expression is the only way in which humans can claim immortality, while the second is a clear expression of spiritual Titanism.

The divinization of humanity and the origins of Indian Titanism most likely have pre-Aryan roots in traditions we now know as Sāṃkhya, Yoga, and Jainism. It is by the perfection of yogic practices that humans such as Divodāsa are best able to challenge the preeminence of the gods. It is no coincidence that the Purāṇic writers blame a Jaina monk for teaching Vena the blasphemy of making himself divine.[27] (The sages call Vena's claim to divinity "nonsensical.")[28] Padmanabh S. Jaini observes that in the Vedic tradition divine attributes were imputed to humans only in a "secondary sense," and that "one looks in vain for even one such reference [divine attributes in the primary sense] in the entire Brahmanical literature, including the Upaniṣads."[29] He also contends that the deification of Mahāvīra and the Buddha was "certainly a unique phenomenon in the entire history of human civilization."[30] Contrary to Jaini, I believe that we can find deification in the primary sense in the Upaniṣads, and one would also have to place Kṛṣṇa and Christ alongside the Buddha and Mahāvīra.

In his book *Presuppositions of Indian Philosophy* Karl H. Potter not only confirms my hypothesis about conceptual similarities between Indian anthropocentrism and the Greek Sophists' *homo mensura*, but he also focuses on the hubris of the Indian yogis. Maintaining that Sāṃkhya-Yoga is "excessively anthropomorphic" and agreeing with Zimmer that asceticism is "an expression of an extreme will for power,"[31] Potter states:

> Indian philosophy *does* in fact elevate power, control or freedom to a supereminent position . . . the ultimate value . . . is not morality but freedom . . . complete control over one's environment—something which includes self-control but also includes control of others and even control of the physical sources of power in the universe.[32]

S. K. Maitra has distinguished between the "freedom of man" and the "freedom of the will."[33] In the former human beings are totally free from all bondage to the body and to nature, whereas the latter is a moral freedom within the limitations of the physical. In Judeo-Christian philosophy the first type of freedom has been attributed to God only, whereas it has been granted to all human beings in the Indian tradition. Potter concludes that Euro-Americans have a better understanding of their limitations than their Indian counterparts. The scientific view of nature as "impersonal neither in our control nor controlling us" is alien to the Indian mind, which has no doubt about "the power of the yogi to control not only his body but the bodies of others—indeed, the whole universe. . . ."[34] This book will offer evidence for Potter's provocative claims.

Uttarāvāda versus Avatāravāda

For our purposes it will be essential to distinguish between Uttarāvāda (lit. "way of the ultimate [one]") and Avatāravāda (lit. "way of the descending [one]"). Less literally one could say that the first way is humans ascending to Godhood, or simply discovering their own divinity; and the second way is God descending into humanity as an incarnation (*avatāra*). As we shall see, Jaina philosophers explicitly choose the first way and reject the second as the preference of the Hindus. This is the principal reason why Jainism becomes our strongest candidate for a theoretical (not practical) expression of spiritual Titanism. One might argue that, as it is impossible to prove a divine incarnation, the two ways actually collapse into one. Without such proof the two views are making the same prima facie claim: a human being is a divine being. But intentions should count for something, so we should respect the incarnationalists' belief that true divinity has somehow made itself flesh and blood. Although there may be logical difficulties in both ways, there is after all a major theological difference between God claiming human attributes and human beings claiming divine attributes. This significant difference will serve to mitigate expressions of spiritual Titanism that one might detect in Christianity and in the *bhakti* forms of evangelical Hinduism.

In his short speech "Incarnations" Swami Vivekananda argues that were it not for divine incarnations human beings would be completely without spiritual guidance. Therefore, according to Vivekananda, ordinary people must worship God as a human being.

Philosophical theologians who attempt to describe God in terms of nonhuman attributes are committing blasphemy and are on par with atheists who reject God. Vivekananda appears to reject Xenophanes' suggestion that human beings, with their superior awareness and cognitive powers, are able and thus ought to conceive of God in nonhuman terms. This reminds us of Vivekananda's point about seeing the Son and not the Father mentioned earlier, but here the context is different. Earlier he was defending the nontheism of Buddhism and Jainism, which "evolve God out of man," but here he is explaining the incarnational theism of Christianity. Perhaps he means to collapse the two into one when, in another article, he claims that Christ is, presumably just as is the Buddha or Mahāvīra, "higher than any God that you can imagine."[35] It seems that he is encouraging Christians to embrace the *Jesuologie* discussed previously.

Returning to the first article, however, Vivekananda does preserve the distinction between Uttarāravāda and Avatāravāda. The former is represented by the exceptional human being, the *paramahamsa*, "who has risen beyond all the weaknesses of humanity and has transcended the limits of his own nature. To him all nature has become his own Self. He alone can worship God as He is."[36] In this case we discover our own divinity rather than worshiping a deity revealed as an *avatāra*. Given Vivekananda's commitment to Vedānta this statement should be given a monistic and not a Titanistic interpretation. This would mean that we understand "God" to stand for Brahman, the ultimate reality of all that exists, and that our worship simply consists in seeing our indivisible unity with Brahman. (By the way, this is a good place to note the obvious difference between a mystic and a Titan; the former uniting fully with ultimate reality while the latter claiming to be that ultimate reality.) Placing the phrase "to him all nature has become his own Self" in a Jaina or Sāṃkhya-Yoga setting gives us quite a different meaning. In both views there is what Eliade calls the "cosmicization of the yogi," in which saints become the entire universe before reaching their final state of perfection and complete self-absorption. As a Vedāntist Vivekananda is free of the anthropocentrism and anthropomorphism implied in "evolving God out of man," but these characteristics are intensified to an extreme in Jaina-Sāṃkhya-Yoga philosophies. Here there is no unity with Brahman (the concept does not even appear in these schools), but the complete isolation of many liberated souls from one another. It is here that we find the basic prototype for spiritual Titanism in India.

Vivekananda also calls the *paramahamsa* a *jīvanmukta*, but this term has a more specific meaning in Indian thought. A *jīvanmukta* is one who is liberated while in a body as opposed to the one who is liberated at death. In Buddhism the difference is sometimes phrased as Nirvaṇa "with qualities (*saguṇa*)" as opposed to Nirvaṇa "without qualities (*nirguṇa*)." Advaita Vedānta supports the idea of the *jīvanmukta*, but Advatins realize that, because such a person would continue to be a karmic being, certain problems are generated. (The Buddha's distinction between craving and ordinary desires may offer a more satisfactory solution to these issues.) In a thorough and insightful article on the *jīvanmukta* Lance Nelson suggests that Advaitins should take Īśvara as a model for liberation while in the world. Śaṇkara himself twice declared that "I am Īśvara," and those liberated have warrant to say this because they know that the distinction between them and the Lord is created by ignorance and does not exist in reality.[37] The principal problem with taking God the Creator as the model for living liberation is that Īśvara will continue to exist as long as there are ignorant ones to support the world's existence. In an odd parallel to the Bodhisattva ideal, the logic of this modeling implies that all saints will have to wait for everyone else for their final liberation. This is definitely not the Advaitins' view, so that means that their liberated ones are spiritual Titans, who, in their independence from created nature, are greater than the Lord of the universe.

While the theistic traditions of Rāmānuja and Madhva reject that idea of a *jīvanmukta* (as Vaiṣṇavas they preferred the Avatāravāda over the Uttarāvāda), Jainism, Sāṃkhya, and Yoga join Advaitins and Buddhists in supporting the possibility of living liberation. As both Hindu and Christian theism has proved to be a guard against extreme humanism, one might be initially inclined to claim that the idea of a living saint necessarily leads to spiritual Titanism. This correlation, however, is mistaken. First, we have seen that the Advaitin view dissolves the saint's identity into Brahman or Īśvara. Second, we will demonstrate that the Buddha can claim liberation in a body without becoming a Titan. In fact, the Buddhist and Tantric valorization of the body constitutes an important counter against extreme forms of spiritual humanism.[38] This book will support the Buddhist view over Vedānta, primarily because the latter gives a premodern solution to the self-world problem while many Buddhist thinkers anticipated a constructive postmodern response.

Summaries of the Chapters

In chapter 1 we analyze several examples of Western Titanism. It is proposed that "dialogical" forms of existentialism (e.g., Martin Buber, Martin Heidegger, and Gabriel Marcel) could serve as an answer to the Titanism of Jean-Paul Sartre's early existentialism, in which the latter declares that the self's goal is to become totally independent from others and from nature. Sartre's Titanism is clear in this famous passage: "The fundamental project of human reality is to say that man is the being whose project is to be God"[39]—a being who is totally self-caused, self-sufficient, and self-determined. This radically autonomous self is the link between Indian and Western Titanism, so the social self of Heidegger, Buber, Marcel, and Confucius is offered as a response to this extreme humanism. In a significant break with Aristotle and modernism in general, Heidegger and Buber redefine human essence as "care" (*Sorge*)[40] and as *Mitmenschlichkeit* (with peopleness) respectively, a position remarkably similar to the Confucian concept of *ren*, literally "two peopleness," translated as "human heartedness," "humaneness," "benevolence," and "compassion." American pragmatism is also an important resource for this comparative project, and Steven Odin's *Social Self in Zen and American Pragmatism* stands as a significant contribution.[41]

Allowing for much sectarian variation, one can profitably divide the world religions among "gnostic" religions (Jainism, Hinduism, and Buddhism); "obedience" religions (Zoroastrianism, Judaism, Christianity, and Islam); and "praxis" religions (Zen Buddhism, Daoism, and Confucianism). In the gnostic religions the basic sin is ignorance; it is disobedience in obedience religions; and malpractice in praxis religions. (Devotees of gnostic religions would find it difficult to understand Yahweh's prohibition about eating of the Tree of the Knowledge of Good and Evil.) In obedience religions it is God who saves us (thus mitigating substantially any Titanism found here), while in the gnostic and praxis religions humans save themselves, which make them both strongly humanistic as well as potentially, at least on the gnostic side, Titanistic. It is important to note that Gnostic Christians differ from their Indian counterparts in that they used the Greek word *gnosis* in its proper sense, that is, a knowledge of acquaintance rather than a knowledge of fact. Whereas the Christian Gnostic claims to have direct knowledge of God as a person, the Indian Gnostic, rarely ever focusing on God(s), speaks about knowledge of the soul and reality in general. (Note: we retain the uppercase *G* in Indian Gnosticism and Gnostic Titanism for stylistic reasons, but still maintain the distinction between gnostic religions in general and the Gnostic religion.)

One of the greatest temptations of the gnostic religions is to assume that spiritual enlightenment results in absolute knowledge. The Gnostic Titan, then, is a religious aspirant who falls into this temptation and who attempts to take on the divine attribute of absolute knowledge. In chapter 4 we will see that Jaina scriptures impute such a position to Mahāvīra, but Pāli scriptures carefully qualify the Buddha's knowledge claims. (In fact, it might be less confusing to say that the Buddha, at least according to the Pāli accounts, was not *omniscient* in the general Indian or Christian sense of that term.) According to the Jainas, the worst sin is to reject the doctrine that absolute knowledge is necessary for salvation. Makkhali Gośāla of the Ājīvikas was condemned to, and was irredeemably lost in, the lowest existence (*nigodas*), because of his rejection of the fully gnostic religion of the Jainas.[42]

It is instructive to contrast Jaina omniscience with the claims of orthodox Christian theology. Following Augustine, the Christian claim is that God knows all time as an Eternal Now without temporal succession. By contrast the Jaina claim is that the saint knows the past in all of its modes, the present in all of its modes, and the future in all of its modes. This means that, again contrary to the Christian correlation of divine omniscience and immutability, "absolute" knowledge changes as more of the future is actualized. As the Jaina philosopher Vijay Bhuvanbhanusuri states: "This omniscience by its nature goes on changing as the knowable things change from time to time. . . ."[43] On the question of the saints' alleged omnipotence, the Jainas seem to have an intractable problem that is absent from monotheism—namely, how can each and every liberated Jaina have *all* power? There does not appear to be a way to redefine omnipotence so that this challenge can be solved. The Jaina saints' omniscience and omnipotence simply may be yet another expression of the hubris of spiritual Titanism, namely, humans taking on divine attributes as their own without any regard for their logical coherence. As we shall see in chapter 4, the Jainas reject the soul's omnipresence, so there are no logical problems on this point.

In chapter 5 we discuss in detail four of the five types of Titanism just listed. We also analyze the Puruṣa hymn of the *Ṛg-veda*, which tells us that the universe originated from the body of a divine man (*puruṣa*). We will show how this Puruṣa motif continues in the Indian philosophical and religious tradition, even the Purāṇas, a comparatively late collection of Hindu myths. Here the sacrifice of the divine man is replaced by a cosmic yogi, who, Titan-like, produces the universe by means of his own yogic powers. The desire to become father of oneself is one of the general features of the psychology of Titanism, and the idea of a human being creating himself, the universe, and the gods is the ultimate expression of extreme humanism. The male Titan also appears to be appropriating the creative power previously invested in the Goddess.

One could say that Titanism is predominantly a male problem. It seems that, using Jungian terms, our *animus* leads us to overstep boundaries (societal, natural, and spiritual) and our *anima* brings us back into balance. Chapter 6 focuses on Śākta philosophy and analyzes this gender dynamic in the Indian context. In the later expressions of the Sāṃkhya-Yoga dualism of *puruṣa* (spirit person) and *prakṛti* (nature, matter) the former is represented as masculine and the latter as feminine; indeed, *prakṛti* is one of primary philosophical designations of the Hindu Goddess. The goal of yogic practice is for each spirit to obtain final release from nature and to achieve par excellence with Īśvara the Lord, the only spirit not to have been entrapped in the material world.

One can observe several interesting and ironic implications in Sāṃkhya-Yoga philosophy. The yogic ideal involves a Titanistic effort to break all ties with nature, but the result is an entity who is totally isolated (there is no union with Īśvara), static, and impotent. Dynamic power, interrelation, and the riches of experience lie with nature and with her alone. This spirit-nature dualism was later infused into the Purāṇic literature, especially into the Śākta works, where the power of male gods is female power (*śakti*). Furthermore, many stories portray inactive male deities (e.g., the sleeping Viṣṇu), whose duties are taken over by activist goddesses. In general it is the Hindu Goddess who brings the Indian spiritual life back to earth, back to the body, and back to ordinary human relations. Traditional goddess theology, however, was always under the control of kings and priests, so we will find that the Goddess does not always speak with a feminine voice. Until recent times Indian kings call on her as they went to war and the priests recited her scriptures only to males.

The only Indian writer who uses the words "Titan" and "superman" is Śri Aurobindo. He uses these words favorably and in his works he outlines the evolution of a superrace of spiritual beings. Although in his attempt to distance himself from Nietzsche he misinterprets the idea of *Übermensch*, Aurobindo's own philosophy avoids most of the liabilities of Titanism primarily because of his commitment to a social self and to the concept of feminine power. The balance of chapter 7 is devoted to Ramakrishna and to his worship of Kālī, which strongly influenced Aurobindo, and to Vivekananda, a follower of Ramakrishna and a leading neo-Vedāntist philosopher. Ramakrishna will be a key figure in understanding the child stage of Nietzsche's Three Metamorphoses, a heuristic metaphor that is used to explain spiritual Titanism and its connection to modernism and postmodernism.

Chapter 8 argues that early Buddhism contains a humanism that does not lead to Titanism. The Buddha's Middle Way and his rejection of all craving—yogic as well as sensual—represents an effective response to Indian Titanism. Zen Buddhism's view of the Middle Way and its adaptation of Chinese naturalism makes an especially significant contribution. To the charge that the Buddha's claim to omniscience constitutes Titanism, the answer is that the Buddha's omniscience is not a divine attribute as it was in his Jaina counterpart Mahāvīra. His disciples also called him *mahāpurisa* (superperson), but it will be shown that this title is not connected to the Hindu Puruṣa tradition and that it means human perfection not divine perfection. The use of a closely related term *uttamapurisa* has the same anti-Titanistic implications.

In the later schools the Buddha is deified and takes on a cosmic body (*viśvarūpa*, an idea borrowed from the Hindus), but here Titanism is mitigated significantly by the presence, in several Mahāyāna schools, of an all-encompassing monism in which individuals are dissolved into a divine one. This is why Hindu monistic schools also escape the charge of spiritual Titanism. Our contention, however, is that a postmodern reconstruction of the self is far preferable to a return to premodern notions of primordial unity and totality. In premodern views the self loses far too much value and integrity, whereas modernism isolates the self in its ideal of autonomy. The constructive postmodern solution is a relational, social self, which some political theorists have called "situated autonomy." The phrase "relational and social" appears redundant, but *relational* is an ontological term indicating the presence of internal relations, while *social* refers to how much stress is placed on social influences. Thus the Buddhist self is fully relational but not as social as the Confucian self, while the Daoist self is also fully relational but, especially in Zhuangzi, exhorted to sever all contacts with society. Chapter 2 contains much more on a constructive postmodern view of the self.

Whereas the yogi's goal is to discover the power of the universe and then to use it as a means to liberate himself from all constraints, both natural and cultural, the Confucian sage's goal is just the opposite—integrative and embracing of others and nature. The last three chapters propose that the Confucian concept of *ren*, which makes human relatedness the essence of human nature, is the best Chinese answer to spiritual Titanism. In contrast to Kṛṣṇa, Gautama, and Jesus, who were deified early by their devotees, the elevation of Confucius came much later in the development of Confucianism. Even here, as we demonstrate in Chapter 9 most Confucian philosophers saw him only as a great sage. The Confucian triad of Heaven, Earth, and humans—in which human beings are not deified, gods are not humanized, and nature is not devalued—contrasts sharply with Christian and Indian incarnational theologies that upset the balance of the Chinese cosmic harmony. Chapter 10 defends Xunzi's view of the Cosmic Triad against commentators who have incorrectly seen him as anticipating scientific humanism and technology. The Daoists are also committed to cosmic balance and Zhuangzi reminds us that it is wrong to take "Heaven as your authority and do without [E]arth."[44]

In contrast to the yogi's identification with Puruṣa, the last chapter demonstrates that the Daoist sage does not identify with the Chinese cosmic giant Panku, but with primordial chaos (*hundun*), an image completely devoid of anthropocentrism and anthropomorphism. Also discussed are issues such as the alleged reference to personal immortality in the *Daodejing*, the nature of the Daoist immortals, and the characterization of the sage as "godlike" or "spiritual" (*shen*). We will also consider Zhuangzi's alleged connection to deconstructive postmodernism and his similarities to Nietzsche, whose relation to spiritual Titanism will be discussed in the next section. The Daoist concept of *wu wei* is obviously an answer to spiritual Titanism, but the socially engaged Confucian solution is much more preferable.

While the issues that Titanism raises are psychological, social, and political, this study is primarily a philosophical enterprise, one inspired by process philosophy and constructive postmodernism. (As already indicated in the preface, a sociological study would be frustrated by the fact that the presence of conceptual Titanism in India is not predictive of the negative practices expected.) This book claims that Titanism is basically a philosophical mistake with theological implications: a conflation of human and divine attributes. Chapter 6 does summarize Stanley Kurtz's psychoanalytic arguments for Indian Goddess worship, but the discussion's focus is on a comparative analysis of the material principle and the various concepts of power in Indian thought. Jainism and Chinese philosophy are criticized and praised respectively on philosophical grounds. Chapter 2 is a philosophical analysis of the self vis-à-vis issues in modernism and postmodernism. Titanism is an extreme form of modernism in which modernist problems have been exacerbated. Modernist alienation is intensified in the Titan's claim of absolute autonomy and independence. This alienation is not only social but it also leads to, in most instances, a separation from the body and from nature. In the case of Sāṃkhya-Yoga the soul-body distinction is absolute (the *puruṣa* has no relations at all with the material world); or in Jainism there are relations with the body and the world, but matter, at least according to some commentators, is made, Manichean-like, the source of evil.

Absolute separation, total self-sufficiency, and perfect knowledge are not attributes that even the most dedicated ascetics can honestly claim for themselves, so we must look to extraexperiential models for the self-aggrandizing self of spiritual Titanism. Commentators are most probably correct in pointing to the Christian God (or alternatively to the physical atom) as the model for the Western autonomous self, but no comparable ideal was present for the early Jaina and Sāṃkhya nontheistic thinkers. Here the concept of the isolated soul must have come from the experience of self-world separation brought about by the practice of extreme austerities. Gautama Buddha's view of self-world interdependence arose from a fresh look at the world made possible by his rejection of the world-denying practices of his contemporaries and by his elimination of all material and spiritual substances. While I offer Buddhism and Confucianism as philosophical counters to spiritual Titanism, it is not my intent to give any detailed philosophical defense of them as answers to spiritual Titanism. (I humbly admit that I do not possess the analytical skills to flesh out, for example, all the characteristics of a coherent concept of a social self.) I simply offer their views on self, body, and nature—sometimes using the best commentaries available—as the best Asian alternatives.

Nietzsche's *Übermensch* Not a Titan

If one looks for Titanism in the West, one might be tempted to say that Nietzsche's *Übermensch* is the highest embodiment of extreme humanism. I believe that this view is mistaken. Nietzsche's Titan is symbolized as a lion, the second of the Three Metamorphoses of *Thus Spake Zarathustra*. The lion, Titan-like, battles the dragon called Thou Shalt, who rules over the camel, the first metamorphosis. The lion takes every "It was" or "it happened to me" and transforms it into a "Thus I willed it and shall will it for eternity." Even though necessary and liberating, the lion's work is ultimately negative and destructive. (The lion is called thief as well as predator and this might provide a link to Prometheus stealing fire to create a new humanity.) The lion opens up unlimited freedom and is thus effective in destroying old values; but because of his nihilism he is incapable of creating new values. The Promethean "No" of the lion must be replaced by the sacred "Yes" of the child, the third metamorphosis, which I believe is Nietzsche's answer to Titanism. "The child," as Nietzsche says, "is innocence and forgetting, a new beginning, a game [of creation], a self-propelled wheel, a first movement, a sacred Yes."[45]

The Titan is a false *Übermensch*, the superman of popular, but distorted Nietzschean interpretation. The true *Übermensch* knows "the meaning of the earth . . . I beseech you, my brothers," says Zarathustra, "remain faithful to the earth, and do not believe those who speak to you of other worldly hopes." In former times the greatest sin was "against God," but "to sin against the earth is now the most dreadful thing."[46] The *Übergang* of the *Übermensch* is also an *Untergang*; and she overcomes herself so that she is "over" herself, not the world or other people. (Actually the play of *Übergang* and *Untergang* works out much better in a Daoist context, where the sage's overcoming always appears as underachieving and self-effacing.) Many of the metaphors of the *Übermensch* are horizontal and immanent, rather than vertical and transcendent—for instance, "Man is a rope, tied between beast and over man—a rope over an abyss."[47] *Übermenschen* never transcend their animal natures, because, as Graham Parkes observes: "It is impossible to go over unless the rope is held in tension; and if one casts off behind and loses the connection back to one's animal past there will be nothing to prevent a plunge into the abyss."[48] *Übermenschen* appear to be true ecological beings: in their *Untergang* humankind will "prepare earth, animal, and plant for [them]."[49] The Overman is a person of the elements: he is the "sense of the earth" and also "a sea" so clean that it will redeem a polluted humanity.[50]

Parkes proposes that we conceive of the Three Metamorphoses as a dialectical triad of "immersion, detachment, and reintegration."[51] A person of the first stage is immersed in society and nature without any clear delineation of self and other. People at this stage typically take on the values that are given them, hence Nietzsche's image of a camel carrying the burdens of a herd morality. Persons in the second stage develop fully self-conscious egos and separate themselves from society/nature either through active protest and rebellion or through ascetic withdrawal. This is the point at which spiritual Titanism is possible, and this book will analyze theoretical instances of its actualization in Indian thought, particularly Jainism and Sāṃkhya-Yoga. A desert father known as Abba Joseph, who once exhorted a fellow monk "to become entirely as fire,"[52] offers a parallel to Indian yogis who claim to become one with the elements, not with society, and to appropriate the power of the universe. We shall see, for example, that the Hindu Śuka, after transcending his body and all the elements of nature, makes himself "a blazing fire without any smoke."

We shall, however, find just as many examples of the third stage of reintegration, which Parkes describes as a "return to participation, but now reflective and self-conscious. The self reengages with the world without being totally taken in by it."[53] The third stage is symbolized in Zen Buddhism in the ninth and tenth Ox-Herding pictures and in Zhuangzi's sage whose "body and vitality are without flaw" and who returns "to become a Helper of Heaven."[54] Parkes's insight reminds us that we are obviously dealing with metaphors in the Three Metamorphoses and that the reintegrated person will be *like* a child in her spontaneity, in her acceptance of things, and in her love of body and the earth. Unlike the literal child, the Overman will have refined raw instincts into a harmonized life of impulse and reflection. This reintegration will not be limited to human beings, but will encompass all of nature: "we [will] begin to naturalize humanity in terms of a pure, newly discovered, newly redeemed nature."[55] Nietzsche's child is like the spiritual pilgrim of T. S. Eliot's *Four Quartets*, who returns to the Garden and truly knows it for the first time. Reinterpreting Wordsworth somewhat, Nietzsche's child will be "Father to the Man," a new humanity beyond the camel and the lion.

Bernd Magnus distinguishes between "lumpers" and "splitters" among Nietzsche scholars, and I side with the lumpers in most of my interpretations. Magnus's distinction is not based on an analytic versus a continental approach or the philosophical versus the literary; rather, it is based on whether one gives any credence to Nietzsche's *Nachla ß*, specifically that material published as *The Will to Power*. Following the lead of other scholars, my comparison between Daoism and Nietzsche draws on *The Will to Power*. Most of my other points, however, come from *Thus Spake Zarathustra*, the book that Nietzsche thought was his best. In the lumpers' defense one could say that historical philosophy would be a rather impoverished resource if we could not consult unpublished works. There would be, for example, no Aristotle at all and a very minimal Wittgenstein, certainly not the "continental" Wittgenstein, which Magnus appears to reject but that some of us have found in his *Nachlaß*.

According to Magnus, the lumpers generally conclude that Nietzsche held specific philosophical positions: namely, a perspectivist epistemology, a will-to-power ontology, an eternal recurrence cosmology (here is where I "split" with the lumpers), and the *Übermensch* as a human ideal. On the other hand, the splitters see Nietzsche as the most brilliant forerunner of deconstructive postmodernism, demonstrating that no philosophical positions are possible. If Parkes is correct that the child metamorphosis goes beyond nihilism to reintegration, the lumpers' Nietzsche should be construed as a constructive postmodernist. In defense of the splitters, Magnus argues that

> no *published* aphorism treats eternal recurrence as a cosmology, . . . and that only two published aphorisms arguably assert will to power as a cosmology or an ontology of sorts. Equally interesting, in my opinion, is that the notion of *Übermensch* virtually disappears from Nietzsche's published *and unpublished* writings after *Zarathustra*.[56]

For our purposes, let us focus on the difference between the two schools with regard to the *Übermensch*. As we have just seen, the lumpers take Zarathustra at his word that common humanity will be overcome and that this transition will lead to a new race of value creators. Magnus summarizes the view of three lumpers on the *Übermensch*:

> Lumpers tend to construe the *Übermensch* as the essence of Nietzsche's notion of a higher humanity: an ideal of perfectibility (Schacht). The *Übermensch* has overcome his animal nature, sublimated his impulses, organized the chaos of his passions, and has given style to his character (Kaufmann). He is a free human being, joyous, without guilt, the master of instinctual drives which do not overpower him (Danto). The *Übermensch* overflows with vitality and health, spirituality, refinement, manners, independence of mind and action, intellectual honesty and astuteness (Schacht).[57]

As opposed to the view that the *Übermensch* is a "goal for human striving or as a recipe for achieving greatness," Magnus believes that the consistent splitter (he admits that some splitters are lumpers on the *Übermensch*) must stress the point that all ideal human types are culturally conditioned. One only needs to be reminded of two examples: Aristotle's "great souled" man, a propertied male beaming with pride, and with the Nazi interpretation of the *Übermensch*. This means that the lumpers would be hard-pressed, considering the great variety of historical preferences, to agree on a single set of virtues for the *Übermensch*. Indeed, Nietzsche's choice of ancient warrior virtues is a source of constant irritation for even his most enthusiastic readers.

Magnus proposes that instead of seeing the *Übermensch* as a normative ideal, we should see it as a particular attitude toward life, in which a person

> would crave *nothing* more fervently than the eternal recurrence of each and every one of life's moments. . . an *Übermensch* cannot lie or imagine his life under erasure, edited, emended in this way or that. Rather an *Übermensch* must love each and every moment of life unconditionally.[58]

Magnus's view of the Overman fits very nicely with a noncosmological interpretation of eternal recurrence, one that I have always supported. Nietzsche did not want us to subscribe literally to a cosmology of eternal return; he only wanted us to live *as if* every moment of our lives would come back again. His pseudoscientific speculations notwithstanding, Nietzsche is using scare tactics; the terror of eternal recurrence (Zarathustra's most dreadful thought) is a psychological ploy to eliminate self-deception, to force us to love our lives, and to get us to take full responsibility for ourselves. The most that eternal return can mean psychologically is that we can expect to be faced with many similar events in our lives and the sooner we remove the shackles of bad faith the better off we shall be. The most that eternal return can mean cosmologically is that the universe has no ultimate meaning—in part or as a whole.

Whether we are lumpers or splitters we should all agree that the *Übermensch* is no Titan. (Even Magnus's suggestion that the *Übermensch* is an "inverted secular god equivalent" does not mean that the Overman takes on divine attributes.) This is not only clear in the strong implication that the Overman is the child, but also in the more indirect indication that all people, regardless of mental or physical powers/appearances, can overcome themselves. Both the *Zhuangzi* and *Zarathustra* play host to large numbers of strange characters, many of them crippled and deformed. For Zhuangzi the real deformity—being crippled by Confucian virtue—is far worse than any physical deformity. Indeed, Zhuangzi's monsters express unconditional self-acceptance and self-love in the Nietzschean sense. While Zhuangzi's characters are generally self-affirming, Nietzsche's motley crew of "higher men" is in constant need of preaching and prodding. Zarathustra's advice to a group of cripples who besiege him is that they should not beg for miracle cures, but that they should perform the greatest "miracle" themselves, namely, to use their own wills to overcome their handicaps.[59] Being an *Übermensch* is a matter of accepting things as they are, the greatest of all challenges in the nonteleological universe of Nietzsche and Zhuangzi. Zarathustra's rough treatment of the cripples is only a way of forcing them to stop their self-pitying and to start them on the road to self-love. In the daily news we are continually reminded of handicapped persons who have overcome incredible odds to lead exemplary human lives. No one can "reach the ultimate in a single leap"[60]—this is the illusion of Titanism—but all human beings can overcome themselves and flow with the Dao of Heaven.

1 Titanism in the West

[Christ] became man so that we might become God.

—Athanasius, *De Incarnatione* (54.3)

To be man means to reach toward being God.

—Jean-Paul Sartre

Learn to live and to die, and in order to be a man, refuse to be God.

—Dr. Rieux, Albert Camus, *The Plague*

O my soul, do not aspire to immortal life, but exhaust the limits of the possible.

—Pindar

Introduction

In American culture *humanism* has not been a term widely used until the 1980s, when the Religious Right began to employ it to execrate everything that it is against. It used to be that all of America's ills were blamed on a "Communist conspiracy," but now this has been replaced with a "humanist" conspiracy. Humanists are being targeted as the one source of every evil, from homosexuality to one-world government. This attack is truly incredible if one considers the fact that humanism is one of the greatest achievements of Western civilization. The humanism of Socrates has become the basis for ethical individualism; the humanism of the Greek Sophists gave law its adversarial system and inspired Renaissance humanists to extend education to the masses as well as to the aristocracy; the Christian humanism of Aquinas and Erasmus helped temper negative views of human nature found in the biblical tradition; and the humanism of the Enlightenment gave us political rights, representative government, and free market economics.

Most of the distortion of the humanist tradition has come from the Religious Right, but equal blame must go to some secular humanists who insist that only their views are "true" humanism. These humanists, fundamentalists, and too many knowledgeable Christians continue to believe that all humanists are atheists. Humanists are most often described as those who attempt to move God aside and to take God's place; in other words, the Religious Right conceives of all humanists as Titans. Such a view simply does an injustice to the Western humanist tradition, which, since Plato and Aristotle, has been dominated by confirmed theists and moderate humanists. Secular humanism has its origins in Protagoras and in his belief that human beings are the measure of all things. This was definitely a minority tradition until the Enlightenment, but even then theistic humanists like the American Founding Fathers still prevailed. It has only been during the last two centuries that secular humanism has made any progress, culminating in our time with atheistic existentialism and other secular philosophies.

Humanism and Superhumanism

Western humanism can be defined as the view that holds that all human beings have intrinsic value and dignity. Humanists believe that human beings are individual centers of value with moral freedom and responsibility. Western humanists also trust reason rather than revelation as a guide to truth, but they must realize that even their own principles cannot be strictly demonstrated as true. The limited scope of human reason does allow theistic humanists to appeal to divine revelation, but only if these revealed truths do not undermine basic humanist principles. For example, Calvin and Luther's rejection of reason (particularly Luther's), their belief in utter human depravity, and their affirmation of total divine determinism definitely remove them from the humanist camp. While humanists in Europe and Asia differ on the exact nature of human freedom (see chapter 8), a basic humanist assumption will be the belief that human beings play a principal role in shaping their own destinies.

If properly conceived, humanism does not involve the displacement of God in favor of humankind. True theistic humanism will let God be God and humans be humans. This is what could be called the "Hebraic principle," based on the greatest discovery of the ancient

Hebrews, namely, the transcendence of God. The Hebrew writers of the sixth century B.C.E. not only overcame the primitive anthropomorphisms of earlier writers, but also made a clean break with Mesopotamian views in which, for example, gods battled with sea dragons or mated with humans. This of course thoroughly confused the distinction between the divine and the nondivine.

Confucianism and Buddhism are the only Asian philosophies that have been called humanisms. (See chapter 8 for more on Buddhist humanism.) Confucius' strong focus on human dignity and right human relationships and on the deemphasis on divine powers establish his humanist credentials. Confucian humanism can be summarized best by a passage from the *Analects*: "It is humans that make the Way great and not the Way that can make humans great."[1] Confucius also respects the Hebraic principle by refusing to humanize Heaven and rejecting the divinization of human beings. This will be the main topic of chapters 9 and 10.

We must be careful in formulating a general definition of humanism that will encompass both Asia and Euro-America. The humanism of the Greeks and the Chinese focuses on this-worldly concerns without giving up the idea of a transcendent realm altogether. In other words, humanism's principal concerns in Greece and China were secular. Both the Greeks (especially after Socrates) and Confucians turned from cosmology and metaphysics to what they considered to be the more pressing concerns of ethics and politics. The crucial agenda for both Socrates and Confucius was to establish proper human relationships. Most Indian thought can hardly be described as secular philosophy; therefore, the common worldly concerns we find in Western and Chinese humanism cannot be the baseline of a comprehensive view of humanism. The emphasis here is more on speculative metaphysics and cosmology, and this contrasts sharply with the humanism of Socrates, the Sophists, and modern existentialists.

As for a comprehensive definition of humanism, the entry from *Websters Ninth Collegiate Dictionary* serves our purposes very well: "A doctrine, attitude, or way of life centered on human interests or values, especially a philosophy that usually rejects supernaturalism and stresses an individual's dignity and worth and capacity for self-realization through reason." The Indian ascetic tradition, by virtue of its focus on humanity and its de-emphasis on the role of the gods, fits this broad definition of humanism. In the Hindu, Buddhist, and Jaina traditions human beings realize themselves through spiritual discipline (*tapas*), not through reason. Reason also plays a more subordinate role in Confucianism. Whereas for Aristotle "reason more than anything else is man,"[2] for Confucius true humanity (*ren*) consists in reciprocity and in loving others. Even with the Buddha's great dialectical skills, it is clear that the lay Buddhist is never liberated by reason but by virtuous action. Therefore, for both Confucianism and for some forms of Buddhism substituting "self-realization through virtue" for reason would serve to make this definition of humanism more universal.

The Greek Protagoras could be called the father of secular humanism in Europe. His *homo mensura* thesis becomes the basis for the extreme humanism of Titanism. Secular humanism need not be Titanistic if it remains within the bounds of human limitations. But when we find that humans are the measure of everything in the universe, then we have encountered the radical anthropomorphism and superhumanism that gives rise to Titanism. In the *Māndūkya Upaniṣad*, the human mouth becomes an analogue for basic cosmic sounds, and the yogi who reaches the third stage of "deep sleep" is able to "measure the whole universe in very deed and is absorbed (into it)."[3] In Western humanism the Titans celebrate their radical autonomy and control over their destinies; likewise, the yogi "attains to independent sovereignty, attains to the lord of the mind."[4] In the *Kauṣītaki Upaniṣad* the liberated one is even beyond good and evil,[5] a point that Karl Potter emphasized in an earlier discussion.

Extreme humanism in Asia and Europe does converge on one pervasive cosmological image: parts of the natural world are analogized as parts of the human body. One widespread expression of this is the idea that human beings are microcosms of the macrocosm. The Church Father Origen said that "you are another world in miniature and in you are the sun, the moon, and also the stars."[6] The Renaissance humanist Robert Grossetteste, in a small piece called "Man Is a Smaller World," suggests that the "head refers to the heavens: in it are the two eyes, like the lights of the sun and moon. The breast corresponds to the air . . . but the belly is likened to the sea . . . [and] the soles of the feet are likened to the earth."[7] The Swedish mystic Immanuel Swedenborg continues this same tradition: "The multitude of these little glands [of the brain] may also be compared to the multitude of angelic societies. . . ." But he also reproduces the Indian cosmotheandric view: "The whole of heaven has this resemblance to man, because God is a Man."[8] This is the ultimate goal of spiritual Titanism: to become God in God's absence or to dethrone the gods and to humanize the entire universe.

Existentialism and Titanism

The existentialist writers offer some of the best examples of Western Titanism. Feodor Dostoevsky's notorious protagonists are the most dramatic expression of this extremes humanism. First, we have Raskolnikov, the existentialist hero of *Crime and Punishment*, who after convincing himself that there is no reason why one should follow moral conventions, attempts to execute the perfect crime. Dostoevsky, simultaneously sympathetic and horrified at his own Titans, chronicles in painful detail the downfall of a man who thinks he can transcend the basic human predicament. The Ivan of *Brothers Karamazov* is also a Titan in his celebration of the death of God and in his famous declaration that if God does not exist then everything is possible. Late in the novel Satan appears to Ivan in a dream to foretell the coming of a man-god who will take God's place when all religious belief is destroyed.

It is with Kirilov of *The Devils* (sometimes entitled *The Possessed*) that the theme of the man-god is played out in some detail. Kirilov is part of a ragtag group of revolutionaries who are planning terrorist actions against the government, and his part in the plan is a prearranged suicide. He has already shown himself to be erratic and unreliable, and he finally explains himself to Stravrogin, one of the conspirators. Kirilov says that he believes that all things and acts are good, and the carrier of this message (obviously Kirilov himself) will be called the "man-god." Stravrogin is confused, for he believes that Kirilov must mean Jesus Christ. He reminds Kirilov that this man who said that all is good (Dostoevsky's oddly unbiblical view of Jesus) was crucified. Furthermore, protests Stravrogin, Jesus was the God-man not a man-god, which he, Kirilov, will become. This is the Western equivalent of the distinction between Avatāravāda and Uttarāvāda that was discussed in the introduction.

Later in the book Kirilov and another conspirator discuss the same subject. Kirilov argues, just like Ivan Karamazov, that theoretically God must exist, but an all-powerful deity would cause all evil and suffering. Such a God would also undermine human freedom, so he has to reject God. But there is even more to Kirilov's Titanistic logic: he now has to kill himself, not for the revolutionary cause, but to bring about the age of the man-god. The crux of Kirilov's argument is the following: "If there is a God, then it is always His will, and I can do nothing against His will. If there isn't, then it is my will, and I am bound to express my self-will . . . [and] the most important point of my self-will is to kill myself."[9] Kirilov believes that his unique suicide will convince all other persons of their own self-will and of their basic potential as the new gods. "I am the only man in universal history who for the first time refused to invent God. Let them know it once for all."[10] Kirilov is the self-proclaimed prophet of a new race of spiritual Titans.

Jean-Paul Sartre continues the existentialism of Dostoevsky's Titans, and the best Sartrean parallel to Kirilov is Orestes in *The Flies*. Taking many liberties with Aeschylus' *Oresteia*, Sartre places Orestes in a Promethean rebellion against Zeus, who is presented as an unflattering mixture of Olympian deity, Yahweh, magician, and fool. Like Kirilov, Orestes also wants to sacrifice himself—Christ-like (but much superior to that failure Jesus, says Kirilov)—so that the human race can be free from both earthly and heavenly tyrants. Both Zeus and Aegistheus must realize that their game is up: "The bane of gods and kings. The bitterness of knowing men are free . . . [and] once freedom lights its beacon in a man's heart, the gods are powerless against him."[11] The impotence of the gods is a theme that will become dominant in Indian Titanism.

Both Kirilov and Orestes celebrate their dreadful freedom; neither of them feel self-pity or remorse; both of them execute actions, which, by virtue of having been freely chosen, are necessarily good; and both have cut themselves off from God's nature and from nature's laws. Both claim to be completely autonomous, guided by their own self-will and by their own laws. Neither of them, however, shuns responsibility, for as Orestes states: "You see me, men of Argos, you understand that my crime is wholly mine; I claim it as my own, for all to know; it is my glory, my life's work, and you can neither punish me nor pity me."[12] At this point it must be observed that the Indian Titans never transcend the law of karma (they simply fulfill it completely); therefore, Western Titanism is much more extreme with respect to natural moral law. But Indian Titans, as Karl Potter observed above, are more extreme in their view that nature can be transcended completely.

Sartre's manifesto *Existentialism Is a Humanism* gives the philosophical basis for his Titanism. First, his humanism is extreme: he declares that "we are on a plane where there are only men" and "there is no non-human situation."[13] With nature out of the way, Sartre turns to God. His Promethean challenge is that "the fundamental project of human reality is that man is the being whose project is to be God."[14] The violation of the Hebraic principle is complete: human beings are exhorted to take over divine prerogatives and divine attributes. Sartre claims that "each of us performs an absolute act in breathing, eating, sleeping, or behaving in any way whatever. There is no difference between being free, . . . an existence which chooses its essence, and being absolute."[15] Traditional theologians have observed that if the will is free, then divine and human wills would be formally equal. A will admits of no degrees: either one has one or not. At the same time, these theologians also conclude that our finitude and relative impotence mean that we obviously cannot do what God can do with unlimited power. Only Titans believe that we somehow have the power to challenge the gods and to dominate the universe.

Christian Titanism and the Incarnation

Direct empirical investigation of the self would never have produced the idea of an autonomous self; indeed, experience shows that the self, embedded as it is in a body and social relations, is anything but self-contained, self-sufficient, and completely self-directing. Therefore, the autonomous self must have been a theoretical invention. Mark C. Taylor proposes that the idea of the autonomous self is basically a theological conception.[16] Catherine Keller agrees with Taylor in her succinct observation that "the atomic ego is created in the image of the separate God."[17] In Christian philosophy and theology the ideal self is modeled on the concept of God as a self-contained, self-sufficient being of pure thought. For example, in his argument for free will, Thomas Aquinas essentially makes the human will an unmoved mover. The following passage is especially revealing:

> The closer an object of nature is to God, the greater in it can be found an expression of a semblance of divine dignity. It is furthermore a matter of divine dignity to move, influence, direct all things and be moved, influenced, and directed by no other thing. Hence, the closer a natural object is to God the less it is directed by an other and the more it is capable of directing itself.[18]

In his moral rationalism Kant presents the same view of the self, but with significant changes. The effect of Kant's reduction of religion to morality is that the transcendent reality of God is replaced by conscience, which is to be interpreted as a source of divine commands. One possible interpretation leads to a humanism of radical proportions: autonomous reason, an unmoved mover, takes over divine prerogatives. In short, there is for Kant a little god, or Titan, in each one of us. Kant's moral rationalism can be seen as the fulfillment of Aristotle's belief that "reason is divine" and that "life according to it is divine in comparison with human life."[19]

Thinkers with any respect for logic must strongly disagree with Sartre's contention that "there is no difference between being an absolute, temporally localized" and being God.[20] Sartre is obviously contradicting himself: an absolute cannot be temporally localized. Even if there were no God, this does not mean that we can take on divine attributes. But if God exists, then the logic of divinity requires that we acknowledge an ontological difference between Creator and creature, between a necessary, infinite being and contingent, finite beings. This is the thrust of the Hebraic principle in the Judeo-Christian (as well as in the Zoroastrian and Islamic) tradition. Jewish and Christian thinkers might, therefore, contend that the lesson of the Garden, the moral of the story of Job, and other examples of God's sovereign control offer the best defense against Titanism.

Even though the Bible warns against extreme humanism—even, some might say, humanism in any form—this does not mean that those who interpret biblical teachings were immune from Titanism. In fact, in the Judeo-Christian tradition, it was only the Sadducees who strictly adhered to the Hebraic principle. Along with the Pharisees, the Sadducees rejected the Christian idea of Incarnation (to them a pagan mixing of human and divine), but the Sadducees, unlike the Pharisees, also eschewed the resurrection of the body and eternal life. In addition to rejecting any idea of incarnation (the humanization of God), a truly Hebraic theology must also avoid any divinization of humans by granting them the divine attribute of immortality. Both concepts involve a clear violation of the Hebraic principle. In rejecting an immortal soul, the Sadducees were being loyal to a preexilic Hebrew tradition that the human soul was thoroughly mortal and corruptible. Furthermore, references to bodily resurrection and to eternal life, except for a few obscure passages in the Psalms, do not appear until after the Babylonian captivity. For the preexilic Hebrews, all human beings, regardless of virtue or vice, went to Sheol, the Hebrew equivalent of the Greek Hades. Walter Brueggemann finds the strongest biblical humanism in the Wisdom literature.[21] Here Brueggemann discovers a reaffirmation of the preexilic belief that "being human is all there is" as contrasted with the orthodox doctrine that "being human is just a stage" in our goal of becoming angels or gods.

At this point the intimate relationship between the two major violations of the Hebraic principle—our own divinization and the humanization of God—becomes clear. In his *De Incarnatione* Athanasius proclaimed that the Logos "became man so that we might become God."[22] This is not just an erratic comment on Athanasius' part, because we can read in Thomist Etienne Gilson that "by the grace of the Incarnation, which made human nature divine, we can have friendship with God because we can live with Him."[23] Drawing on Kirilov's point that the God-man is not the same as the man-god, some might claim that the doctrine of Incarnation is a sort of "reverse" Titanism. (There is some truth in this contention, and that will be discussed at the end of this section.) Incarnational theologies might be yet another Promethean way to humble and to humiliate God—to manipulate God for our own project of divinization. (The subordination of God is particularly evident in the concept of *kenōsis*, in which God empties himself and takes on "the form of a servant.")[24] The humanization of God through incarnation could be just another example of the vanity of our species. It becomes a vindication of Xenophanes dictum that all creatures make gods in their own image.

The English debate on the Incarnation in the late 1970s offers some evidence for this hypothesis. Michael Green, editor of *The Truth of God Incarnate* and leading critic of the liberals of *The Myth of God Incarnate*, quotes Michael Ramsey favorably: "God is Christlike, and in him is no un-Christ-likeness at all."[25] "Christ" is the New Testament equivalent of the Hebrew "Messiah," which was originally the name for the future warrior-king who would destroy the enemies of Israel and set up God's kingdom on earth. Although Messiah meant much more than this for most early Christians, it is nonetheless significant that contemporary evangelical Christians choose to characterize the *entire* nature of God in terms of this human concept.

When Green demands a "revelation of [God] that necessarily corresponds to this real nature,"[26] he is essentially saying that God's real nature is somehow basically human. Confirming my point about Xenophanes, Green argues that "God deign[ed] to show me what he was like in terms I could understand, the terms of a human life."[27] Joining Green against the liberals in the incarnation debate, Brian Hebblethwaite argues against John Hick's idea of multiple worldwide incarnations: "For only one man can actually be God to us, if God himself is one. . . . And the Son, we discover, is very God of very God, God's human face, reflecting God's own glory, and bearing the stamp of his nature."[28] Are these conservative evangelical Christians implicitly agreeing with Vivekananda that it is legitimate to "evolve God out of man"?

Among the liberals it is Don Cupitt who best unveils the profound mistakes of the literal incarnationists. Significantly, it is Cupitt who best expresses the Hebraic principle in *The Myth of God Incarnate*.

Cupitt contends that a literal incarnation made it easy for the Church to substitute a worship of Christ for the worship of God. This development was subtle, but deeply rooted, and broke through dramatically in the Christocentrism of the Reformation. As Cupitt states:

> Perhaps it was only when Christocentric religion finally toppled over into the absurdity of "Christian Atheism" that some Christians began to realize that Feuerbach [and Xenophanes] might have been right after all; Chalcedonian Christology could be a remote ancestor of modern unbelief, by beginning the process of shifting the focus of devotion from God to man . . . . [Chalcedon led to] a cult of humanity. Similarly, it could not resist the giving of the title *theotokos*, Mother of God, to Mary. The phrase "Mother of God" is prima facie blasphemous.[29]

This is yet another aspect of the Christian project of humanizing God.

While American fundamentalists agree with these English evangelicals about a literal Incarnation, they violate the Hebraic principle in another way. Many in the Religious Right preempt God's role in the universe by making judgments for God. The most famous example of this, of course, is Jerry Falwell's claim that God does not answer the prayers of Jews. More general, however, is the tendency for fundamentalists to identify who the real Christians are—usually themselves. In his incisive *Religious Right and Christian Faith*, Gabriel Fackre charges that fundamentalists who attempt to attain God's goals through political means are actually embracing a humanist ideology. Insofar as fundamentalists are attempting to do God's work for him in the world, they are just as humanist as the secularists they have railed against. Not unlike the ancient Gnostics, the fundamentalists claim infallible knowledge in all things spiritual. This claim is obviously an expression of Gnostic Titanism, and combined with the gnostic axiom of biblical inerrancy, it allows fundamentalists to profess to know what God exactly said and what God actually wants us to do.

In the evangelical rationalism of Ronald H. Nash and Gordon H. Clark, who resurrect the Logos doctrine of the early Church Fathers, we find the claim that, insofar as the divine Logos is in the human *imago dei*, we are able to think God's thoughts after him.[30] Especially striking is the following motto by Stuart C. Hackett, another evangelical rationalist: "I think, Therefore God is."[31] Titanistic elements in fundamentalism also appear among the creationists, who presume to know, for example, that the search for extraterrestrial life is unnecessary because they already know for sure that earthly life was the only life that God planned for cosmic history.[32]

Before ending this section, we have to qualify, in a significant way, the elements of Titanism that we have discovered in the Judeo-Christian tradition. Religions of obedience stress "other-power" in their belief in a transcendent, omnipotent God as sovereign ruler of the universe, while gnostic religions focus on "self-power" and explicitly subordinate the role of the gods. In religions of obedience, God saves us, but in religions of knowledge we save ourselves. A major exception in the Asian tradition is Pure Land Buddhism. Shinran (1173–1262), Buddhism's Luther, radicalized a tradition that had already placed emphasis on human depravity and reliance on "other-power" rather than on "self-power."[33]

Even though orthodox Christianity promises eternal life, it is clear (despite theologians like Hackett who hold to a "natural" immortality)[34] that the correct teaching should be a "bestowed" immortality. (Recall that Adam and Eve ate only from the "knowledge" tree, and Yahweh removed them before they could eat of the Tree of Life.) According to Christian doctrine, it takes a special act of God to restore the tarnished *imago dei* and to transform the mortal soul into something fit for the divine presence. Gilson made this point clear: God's grace makes "human nature divine."[35] By contrast immortality in Hinduism and Jainism is "natural," an essential attribute of the human soul. Therefore, the Titanistic elements of Christianity are mitigated by the fact that the Hebraic principle, while substantially compromised by the Incarnation, human immortality, and some gnostic elements, is still intact. In short, God is still in control and still makes the final decisions. (Recall that the yogi can "roll up space as it were a piece of leather," but only Yahweh can "roll up the skies like a scroll.")[36] Therefore, there is no extreme humanism in Christianity (unless one agrees completely with Cupitt's analysis of the Incarnation), but it is found in Hinduism, Jainism, and existentialism. The yogi discovers his own divinity, Kirilov tries valiantly to make himself God, but the Christian God bestows immortality by means of divine grace and our obedience.

Western Answers to Titanism

It is clear that theistic humanists must have a better theological model than that of divine master-obedient servant. Kant was entirely correct when he observed that the practice of religious subservience is nothing but an extension of our ancestors' "courtly obligations" to kings and emperors. But human beings have come of age: they have thrown off authoritarian governments and they now must reject all authoritarian forms of religion as well. Theistic humanism, therefore, must join the gnostic religions, but it must beware of the dangers of Titanism. In eschatology and ethics this means that the humanist must reject God as cosmic moralist and final judge. Among the current options in Protestant liberalism, the process theologians are correct in their rejection of God as a cosmic moralist,[37] and their denial of divine omnicausality and divine foreknowledge offers the best protection for human freedom.[38] At the same time, their organic view of reality and their relational view of the self allow humanists to avoid the alienation caused by the absolute autonomy claimed in Sartrean existentialism. Furthermore, the process theists propose an intelligible theory of divine immanence that tempers the extremes of the *via negativa* and its overemphasis on divine transcendence. (There are dangers in applying the Hebraic principle too strictly and thereby making any relation between God and the world impossible.) Finally, the process theists, particularly David R. Griffin, have proposed a "constructive postmodernism," which offers a middle way between the liabilities of both premodern and deconstructive views. This particular postmodern vision will be the principal theoretical framework for this book. Constructive postmodernism can also be found in the "dialogical" existentialists whom I will discuss presently.

One of the trademarks of humanist philosophers, especially under the influence of Kant, has been the use of the term *autonomy*. The word comes from the Greek words *autos* (self) and *nomos* (law), so that an autonomous person is a self-governing being. In many minds the idea of autonomy conjures up visions of isolated individuals vying for dominance over nature and over their fellow human beings. It gives the mistaken impression that people can and should be able to live without each other's support. Emphasis on autonomy seems to preclude any real basis for human community and social interaction. The possibility of moral and political anarchism created by self-legislating individuals, attested to by Dostoevsky and Sartre's heroes, is something that contemporary humanists must guard against.

One of the best critiques of autonomy is found in Gabriel Marcel's *Being and Having*, a crucial text for what could be called dialogical existentialism. The concept of self-sufficient, self-contained, self-governing individuals, just like the idea of the material atom, comes from "first reflection" and from the "realm of having," a "zone of separation." (It is no accident that a move to a relational self and to a more holistic social philosophy has gone hand-in-hand with a move to relational entities and to an "organic" universe in contemporary physics.) Marcel observes that the motto of the autonomous person is "I want to run my own life," which then leads to defensive and protective maneuvers that all come under the rubric of "Don't tread on me." For Marcel true freedom is not based on autonomy, but on a relational self that is fully engaged with other people and with the world. True freedom is "rooted in Being," not having, and "transcends all possible possession. . . ."[39] That means, for example, that "we *are* our bodies" instead of "we *own* our bodies," as many contemporary feminists and libertarians are prone to say. The former view is one that we will also find in Confucianism and in many Buddhist schools.

If we take Marcel seriously, then all language about us "owning" ourselves (some humanists) or God "owning" us (fundamentalism) must be given up. A campus poster once announced a talk, sponsored by the Campus Crusade for Christ, entitled "Whose am I?" This was obviously a fundamentalist response to the humanistic question of "Who am I?" and in turn a derivation of the Socratic "Know thyself." It is distressing to discover that John Locke, a great humanist in all other respects, supports the fundamentalist view: "As a work of God, [man] remains always not only God's servant but forever God's property."[40]

In their introduction to process theology, John B. Cobb and David R. Griffin praise the existentialists for their contributions to our understanding of human nature. I believe that this praise ought to be more discriminatory in light of the Titanism that we have discovered in the "monological" existentialists—Dostoevsky's heroes and Sartre. The key to dialogical existentialism (Heidegger, Marcel, Buber, and Merleau-Ponty) is an explicit critique of a Cartesian methodology which, from the beginning, perpetuates an alienating gap between the self and the world. Descartes's method of systematic doubt leads to the isolated *ego cogito* and then to the problem of this ego's relationship to the world. Descartes solves this problem positively with a confident flourish of arguments for the existence of God and for the external world.

The "monological" existentialists, rejecting these arguments for God but retaining the Cartesian starting point, leave us at the nadir of doubt with at best a paradoxical idea of God (Kierkegaard) or at worst a thoroughgoing atheism and solipsism (Sartre). Using the advantages of the literary medium, these thinkers are only dramatically expressing what many academic philosophers have thought for a long time: that the inevitable result of the Cartesian method is solipsism and skepticism. Sartre's Cartesian starting point is perfectly clear in his manifesto *Existentialism Is a Humanism*. He states confidently: "Subjectivity of the individual is indeed our point of departure, and this for strictly philosophic reasons. . . . There can be no other truth to take off from than this: *I think; therefore, I exist*. There we have the absolute truth of consciousness becoming aware of itself."[41]

Marcel, Heidegger, Merleau-Ponty, and Buber explicitly reject this Cartesian starting point, and Marcel suggests that philosophy must move from "intrasubjectivity" to "intersubjectivity"—hence, the two types of existentialism: monological and dialogical. Sartre does in fact use the term "intersubjectivity," but his way of explaining it is not dialogical: "This is the [intersubjective] world in which man decides what he is and what others are."[42] Although in the preceding discussion Sartre appears to understand the implications of a legitimate dialogical view (e.g., "he perceives them as the condition of his own existence"), the conclusion just quoted indicates that he does not leave his Cartesian isolation and his radical humanist notion of total self-determination. In a famous 1970 interview, Sartre confesses that he had finally learned the "power of circumstance," and that although he had used Heidegger's concept of "Being-in-the-world" in *Being and Nothingness*, he had not realized that this was incompatible with radical subjectivity and freedom.[43]

Although Albert Camus maintained a Cartesian methodology and preserved a Sartrean dualism of consciousness and the world, he nonetheless recognized the meaning of limits and always knew the dangers of Titanism. Camus's comment that we must imagine "God without human immortality" shows that he has a full understanding of the Hebraic principle.[44] Camus also criticizes spiritual Titanism in his concept of "philosophical suicide," the heroic attempt to transcend basic human limitations. In his 1970 interview Sartre admitted that he had once been captured by the "myth of the hero." Camus, therefore, deliberately creates an antihero as a substitute for the Titans—Ivan, Raskolnikov, Kirilov, and Abraham—of earlier existentialist literature. Instead of Prometheus and Sartre's Orestes, Camus offers us Sisyphus, "proletarian of the gods," who instead of battling Zeus and protesting his punishment, accepts the lesson not learned by extreme humanists: "The wholly human origin of all that is human."[45] One of Camus's strongest comments against Titanism is the following: "By what is an odd inconsistency in such an alert race, the Greeks claimed that those who died young were beloved of the gods. And that is true only if you are willing to believe that entering the ridiculous world of the gods is forever losing the purest of which is feeling, and feeling on this earth."[46]

Dostoevsky also knows that we have to be true to the earth. In *Crime and Punishment* Raskolnikov's Titanism is countered by the childlike innocence and acceptance of Sonya, who, after hearing Raskolnikov's confession, tells him to go to the "Four Corners" and to kiss "Mother Earth." Dostoevsky realizes, as Nietzsche did, that extreme humanism is ultimately destructive of every human value. Late in the novel Raskolnikov has a dream, which Dostoevsky obviously designed as a warning:

> He had dreamt in his illness that the whole world was condemned to fall victim to a terrible, unknown pestilence which was moving on Europe out of the depths of Asia. All were destined to perish, except a chosen few, a very few. . . . People who were infected immediately became like men possessed and out of their minds. But never, never, had any men thought themselves so wise and so unshakable in the truth as those who were attacked. Never had they considered their judgments, their scientific deductions, or their moral convictions and creeds more infallible. Whole communities, whole cities and nations, were infected and went mad. All were full of anxiety, and none could understand any other; each thought he was the sole repository of truth and was tormented when he looked at the others, beat his breast, wrung his hands, and wept. They did not know how or whom to judge and could not agree what was evil and what good. They did not know whom to condemn or whom to acquit. Men killed one another in senseless rage. . . . In the whole world only a few could save themselves, a chosen handful of the pure, who were destined to found a new race of men and a new life, and to renew and cleanse the earth; but nobody had ever seen them anywhere, nobody had heard their voices or their words.[47]

This nihilistic vision represents Dostovesky's acute perceptions of the dangers of modernism. His diagnosis is, in short, that modernism leads to Titanism, both spiritual and technological. (It is indeed incongruous that madmen making scientific deductions come out of Asia, but it is consistent with Indian yogis who claim to be beyond good and evil.) Dostoevsky's answer, much like Solzhenitsyn's, is a call for a return to Mother Earth, Mother Russia, and the Russian Orthodox Church—a decidedly premodern solution to modernism's radical individualism and alienation. Keeping the dialogical existentialists and process theists in mind and drawing on Hebrew and Buddhist sources, we will now turn to a consideration of some postmodern solutions.

2 The Self and Constructive Postmodernism

God versus Satan becomes Pure Soul versus Matter. God is Pure Soul. Satan is Pure Matter, the tempter, seducer, deluder and Jailor of the Soul.

—J. L. Jaini[1]

"Body am I, and soul"—thus speaks the child. And why should one not speak like children?

—Zarathustra[2]

A dawning realization that I have no idea what "postmodernism" means has led me to wonder whether I ever knew what I meant by "modernism."

—Richard Rorty[3]

Introduction

A major focus of this study is the concept of self and its relation to others and to the universe. If we say that the primordial unity of the Upaniṣads offers a premodern view of the self, and recognize the Jaina-Sāṃkhya-Yoga philosophies as anticipating modern selfhood, then Buddhist and Chinese philosophy may have the potential of a postmodern interpretation. (This means that the seeds for both modernism and its postmodernist critique were already present in the Axial Age.) Many commentators have spoken of the Buddha's anticipation of postmodernism, and David J. Kalupahana is correct in aligning him with constructive postmodernism rather than with French deconstruction.[4] The response of deconstruction to the autonomous self is to negate it completely, but constructive postmodernism seeks to reconstruct the self as relational and social. In their innovative book *Thinking Through Confucius*, David L. Hall and Roger T. Ames, drawing on both the pragmatic and process traditions, have proposed a similar postmodern interpretation of Confucius.[5] Joining in Hall and Ames's "cross-cultural anachronism," the task of this chapter is to join dialogical existentialism and process philosophy with Hebrew, Buddhist, and Confucian views to sketch a constructive postmodern view of the self.

The first section will explore the dialectical development of *premodernism*, *modernism*, and *postmodernism* and it will give these terms a fully conceptual, rather than chronological, interpretation. The second section finds that, opposed to Sāṃkhya-Yoga and Jainism, Hebrew and Buddhist ideas of self share both somatic and relational qualities, characteristics also found in the Confucian self. The third section continues with a discussion of further liabilities of Sāṃkhya-Yoga and Jaina dualism. The fourth section demonstrates that the metaphysics of Advaita Vedānta contains a basic contradiction with regard to individual selves. The fifth section shows how a Buddhist triadic dialectic produces constructive postmodern solutions to basic problems. The concluding section summarizes the basic elements of a constructive postmodern self as an answer to Titanism.

Premodernism, Modernism, and Postmodernism

The modernism of this chapter does not mean modernization in the sense of industrialization and urbanization. Modernism is also not necessarily European and premodernism is not primarily Asian. Furthermore, modernism is not something new and recent and premodernism something old and ancient. Modernism has been described as a movement from *mythos* to *logos*, and this replacement of myth by logic has been going on for at least 2,500 years. Almost simultaneously in India, China, and Greece, the strict separation of fact and value, science and religion, was proposed by the Lokāyata materialists, the Greek atomists, and the Chinese Mohists. Finally, one can also discern the beginnings of a postmodernist response in philosphers such as Confucius, Zhuangzi, and Gautama Buddha. (For Zhuangzi and postmodernism see chap. 11.) There are some commentators who also take Śaṅkara as a forerunner of postmodern thought,[6] but it seems more probable that Brahman as the ultimate, undifferentiated substance is a premodern concept.

The crisis of the modern world has led many to believe that the only answer is to return to the traditional forms of self and community that existed before the Modern Age. Such a move would involve the rejection of science, technology, and a mechanistic cosmology. Ontologically the modern worldview is basically atomistic, both at the physical and at the social level. The cosmos is simply the sum total of its many inert and externally related parts, just as modern society is simply the sum total of social atoms contingently related to other social atoms. The modern state is simply the social atom writ large on an international scale, acting as dysfunctionally as the social atom does in smaller communities. The modernist view of time is also linear, with one event happening one after the other, with no other purpose than simply to keep on continuing that way. The modernist view of the sacred has been to reject it altogether, or to place God in a transcendent realm far removed from the material world. The latter solution is the way that some Christian theologians have reconciled themselves with mechanistic science. The authors of *The Reenchantment of Science: Postmodern Proposals* have argued that this reconciliation began early on and that orthodox theologians found mechanistic science an effective foil against a resurgent pantheism and panpsychism coming out of the Renaissance.[7]

Modernism also gave new meaning to what it means to be a subject, and the primary source of this innovation was the *ego cogito* of Descartes's *Meditations*. The pre-Cartesian meaning of subject (Gk. *hypokeimenon*; Lat. *subiectum*) can still be seen in the "subjects" one takes in school in or the "subject" of a sentence. In this ancient sense all things are subjects, things with "underlying [essential] kernels," as the Greek literally says and as Greek metaphysics proposed. (As opposed to substance metaphysics, the process view of pansubjectivism makes all individuals subjects of some sort of experience.) After Cartesian doubt, however, there is only one subject of experience of which we are certain—namely, the human thinking subject. All other things in the world, including persons and other sentient beings, have now become objects of thought, not subjects in their own right. Cartesian subjectivism, therefore, gave birth simultaneously to modern objectivism as well. With the influence of the new mechanical cosmology, the stage was set for uniquely modern forms of otherness and alienation.

By contrast the premodern vision of the world is one of totality, unity, and above all, purpose. These values were celebrated in ritual and myth, the effect of which was to sacralize the cycles of seasons and the generations of animal and human procreation. The human self, then, is an integral part of the sacred whole, which is greater than and more valuable than its parts. And, as Mircea Eliade has shown in *Cosmos and History*, premodern people sought to escape the meaningless momentariness of history (Eliade called it the "terror of history") by immersing themselves in an Eternal Now. Myth and ritual facilitated the painful passage through personal and social crises, rationalized death and violence, and controlled the power of sexuality. One could say that contemporary humankind is left to cope with their crises with far less successful therapies or helpful institutions.

In addition to the terror of history, many premodern people also saw the body and senses as a hindrance to the spiritual life. This view was later connected, as it was in Advaita Vedānta, with the view that the natural world as a whole is illusory or at most only a derivative reality. The alternative to Vedāntist monism was a dualism of soul and body; and, in its most extreme forms, Manicheanism and Gnosticism, one is presented with a fierce battle between our spiritual natures and our animal natures. Interestingly, a mind-body dualism characterizes some of modern thought, but it is formulated in a much more subtle and sophisticated way. Most importantly, matter is not considered the embodiment of evil.

It is important to observe that the doctrine of karma is modernist in assuming the concept of individual moral responsibility. It is also significant that individual karma is most consistently expressed in the Jaina-Yoga-Sāṃkhya philosophies that hold to the modernist idea of autonomous selves. Individual moral responsibility becomes problematic only in the *bhakti yoga* of Hindu saviors' forgiveness of human sins and in the distribution of the Boddhisattvas' excess merit. Some philosophers have struggled to make intelligible the idea of collective karma,[8] but the basic logic of karma dictates individual responsibility for individual acts and a corresponding individual resolution of guilt related to these acts.

A related contrast is the idea of premodern shame cultures based on collective guilt and on the modern concept of guilt based on personal moral responsibility. John Kekes has illustrated this distinction very well by an analysis of the story of Gyges and the Lydian queen.[9] Shame cultures are premodern and assume no distinction between the inner and the outer, a realm of private as opposed to public morality. Therefore, the only way for the queen to save her honor was to make public the disgrace she experienced when the king arranged for Gyges to see her naked. Kekes claims that shame is a destructive emotion, because shame cultures are basically reactionary and do not allow constructive criticism of social norms or proper resolution of conflicting personal feelings. In short, Kekes concludes that there can be no moral progress if shame is central to personal action. If Confucian *yi* (usually mistranslated as "righteousness") is simply an internalized *li* (social norms), then Confucian culture is a shame culture with exactly the same problems. A typical modernist and also deconstructionist answer to this problem is to reject or to completely relativize moral standards. But if Hall and Ames are correct in their interpretation of *yi* as a personal appropriation of *li*,[10] we then might well see this as a constructive postmodern solution to the conflict between private and public morality. Such an interpretation essentially makes *yi* the Confucian equivalent of the act of personal appropriation that is present in Aristotle's mean, one that is objective but yet "relative to us."[11]

Modern philosophy generally separates the outer from the inner, the subject and the object, fact and value, the is and the ought, science and faith, politics and religion, the public from the private, and theory from practice. Following Descartes's insistence on a method of reducing to simples and of focusing on clear and distinct ideas, modern humans have made great strides conceptually and theoretically. The practical application of modernism has extended the rule of science and conceptual analysis to all areas of life: personal machines of all sorts, a fully mechanized industry, and centralized bureaucratic administration. Critics of modernism observe that it is a great irony that the modern state celebrates human rights but at the same time its state organization has destroyed the basis for personal autonomy. It has also eroded the intimate ties of traditional community life, and it has threatened the ecological balance of the entire planet.

Earlier it was suggested that Śaṅkara represents premodern thinking, but it is probably more accurate to say that, as opposed to premodern views unaffected by modernist dichotomies and alienation, Śaṅkara's absolute monism is in part a response to Jaina-Sāṃkya-Yoga dualism. It is a significant fact that absolute monism is not found in any premodernist worldview, which, in its search for unity does not eliminate the individual completely and certainly does not declare plurality an illusion. The uncompromising monism found in Śaṅkara and in his predecessor Gauḍapāda is a comparatively late development, which could lead one to conclude that absolute monism represents a reflective and deliberate return to premodern unity with a vengeance, at least an intellectual vengeance. It should also be acknowledged that both Gauḍapāda and Śaṅkara may well have been influenced by Buddhist absolutists such as Aśvaghosa, who declared that the world of the "birth-and-death" soul has no "genuine reality."[12] Therefore, "illusionism" may have had its origins in Mahāyāna Buddhism not in Hinduism. Reacting against the modernist dualism and realism of the Sautrāntikas and Sarvāstivādins, many Mahāyāna philosophers returned to premodern modes of thinking.

Constructive postmodernists wish to reestablish the premodern harmony of humans, society, and God without losing the integrity of the individual, the possibility of meaning, and the intrinsic value of nature. They believe that French deconstructionists are throwing out the proverbial baby with the bathwater. The latter wish to reject not only the modern worldview but any worldview whatsoever. Constructive postmodernists want to preserve the concept of worldview and to propose to reconstruct one that avoids the liabilities of both premodernism and modernism. They would be very comfortable with Graham Parkes's interpretation of Nietzsche's Three Metamorphoses as representing immersion, detachment, and reintegration. They could take the camel stage as symbolizing the premodern self immersed in its society; the modern lion as protesting the oppressive elements of premodernism but offering nothing constructive or meaningful in return; and the child as representing the reintegrative task of constructive postmodernism. As Parkes explains: "The third stage involves a reappropriation of the appropriate elements of the tradition that have been rejected. . . . The creativity symbolized by the child does not issue in a creation *ex nihilo*, but rather in a reconstruction or reconstrual of selected elements from the tradition into something uniquely original."[13] It must be stressed that Parkes is attributing this view to Nietzsche, who is generally taken to be the nineteenth century's leading prophet of deconstructive postmodernism.

Constructive postmodernists are also concerned about a logocentric society and the dominance of calculative and analytic reason, but instead eliminating reason altogether, they call for a reconstruction of reason. A working formula would be the following triad: *mythos* > *logos* as analytic reason > *logos* as synthetic, aesthetic, dynamic reason.[14] The best example of aesthetic reason is the unity of fact, value, and beauty that we find in Confucian virtue ethics—namely, the act of self-cultivation is analogous to the cutting and polishing of a gemstone. A more recent example of a reconstructed *logos* is found in the new "logic" of European art since the late nineteenth century. Cezanne rejected the classical (read: logocentric) perspective and initiated a revolution that opened up new ways of looking at the world. Drawing on Japanese and African themes at the turn of the century, artistic revolutionaries synthesized the premodern and modern in the same way that Gandhi did in his social and political experiments.[15] In a chapter entitled "The Reenchantment of Art: Reflections on the Two Postmodernisms," Suzi Gablick presents both deconstructive and reconstructive examples of contemporary art and finds that the latter movement is a continuation of the artistic revolution just described. Gablick states that

> Reconstructionists . . . are trying to make the transition from Eurocentric, patriarchal thinking and the "dominator" model of culture to a more participatory aesthetics of interconnectedness, aimed toward social responsibility, psychospiritual empowerment, deep ecological commitment, good human relations, and a new sense of the sacred. . . .[16]

This view of art reintegrates premodern elements but emphatically rejects the modernist view of art for art's sake, which is yet another result of the alienation of the private and public that we find in modern culture.

Hebraic and Buddhist *Skandhas*

There is still much truth in Karl Jaspers' belief that the origin of the world's great philosophies and religions came during an "axial" period (1,000 B.C.E. to 300 B.C.E.) in world intellectual history. The major discovery of this period was the self and the problem of its relationship with the world. Generally speaking, Asian and European responses to the "axial" self were positive. The Greeks celebrated this discovery by creating works of art glorifying the human form, speculating about the nature of reality, and offering rational arguments about the proper role of humans in society. The Hebrew prophets' contributions were just as profound, with their concern for social justice and their shift from a collective to an individual view of moral responsibility.

The Hebrew relational self—although not phrased in sophisticated terms—is superior to Greek dualism, which of course has had a profound effect on Western conceptions of self. Both Hebrew *nephesh* and Greek *psychē* originally referred to the unity of soul and body, a somatic soul as it is sometimes called. But later developments in Greece culminating in Plato broke the psychophysical unity of *psychē* into a disjunctive dualism. Although the Hebrew somatic soul is partially preserved in the doctrine of the resurrected body, the physical body, following the Platonic prejudice, was still denigrated in the Judeo-Christian tradition and the Hebrew relational self was almost entirely eclipsed. In his interpretation of Charles S. Peirce as a constructive postmodern thinker, Peter Ochs observes that Peirce reaffirms the Hebraic view that relationality is knowledge at its most basic level. As Ochs states: "Peirce did not read Hebrew, but the ancient Israelite term for 'knowledge'—*yidiah*—may convey Peirce's claim better than any term he used. For the biblical authors, 'to know' is 'to have intercourse with'—with the world, with one's spouse, with God."[17]

Interestingly enough, Gautama Buddha generally agreed with the Hebraic idea of an integral mind-body. Specifically, some Buddhist and Hebrew texts share the view that the heart is the physical basis of mind.[18] Furthermore, relationality is strongly implied in the six Hebraic *skandhas* (*nephesh*-soul; *ruah*-spirit; *hayyim*-life; *dam*-blood; *basar*-flesh; *leb*-heart-mind), which are best seen as functions rather than as entities. A comparison with the Buddhist soul constituents shows, somewhat surprisingly, that the Hebrews emphasize the somatic more than the psychological. At the same time, however, both David Kalupahana and Peter Harvey demonstrate how much influence material form (*rūpa*) has on Buddhist personality, even at the highest stage of spiritual development.[19]

The other Indian response to the axial discovery of the self was far less celebratory. The Jainas, the proponents of the Śāṃkhya-Yoga system, and the Upaniṣadic writers all feared that the self's unavoidable attachment to the phenomenal world would undermine any possibility for spiritual liberation. The response of those with monistic tendencies, first expressed in the Upaniṣads and radicalized in Advaita Vedānta, was to declare the world and the plurality of selves illusory (or at most only derivative in nature) and to urge total union with Brahman. Strictly speaking, since Śaṅkara held that all separation is illusory, there can be no actual reunion with the divine One. Some contemporary commentators object to the use of the term *illusion* as an appropriate description for the ontological status of the Advaitin world, but one must acknowledge the fact that in Śaṅkara's famous example of taking a rope for a snake the perception of the snake is indeed an illusion.

The retreat from the world was just as strong in Jainism and Sāṃkhya-Yoga. Their difference from Vedānta lay in their insistence on the autonomy and plurality of *jīva* or *puruṣa* selves respectively. The vision of spiritual liberation for each is very different from the Upaniṣadic writers: isolated, individual souls enjoying complete freedom from the attachments of a real material world. The Sāṃkhya-Yoga *puruṣa* is even more isolated than the Jaina *jīva*, because its involvement in matter is illusory while the Jainas believe that the soul is actually contaminated by karmic matter. (Vedānta's appropriation of the Sāṃkhya-Yoga system obscured the latter's extreme dualism in the same way that Judeo-Christian dualism overshadowed the Hebrew relational self.) Even though their goals are radically different, it is essential to keep in mind the conceptual parallels between the Europe and Jainism-Sāṃkhya-Yoga on autonomous selfhood.

Siddhartha Gautama's response to the axial discovery of the self was strikingly unique: he proposed the doctrine of no-self (*anatman*). This conceptual innovation was so provocative that it was bound to invite misinterpretation, and unfounded charges of Buddhist "nihilism" continue even to this day. Gautama anticipated Hume's view that the self is the ensemble of feelings, perceptions, dispositions, and awareness that is the center for agency and moral responsibility.[20] (The Buddha's view, however, is superior to Hume's, primarily because Gautama supported real causal efficacy among internally related phenomena. While Hume deconstructed any theory of causality, the Buddha reconstructed causal causality as conditionality relations within his theory of interdependent coorigination.) Gautama rejected the soul-as-spiritual-substance view of the Upaniṣads, Jainism, and Sāṃkhya-Yoga, and he deconstructed the "spectator" self of these philosophies twenty-five hundred years before recent thinkers dismantled the Cartesian self.

As opposed to strict deconstruction, for example, Buddhists hold that selves, though neither the same nor different throughout their lives, are nevertheless responsible for their actions. These selves are also real in the sense that they are constituted by relations with their bodies, other selves, and all other entities. This is why the Buddhist self should be viewed in relational or process terms rather than in the negative implications of the no-self doctrine. The Buddhist self is relational primarily in the sense of its dependence on the five *skandhas* and the internal relations this dependence entails. While Buddhism's relational ontology certainly implies social relationality, the Buddhist self is definitely more individualistic than either the Hebrew or Confucian view. In chapter 11 we shall see that Zhuangzi's fully relational ontology does not lead to a commitment on his part to any social relations at all. This is one of the principal reasons why a Confucian rather than a Daoist answer to spiritual Titanism will be preferred.

Another positive way to express nonsubstantiality is to describe the Buddhist self as "functional." In fact, each of the *skandhas* should be seen as functions rather than as entities. On this point, Kalupahana makes good use of William James (a far better Western counterpart than Hume), who, while denying a soul substance, maintained that consciousness is a function. As Kalupahana states: "*Rūpa* or material form accounts for the function of identification; *vedanā* or feeling and *saṃjñā* or perception represent the function of experience, emotive as well as cognitive; *saṃskāra* or disposition stands for the function of individuation; *vijñāna* or consciousness explains the function of continuity in experience."[21] Both Kalupahana and Peter Harvey describe the Buddhist self in the positive terms of psychophysical unity, process, and interrelation. According to Harvey, the Buddha never rejected the existence of a life-principle (*jīva*), which "is not a separate *part* of a person, but is a process which occurs when certain conditions are present. . . ."[22] This point as well as the previous observation about causality make the Buddha's philosophy much different from David Hume's.

Problems with Indian Dualisms

The primary discovery of Gautama's spiritual search before his enlightenment was that the substance metaphysics common to all Indian philosophical schools constituted the greatest obstacle to the religious life. The problem of selfishness is due to, or at least aggravated by, the false belief that there is a permanent self underlying the phenomenal self. Gautama concluded that the Jaina *jīva*, the Sāṃkhya *puruṣa*, and the Upaniṣadic *ātman* each constitutes a point of attachment that is just as addictive in asceticism as it is in sensualism. In other words, one can become just as attached to the idea of a substantial self (either in meditation or speculative thought) as one can become enslaved by the objects of sense. Gautama believed that the temptations here are so subtle and deep-seated that the craving for a permanent self is the greatest obstacle to overcome. As Kalupahana states: "The elimination of such obsessions . . . turned out to be more difficult than abandoning pleasures of sense, for if by freedom was meant only the latter, the Buddha could have attained enlightenment during the time he was practicing self-mortification."[23] Ultimately the meaning of Buddhist freedom lies in the freedom from reifying either external objects or internal subjects.

In Jainism and Sāṃkhya-Yoga there is an implicit Manicheanism, which has implications for moral responsibility and also the ecological values that are now being universally affirmed. (In contrast, the Buddha, like the Hebrews, always affirmed the self as a somatic soul—a psychophysical personality.)[24] The problem is mitigated somewhat in Sāṃkhya-Yoga, because *prakṛti* is sometimes portrayed as a positive partner in spiritual liberation. Once nature has played its part, however, it becomes inert and useless, and this is incompatible with the contemporary call for the full integration of the natural world. When Jainas speak of the "defiling corruption of . . . matter,"[25] we can see that the role of matter (*ajīva*) in Jainism is much more negative. Despite Buddhism's somatic selfhood and a later doctrine of universal Buddha-essence, its strong ascetic traditions did not allow Buddhist practice to be as body or world affirming as it could have been. The influence of Chinese naturalism (especially in its influence on Zen) and the Buddhist-Christian dialogue have turned contemporary Buddhism much more in this direction.

All experience, according to Gautama Buddha, is an interdependent web of causes and conditions, and the human self is constituted within this web. He concluded that the human self is possessive and aversive primarily because it views itself as an autonomous substance independent from other selves and things. The Buddha also established an important distinction between basic desires that can be fulfilled without accruing karmic debt, and cravings that could never be satisfied and are therefore karma crediting. Even enlightened beings, while still living, will have basic desires that can and must be fulfilled. Contrary to later transcendentalist interpretations, the Buddha also supported the use of concepts, as long as those concepts are, according to early Buddhist empiricism, of the "evident" rather than the "nonevident."

Ironically, the Jaina self is more extreme than most Western views in its insistence on total personal self-sufficiency and isolation. Although directed inward rather than outward, the Jaina goal of absolute freedom has significant parallels with Sartre's early existentialism, where human agents are exhorted to transcend all material causes and conditions. Sartre once said that even if behaviorism were true, we should reaffirm our freedom with Promethean defiance. The interesting fact is that Jainas believe that behaviorism and biological determinism are both true.[26] The thesis of this book is that both views are based on a false view of the self and on its relation to the world.

Jaina hylozoism is probably the most significant contribution to Indian philosophy and to contemporary environmental ethics. The value of Jain hylozoism, however, is mitigated considerably by Jaina dualism. Jainas cannot easily convince us of the unity of sentient creation on the one hand, and also insist on the eternal antagonism of mind and matter on the other. The radical dualism of *jīva* and *ajīva* produces the same dilemma as Cartesian dualism does. If matter does actually infect the Jaina soul, how, if the two are externally related substances, is this accomplished? The Jainas were no more successful in solving this problem than the Cartesians were. As we shall see later, Nāgārjuna had to deconstruct a similar metaphysical dualism that arose in the Buddhist Abhidharma, one that was not there in early Buddhism.

Sāṃkhya dualism is even more extreme than the Jainas, and it is so different from Western dualisms that Gerald J. Larson can only call it eccentric. Without the *puruṣas* Sāṃkhya philosophy would be just another form of reductive materialism, because every thing and event is explained in terms of a basic material principle. Both contemporary and Sāṃkhya versions of materialism exorcise the traditional "ghost in the machine" by explaining all mental events and activities in material terms. But the Sāṃkhya thinkers reintroduce the spirit in the most strikingly odd way. Larson explains:

> Sāṃkhya as it were refurbishes the "ghost," stripping it of its conventional attributes and reintroducing it in the framework of an "eccentric" dualism in the sense that the Sāṃkhya "ghost" no longer has to do with "mind talk," "mentalist" talk, or "ego" talk, all of which . . . are fully reducible to *guṇa* talk in good reductive materialist fashion.[27]

The *puruṣa* is pure conscious presence and nothing more. It has no other qualities and it is not a subject of any action. (Using the principle of the identity of indiscernibles, an Advaitin could argue that Sāṃkhya-Yoga pluralism does indeed dissolve into absolute monism.) Moral action for such souls, as completely passive entities, must take on a totally negative meaning. These selves, along with the Upaniṣadic *ātman* and Jaina *jīva*, transcend everything worldly, including of course the social, the ethical, and the political. The Jaina saint or Hindu yogi is literally beyond good and evil. It is difficult to see how the pure spiritual substances of Indian philosophy can possibly have any relation to the world of moral and practical affairs.

A Critique of Advaita Vedānta

In his book *Ahiṃsā: From Gautama to Gandhi* George Kotturan states that "there is no religious philosophy in the world which gives so much dignity to the individual as the Upaniṣads."[28] If Kotturan were reading the Upaniṣads through the eyes of Rāmānuja or Madhva, then he would have a better argument. But his interpretation is clearly that of Śaṅkara's Advaita Vedānta, which holds that individuals are ultimately unreal. If we take total negation in *nir-guṇa* Brahman seriously, the logical implication is that Brahman is totally devoid of all qualities, including moral ones.

Kotturan contends that nondualism makes love easy, because there is nothing easier than loving one's own self. The problem, however, is that, according to Śaṅkara, we actually do not have a true self of our own. In his view love must amount to Brahman loving himself, but even this cannot be correct because, again, ultimate Brahman, *nirguṇa* Brahman, is totally devoid of qualities. The great moral exhortations of the Upaniṣads make no sense if nondualism in this sense is true. To be self-controlled, to give to others, and to be compassionate (see the *Bṛhadāraṇyaka Upaniṣad* 5.2.3) are intelligible imperatives only if there are individual selves who have reciprocal relations with other beings. Upaniṣadic monism is shallow and empty of meaning if it is not interpreted to include the rich diversity of individual lives and situations. Upaniṣadic monism is better conceived as a panentheism that resacralizes the world rather than a transcendental monism that desacralizes it.

Kotturan's discussion of love manifests another problem—the self-regarding self—which has already been noted in Jainism and Sāṃkhya-Yoga. Kotturan claims that "it is not for the love of the neighbour that the neighbour is important, but for the love of the self that [the] neighbour is important. It is not a question of doing good or wrong to one's neighbour, it is the question of doing good or wrong to one's own self."[29] If this "self" is Ātman then it cannot be called one's own self. It is also hard to believe that Kotturan does not see how problematic it is to define the value of the neighbor in terms of self-love. Love and compassion must be based on a relational, other-regarding philosophy, rather than on a self-centered mysticism. Kotturan might respond that the distinction between the inner and the outer is an illusion, but this appears to contradict our ordinary experiences of the world. It also shows that the only self is Ātman, which is neither plural nor individual, and therefore it cannot be an agent in the world as either a subject or object of love.

An effective way of conceiving absolute monism is the prism analogy. If Brahman is white light, and if the color spectrum is the phenomenal world, then the prism that refracts the light stands for ignorance. If one eliminates ignorance, then one can see that everything is just an undifferentiated one. Due to ignorance, the world and its qualitative differences have a derivative reality only. Realizing the identity of Ātman and Brahman is like waking up from a dream and discovering that those images were only fleeting agitations of the mind.

John D. White has offered a criticism of Advaita Vedānta that fits nicely with the prism analogy.[30] If Śaṅkara assumes that some people are enlightened, while many others remain in ignorance (which he must obviously hold), then clearly his transcendental monism (White's phrase to distinguish Advaitins from pantheists) is untenable. The world will continue to exist for the unenlightened, but somehow it has ceased to exist for the liberated ones. (As White points out, the only way that the Advaitin can answer his argument is to deny the validity of the law of contradiction.) The result is that Śaṅkara's alleged nondualism is, at least until the liberation of all souls, a transcendental dualism, roughly similar to Christian orthodoxy. Furthermore, it means that, if some selves are liberated and some are not, there must also be a real plurality of souls—that is, many different soul-prisms refracting their own perspectives of the world.

The use of a holographic analogy (anticipated beautifully in the story of Indra's pearls) is also not compatible with Advaita Vedānta. The holograph can be broken into any number of parts, each of which contains the exact contents of the whole. The holograph is a differentiated whole with qualitative differences, not the undifferentiated one that Advaita assumes. The holographic analogy is very useful for those who support an organic holism that preserves real qualitative differences in the world. Note, too, that it preserves unity, but denies undifferentiated oneness. There is, after all, a difference between organic unity and the total oneness of *advaita*. The holographic analogy, however, does have its limits: it does not serve as an analogue for the experience of individual selves. Our experiences, unless they are illusory, are obviously not exact replicas of the experience of the whole. The holograph is rich in a single vision of diversity, but is not able to portray individual differences. In other words, our "piece" of the whole not only contains part of the big picture, but also a picture that is truly our own perspective on the whole.

The holographic analogy aptly represents Hua-yen Buddhism's view of the complete interpenetration of every thing in everything else. Steven Odin, however, has shown, in his brilliant comparative study of Hua-yen and Alfred North Whitehead,[31] that the latter's doctrine of negative prehension is the best way to make organic holism intelligible and compatible with experience. The totally mutual and symmetrical relations of Hua-yen eliminate real history as well as real individuals. Whitehead, on the other hand, holds that each new actuality is internally related to the past, but it takes, by virtue of negative prehensions, only a small portion of it into its own "concrescence." (And even that portion is made unique by the actual occasion's subjective aim.) The relations between an actual occasion and its past are asymmetrical, a doctrine that establishes both the arrow of time and the unique individuality of each and every actual occasion.

Several books have been written proposing that the general conclusions of contemporary physics were already anticipated by the Asian mystics. The view usually attributed to these mystics is the absolute monism of either Advaita Vedānta or of some forms of Mahāyāna Buddhism. These authors (e.g., Fritjof Capra and Gary Zukav) consistently confuse organic unity with Śañkara's oneness-without-a-second. And they are definitely misled if, following Sir James Jeans and/or Yogācāra idealists, they say that the universe is some sort of cosmic mind. Contemporary theories of matter and energy do confirm a basic unity in the universe, but this it best conceived as an organic whole with internally related parts. The Chinese word for physics—*wuli* (patterns of organic energy)—expresses this organicism beautifully.

If contemporary physics proves anything metaphysical, it is holistic pluralism, not absolute monism. Every subatomic particle has its own unique signature (otherwise it could not be detected), and these particles, qualitatively different from one another, could serve as rough analogues to individual souls. (If Whitehead is correct about subjective aim, then the principal criticism of this analogy is met. Hydrogen atoms, quantitatively identified by the same wave length, are qualitatively real individuals, not just empty entities.) Though each particle-soul has its own identity, both physics and the social sciences have taught us that these identities are not *sui generis*, self-contained, nor self-sufficient; rather, they are internally related to their environments and partially constituted by them. From this standpoint, the Jaina or Yogic goal of utter self-absorption and isolation as well as the island of conscience that many have admired in Socrates and Kant are all illusions. What is needed is a view of identity-in-difference that is found in most Buddhist schools or in the panentheism of Rāmānuja and American process philosophy.

A revised prism analogy with many different soul prisms refracting their own perspectives gives us both the plurality and equality of souls that experience and justice require. Advaita Vedānta does not do justice to the rich and dynamic diversity of life and the intrinsic value that ecological consciousness gives even to the smallest species. In contrast to Advaita Vedānta, the prism no longer stands for an ignorance that must be removed, but a window on reality through which we perceive the world. Following Rāmānuja, this aperture of the soul remains for all incarnations and after liberation as well. Finally, the revised analogy still confirms the validity of mystical experiences: through spiritual exercise soul-prisms are able to make themselves, momentarily, transparent to the One. In the mystics some of Indra's pearls sometimes become wondrously white with the light of Brahman.

A Buddhist Dialectic of Reconstruction

Authors who claim that Advaita Vedānta gives a basis for interdependence and interrelatedness do not realize that, strictly speaking, relations do not exist for an absolute monist. (F. H. Bradley makes the best attempt at proving this remarkable conclusion.)[32] If there is only one substance, then it obviously can have no relations with anything else, and ironically, this makes the much celebrated "union with Brahman" an oxymoron. Although Aristotle is not an absolute monist, both Bradley and Sañkara would agree with his claim that "relatedness is . . . a logical accident of substance."[33] (This remnant of Parmenidean monism here in Aristotle forms the basis of the entire Western metaphysics of substance.) The Buddhists, however, disagree: relatedness and interdependence are the very essence of reality.

If one is looking for parallels between Buddhism and contemporary physics, Sarvāstivādin atomism initially seems to be a good place to begin. Here one finds momentary units (*dharmas*) that are qualitatively different; but, contrary to both contemporary physics and early Buddhism, these atoms are externally related substances. In their attempt to return to original Buddhism, the Sautrāntikas criticized the Sarvāstivādins for giving mind and matter self-nature (*svabhāva*), but even some of them succumbed to substance metaphysics by insisting on a subtle personality (*pudgala*) that carries karma and survives death. The Buddha did not reject the concept of reincarnation, for he could verify that by retrocognition, but even the most acute ESP could not detect a transmigrating soul substance. While the Buddha concentrated on deconstructing the soul substances of his day, Nāgārjuna and Vasubandhu focused their dialectical skills on Abhidharma realism.

Instead of a two-moment dialectic of dismantling Indian metaphysics, many Buddhist texts offer a three-moment procedure of metaphysics > deconstruction > reconstruction. The first diad would be the antinomy of being (*sat*) and nonbeing (*asat*). The deconstructionists would leave this as undecided or appeal to transcendentalism, but many Buddhists resolved the antinomy with a third moment of "becoming." For Buddhist process philosophy we can expand the triad as substantial being > no substantial being > "being" as becoming. In Europe Kant offered the transcendentalist solution, while Hegel gave us a process philosophy that was thoroughly rationalist and absolutist. Returning to the concept of self, deconstructionists leave us with the negation of the second moment, while the Buddhists and contemporary process philosophers offer us a reconstructed self. We can now formulate the triad for the reconstructed soul as self > no self > "self," which can be expanded as substantial self > no substantial self > relational process self.

Any number of Pāli *sūtras* could be used to support this view, but it is significant that it is also found in some Mahāyāna *sūtras* as well. Kalupahana has thrown new light on a subtle argument about karma that appears in the *Vajracchedikā* : "What was taught by the Tathāgatha as heap of merit, as no heap of merit. . . . Therefore, the Tathāgatha teaches 'heap of merit, heap of merit.'"[34] The key to understanding this passage as a positive conclusion about karma is the set of quotes around the last double phrase. (These inverted commas are indicated in Sanskrit by the word *iti*.) It indicates that the negation of karma as a substance (the Jaina view most exactly) has allowed us to reconstruct karma as a meaningful concept within the doctrine of interdependent coorigination. This means that we now understand karma correctly as a process of psychological conditioning. Kalupahana's analysis can be applied to the following discussion about the nature of beings in the *Vajracchedikā*: "They, Subhuti, are neither beings, nor no beings. And why? 'Beings, beings,' Subhuti, as no beings have all these been taught by the Tathagatha. Therefore are they called 'beings.'"[35] This passage confirms our three- moment dialectic of being that was just stated.

In the *Vajracchedikā* other concepts are deconstructed and reconstructed much more subtly and indirectly than these examples of being and karma. Subhuti knows what to answer when the Buddha asks him about the nature of the Arhat: he must answer that the Arhat is not a perfect being. Following this dialectical model of karma, we interpret the resolution of the issue in this way: Arhat as perfect being > no perfect being > reconstructed as Arhat as a being without craving but living in a world of ordinary desires. There is also a brilliant critique of the virtues (*pāramitās*) as perfections, in the way that Plato conceived them as Forms. Following Kalupahana's suggestion that we should see the perfection of virtues morally rather than ontologically, we construct the following triad: virtues as ontological perfections > no virtues as such > the virtues reconstructed as perfected dispositions. Therefore, when Subhuti hears the Buddha proclaim that the Tathagatha's "perfection of patience . . . is no perfection,"[36] we are not to take this to mean that the Buddha does not have the virtue of patience. It is very clear from the story of his appearance as Kṣanti that he was indeed a very patient sage. The Buddha explains that if he had assumed a substantial concept of the self, he "would also have had a perception of ill will at the time." On our model this means that the Buddha, while deconstructing the idea of a substantial self and a corresponding notion of perfect virtues, is reconstructing the virtue of patience on the basis of a reconstructed process self.

Conclusions

Let us now summarize the view of self that we have presented in the last two chapters. First, the self is "dialogical" not "monological," corresponding to the two types of existentialism discussed at the end of chapter 1. Second, the self is constituted intersubjectively rather than as the intrasubjective constitution of the Cartesian self. Third, the self is somatic, that is, the body is constitutive of personal identity. The soul, as Merleau-Ponty, the Jainas, and the Confucians have independently discovered, is also coextensive with the body. This means, repeating Marcel's language, that "we *are* our bodies" rather than the modernist view that "we *own* our bodies." Fourth, the soul is not a social atom, analogous to the physical atom, moving accidentally through social space. In this view society and community are simply abstractions; for the social atomist the only true realities are individuals. The constructive postmodern self, using Whitehead's analogy of organism, is thoroughly social and relational. If we are constituted just as much by others as we are by ourselves, then society (and nature, too) is an interrelated whole rather than the simple sum of existing individuals. Finally, the constructive postmodern self is not an enduring substance (either material or spiritual), but an ever-changing unity of personal events intimately related to all other events. It is this process self that is offered as a replacement for the autonomous selves of Western modernism, Jainism, and Sāṃkhya-Yoga.

3 Prometheus East—Greek and Hindu Titans

I alone am the highest religion; I alone deserve to be worshipped.

—The human Vena[1]

By rituals one reaches the world of the gods; and the gods do not wish that mortals should live on high.

—The sage Vyāsa[2]

The Titan [*asura*] is potentially an Angel [*deva*], the Angel still by nature a Titan.

—A. K. Coomaraswamy[3]

Introduction

This chapter will investigate the phenomenon of Asura Titanism and evaluate Indian mythological parallels to the story of Prometheus. The Sanskrit *asura* is usually translated as "demon," but sometimes as "Titan" or "antigod." We shall see that "demon" is not appropriate for the earliest Vedic use of the term, which, according to W. H. Hale, could apply to gods, demons, and humans. The *asuras* do, however, become the principal antagonists of the *devas* of Hindu religion, especially as it is embodied in the Purāṇas. We will usually avoid calling the *asuras* "demons," because although they are antagonists, they are sometimes more virtuous and superior in spiritual practice than the gods with whom they compete. Nevertheless, the pejorative meaning of Asura and Titan eventually dominated Greek and Indian mentalities. Just as Plato blamed evil on "an ancient Titanic nature,"[4] so did later Indians blame it on one's "asuric" nature.

The traditional theory about the origin of the Asuras is that they parallel the Greek Titans—the older ancestors of the younger Olympian-like Devas. Greek Titanism, then, is a form of Asura Titanism, where the main conflict is between two classes of mythical beings. We also find that the Titans, especially Prometheus, turn out to be more virtuous, at least in terms of his love for humanity, than the Olympians. We will discover that the Purāṇic form of this Titanism will be the weakest form of Hindu Titanism. The most troubling forms are the ones in which human beings themselves take on divine attributes and prerogatives. In addition to the fact that Prometheus is an Asura and not a human being, we will also find other instructive differences between him and the spiritual Titans of the Indian tradition. The chapter will begin with a discussion of Asura Titanism in the Hindu tradition, will then turn to the human Titans of the Purāṇic tradition, and will conclude with a comparative analysis of the Prometheus myth.

Asura Titanism

One Vedic myth about the origin of evil indicates that it was a combination of Prajāpati's creative fiat and the spiritual geography of the cosmos itself. When Prajāpati created the gods "they entered the sky (*divam*); and this is why the gods are gods (*devas*)."[5] The Asuras, on the other hand, entered the darkness of the underworld and Prajāpati "pierced them with evil." As a result the Devas and the Asuras became "hateful fraternal enemie[s]." Prajāpati's act of disapproval might be seen as simply a confirmation of the lower (= less good) domain that the Asuras had occupied. (In contrast the Greek Titans are sent to the underworld by a deliberate act of Zeus.) A similar explanation, employing the *guṇa* theory of Sāṃkhya, is found in the *Bhāgavata Purāṇa*. According to this account the gods are made of *sattva*, the purest quality; the *asuras* are composed of the passion of *rajas*; and the *yakṣas* and *rākṣasas* are constituted by *tamas*, the lowest, most impure quality. This *guṇa* determinism not only explains the behavior of these beings, but it also explains that why in an age in which *rajas* is dominant, the great god Viṣṇu is inclined to grant the wishes of the Asuras.[6] As pure spirit (*ātman*) Viṣṇu is devoid of *guṇas* and he cannot be partial to any being. It only appears that he is partial because of the ascendency of one quality of any particular age. And even though Viṣṇu is the creator of time, it is time not he that determines the dominant qualities of the ages.

The *Śatapatha Brāhmaṇa* has a very different view of the origin of evil, one that parallels an Iranian myth. In this story Prajāpati creates the Devas and the Asuras as equals and gives them speech: "Both of them spoke the truth, and both of them spoke falsehood; and as they spoke alike, they were alike. The gods gave up falsehood and kept truth, and the demons gave up truth and kept falsehood."[7] In the *Gathas* of Zoroaster we find that Ahura Mazda creates two spirits, one who chose the good (Vohu Manah) and one who chose evil (Angra Mainyu). "Of these two spirits, the evil one chose to do the worst thing, but the Most Holy Spirit, clothed in the most steadfast heaven, joined himself unto Righteousness."[8] We find yet another view of the origin of evil in Greek philosophy when we analyze the Prometheus myth in the last section of this chapter.

In the beginning the Devas and the Asuras shared the same *loka* and feasted on the same divine food (*soma*). The Asuras were not yet evil in any respect, because Varuṇa is described as the "wise sovereign (*asura*) king."[9] This again reminds us that the ancient Iranians, who once shared the same religious practices with the Indo-Aryans, called their god the Wise Lord (*ahura* [= *asura*] *mazda*) but called their demons *devas*. The word *yakṣa*, used to describe a large category of demons, literally means "honored ones." Their origins are most likely pre-Aryan, making them older, in terms of Indian worship, than the Vedic gods. The pre-Aryan Jaina tradition, for example, regarded the *yakṣas*—along with *rākṣasas*, *bhūtas*, and *piśācas*—as deities, and contemporary Jainas regard them so to this day. The Hindus of course consider all these beings to be demons, although usually in a lower class than the Asuras.

The traditional theory is sometimes called functional in the sense that although the Devas and the Asuras share the same nature, the former usually function as divine beings while the latter function as antigods. A. K. Coomaraswamy expresses the functional theory like this: "Although distinct and opposite in operation, [Devas and Asuras] are in essence consubstantial, their distinction being a matter not of essence but of orientation, revolution, or transformation. . . . The Titan is potentially an Angel, the Angel still by nature a Titan."[10] In one Vedic account, both Agni and Soma are former Asuras, who are won over by Indra, king of the gods. The best example, however, is the great god Śiva, who is known as the Slayer of Titans on the one hand but as the Lord of the demons (*bhūtas*) on the other. Indeed, all of the Asuras, except Prahlāda, are Śiva devotees.[11] The Asura Andhaka and Śukra, the Asuras' priest, are born of Śiva's body. His son Gaṇeśa is the head of a host of demons/demigods called *gaṇas*, and, according to one story, is the origin of evil in the world.[12] In both Greek and Hindu mythology the Angels and Titans trade places: Kṛṣṇa dispatches Asuras to heaven without even giving them a choice, and Prometheus finally regains immortality and joins his former enemies on Mt. Olympus. The functional theory explains why the Asuras and the Devas form friendships such as the one between Indra and Namuci. It also explains why Asuras such as Bali are capable of great virtue while the Devas can be devious and full of vice. For example, the Devas betray the Asuras after requesting their cooperation in the churning of the cosmic ocean, and Indra turns on Namuci and decapitates him.

The Buddhist view of the Asuras confirms the functional theory just as well as does the Jaina tradition. In some Buddhist texts the Asuras are known as the "older *devas*," who originally dwelt in the Tāvatimsa Heaven. For example, Sakka refers to them as such in the *Saṃyuttanikāya*, and it is said that they lost their morality by attacking the Devas.[13] The *Bardo Thödol* describes the Asuras as jealous, prideful, quarrelsome, and forever warring with the gods. One Buddhist story tells of the Asura Rahu, who caused the eclipses of the sun and moon by taking them into this mouth. One day the Buddha made himself taller than Rahu, and with the Buddha towering over him, he saw his Titanic folly and became a disciple.[14] The Buddhist Satan Mara is alternatively called an *asura* and *yakṣa*, and his battle with the Buddha could very well be seen as a battle of *asura* against *devatīdeva* (god beyond god), a term used in Mahāyāna Buddhism. The Buddhist texts offer two interesting etymologies of *asura*. The first simply takes the stem *-sura* to mean god and the a-privative makes *asura* the antigod. The second is more fanciful: the stem *-sura* refers to an intoxicant by which the Asuras once drank themselves unconscious.[15] By this account the term means "teetotaler," because they took a vow never to drink *sura* again.

In his thorough study of the Asuras, W. H. Hale qualifies the functional theory by demonstrating that in the early Vedic period the Asuras were not a separate class of gods/demons. Hale produces a much better etymology of the word *asura*. Its roots are *asu* + *ra* and its literal meaning is "one who possesses *asu*"—life-power, connected to both *māyā* and *brahman*, the power of creation and the power of the sacrifice respectively. Therefore, for the early literature Hale translates the word as "sovereign lord," and both gods and humans took on this title by successfully exercising their powers. One is not born with asuric power; rather, one must achieve it in an heroic act. Indra as the "slayer of Asuras" most likely implies human, not divine, but nonetheless powerful enemies. According to Hale, after the Aryans had settled in their newly conquered territories, their earlier enemies—the *dasyus* and the *dāsas*—were then mythologized as demons who battled, Titan-like, with the gods at the beginning of time. Therefore, Asuras, either early Vedic or Puranic, can be seen as powerful lords—divine, demonic, or human. Hale explains:

> An *asura* seems to be some sort of leader who is respected and has at his command some fighting force. In addition, he may wield a sort of magical power called *māyā*. Such a lord can be either a god or a human, but since the *Ṛg-veda* is a collection of hymns to gods, *asura* occurs much more often of gods in that text.[16]

There is a gradual shift in meaning from lord and from any being having power, to enemy lord, then to enemy, and finally to the antigods of the Purāṇas and popular Hindu imagination.

The soma communion of the Devas and Asuras was broken after one of the most amazing episodes in Indian mythology. One particular cycle of creation failed to provide enough soma, so the gods persuaded the Asuras, with the promise of an equal portion, to help them churn the cosmic ocean to produce the nectar of life. After the churning was complete, Viṣṇu, disguising himself as a beautiful woman, managed to deceive the Asuras and to cheat them out their share. A great battle broke out between the two parties, and the Devas, empowered by their access to the fresh soma, easily defeated the Asuras. Endless other battles ensued, usually in the form of the Asuras attempting to steal the sacrifice or each seducing the others' wives. The Asuras most powerful weapon, however, against the gods was their perfection of ascetic practices. Self-suffering (*tapasyā*) as a way for the Asuras to gain power contrasts sharply with the Greek Titans, nonascetics all, whose suffering was imposed upon them by Zeus.

Etymologically, the Sanskrit equivalent of Prometheus is *pramatha*, whose verb stem is *manth*, which means "to churn," "to rob," or "to attack." Wendy Doniger expands on this derivation by observing that *manth*

> indicates vigorous backwards and forwards motion of any sort: in the Vedas, it refers primarily to the twirling of the two fire-sticks to produce the sacred flame, an act often given sexual connotations. . . . *Manth* also applies to the churning

of milk into butter and, in addition, often describes violent attack.[17]

The "churning" of the cosmic ocean, the sages "churning" the wicked king Vena, Indra "churning" the head of Namuci, and Vyāsa using fire sticks to churn out his son Śuka are examples of these meanings of *manth*. It is commonly assumed that the meaning of Prometheus is "forethinker" (from *mantháno*, "to learn" or "to know") with his bumbling brother Epimetheus as "afterthinker," but the Indo-European root indicates meanings of "churner" or "robber" instead.[18] Already we can see some interesting connections: Prometheus steals fire from Zeus and the Asuras attempt to rob the gods of their divine soma. It is also significant to note that Śiva, Lord of the Bhūtas, including the *gaṇas* and *pramathas*, is also known as the fire god. More figuratively, we have seen that the Asuras are related to the *rajasguṇa*, the quality of fiery passion.

According to the *Harper's Dictionary of Hinduism* the *pramathas* (here the authors' etymology is "tormentor" or "smiter," focusing presumably on *manth* as "to attack") are first mentioned in the *Atharvaveda* and are described as demons who are "bearded, terrific, pot-bellied, hunch-backed and dwarfish" and "appear to be the same as the *gaṇas*."[19] The *gaṇas* are under the command of Gaṇeśa, hence one of his names, Gaṇapati. (Like the *yakṣas* Gaṇeśa also had a pre-Aryan origin before being appropriated by the Śiva cult.) Switching playfully to the divine side, the *gaṇas* are also called *gaṇadevatās*, attending not only to Śiva and Gaṇeśa, but also to Indra's court. If our task is to find Hindu equivalents of the Greek Titans, we have certainly not found them in such minor beings as the *gaṇas* or the *pramathas*. The *rākṣasas*, just as fearsome as the *pramathas*, fare no better, because they are enemies of the human race, for instance, Rāma's enemy Rāvaṇa as the most powerful and famous.

Some of the most famous Asuras trace their lineage from Rambha. One day he and his brother Karambha were practicing austerities and Indra brutally murdered Karambha. So distressed was Rambha that he decided to cut off his head and throw it into the sacrificial fire. Agni intervened, warned him that suicide was worse than killing, and offered to grant him any wish that he desired. Rambha said: "Grant my desired boon that a son be born unto me, who will destroy the forces of my enemy and who will conquer the three worlds."[20] The son requested was none other than Mahiṣa, the great Asura of the Durgā myth, to which we shall return in chapter 6. Mahiṣa's son Rakta also won a victory over the Devas and ruled the triple world. He decreed that no contributions should be given to any priest, and that his fellow Asuras should make sacrifices to him only. Without the ritual sacrifice the Devas became impotent and the Asuras easily defeated them. Bṛhaspati, the priest of the Devas, requested the intervention of Devī and she restored divine rule.[21]

Mahābali, the most virtuous of Asuras, was principal Titan during the churning of the ocean and in a later battle he thoroughly vanquished the Devas. Mahābali's grandfather Prahlāda annointed him as king of heaven (i.e., as Indra); but, without hubris, Bali "had no aspiration for sovereignty over the gods."[22] In response to his grandson's question about how to rule, he said: "Only virtue will always win. Rule the kingdom without deviating from virtue."[23] Bali did indeed establish a kingdom of virtue and everyone was happy and prosperous, except of course the Devas, whose mother Aditi had a plan. She performed twelve days of austerities, after which Viṣṇu appeared to her and granted her wish that a son born of him would overthrow Bali's rule. Vāmana, the dwarf incarnation, appeared before Bali, who treated him with the utmost respect and hospitality. Even though he was warned that an incarnation of Viṣṇu would defeat him, he nonetheless granted Vāmana's wish that he be given all the land that he could pace off in three steps. Bali even offered his head as the final resting place of Vāmana's third cosmic stride. Bali was crushed down into the netherworld, where the rest of the Asuras, they too being defeated, followed. The combination of Viṣṇu's deviousness and Bali's righteousness is reminiscent of the story of Job. Just as Job is rewarded with a new family, so is Bali eventually given the kingdom of Sutala.

The story of Jalandhara is another story of the exploits of the Titans. Out of regret for granting a boon to Indra for extra power, Śiva, with Brahmā's help, created an Asura with equal powers. Jalandhara was meant to be a counter to the excessive pride Śiva now detected in Indra. (Jalandhara's creation from the ocean serves as an interesting parallel to Prometheus' close alliance with Oceanus and his daughters.) Jalandhara performed childhood miracles and he wed the nymph Vṛṇḍā and the power of her faithfulness aided him in his later battles with the Devas. (In one variation on this story Viṣṇu tricks Vṛṇḍā into making love to him thereby eliminating the advantage that Jalandhara obtained from his wife's faithfulness. In return, however, Vṛṇḍā cursed Viṣṇu and in his Rāma incarnation he was forced to suffer the long separation from Sīta because of his deception of Vṛṇḍā.)[24] Jalandhara established a great kingdom and ushered in a Golden Age. Seeking to address the injustice of the Devas' deception in the churning of the ocean, Jalandhara declared war on them. A great battle ensued; the Asuras got the upper hand; Viṣṇu intervened, but Jalandhara defeated him as well. Viṣṇu was spared only after his wife Lakṣmī pleaded for his life. Ever gallant even in battle, Jalandhara acceded to her wishes. The gods retreated and sought Śiva's help, and he fashioned a fearsome weapon, a fiery discus called Sudraśana that blinded the gods and that singed Brahmā's beard. With this awesome tool Śiva was able to decapitate Jalandhara, but innumerable Asuras sprang from his blood and engaged in fierce battle. Only after Śiva called on the gods' *śaktis*, who Kālī-like drank all of Jalandhara's blood, was the great Asura defeated.[25]

The first conclusion of this chapter is that Asura Titanism, as the first expression of Indian Titanism, turns out to be its weakest form. First, of all the beings who have a claim to heaven, it is the Asuras who have the strongest case. After all, they were consubstantial with the Devas—"we are all of equal birth, the gods and we"[26]—Prājapati made them equal or alternatively both are sons of the sage Kaśyapa. Furthermore, the Devas' devious ways are at least equally responsible (if not more) for the Asuras' demise. As there is no ontological difference between them, the only way to make a distinction is to create strife. Therefore, if the Devas want to be different from the Asuras, then it makes sense for them to promote these cosmic battles. Furthermore, since the Devas depend on human sacrifice for their sustenance, and if the best way to get humans to make offerings is to scare them with demons, then it also makes no sense to eliminate the demons altogether.[27] Second, the revolt and subsequent defeat of the Asuras is, as we have seen, rather predictable and anticlimactic. They do achieve a few victories, but we all know that the gods will trick them into giving up their hard-won gains. Their victories are not that impressive, since the gods (or time-destiny itself) empower them in their rebellion. Brahmā and Śiva seem bent on aiding the Asuras (rewarding them for their virtue or for their extreme austerities), and it is usually Viṣṇu who has to come to the rescue. Our first conclusions are doubly ironic: (1) the beings who have the best claim to heaven do a rather poor job of making good on that claim; and (2) the beings with no natural claim to heaven (viz., human beings) contend, according to many versions of Hinduism, Jainism, and Buddhism, that they can achieve divinity on their own power.

If it is immortality that defines divinity, then neither the Devas nor the Asuras are true deities. They are born, they die, and they depend on the sacrifice for their continued existence. In the Hindu tradition one should distinguish between a strong and a weak conception of immortality. The strong notion is contained in *ātman*, a perfect immutable being with no beginning or end. Doniger explains the weak form in this way: "The gods take the ambrosia from them [the Asuras] and use it for the only immortality which is natural and in order, even for the gods—'a full life-span.'"[28] Even the high gods Śiva, Viṣṇu, and Brahmā appear to be subject to weak immortality. And only insofar as these gods—usually only the first two—are later identified with Brahman do they take on immortality in the strong sense. We will see that the Goddess is also identified with Brahman, but, if *śakti* is the only cosmic power, then the Goddess is ontologically supreme. Therefore, there is a third irony in Indian Titanism: Hindu sages, Jaina saints, and Yoga adepts are claiming divine attributes that even the Vedic gods do not have.

Human Titans in the Purāṇas

During the Golden Age humans were able to travel between earth and heaven at will. One day they ate some barley corn that belonged to Varuṇa. As punishment Varuṇa, god of waters, inflicted them with dropsy, but Prajāpati "healed them and freed them from Varuṇa's snare."[29] Here one could say that Varuṇa represents Zeus, and Prajāpati, as humankind's advocate, stands for Prometheus. Even more significant for my thesis is the fact that Prajāpati, as a successor to the human giant of the Puruṣa hymn (discussed in chap. 5), is a "god" of a different sort—a true Titan, according to our definition, not an Asura nor a Deva. It has been argued that Puruṣa and Prajāpati are divinized human forms, and that the successor to both is holy power (*brahman*), which in the Upaniṣads became the Godhead and ultimate reality. Therefore, a human appropriated power displaces the Vedic gods and their sovereignty.

According to the Purāṇas, Brahmā, in answer to the gods' constant lack of sacrificial food, created kings to establish *dharma* and to offer regular sacrifices. The first king, Vena, did not turn out so well, but his son, Pṛthu, fared better. Vena shocked his subjects by declaring that all the gods were merged in himself: "I am the eternal Viṣṇu, I am Brahmā, I am Rudra, I am Indra."[30] Vena declared himself lord of the sacrifice and boasted that "I alone am the highest religion; I alone deserve to be worshipped."[31] Both the gods and sages were shocked by Vena's arrogance and impiety, clearly indicating the presence of the Purāṇic equivalent of the Indo-Iranian theistic principle. (See *supra*, p. 7.) The gods condemned Vena and the *ṛṣis* killed Vena with some sacred *kuśa* grass. The gods churned (*manth*) the thigh of the dead Vena and produced Niṣāda, who carried the sins of Vena into the Vindhya mountains.

Churned from Vena's right hand, Pṛthu was big as a mountain, shone "on the earth as Indra in heaven,"[32] manifested divine signs, and was omniscient and omnipresent. Under his wise and virtuous rule, the earth enjoyed a Golden Age: there was great prosperity, religious practices flourished, and the gods received their soma. After faithfully producing great abundance, the earth goddess Bhūmidevī withdrew her fertility by taking all seeds into herself. Pṛthu's new subjects complained bitterly that the earth was becoming a great desolation. Pṛthu pursued the goddess vigorously to the ends of the universe, repeatedly impaling her with his arrows. (The story takes the converse form of the Durgā's pursuit of Mahiṣa: Bhūmidevī takes on various disguises, including that of an elephant, a buffalo, and a cow.) Failing to find refuge in the gods, she had no choice but to confront Pṛthu and to ask him why he persecuted her so. Did he really think that by killing her he could solve his problems? Furious at the goddess's impudence, Pṛthu said that he would nourish and protect his people by his yogic power alone. Finding this a bad idea, Bhūmidevī said: "Control your anger. I shall be full of food and will support these subjects."[33] In the form of a cow she was "milked" for every need and by every being in the universe. (In chap. 6 we shall investigate in some detail the claims of Yoga Titanism. We will also find that Śiva claims that he can rule exclusively by his yogic powers, only to be castigated by Pārvatī for his ignorance, arrogance, and presumption. We will also analyze the problem of the raging anger of many Hindu Titans.) The writers of the *Padma Purāṇa* display the complete dominance of Pṛthu over Bhūmidevī by making her his adopted daughter and by naming her Pṛthvī.

In another story from the *Mahābhārata* a different Pṛthu is a Vasu, who along with Dyaus and other Vasus, stole the cow Nandinī from a sage by the name of Vasiṣṭha. They did this so that the cow's magic milk would make a beautiful princess immortal. In terms of our search for Prometheus equivalents in Indian mythology, Doniger's comments are significant:

> [Pṛthu] helps to steal this cow (as Prometheus steals the fire from Zeus) in order to help a mortal defy the challenge of the gods, to become free from age and disease—the definitive

> crime which the jealous Hindu gods cannot tolerate. It is ironic that the Indian counterpart of Zeus—Dyaus, now demoted in status— is the would-be thief of immortality.[34]

Pṛthu is like Prometheus: he steals divine power and saves the human race from a wicked father. It is interesting to note that Vena's rehabilitation and deification (a *bhakti* innovation) parallels Prometheus' final elevation to Olympus.

The myth of Divodāsa offers yet another instructive parallel to the Prometheus myth. Impressed with his ascetic practices and virtue, Brahmā asked the human Divodāsa to rule Benares and to save humanity from its sin. Divodāsa accepted the offer on the condition that all the gods, including Śiva who had made Benares his home, leave the city and return to heaven. (This is an interesting reversal: Titans usually want to move the gods out of heaven; here the superman, known as the godless king, commands the gods to return to their proper abode.) Divodāsa did as he was instructed: he was so successful in producing virtue in his subjects that the gods became jealous and angry. They retaliated by bringing natural calamities to Benares, but Divodāsa, by his ascetic powers alone, was able to make rain, fire, water, and everything else his kingdom needed. The gods eventually made Divodāsa a Deva, primarily to prevent him from ever again upsetting the balance between gods and humans.

The Vedic sages were so special that they are sometimes listed as a separate class of beings.[35] The *ṛṣis* were considered to have powers that exceeded the gods: Indra's thunderbolt, for example, was made from a sage's bones. Insulted by Indra's elephant the sage Durvāsas caused famine in all three worlds, which set the stage for the unprecedented cooperation of Devas and Asuras in the churning of the ocean.[36] To avenge the murder of his clan, the sage Aurva practiced such fierce *tapas* that the gods feared that he would burn up the world. Aurva's fire was relegated to the bottom of the ocean, but it, by some accounts, will be the all-consuming fire that will bring each age to its end.

In addition to gaining power by practicing austerities, the seer-poets also attained it through the speaking of mantras. By the use of mantras, the sages "possess[ed] the magic power to conjure up immediate reality—be it in [the] form of gods or in the play of forces."[37] Their supreme power was such that they were said not only to have created all beings—Devas, Asuras, and humans alike—but themselves as well—for instance, both Puruṣa and Manu were considered self-created. In the Hindu Genesis it is not God who creates, but

Svāyambhu, the first Manu: "Then the Lord who is Self-existent [Svāyambhu], himself unmanifest, caused this (universe) to become manifest; putting his energy (*ojas*) into the great elements and everything else, he became visible and dispelled the darkness."[38]

The great sage Kaśyapa gave birth to the Devas through his wife Aditi and to the Asuras by his wife Diti. Kaśyapa also sired two races of giants—*daityas* and *dānavas*—and was also the father of the terrible *rākṣasas*. Two *daityas*—Hiranyakaśipu and Hiraṇyākṣa—caused so much trouble that Viṣṇu had to become an avatar twice to repair the damage. Hiranyakaśipu—an incarnation of Rāvana—was able to dethrone Indra with power granted him by Brahmā. One commentator suggests that the tracing of all beings to Kaśyapa "was an attempt to emphasize a sort of universal brotherhood."[39] Compared to the universal humanity under God, Allah, or the Chinese Heaven (*tian*), however, this Purāṇic version with a human being at the head of creation is conspicuously anthropocentric. In terms of the indigenous origins of Indian Titanism, it is also significant to note that the earliest Vedas do not indicate that Aditi, mother of the gods, had a human father. Finally, while Vedāntists claim that any person can say "I am Brahman," it would be blasphemous to say "I am Īśvara." But this is exactly what the Purāṇas are claiming about Kaśyapa, the cosmic yogi, and the "sinless lord of creation."[40]

The *Mahābhārata* tells the story of the great sage Vyāsa and of his desire to have a son whose virility (*vīrya*) would be equal to that of the elements. (The various Sanskrit terms for power—*tejas, ojas, vīrya,* and *śakti*—will be discussed in chap. 6.) After practicing great austerities for a hundred years, Vyāsa churns (the crucial verb *manth* again) a son out of his fire stick: "Śuka of great ascetic power was born, the great yogi whose womb was the fire stick. And as soon as he was born, the Vedas came to dwell in him, as they dwelt in his father."[41] Again we see a trademark of some forms of spiritual Titanism: ordinary procreation is replaced by a Promethean churning—an act of self-creation in which Śuka arose "looking like a second Vyāsa."[42] Śuka is destined to surpass his father and is determined not only to return to the elements but to transcend them:

> Then Śuka abandoned the four sorts of worlds. He gave up the three strands that compose all matter [the three *guṇas* of *prakṛti*]: the eight forms of darkness [*tamas*], the five forms of energy [*rajas*], and goodness [*sattva*]. Free of the strands of matter, dwelling in ultimate reality [*brahman*], he was like a blazing fire without any smoke.[43]

In his rejection of, and alienation from, the elements of the world, Śuka is a perfect candidate for the definition of Yoga Titanism discussed in chapter 5.

In addition to this epic account of Śuka there are two Purāṇic versions that offer similarities as well as some significant variations. Common to the *Mahābhārata* and the *Devī-Bhāgavata* is a visit to King Janaka, famous for his status as a *jīvanmukta* (liberated while embodied). Śuka asks Janaka about the proper means of liberation and the king responds with the traditional view of an orderly progression through the four stages of life (*āśramas*). Śuka has nothing but loathing for the householder's life, so he presses the king about the necessity of committing himself to activities he detests. Realizing Śuka's advanced state of spiritual development, Janaka finally acknowledges that Śuka is indeed an exception and that all he needs is to recognize his perfected nature. Śuka returns home to his father, who reluctantly blesses his spiritual journey, ending in the self-apotheosis just described, which actually transcends all the *āśramas*.

The *Bhāgavata Purāṇa* continues the theme of alienation from the world but the *jñāna* yoga of the epic is replaced by *bhakti* yoga. Although completely indifferent to, and immune from, the sensible world, Śuka still has love and compassion for all those still caught in the web of Saṃsāra. The *Devī-Bhāgavata Purāṇa*, however, makes significant changes to the story that are characteristic of its Śākta (i.e., Goddess) orientation. This time Janaka does not make Śuka an exception and insists that he commit himself to the prescribed life stages. Śuka is able to hold his own in argument until Janaka observes that he is the one who is completely at ease in the world while Śuka is miserable and full of doubt. Śuka returns home to his father, marries a woman named Pīvarī, and they have four sons and a daughter. Like Janaka he, too, becomes one who is liberated while in a body (*jīvanmukta*), but Śuka attains this not so much because of his yogic power but by virtue of his worship of Devī Māhā Māyā. The Śākta Purāṇas incorporated many Advaitin terms, but, as C. Mackenzie Brown says, "*māyā* becomes radically revaluated, becoming more a means than an obstacle to liberation, a view reinforced by the Tantric currents of the day."[44] While the *Devī-Bhāgavata* version of this story contains typical Śākta themes—an affirmation of the world through a coincidence of enjoyment (*bhukti*) and liberation (*mukti*)—Śuka, "always averse to any company," finally left his family and traveled to Mt. Kailasa.[45] There he attained *siddhi* powers and became like a second Sun. Although this apotheosis is not as grand or as transcendent as the epic version that was just discussed, this ending mitigates somewhat the effect of the general Śākta solution to the problems of Yoga Titanism that we explore in chapter 6.

Titans and Olympians

The Greeks did not have a category for devils or evil ones. The word "demon" comes from the Greek word *daimon*, but for the Greeks *daimon* usually meant good "spirit"—the most illustrious example being Socrates' *daimon*. Rather than stipulating some thing's nature as either good or evil or that one becomes evil by deliberate choice, the Greeks, like the Chinese, saw the problem as a matter of balance. Heraclitus, for example, did not condemn war and strife; rather, he saw them as an integral part of a cosmos ordered by *logos*. Anaximander proposed that all opposites, none of them evil in themselves, emanate out of the *apeiron*; but *dikē* makes them "pay" for their separation and all opposing forces are reconciled in cosmic justice. Anaximander demythologized earlier views about the devastating results of the castration of Uranus, which spawned all sorts of evils (i.e., imbalances) in the world, including a race of rebellious Titans.

The evil of hubris, then, is not so much a matter of deliberate willing as it is a consequence of cosmic imbalance. The Titans' pride and violence were futile in a world destined to be ruled by Zeus. In *Prometheus Bound* Prometheus' crime is described as one "in excess of justice" and Prometheus admits that he "loved men too well."[46] In addition to favoring creatures whom Zeus chose to suppress, Prometheus and his fellow Titans coveted divine prerogatives that were no longer theirs. Therefore, Prometheus was viewed as both a thief (one meaning of *manth* in *pramatha*) and an usurper. Like the Asuras he was not a demon but simply a god who had been overthrown. Zeus' goal was to establish justice and order no matter what the cost, and according to the Greeks, he succeeded. He was able to win the battle with the Titans only by buying off their brothers—the Cyclopes and the Hundred-handers—by offering them a feast of divine ambrosia.

Let us begin with Hesiod's description of the Greek Golden Age, in which the gods and humans live happily together and ate the same divine food at a common table. The Titans had failed because they thought they could win with brute force, but Prometheus realized that *mētis*—"cunning or wily intelligence"—was Zeus' advantage and that he had just as much *mētis* as his antagonist. Prometheus decided that it was best to join Zeus and the Olympians and due to his diplomacy he was chosen to divide up the first sacrifice. At the sacrifice Prometheus hid the meat for humankind under the disgusting skin and stomach, while he disguised the bones for the gods with the favored fat. Zeus fully expected Prometheus to play such a trick, so Zeus countered by hiding the heavenly fire so that human beings could not cook their meat or stoke their forges. He also withdrew the cereal grains that had grown spontaneously during the Golden Age.

Parallels with Hindu mythology here are not exact, but they are still significant and instructive. Rather than steal fire, the first Indians stole grain instead: they ate Varuṇa's (=Zeus) barley, he punished them with dropsy, and Prajāpati (=Prometheus) saved them. Bali, Pṛthu, and Divodāsa were also committed to human welfare, even if it meant creating envy in the gods. Significantly, *mētis* and *māyā* are Indo-European equivalents,[47] but the latter term has a much closer link with the power of the sacred. Employing his *mētis* or *māyā* Viṣṇu turned himself into a seductive woman, whom the Asuras now trusted to hand out the hard-won and newly churned soma. The Asuras and Devas lined up across from one another, Viṣṇu distributed the soma down the Deva side first, and then he disappeared. If C. Kerényi is correct in assuming that the original Greek story paired Olympians and Titans (rather than humans) at the sacrifice,[48] then the parallel of Prometheus using his *mētis* to fool Zeus is much more exact. It is also significant to observe that more battles were won in Hindu and Greek mythology by trickery and deceit than by brute force.

In patriarchy the name of the game is power and the desire for total control and total sovereignty. Zeus and the Judeo-Christian God reached this goal, at least as far their devotees claim, but the Indian gods never attained such supremacy. One could speculate that it was Hindu polytheism that prevented this from occurring, but it would follow that Greek polytheism would also have led to some limitation to Zeus' sovereignty. So the reason must be more fundamental than this, and it may have to do with the role of the Goddess. As we will see in chapter 6, the Goddess's power is one that she shares with all beings. Her power is *śakti*, the source of all being, not *tejas*, a power that waxes and wanes according to the dominance of the Devas or the Asuras. The Goddess's agenda is not the zero-sum power game that the patriarchs play, but a game with totally different rules. *Śakti* is not a power that is won, but one that is simply given unconditionally to all beings.

Kerényi observes that most of the Titans, the gods before the gods (*prōteroi theoī*), were "violently solar" but the "moonlike Prometheus" was connected to the worship of the Goddess.[49] Ovid relates that Athene provided the breath of life to animate the clay figures that Prometheus had formed as human beings.[50] In one account it is also Athene who helped Prometheus steal fire. It is significant that in *Prometheus Bound* Prometheus called on the earth goddess Gaia immediately after he was chained and also turned to her in the end as the mountain collapses on him. Prometheus was also consoled by a Chorus of the daughters of Oceanus, a Titan who reluctantly allowed them to come to Prometheus' aid. (Prometheus married Hesione, one of Oceanus' daughters, and her sisters remind Prometheus of the times when he was gentle, humble, and far less angry.) Although male, Oceanus has deep feelings and moral qualities, and paired with his wife Tethys, they together represent a Greek equivalent of *prakṛti*, the dynamic material principle of Sāṃkhya philosophy and later Goddess philosophy. The Greek attribution of primordial waters as male is unusual in world mythology; they are generally female in other traditions, most notably Babylonian and Hindu. Hesiod's view that Oceanus and Tethys were children of Gaia is a later one, but it returns us to the more universal view that a feminine material principle—either water or earth—is the source of all things. For Hesiod, Night is the dark side of the material principle, called by Homer "the subduer of gods and men,"[51] and it is so powerful that even Zeus stands in awe of her.

Zeus' relationship with feminine forces is not one of alliance but of conflict and domination. After the defeat of the original Titans, the great Goddess Gaia produces one last antagonist for Zeus, the serpent-headed Typhon, a true god of chaos. With the thunderbolt that the Cyclopes have given him, Zeus easily defeats Typhon, although his maritime storms still remain to wreak havoc on earth. According to the Pseudo-Apollodorus, Gaia makes one last attempt to defend the old (dis)order: she sends the Giants, a race of fierce warriors, whom she attempts to immunize with a potion of immortality. The wily Zeus steals the potion before she can administer it, and Heracles wins the victory over the Giants. Zeus does not battle the Goddess directly, as Mahiṣa engages Durgā, but a basic conflict with feminine power remains. Zeus' supremacy over this power is symbolized in his decision to swallow his first wife Metis. By this act he preempts the birthing process by having Metis' child Athene issue from his head rather than from her womb.[52] (Another womb substitute is Zeus' use of his thigh to give birth to Dionysos.) We have already seen that the Hindu Titan expropriates the creative powers of the female and seeks to take all power unto himself. The converse is seen in Ramakrishna's Goddess religion where Śiva is swallowed by Kālī and is born again out of her thigh.[53]

It must be said, however, that Gaia's position in the Titanomachy is ambivalent. Gaia conspired with Rhea in the hiding of Zeus, and it was at her suggestion that Zeus was made king of the gods. Gaia also advised the Hundred-handers to ally themselves with Zeus. Finally, Gaia and Uranus urged Zeus to swallow Metis so "that no one but Zeus would hold the title of king among the eternal gods."[54] It is Hera who has the proper feminist response to Zeus' presumption of reproductive power: "furious at her husband, [she] bore a child without making love, glorious Hephaistos."[55] (One is reminded of Pārvatī creating Gaṇeśa without the aid of Śiva.) Gaia's equivocal role in the Titanomachy may be due to the fact that the worship of the great Goddess was already well into decline and that patriarchal gods such as Marduk, Yahweh, and Zeus had already established supremacy in their respective cultures. Many of the daughters of Oceanus had gone over to Zeus, just as Sophia had become a handmaiden to Yahweh.

Prometheus is not completely free of the negative traits of Titanism. Titans suffer from a surfeit of pride, anger, and resentment and an extreme stubbornness not to lose face. In *Prometheus Bound* Oceanus warns Prometheus that he is too proud and that his "anger is a disease."[56] Later Hermes suggests that Prometheus is insane, and the latter offers a qualified confession: "Perhaps—if to hate enemies is insanity."[57] Prometheus' alliance with the Goddess does not mean that he is a *feminist* in any modern sense of the term. Prometheus' pride and stubbornness are seen in these sexist comments to Hermes: "Never persuade yourself that I, through fear of what Zeus may intend, will show a woman's mind, or kneel to my detested enemy, with womanish hands outspread in supplication for release."[58]

The Chorus, the daughters of Oceanus, tells Prometheus that "there is too much freedom in your words" and that "your spirit . . . yields not an inch."[59] Not only is stubbornness a vice, but also seeking too much freedom as well. This is especially true in worldviews where natural necessities play such a strong role. Zeus is destined to rule the universe, so the Chorus warns Prometheus that he should not exhaust himself against the dictates of fate. (If the *rajasguṇa* rules the present age, then not even the most powerful Hindu god can do anything about the fact that Asuras are bound to rule.) Hermes tells Prometheus that "time has not taught [him] self-control or prudence,"[60] so Prometheus joins Hindu protagonists who practice what Doniger calls the Doctrine of the Golden Extremes rather than the Doctrine of the Golden Mean proposed by the Buddha and Aristotle.[61] Even more than pride, the anger of the Hindu gods and the sages was their fatal flaw, and the Buddha made the elimination of anger the centerpiece of his moral psychology.

Prometheus is also intimately connected to what we have called technological Titanism. The Greek *titanos* literally means the quicklime made from an earthly element and fire,[62] and the Titans were closely connected to the forge and to the art of smithing. Both Prometheus and Hephaistos were said to have been Kabeiroi, an ancient race of men-gods who were great blacksmiths. The original Cyclopes were probably bronze smiths, who, according to Robert Graves,[63] were one-eyed because of the practice of covering one eye as protection at the forge. Therefore, the fire of Prometheus is not only the cooking fire and the lighted torch, but the alchemical fire of the smelter. Two fragments from Aeschylus' now lost Prometheus plays—"do thou guard thee well lest a bubble strike thy face; for it is bitter, and deadly-scorching its vapors" and "like the goat, you'll mourn for your beard, you will"[64]—are clear allusions to the dangers of working too close to molten metal. Although the connection is not made in the Greek myths, the fact that smelting and mining are intimately connected leads, at least retrospectively in some minds, to protest a major violation of the sanctity and integrity of Mother Earth. Until the industrial age smelting and mining were relatively small scale, so preindustrial peoples could not have predicted the catastrophic implications of their powerful pyrotechnology.

Conclusions

In conclusion we can see that Prometheanism and technological Titanism are clearly linked, but Prometheanism and the spiritual Titanism found in India have significant differences. First, Prometheus is a god and not a mortal, so he cannot be accused of illegitimately claiming divine attributes or coveting divine prerogatives. Second, although Prometheus does suffer from hubris and even from a touch of insanity, he does not reject nature and the earth mother. This is true only of Indian Titans not Prometheus, who has very close ties with his grandmother Gaia. If bringing together Jungian *anima* and the *animus* represents the overcoming of Titanism, then it is Prometheus, ironically, who embodies this reconciliation, a Greek Titan rather than Zeus the chief Olympian. Third, Prometheus is not an ascetic and he does not seek isolation from either nature or society; on the contrary, he is fiercely committed to the flourishing of human community and civilization.

Although they practiced austerities, the Hindu kings Divodāsa and Pṛthu also supported humankind and established kingdoms of virtue. On this point the Devas and the Olympians share the same distrust of humanity. There is a constant tension between the Devas and human kings, because the more the latter establish virtue the less inclined humans are to sacrifice to the gods. The social and moral commitment of Divodāsa and Pṛthu mitigate the effects of their Yoga Titanism, whereas there appears to be little to qualify the preference for isolation in other yogis and the sages, the latter usually allying themselves with the gods against humankind. Finally, it is interesting to note that it is the Devas who can always count on the Goddess's help, while it is Prometheus who is closest to her. Not only does the yogi believe he can live without the human community, but he, at least according to Sāṃkhya-Yoga, also maintains that final liberation depends on the complete elimination of the material principle and of the Goddess who embodies it.

4 Jaina Superhumanism and Gnostic Titanism

[The Jinas] attained fullest self-realization and absolute perfection, bringing out to the full the divinity or godhood inherent in man.

—Jyoti Prasad Jain[1]

There is no *deva* but the Jina.

—Medhāvin[2]

Virtually no tradition other than Jainism has dared to attach so cosmic an attribute [absolute knowledge] to a human being.

—Padmanabh S. Jaini[3]

Introduction

The previous chapter concluded that Asura Titanism is the weakest form of Indian Titanism. It is essentially nonexistent in Jainism because the conflict between the Devas and the Asuras found in Hinduism is not present in Jaina mythology. As in the earliest Indo-Iranian traditions, the Devas and the Asuras are, for the Jainas, simply different types of divine beings. In Jaina mythology the Devas are portrayed as completely devoted to the Tīrthaṅkaras (lit. "ford-crossers")—a typical Titanistic reversal—so the Hindu tension between the gods and humans is also virtually absent in Jainism. The Jainas vigorously rejected the Vedic sacrifice and priestly prerogatives, so Brahmin Titanism is obviously not an issue. One can, however, discern the existence of two other forms of Titanism—namely, the Tīrthaṅkara as perfect yogi and as perfect knower.

In this chapter we shall investigate possible Jaina contributions to Yoga Titanism and to Gnostic Titanism. The next three sections present the case for Jainism's superhumanism, demonstrating how the Jaina saints claim divine attributes and prerogatives. The fourth section discusses the issue of Gnostic Titanism by contrasting omniscience in Mahāvīra and in the Buddha. The fifth section demonstrates that the Jaina doctrine of many-sidedness (*anekāntavāda*) does not serve as an answer to the charge of Gnostic Titanism. The final section presents Jaina panzooism and the interdependence of mind and body as mitigating factors against Jaina Titanism. Finally, it must be said at the outset that even though Jaina superhumanism is theoretically one of the strongest forms of Indian Titanism, this fact has not affected Jaina behavior in any deleterious way.

Jaina Colossi and the Cosmic Man

Technological Titanism usually expresses itself in powerful machines, techniques, and other external artifacts, while spiritual Titanism is primarily an internal affair. The exception to this is the gigantic statuary of the Buddhists and the Jainas, which represent some of the largest free-standing figures in the world. The Jaina Tīrthaṅkaras themselves were veritable colossi, who, leading back from Mahāvīra (the twenty-fourth and Buddha's contemporary), are described as retrogressively larger in size, strength, and virtue; they are also retrogressively longer lived, producing incredible life spans and chronologies that antedate the present scientific estimate of the birth of the universe. For example, Ṛṣabha, the first Tīrthaṅkara, was born 100 billion sagaras ago and he lived for 8,400,000 years. (A sagara is 100 billion palyas, which is a period in which a well 1 mile deep filled with fine hairs can be emptied if one hair is drawn out every 100 years.) Ordinary people were giants as well. In the first Golden Age people had 256 ribs and were 6 miles tall. In the next age they lived only 2 palyas and had shrunk to 4 miles and 128 ribs. The *Tattvārtha Sūtra* tells us that just before liberation the soul ranges from 3,000 feet to 14 feet tall, the difference being due to the progression of the ages.[4] The mothers of liberated Jainas are even larger and, for some unstated reason, souls lose one third of their height just after liberation. This same text also claims that just before liberation the soul expands to fill up the entire cosmos but then returns to its previous shape.[5]

The most famous Jaina statue, lavishly anointed every twelve years, is found at Śravanabelgola in Karnataka state. This 57-foot monolith, reproduced on the cover of this book, was superbly sculpted in 983 C.E. in the form of Bāhubali (sometimes called Gommaṭeśvara), the second son of Ṛṣabha. Although not a Tīrthaṅkara, Bāhubali is revered, especially by the Digambara sect, for his extreme ascetic practices. Deep in trance, Bāhubali is depicted standing in *kāyotsarga* (a yogic posture for leaving the body), with vines climbing up his totally immobile body and anthills at his feet. Heinrich Zimmer describes the Śravanabelgola statue as follows:

> The majestic aloofness of the perfected, balanced, absolutely self-contained figure of the [Jaina] saint becomes emphasized in its triumphant isolation. The image of the released one seems to be neither animate nor inanimate, but pervaded by a strange and timeless calm. It is human in shape and feature, yet as inhuman as an icicle; . . . [the saint] stands supernally motionless, absolutely unconcerned about the worshipping, jubilant crowds that throng around his feet.[6]

Isolated, aloof, indifferent, emotionless, self-contained, timeless, and immobile ("motionless as a mountain rock")[7]—these are the attributes of the soul that we find in spiritual Titanism.

These images of the Jaina saints appear to distort the human place in the world, and the Jaina belief in a cosmic man takes anthropomorphism and anthropocentrism to their extreme. (It is also sexist in the Digambara sect where women have to be reincarnated as males before they can be saved, so the cosmic being is a male person for both Jainas and Hindus.) One could say that the cosmic man of the Vedic Puruṣa hymn is nothing more than a figure of speech, but for some Jainas a human-shaped cosmos is a literal belief. (This belief is not found in the canonical scripture, but it is found in Jaina art and in the commentary on the *Tattvārtha Sūtra*.)[8] Below the feet of the cosmic man are innumerable *nigoda*, primitive one-celled souls who live in colonies. Some of these beings (called *nitya-nigoda*) will never achieve liberation; nothing they can do will allow them to advance their spiritual prospects. Residing in the feet and legs of the cosmic man are various hell beings, who are experiencing the results of their evil acts and are undergoing incredible tortures. Their bodies immediately heal so that the burning, cutting, piercing, pinching, and crushing of the wicked souls can begin again.

The Jaina Puruṣa's waist contains the middle regions, where human, animals, and plants are found. The lower levels of the celestial realm are found in the chest, and there the peripatetic gods (*gandharvas, yakṣas, rākṣasas, bhūtas*, and *piaścas*) move freely between the celestial and the terrestrial. The higher gods are found in the head and the Tīrthaṅkaras float free in the crown of the cosmic man. Jaina *jīvas* are naturally self-moving, like Plato's soul, and if not weighted down by karmic matter, they will immediately shoot up to the top of the universe. Crooked is the path of the evil soul, but straight upward motion is perfect, in contrast with the Greek's circular motion.[9]

The Status of the Jaina Gods

Jainism is usually conceived as atheistic or nontheistic, but we have just seen that gods do in fact play a role in Jaina cosmology. These gods are not the Hindu deities whom the Jains call false gods—primarily because of their violence and lust. This is rather ironic because the Jaina gods also have weapons, battle with one another, and cavort with goddesses, although the highest gods have no sexual appetites.[10] Another irony is that though most Jainas vigorously reject the caste system, their gods have a stratified class system—ranging from menials to lords. (There are, amazingly enough, ninety-nine types of menial gods.) Yet another point against Jaina egalitarianism is the fact that Tīrthaṅkaras can arise only among Aryans not among the "barbarians."[11]

The Jaina gods are, however, clearly subordinated to the Tīrthaṅkaras, who are considered the real divinities. In his *Yogaśastra* the great Jaina philosopher Hemacandra defined a *deva* as an omniscient being who knows the true nature of reality, and only the Jaina saints meet this qualification.[12] The Jaina gods, says Jyoti Prasad Jain, "are superhuman but not supermen, are divine beings but not divinities or deities. The only divinities or deities are the Arhantas and the Siddhas, who are adored and are worth adoring."[13] As in the case of the Buddha, the gods were the first to praise each of the Arhantas (a liberated Jaina but not the same as a Tīrthaṅkara) and offered aid in all their efforts. The saints are also called Jinas ("conquerors") or Kevalins ("liberated ones"). The term *siddha* is usually used for the disembodied souls at the top of the universe.

At this point Jainas would be eager to explain that the worship of these liberated humans is not the same as in Hinduism and in other religions. The Jinas are not requested to bestow favors nor could they; they are, like Aristotle's unmoved mover, far beyond any form of communication or causality. Instead, the Jinas are praised for their supreme ascetic achievements and these efforts constitute the ideal for aspiring Jainas. The point, however, at least for our thesis, is that the Jinas are alleged to be divinized human beings and that they have taken the place of God or the gods. The ritual called *pañca-namaskāra* involves bowing to each of the five holy ones as a supreme divinity (*parameṣṭhin*): the Jinas, the Siddhas, the monastic leaders (*ācāryas*), monastic preceptors (*upādhyāya*), and all Jaina *sādhus* in the world.[14] This ritual is also simply called *devapūja*, and here we see very clearly that these Jaina holy men have taken on the divine name and divine worship. In fact, *deva* is commonly added to the name of the Tīrthaṅkaras, as in the Hindi Mahāvīrdev. The most dramatic expression of this direct substitution of man for God comes from a sixteenth-century Jaina philosopher Medhāvin, who responded to the Muslim Firūz Khān of Nagpur by provocatively declaring: "There is no *deva* but the Jina."[15]

Other divine images, however, did appear in some Jaina temples during the medieval period. There were statues of the snake god Dharanendra and of his consort Padmāvatī, who, just as in the story of the Buddha, protected Pārśva (the twenty-third Tīrthaṅkara) during his spiritual quest. These beings, generically called *śāsana-devatā*, are able to grant boons to pious supplicants.[16] Each Tīrthaṅkara is accompanied by two *śāsana-devatās*, and five of the best known are goddesses. The consort of the twenty-second Tīrthaṅkara Nemi is Ambikā, whom we know from Hindu mythology as either Śiva's sister or as a form of Durgā. Interestingly enough, the Śvetambara sect ranks a woman Malli as the nineteenth Tīrthaṅkara, and today the worship of the *yakṣi* Kushmandini Devi is an integral part of the Jaina ritual at Śravanabelagola.

The contemporary Jaina philosopher Vija Bhuvanbhanusuri confirms the fact that some Jainas still believe that the gods can bestow grace.[17] Surprisingly enough, he also appears to commit himself to what I have called the Indo-Iranian theistic principle. Bhuvanbhanusuri cautions those who take attributions of divinity to humans (e.g., "he is like a deity") as actually meaning that the man is divine, because *deva* is used only for gods not mortals.[18] On the same page, however, Bhuvanbhanusuri reaffirms the general Jaina position that the Tīrthaṅkaras are divine. This inconsistency could be resolved by maintaining that mere mortals are transformed into deities at liberation, but as we shall see presently, this is not the Jaina view at all.

Man Is God and *Homo Mensura*

It is actually incorrect to say that the Jinas have been divinized, because, according to Jaina authorities, divinity is their inner nature. Liberation does not involve a transformation of their basic natures; rather, the Jinas simply discover their own divinity. God is not an indwelling presence, as in Christian mysticism, but human essence is literally divine essence. As we have seen, the Jainas believe in Uttarāvāda (the "ascendence of man to Godhood")[19] rather than Avatāravāda, which they impute to Hinduism and Christianity. Prem Suman Jain states that a person has "infinite powers" and that "the individual is capable of reaching such divine heights because the pure form of the self is itself divine and therefore relies on its own efforts."[20] This appears indeed to be an extreme humanism and a supreme form of spiritual Titanism.

Jyoti Prasad Jain uses the phrase "man is the measure of all things" as a way of describing the Jainas' humanistic belief that human beings are in control of their own destiny.[21] The Greek *homo mensura* can also be used to describe the extreme anthropomorphism and anthropocentrism of Jaina humanism. As we have seen, the cosmos for some Jainas is human-shaped and the human realm, where true spiritual deliverance is found, is the center of the cosmos. Krishna Prem and Madhava Ashish express the Hindu version of this: "The divine purpose cannot be effected except through its highest creation, Man. . . . Man is indeed the measure of all things. . . . Other than this, divinity has no aim. . . . Here at last is Man, to whose evolution the totality of universal power has contributed."[22] *Homo mensura*, the watchword of Western humanism, is more cosmic and comprehensive here in Jainism and Hinduism than it ever was in Greek Sophism.

The interpretation of the word OM (sounded as three letters: AUM) becomes radically anthropomorphic in Jainism. First, the Vedic reading was geographic with the three letters representing earth, the atmosphere, and the heavens. This view appears to efface the human place and to emphasize the cosmic source and meaning of the word. Second, the *Māndūkya Upaniṣad* added a fourth element to represent the silence between the sounding of the sacred word. While this Upaniṣad maintains the macrocosmic origin of OM—"this syllable is this whole world"[23] and contains all of time—it also offers a microcosmic interpretation as well. The letter *A* stands for the waking state; the letter *U* symbolizes what we would now call rapid-eye-movement sleep; the *M* expresses deep sleep; and the silence stood for the trance state of the liberated yogi. The interpretation was also intimately connected to the human body in that the speaking started at the back of the mouth (*A*), moved through the middle (*U*) and closed with the pursed lips of the *M*. Further intensifying the anthropomorphizing of AUM, the Jainas made the three letters represent the five supreme deities just mentioned. Jinas, Siddhas, monastic leaders, monastic preceptors, and *sādhus*.[24] The Jainas also believed that all mantras emanated from their Tīrthaṅkaras, not from the cosmos. Therefore, one can see a clear movement from a cosmic word that sacralized human beings to a word, characterized exclusively in human terms, which sacralizes the world in the act of human speech.

Descartes once said "conquer yourself rather than the world,"[25] but this imperative has been obeyed far more in India than in Europe, where technological Titanism has attempted to conquer the world. The language of conquest (annihilation of karma, the senses, and the body as the "enemy") and words of hubris, mastery, and power are pervasive in the Indian ascetic literature. Both the Tīrthaṅkaras and the Buddha are called Jinas—conquerors of the self. (Note again Prem and Ashish's claim just cited that "the totality of universal power" has been given to the yogi.) A contemporary Jaina philosopher claims that the soul "has the power of attaining an absolute victory over the inner enemies like attachment, etc. . . ."[26] The Jaina philosopher M. G. Dhadpahle suggests that the Jaina monk is a hero, solider, and conqueror in the same vein as the Greek "spiritual athletes."[27] (Interestingly enough, the Greek root for "ascetic" means "athlete.") The following exhortation from Jyoti Prasad Jain could very well be adapted as a Jaina equivalent of "Onward Christian Soldiers": "Greater is the victory of one who conquereth his own self than of him who conquereth thousands and thousands of formidable foes in a valiant fight. Fight with thyself, why fight with foes external? Happy is he who conquereth his self by his self."[28] The Jainas are certainly not alone in using militaristic images to express spiritual battles, because Buddhist texts, such as chapter 8 of the *Dhammapada*, use this imagery as well.

Omniscience: Mahāvīra and the Buddha

In the thirteenth year of Mahāvīra's ministry he reached a state the Jainas call *kevalajñāna*—"the supreme knowledge and faith, *kevala* by name, unsurpassed, unobstructed, unlimited, complete, and full."[29] Specifically, it meant that Mahāvīra had direct and complete knowledge of all that there was to know. The claim is rather remarkable: taking the "all" (*sarva-*) of *sarvajña* quite literally, Mahāvīra knows *all* objects of knowledge—past, present, future, actual, and possible—all at the same time.[30] Noting that absolute knowledge has always been ascribed to God in the theistic schools, P. S. Jaini states: "Virtually no tradition other than Jainism has dared to attach so cosmic an attribute to a human being."[31] This seems to be convincing evidence for Gnostic Titanism in Jainism.

For the Jainas omniscience is an innate quality of the soul that has been covered up by karmic accretions. This means that when all karma is removed, as was the case with Mahāvīra, then omniscience is fully revealed and actualized: "unlimited perception and unlimited knowledge are inseparable from the nature of the *jīva*."[32] Jainas believe that this state is completely pure, irreversible, and independent from the senses, the body, and all matter. Like the yogis of Sāṃkhya-Yoga, the liberated Jaina attains complete autonomy and isolation, not only from the world but also from other liberated souls. Spiritual Titanism is a very solitary occupation indeed. As we have seen, the literal meaning of *kevala* is "alone," "independent," or "isolated."

The differences with the Buddhism of the Pāli scriptures are instructive and significant. While Mahāvīra's omniscience consists in simultaneous knowledge of all six substances in all of their modes and in all three aspects of time, the Buddha's knowledge is all that can be experienced by the six senses (and by their ESP extensions) and the correct philosophical view of this experience. True to the Buddhist Nikāya's strict empiricism, only knowledge of the present could be directly experienced. The past would have to be remembered simply as it was, and the future, since it has not been actualized, would have to be predicted, not known in any actual sense. Furthermore, the Buddha usually prefers an "all-knowledge" with a definite soteriological focus. Here omniscience consists simply in all that one needs to know for salvation or for simply knowing the Truth (*dharma*). In a succinct response to the Jaina view the Buddha states: "Wherefore, Udāyin, let the past be, let the future be. I will teach you *dhamma*,"[33] and he then defines *dharma* in terms of interdependent coorigination and its moral implications.

In Mahāyāna scholasticism the Buddha's omniscience takes on much grander proportions, primarily because the metaphysics is much grander. (Kalupahana demonstrates that the absolute view of the Buddha's omniscience was already present in the Sarvāstivādins.)[34] The Pāli view is, of course, still preserved: a threefold knowledge of previous lives, the six realms of karmic rebirth, and a knowledge of the end of craving; and a completely accurate philosophical knowledge. Siddhartha Gautama appeared to have emotions and intentions; he deliberated, he hesitated, generally willed his actions to happen, and knew objects as we would know them if we had his ESP powers. For Asaṅga and Vasubandhu, however, the true Buddha-mind has none of these qualities. Assuming that the extent of Buddha awareness is universal, the Mahāyāna scholastics debated the question of whether there were any limits to it. They agreed that such objects as "a barren woman's son" and "an eternal self" were not possible objects of Buddha awareness. They also rejected the notion that the Buddha-mind was only potentially aware, because this would require that intention and volition would be necessary for the actualization process. To this significant break with the Pāli accounts, there came another change, at least insofar as knowing the Dharma was the focus of the Buddha's omniscience. Asaṅga and his associates affirmed that the prefix *sarva-* means all actual states of affairs and rejected the lesser alternative of all knowledge that has salvific importance.

In a thorough and insightful discussion Paul J. Griffiths demonstrates how radically the Buddha-mind is totally free of intentions and constructions. Using Thomas Nagel's famous article "What Is It Like to Be a Bat?" Griffiths demonstrates that the Buddha-mind is much more inaccessible than a bat's mind.[35] Indeed, nothing in true Buddha awareness corresponds to any awareness that we can experience or imagine. (Just as in the Christian *via negativa,* the use of terms becomes equivocal rather than univocal.) In the case of the bat we can at least imagine the types of perceptions and mental states it might have. In the case of the Buddha-mind, however, we might as well imagine what it is like to be a rock. This point is not as facetious as it might first appear, because a common image for the Buddha mind is a completely still lake perfectly reflecting its surroundings. According to Mohist logic, the lake and its surroundings are not analogues; rather, they are "parallel" to the Buddha mind and to its contents. The terms of parallel arguments have similar syntactic structures—they are much more like mathematical ratios—whereas the terms of analogical arguments have different syntactic structures.[36] Any comparison between our minds and inanimate objects would be analogical, but for the Buddha-mind, it being more inanimate than anything mental we know, it is parallel.

The content of the Buddha-mind is not the result of sensation or intention, so it is, strictly speaking, uncaused and has always and necessarily existed. This also means that it is eternal and unchanging, a claim that appears to undermine the doctrine of impermanence. The Mahāyāna scholastics attempt to reconcile this by saying that the Buddha-mind has eternal and unchanging awareness of "all reals without exception" in "all modes of appearance" and impermanence is simply one of these modes.[37] We now have a view much more like Jaina "all-knowledge" and are epistemologically worlds apart from the Pāli accounts of the Buddha's omniscience. Specifically, the Pāli view would be that objects of knowledge are always changing and always have perceptual and intentional content. Furthermore, the Mahāyāna view maintains that the future is already contained in the Buddha mind, while the Pāli view would be that it is not yet actualized and, therefore, cannot be known.

Some recent theories in quantum mechanics suggest a cosmology that coincides with Mahāyāna and Jaina views of omniscience. Hugh Everett's theory, here described by Nick Herbert, is particularly apt:

> Everett's quantum theory without collapse describes the world as a continually proliferating jungle of conflicting possibilities, each isolated inside its own universe, . . . a super-reality. Humans do not happen to live in super-reality, but in the world of mere reality where only one thing happens at a time. We can picture Everett's super-reality as a continually branching tree of possibilities in which everything that can happen actually does happen.[38]

Even if Everett's theory were proved to be true, he would never propose that a human mind could actually know all these worlds. There is after all a distinction between ontology and epistemology. Moreover, the law of contradiction prevents us from knowing two contradictory states of affairs in the same time, place, and manner. In other words, the charge of Gnostic Titanism for Jainism and Mahāyāna scholasticism still stands.

Jaina philosophers realized that they had to address the problem of how Mahāvīra could maintain the state of *kevala-jñāna* and still function in the ordinary world. The solution was this: while maintaining complete separation between his pure soul and his body, the Tīrthaṅkara has "such a body and such an organ of speech that he will be able to impart the knowledge of truth without engaging in a volitional act."[39] (According to some accounts, Mahāvīra did not preach with ordinary words, but simply emitted mysterious sounds, which were intelligible only to his closest disciples.) In Jainism the pure soul is a knower apart from the will and the sense organs. Pāli Buddhist epistemology is entirely different from this: the five *skandhas* (one of which is the body itself) correlate with sense/mind objects in the production of any knowledge. This means that the

Buddha had to reject the Jaina idea of an independent, pure knowledge as impossible. Both the *skandha* psychology and the process ontology of no-substance/no-self precludes anything at all similar to Jaina omniscience. The Buddha constantly disabused people of the idea that he possessed the same knowledge as Mahāvīra did. His most emphatic denial was spoken in the presence of King Pasenadi of Kosala: "There is neither a recluse nor a Brahman who *at one and the same time can know all*, can see all—this situation does not exist."[40]

Jaina and Mahāyāna scholastic positions are obviously docetic theories of the saint's nature, just as docetic as the early Christian fathers' attempt to explain Christ's nature. All three religions ascribe divine attributes to their saviors while at the same time trying to preserve their humanity, that is, their ability to function in a body and to relate to other people in the world. All three present us with the notion of perfect beings *appearing* to use sense organs and their bodies, but in fact they were not really doing so. It seems clear that both Jainas and Mahāyānists undermine their saviors' humanity as badly as Christian theologians did.

Pāli Buddhist views on omniscience are made especially clear in a conversation the Buddha once had with a prominent disciple. In the *Mahāparinibbāna suttana* Śāriputra greets the Buddha and proclaims that no one is "greater or wiser than [he]," especially with regard to omniscience.[41] The Buddha asks his disciple if he had personally known all these religious teachers. Śāriputra is embarrassed and has to answer "no." The Buddha further chides him for not realizing that one would have to be omniscient in order to recognize omniscience in another. Nathan Katz aptly summarizes the Buddha's reasoning: "he does not want anyone to be hailed as omniscient, be it Mahāvīra or himself, because for Buddhism a highly serious human disease is the tendency to claim, despite the lack of grounds for such claiming, an expression of the craving for speculation."[42] To avoid confusion Katz suggests that we view the Buddha's knowledge claims under the rubric of *tivijja* rather than *sabbañña*. When Vacchagotta imputed Jaina omniscience to him, the Buddha categorically rejected it and instead claimed a threefold knowledge (*tivijja*): namely, former lives, the karma of others, and his complete escape from rebirth.[43]

The limited nature of the Buddha's claims in the Pāli scriptures militate strongly against the hypothesis that he was a Gnostic Titan. It should be mentioned that Nāgārjuna refines Buddhist dialectic so masterfully that it protects his Madhyamaka school from any hint of Gnostic Titanism. Kalupahana finds it significant that nowhere in the *Kārikā* does Nāgārjuna refer to omniscience.[44] Indeed, the ultimate effect of Nāgārjuna's dialectic is the realization that the negation of knowledge is the means to liberation. Nāgārjuna's concept of *śūnyatā*, however, is not at all nihilistic; rather, it simply means that no one thing is self-contained or self-sufficient. *Śūnya*tā is "relative" nonbeing while at the same time it is relative being as well; all things are interdependent and relative to one another. *Śūnyatā* means that there are no substances—either physical (matter) or mental (soul or *ātman*). Nāgārjuna's doctrine destroys the very idea of autonomous selves, the foundational idea for all Titanistic philosophies. We shall have occasion to disconfirm the general thesis of a Buddhist Titanism in chapter 8.

Anekāntavāda and Gnostic Titanism

Let us now look at aspects of Jainism that might mitigate the charges of Jaina Titanism in the previous sections. With regard to Gnostic Titanism one could offer the Jaina epistemology of *anekāntavāda*. This famous doctrine of many-sidedness—contrasted with the one-sided (*ekānta*) views of Vedānta and Sāṃkhya—is dramatically expressed in the story of the partial knowledge that five blind men have of an elephant. It is clear, however, that the omniscient Jinas are no longer "blind," because they now know all aspects of all things at once. Even at the fourth level of a fourteen-stage spiritual practice, the Jaina monk is "like a person born blind who sees the world for the first time on the sudden acquisition of eyesight, so the soul now sees the truth."[45] The epistemological mode of *anekāntavāda* is no longer operational, because at this stage, as P. S. Jaini states, the monk has an "absolutely undistorted view of reality."[46]

Jaina writings are filled with incredible knowledge claims, and it appears that all of us are able to get a taste of the saint's perfect knowledge. The author of the *Gommaṭsāra Jīva-Kanda*, for example, presumes to tell us the exact number of hell beings or celestial beings and many other precise calculations. He also categorically states that every six months 608 souls leave the *nigoda* realm. In the same time, at the top of the universe, exactly the same number of souls are liberated.[47] In his commentary J. L. Jaini attempts to enhance the accuracy of this knowledge by presenting many of the calculations in elaborate algebraic formulations. For example, Jaini is able to calculate that at any one instant there can be a maximum of

898,502 vibratory omniscients in the cosmos.[48] (The presence of "vibration" means that the soul is still being affected by the body and the senses, so that a Tīrthaṅkara is a nonvibratory omniscient.) Such claims of precise knowledge and the Jaina's taxonomic exuberance (found in other Indian treatises as well) tends to close philosophical discourse rather than open it up. One would think that the doctrine of many-sidedness would lead to the latter rather than to the former. The ramifications of this Gnostic Titanism are not salutary: the imputation of perfect knowledge to Mahāvīra leads to excessive knowledge claims on the part of his followers.

A possible Jaina response to the foregoing is that *anekāntavāda* is the condition of the vast majority of Jainas and that this limitation instills humility and encourages an epistemological tolerance that makes Gnostic Titanism impossible in practice. Furthermore, the complete knowledge that the Jina has of the world is ultimately irrelevant. The most important aspect of *kevala-jñāna* is self-knowledge—seeing that our inner natures are divine—rather than any knowledge about the world. World knowledge is not used, as it is in technological Titanism, for domination and exploitation.

With regard to epistemological tolerance the Jainas could use Gandhi's words very profitably. In a response to queries about apparent inconsistencies—for instance, holding to *advaita* and *dvaita* at the same time—Gandhi answered that he believed in the Jaina view of many-sidedness, and that his "*anekāntavāda* is the result of the twin doctrine of *satya* and *ahiṃsā*."[49] If one thinks of Gandhi's view of relative truth and how this would preclude one thinking ill of others with differing beliefs, then the alliance with Jaina *anekāntavāda* is a natural one. In the same passage Gandhi continues: "Formerly I used to resent the ignorance of my opponents. Today I can love them because I am gifted with the eye to see myself as others see me and vice versa."

Surprisingly, P. S. Jaini offers a strong disclaimer on the point of epistemological tolerance: "This practice [*anekāntavāda*] probably does not really increase tolerance of others' views; nevertheless it has generated a very well-informed (if not always valid) sort of criticism."[50] In a very sympathetic appraisal of Jainism, Christopher Key Chapple describes Jainism as a friendly form of religious fundamentalism, in which Jainas are firmly committed to their own views and have no intention of ever changing them. At the same time *anekāntavāda* allows them to be tolerant of other views, which are seen as "incomplete" rather than "incorrect."[51] The Jainas' resistance to accepting other views is most likely the principal reason why Jainism survived in India, whereas Buddhism's demise was partially because Buddhists allowed too much syncretism with Hinduism.

Another Jaina response might be to call our attention to the fact that *anekāntavāda* is primarily a logical, not an epistemological doctrine. *Anekāntavāda* lays out seven logical possibilities with regard to a thing's existence and to its expressibility: (1) from one standpoint, my computer exists; yet (2) it did not exist before it was produced nor will it exist after it is destroyed; but now we can see that (3) because my computer presently exists but will cease to be, we can say that it both exists and does not exist; (4) if (3) holds, then it is impossible to express everything definite about my computer; therefore, we must conclude that (5) things are existent and expressible; (6) nonexistent and inexpressible; or (7) existent, nonexistent, and inexpressible.[52] These logical possibilities exist independent of whether one is omniscient or not, and can be immediately recognized by any rational person.

The foregoing appears to be an answer to our charge that the Jaina saints are exempt from *anekāntavāda*. But is this actually so? The doctrine of many-sidedness makes every truth provisional, but does the omniscient saint know only provisional truths? Is Jaina omniscience simply the sum total of all partial truths? No, it is in fact very different from this. As we have seen, Jaina omniscience literally means having total and complete knowledge of all things in all of their possible modes. This is the very opposite of *anekāntavāda*. The other point to observe is that our division between the logical and the epistemological is quite artificial. Not only can we not really separate the two, but there is also, at least for most ancient philosophers, a necessary connection to metaphysics. Even one as skeptical as the Buddha held that truth, knowledge, and reality are all interrelated. We are, after all, speaking about being and nonbeing, not simply affirmation and negation.

Panzooism, Mind-Body, and Process Philosophy

The Jainas have always been known for their unwavering practice of nonviolence (*ahiṃsā*), most dramatically expressed in their care for animals (especially those that have been harmed or neglected), and contemporary Jainas have been at the forefront of expressing and practicing ecological concerns. Central to these admirable practices is the Jaina view of the equality of all souls. In the *Uttaradhyayana Sūtra ahiṃsā* is defined as being "equal-minded to all creatures and regard[ing] them as one's own self. . . ."[53] Compared to Hinduism and Buddhism, where there is a hierarchy of consideration (viz., higher-"minded" creatures have priority over the lower),[54] Jainism attempts to enforce a strict egalitarianism regarding the objects of injurious action. Simply put, every life unit (*jīva*) has equal value. Therefore, Jaina *ahiṃsā* is based on the equality and universal kinship of all souls.

This egalitarianism is a great Jaina achievement, but the philosophical formulation is questionable. First, every Jain *jīva*, just as every Sāṃkhya *puruṣa*, is distinct and separate from every other, so a Jaina cannot, strictly speaking, regard another self as her "own self." Second, sympathy and reciprocity, along with equality, must be necessary conditions for *ahiṃsā*. True sympathy and reciprocity are possible only in a system of internal relations. Jaina spiritual atomism, insofar as it pertains to personal salvation, is based on external relations, that is, the possibility of the soul to become completely independent from everything else in the cosmos. A Jaina may, theoretically, be able to recognize another soul as equal; but it is difficult to see, given the insistence on the isolation of the liberated soul, how souls can be truly sympathetic ("feeling with" is the literal meaning) with one another. In Buddhism, on the other hand, we find that relatedness and interdependence are the very essence of reality, so that there is a near perfect match between ontology and ethics. Unfortunately, the Jaina's theoretical Titanism is at odds with the practice of its most treasured virtue.

A contemporary Jaina philosopher reaffirms the theory of absolute independence and its relation to *ahiṃsā*. N. D. Bhargava argues that *ahiṃsa* must be totally unconditional and unrelational, that its practice is successful only by disengaging from the world of "give-and-take." Bhargava contends that such a world, based as it is on possession and domination, is necessarily violent. In their practice of *ahiṃsā* Jaina saints cannot depend upon the existence of others or the action of others, because nonviolent action is "independent of society." Bhargava states that "the world of relationship is a world of attachment and aversion. But nonviolence is possible and possible only without interrelationship, because interrelationship is dependent on others and cannot be natural."[55] The ultimate implication of Bhargava's view is a *reductio ad absurdum*: liberated Jaina saints are the only ones who can practice nonviolence, but their isolated *lokas* are the only places in the universe where such practice is not necessary—indeed, it has no meaning at all there. Saints in the world, going from town to town for food and teaching, are still presumably in the world of "give-and-take" and are still unable to fulfill the requirements of nonviolence as Bhargava defines it. While Bhargava finds interrelationship unnatural, both Buddhism and Chinese philosophy find it eminently natural.

Given Bhargava's position it is not surprising that he defends the negative formulation of *ahiṃsā*, as opposed to Gandhi's positive formulation that includes not only noninjury but sympathy, love, and compassion as well.[56] Bhargava's reason is that "if we speak of love, we can [only] think of one form or the other of attachment. . . ."[57] Bhargava is certainly correct about the dangers of self-centered love, but his extreme caution on this point again reveals the extreme nature of the Jaina approach. By removing the self from its social and ecological relations, one can obviously remove most of the dangers of attachment and the injury that necessarily follows. But one also risks another danger: alienating people from one another and removing the content and meaning of a whole range of virtues that are arguably more important than *ahiṃsā* itself. Both Gandhi and the Buddha believed that without sympathy and compassion, virtues intelligible only within a world of interdependence and relation, *ahiṃsā* is not worth anything at all. In my own work I have argued that nonviolence is at most an "enabling" virtue, a necessary means to the "substantial" virtue of love and compassion.[58]

Coupled with the equality of the souls is the Jaina doctrine of panzooism, which conceives of *jīvas* of one sort or another inhabiting every part of the universe. Even though the Upaniṣads and Vedāntist philosophy frequently indicate that all things have *ātman*, Hindu beliefs about an intermediate state for the departed soul are not consistent with this view. After death the soul wanders in the atmosphere for some time before falling in raindrops to earth. There it becomes part of the plants that human beings ingest, so that individual souls finally make their way to a male's testes. The Jainas reject this view as incoherent and have instead committed themselves to a doctrine of instantaneous reincarnation. Their argument is simple: if everything is ensouled, then the *ātman* cannot displace any living air bodies, water bodies, or earth bodies; nor can it compete with any plant *jīva*.[59] Again we see the Jainas' firm commitment to the equality, integrity, and value of all souls.

Part and parcel of the Jainas' view of instantaneous reincarnation is their rejection of the soul's omnipresence, a view found in Vedānta, Nyāya, and Sāṃkhya-Yoga. (This position, however, appears to conflict with Nathmal Tatia's description of the Jina's soul filling up, Titan-like, the entire cosmos.)[60] The omnipresence of every soul not only raises problems of spatial inclusion and personal identity, but also forces its proponents to provide various ad hoc mechanisms to facilitate reincarnation in individual bodies. The advantage of the Jaina position is that it eliminates the necessity of a "subtle" body to accompany the soul during its intermediate state. The Jaina position is that the soul is always coterminous with its body, and that the soul can adjust its size appropriately for each bodily existence. As the *Tattvārtha Sūtra* states: "Like the light of a lamp, the soul assumes the size of the body it happens to occupy. . . ."[61] The fact that the Jainas believe that even the souls of the Tīrthaṅkaras take the shape of their last bodies has led P. S. Jaini to the following observation: "One can only conclude that the idea of this interdependence [of soul and body] so dominated the minds of Jaina thinkers that they were somehow reluctant to dispense with the body completely even in the case of *mokṣa*."[62] Early Christian philosophers, even though greatly enamored by neo-Platonism, were likewise reluctant to give up completely the Hebrew somatic soul.

The Jaina doctrine of a coextensive body-soul appears to anticipate modern somatic philosophers such as Merleau-Ponty, Gabriel Marcel, and Michael Polanyi, but Jaina dualism ultimately prevents a successful comparison here. One of the greatest contributions of these somatic philosophers is the recognition that the body is constitutive of the emotions. But, true to traditional dualisms, the Jaina body can have only physical qualities, not affective ones. (With its view that *prakṛti* carries both psychological and physical qualities, Sāṃkhya dualism is superior on this point, but it still leaves the soul totally isolated.) This is so because Jaina philosophy has anticipated Descartes's analogy of the soul as the pilot in a mechanical body. The soul is the "proprietor-sovereign" over the body and its "machine-like system."[63] Bhuvanbhanusuri offers the following as one of his proofs for an independent soul: "A machine manifests a regular and particular kind of working, but the body as opposed to the machine manifests many strange activities. Therefore, we have to infer the existence of some entity dwelling inside the body as the case of a body possessed by a ghost."[64] Unfortunately, contemporary Jaina philosophers appear to be ignorant of the subtleties of the mind-body debate that has flourished in twentieth-century Western philosophy. Only the Buddha and his current interpreters have been able to join this debate successfully.

A sound ecological ethics requires a positive view of the body as well as the earth. Unfortunately, we must conclude that Jainism does not meet these criteria. The Jaina dilemma is somewhat parallel to Christianity. While the Jainas rejected the disembodied soul of the Hindus, the Christians eschewed the Greek soul in favor of the Hebrew somatic view. As a result the body in Jainism and Christianity has somewhat more value than it had in Hinduism or Greek philosophy. Jaina and Christian scriptures, however, are ambiguous on the value of both the body and the earth, with the Jaina view tending to be much more negative than the Christian view. (At times some Jainas sound strongly Manichean,[65] but at least matter is not destroyed at the end of history as some Christians believe.) Furthermore, the Jaina and Christian spiritual bodies are not actually material at all; besides the physical body, the Jainas posit four other types of bodies, each more abstract and nonmaterial than its predecessor.[66] A doctrine of the intrinsic value of the physical—essential for ecological ethics—is nowhere to be found in these religions, except for some Christian theologians who have made the necessary metaphysical adjustments, most successfully achieved in contemporary process theology.

Process theologians argue that a true ecological ethics requires that substance metaphysics be replaced by process metaphysics. Vedānta and Sāṃkhya-Yoga are clearly within the substance tradition, although one could say that *prakṛti* and its constituent *guṇas* indicate an incipient process position. (Process and change, however, are absolutely alien to the Sāṃkhya *puruṣa* and the Vedāntist *ātman.*) To their credit Jaina philosophers attempt to take process seriously, and are rightfully proud of their advance over their Indian counterparts. Reflecting on their doctrine of substance, mode, and qualities using step three of *anekāntavāda* (see the previous section), Jaina philosophers conclude that "all things are unchanging," which is only partially true. The unqualified proposition ignores the fact that *jīva* and *ajīva* change according to their modes, while remaining unchanged in themselves.

Describing Jaina philosophy as a "dynamic realism," A. Chakravartinayanar states that the "Jaina system admits only the dynamic reality or *dravya*. *Dravya* then is that which has a permanent substantiality which manifests through change of appearing and disappearing."[67] Even though Chakravartinayanar claims that the Jaina view is compatible with "the modern conception of organic development" à la Bergson, he also compares it with Spinoza's philosophy of substance and modes. It is unclear whether Jaina philosophers can make coherent a metaphysics of dynamic substance. Most challenging would be arguments against eternal, immutable souls and enduring objects (Jaina *jiva* and *ajiva* respectively) raised by the Buddha, contemporary process philosophers, and contemporary physics. The fact that Chakravartinayanar compares the Jaina solution to the middle ground between Parmenides and Heraclitus suggests that the Greek equivalent of Mahāvīra is Aristotle, who of course is Europe's prime example of a substance metaphysician.

Conclusions

On a practical level the Jainas are to be commended for their fierce commitment to the ideal of nonviolence and to their success in helping to eliminate animal sacrifice and to diminish cruelty to animals and meat eating in India. With their ethics of minimal impact on the environment and their panzooism, the Jainas could be hailed as the world's first ecologists. (The ancient Zoroastrians, with their protection of fire, water, earth, and air, are perhaps runners-up for this honor.) On the theoretical side, however, we must conclude that Jainism does constitute a form of spiritual Titanism. This of course is one of its most benign forms and Jaina monks are no obvious no threat to other humans and the environment. Practically, the Jainas have been able to meld self and world rather successfully. Philosophically, however, their strict dualism, substance metaphysics, extreme anthropocentrism, and hyperbolic knowledge claims remain fundamental problems.

5 Hindu Titanism

Deep in the tiny atom of the psyche lies hidden a tremendous force which will lead the psyche to the point of omniscience, omnipotence, and omnipresence if this force is released properly, systematically, and chronologically.

—Rammurti S. Mishra[1]

In the beginning was yoga, and no longer the sacrifice. The Absolute is that of the yogi. . . . Yoga thus becomes the supreme value, and the Absolute is that of the yogi. . . . The starting point for everything, the ground zero of cosmogony, thus takes the form of a projection of the yogi into the absolute.

—Madeleine Biardeau[2]

Enough of this asceticism, my son. By your dharma you have conquered all worlds, now you should protect the world, for there is no other dharma like that.

—Brahmā to Divodāsa[3]

Introduction

Chapter 3 demonstrated why Asura Titanism is the weakest form of Hindu Titanism, and chapter 4 presented the evidence for Yoga and Gnostic Titanism in Jainism. The first section of this chapter will continue the discussion of these two types as well as Brahmin and Bhakti Titanism. The second section discusses the Yoga Titanism of Sāṃkhya-Yoga philosophy. The third section analyzes the Puruṣa hymn of the *Ṛgveda*, which serves as the prototype for divinized humanity in the Indian tradition from the Vedas to the Purāṇas. The fourth section shows how Puruṣa becomes a cosmic yogi in the Purāṇas. The final section takes issue with claims that Vedāntist monism is the best grounds for ecological ethics and that this monism is the best answer to Indian Titanism.

Types of Indian Titanism

The original offering of the Vedic sacrifice was most likely a human being, with animals, then food and flowers substituted in evolutionary stages. In a provocative article, Brian K. Smith has demonstrated the close connection between eating and power:

> In the Veda, violence and power—that is, power *over* another, the power the eater has over food—were celebrated on their own terms. . . . The texts depict a life where I gain only at your loss, my prosperity entails your ruin, my continued existence depends on your death, my eating requires that you become food.[4]

The main conflict between the Devas and Asuras was concerned with sacred food, and because the brahmin priests had control of this food, they could make a claim to divinity. The priests declared that they were "gods on earth" or "human gods (*manuṣyadevas*)."[5] The *Laws of Manu* confirm their claim: the priest is "the supreme deity" even if he is unlearned and acts immorally.[6]

As early as the *Atharva-veda*, one can see the priestly expropriation of the sacred power (*brahman*) of the Vedas, which the Upaniṣadic writers then expanded, by their own religious innovation, into Brahman, the Godhead itself.[7] (The surest clue that Brahmanism is post-Vedic and essentially a new religion is the fact that neither the Devas nor the Asuras know who Brahman is.)[8] There then occurs a gradual displacement of the Devas from the center of post-Vedic religion. Wendy Doniger describes the process aptly: "By performing the sacrifice, [the priests] could ensure the achievement of [its] ends . . . without the participation of the gods at all. . . . A man could achieve a kind of immortality equal or indeed superior to that of the gods, through his own individual efforts."[9] With the gods in eclipse, the chief antagonists for the priests were the ascetics. Since the greatest threat to the Devas came from Asuras practicing austerities, the priests acted like the Devas in attacking the ascetics. The yogis and the Asuras found themselves in an unspoken and unofficial alliance against the sacrificial religion, whose priests despised those who claimed to have divine power outside the prescribed rituals. The medieval church reacted the same way toward its mystics.

The discovery of the power of ascetic practices and intellectual reflection gave rise to Yoga and Gnostic Titanism respectively. In distinguishing between Gnostic and Yoga Titanism we have separated those who are divinized through meditation (*dhyana*) and ascetic practices (*tapas*) and those who claim divinity through knowledge (*jñāna*; Gk. *gnosis*). Sāṃkhya-Yoga philosophy therefore combines both Gnostic and Yoga Titanism—with Sāṃkhya as the *jñāna* system and Yoga representing *dhyana*. The Sāṃkhya emphasis on knowledge—specifically the discrimination (*sāṃkhya*) and separation of all spiritual entities from material things—led it to ignore ethical development and spiritual purification. As in Śaṅkara's intuition of the Brahman-Ātman identity, the jñāna yoga of both views appears to imply that knowledge alone is sufficient for salvation. In contrast to Yoga, Christopher K. Chapple observes that "the relative absence of emphasis on purity and virtue within the Sāṃkhya system . . . seems striking."[10]

Finally, there is Bhakti Titanism, which, as was shown in chapter 1, has its counterpart in Christianity. One might contend that this must be the weakest form of Titanism, or surely not Titanism at all. In Hindu and Christian bhaktism, God and humans have passed beyond the petty jealousies that characterized earlier forms of religion. The vain Devas and the jealous Yahweh have been replaced by a God of love. The original interdependence of Creator and creature is reaffirmed in *bhakti* yoga, and everyone, including selected Asuras in evangelical Hinduism, are eligible for salvation. By seeing bhaktism as a true Avatāravāda one could easily eliminate the category of Bhakti Titanism. At the end of the third section, however, we will see that Kṛṣṇa's appropriation of the *puruṣa* motif, enhanced by many Upaniṣadic confirmations that the Person is higher than Brahman,[11] makes his position arguably much more like the Uttarāravāda, an ascent of the ultimate one.

An alternative approach, focusing on the concept of play (*līlā*) and linking it to Nietzsche, could claim that Kṛṣṇa has passed beyond the Titan (the "lion" stage of Nietzsche's Three Metamorphoses) to the "child" stage of reintegration. Nietzsche's *Übermensch* should not be identified, as argued in the introduction, as the lion, but as the child. Other than the antibody polemic, one might see both an Upaniṣadic *Übermensch* and a precursor Kṛṣṇa in the following passage: "Such a one is a superman (*uttara puruṣa*); and there he roves around, laughing, playing, taking his pleasure with women, chariots, or friends and remembering no more that excrescence [which was] his body."[12]

Yoga Titanism

The Kānphata yogis claim that their sect existed before creation, and that their guru Gorakhnāīh had Brahmā, Viṣṇu, and Śiva as his first disciples.[13] Practicing austerities could generate power equal to, or superior to, that of the gods. An angry glance of an ascetic, for example, could reduce any being to ashes. Kapila, the reputed father of the Sāṃkhya system, was said to have incinerated sixty thousand of King Bhagīratha's ancestors. Called the God of Sāṃkhya or even Īśvara himself, Kapila was known also as the mind-born son of Brahmā, present at the beginning of each cycle of creation with perfect knowledge and disposition.[14] Another aspect of *tapas* that frustrated the gods was the fact that the ascetic was usually immune from sexual temptation, the most successful strategy that the gods had always used against their antagonists. The story of Gautama's rejection of Māra's daughters and Divodāsa's steadfastness in the face of the sixty-four yoginis Śiva sent to seduce him are good examples. (Divodāsa was finally defeated by Viṣṇu and his associates disguised as Buddhist missionaries.) Again, contrary to Greek myth, it is the gods, not the Titans, who are prone to deception.

As we have already seen, the Sāṃkhya-Yoga philosophy contains a strict dualism between the soul (*puruṣa*) and matter (*prakṛti*). As opposed to the pantheism of Vedānta in general and of the absolute monism of Advaita Vedānta in particular, Sāṃkhya-Yoga claims that individual souls are real, eternal substances and that matter is equally real, even in its inactive and nondifferentiated state. Contrary to popular views, the yogi does not unite with any divine reality, not even with Īśvara the Lord. *Puruṣa* souls are self-contained and self-sufficient substances, so they are by nature similar to the autonomous selves of Western philosophy.

As would be expected the gods have a subordinate role in Sāṃkhya-Yoga, and Mircea Eliade gives the reason for their inferior position: "It is only through experiences that one acquires freedom. Therefore, the gods (*videha*, "disincarnate")—who have no experience because they have no bodies—have a condition of existence inferior to the human condition, and as such they cannot attain to total deliverance."[15] Again we see the Titanistic insistence that human experience be the norm. The gods are actually defined in a negative way: the disincarnate ones, those beings without bodies; but, ironically, the final goal of all *puruṣas* is a disembodied state. The being that takes the place of God is the Lord Īśvara, who is a projection of the perfect human—the yogi himself writ large on a cosmic scale—the one *puruṣa* who has escaped entrapment in nature. Eliade describes the yogi's technique as a process of "cosmicization"—"recasting man in new, gigantic dimensions, of guaranteeing him macranthropic experiences." Eliade observes that this Titanistic attempt to identify with all aspects of the macrocosmos—the sun, the moon, and the stars—is temporary, because the yogi ultimately withdraws "to his own center and completely dissociat[es] himself from the cosmos, . . . impervious to experiences, unconditioned, and autonomous."[16] The macanthropos is not dissolved into Ātman-Brahman, but, as in Jainism, is set free to contemplate his own pure essence and an eternally independent and individual being.

The *Sāṃkhya-kārikā* contains an argument for the existence of *puruṣa* that is valid but, to many readers, not sound. Here it is in my formulation:

1. All composite objects are for another's use.
2. All of nature is composite (i.e., made of *guṇas*).
3. If the user is composite, there would be an infinite regress of composite users.

∴ 4. A simple (noncomposite) thing must exist apart from Nature.[17]

To the Western mind the first premise appears to be clearly false, and some of us might be amazed that Īśvara Kṛṣṇa has somehow overlooked the obvious distinction between natural things and things of use. As it turns out, however, Sāṃkhya philosophy is even more anthropocentric than Western thought. The first premise is true for Sāṃkhya philosophers because for them all of nature is merely a means to liberate human spirits. The fourteenth-century *Sāṃkhya-pravacana-sūtra* makes this point very clear: "From Brahmā down to a stock [blade of grass], the creation is for sake of Puruṣa, till there be discrimination [supreme knowledge]."[18] This extreme anthropocentricism and total devaluation of nature is a feature of both spiritual and technological Titanism, and it is a deficiency that Śākta theology is committed to overcoming.

In his commentary on the *Yoga Sūtras* Rammurti S. Mishra claims that "deep in the tiny atom of the psyche lies hidden a tremendous force which will lead the psyche to the point of omniscience, omnipotence, and omnipresence if this force is released properly, systematically, and chronologically."[19] Mishra has essentially confirmed our thesis about Yoga Titanism, but he does not realize that the attributes he ascribes to the yogi are actually not compatible with the *puruṣa* nature. If *prakṛti* is the only source of power, as Sāṃkhya-Yoga teaches, then the liberated yogi is completely impotent not omnipotent. If power is relational and socially constructed, as more and more commentators on this issue realize, then the free and independent yogi can have no power. Furthermore, the *puruṣa* is not omniscient as the Christian God is—knowing everything past, present, and future—but more like Aristotle's God, a being knowing only its own perfect nature. Finally, the yogi cannot properly claim omnipresence, because he must contend with the infinite number of individual spirits who have a claim on the same spiritual space. (As we saw in the last chapter, the Jainas solve this by saying that the soul takes on the bodily shape of its last incarnation.) The *puruṣas* are totally isolated and inactive, completely cut off from everything else, including the Lord Īśvara, who inspired the *puruṣas* to become like him in the first place. The lives of spiritual Titans are exceedingly solitary experiences. The *puruṣa* is like the "perfectly pure" and "victorious" Jaina saint, but is also "absolutely alone."[20]

The *Puruṣa* Hymn and Its Legacy

A common feature of Titanism in general is the tendency to describe the universe in human terms and form. The most striking examples of the humanization of the cosmos can be found in Indian literature, particularly in one Vedic hymn known as the Puruṣa hymn. Already we see a Titanistic reversal in that the *ṛṣi* of the hymn is identified as Nārāyaṇa (=Viṣṇu) and Puruṣa himself is the hymn's self-existent God.[21] *Puruṣa* is the masculine Sanskrit word for "person," and this hymn portrays the birth of the universe in terms of the sacrifice of this cosmic Man. Because of this, some commentators have called it a cosmotheandric hymn; that is, it assumes the identity of God, man, and the cosmos.[22] This cannot, however, be correct because the human element reigns supreme in this cosmic triad. Instead of a long process of prehuman evolution and an eventual human appearance, here the universe evolves out of a cosmic Man. The Puruṣa hymn proclaims that "Man is this whole universe,—what was and what is yet to be, the Lord of immortality. . . . This is the measure of his greatness, but greater yet is (primal) Man: All beings form a quarter of him, three-quarters are the immortal in heaven."[23] The Titanistic subordination of the world and the gods culminates in the declaration that Indra is born from the Puruṣa's mouth.

The Puruṣa hymn is reworked in the *Atharva-veda*, where the demotion of the gods is well advanced. As builders of the Primal Man, it is easy to imagine them as Lilliputians swarming around the giant body, erecting scaffolding and fashioning the "breast and neck of Man."[24] But these godlings are not the real creators, for we learn that it is Brahman, "the single God [who] put sacrifice in Man."[25] The reference to Brahman, however, is self-reflexive, for "Brahman [as] Man [acquires] this fire,"[26] so the Primal Man is creator of himself. The identity of Puruṣa and Brahman is clear, when we are given an interesting, but probably bogus, etymology of *puruṣa*:

> Brought forth above, brought forth athwart,
> All cardinal points did Man pervade,—
> [Yes, Man] who Brahman's city (*pur*) knows,
> By which he is called "Man" (*puruṣa*).[27]

Brahman's city is "radiant . . . yellow, gold, compassed with glory round about"—just as the Puruṣa is always described—and the Creator "Brahmā has entered in."[28]

In the *Bṛhadāraṇyaka Upaniṣad* we find the *puruṣa* motif refashioned once again: "In the beginning this [universe] was the Self alone,—in the likeness of a man (*puruṣa*)."[29] In this same *brāhmana* we also see the post-Vedic tension between the sacrifice, which the gods desperately need, and the Upaniṣadic discovery of the Ātman within, which makes the sacrifice unnecessary. "Whoso thus knows that he is Brahman, becomes this whole [universe]. Even the gods have not the power to cause him to un-Be, for he becomes their own self. . . ."[30] In a word (viz., *ātman*), the gods are being converted to Brahmanism against their will! Here is their complaint:

> Just as many animals are of use to man, so is each single man of use to the gods. To be robbed of even a single animal is disagreeable. How much more to be robbed of many! And so the [gods] are not at all pleased that men should know this.[31]

The gods' pleas are in vain, for the new religion of Puruṣa=Ātman=Brahman, and the immediate divine power that it promises, is solidly entrenched: "I worship (*puruṣa*) as the pre-eminent, the head and king of all beings. He who worships him as such becomes preeminent, the head and king of all beings."[32]

In the *Śvetāśvatāra Upaniṣad* we find an incipient personal theism—a "Blessed Lord" (identified as Śiva) higher than Brahman—developing around the *puruṣa* idea: "I know that mighty Person . . . beyond Him is nothing whatsoever, no other thing . . . the One, the Person, this whole universe full filling!"[33] The Puruṣa hymn is once again rephrased in the third *adhyaya*. In these passages the divine Person is thoroughly anthropomorphic, but a later passage describes the "one God" as "devoid of attributes."[34] Passages from other Upaniṣads also counter Puruṣa personalism by describing him as "formless," "other than human," and also as a cosmic horse.[35] Returning to the context of the phrase "devoid of attributes," one can safely interpret this as Sāṃkhya influence, rather than as Vedāntist impersonalism. This Puruṣa is described as a spectator—an "overseer . . . witness, observer, absolute, alone (*kevala*), devoid of attributes."[36] This is unmistakable Sāṃkhya terminology. A similar passage from the *Maitrī Upaniṣad*—"He is indeed the pure, the stable, the unmoved, the unaffected, unflurried, free from desire, standing still like a spectator, self-subsistent"[37]—is connected to a reference to Sāṃkhya's three *guṇas*. In Sāṃkhya it is assumed that *puruṣas* are creaturely souls, not gods, who must take on human form in order to be liberated. Furthermore, the yogi who "attains to absolute isolation (*kevalatva*) . . . through self-dependence"[38] is not the description of a soul merging with Brahman.

Therefore, this strain of Upaniṣadic Titanism that we have identified contains a very extreme view of human autonomy and superiority. In the *Kauśītaki* the gods flee before the righteous man; and this same man, identified with the Puruṣa, discovers that he is the "Self of every single being," the "Real," and the "entire universe."[39] The *Taittirīya* tells us that the yogi "attains to independent sovereignty, attains to the lord of the mind"; and enjoys a bliss that is a billion times greater than that of the highest gods.[40] In the *Maitrī* the ascetic will surpass Brahman and "will go [yet further], he [will surpass] the gods in the realm of divinity. . . ."[41] What Indian Titans lack in external action and domination, they make up for in elaborate and grandiose internal journeys of conquest and liberation. In the *Śvetāśvatāra* they gain incredible powers: "When men shall roll up space as if it were a piece of leather";[42] and a yogi in the *Taittirīya* boasts that "I am the first-born of the world-order, earlier than the gods, in the navel of immortality. . . . I have overcome the whole world."[43] For the Titans of India everything appears possible. These are veritable Indian supermen. Potter's claim that Westerners actually appreciate human limitations better than Indians appears to be dramatically confirmed.

It is in Kṛṣṇa, however, that the ultimate expression of the *puruṣa* motif is conceived. Kṛṣṇa makes explicit his connection with the Vedic tradition: "Through all the Vedas it is I that should be known, for the Maker of the Veda's end am I; . . ." and "so am I extolled in Vedic speech as . . . the 'Person [All-]Sublime.'"[44] Kṛṣṇa declares himself "God of gods" and the "beginning of the gods"; and he transcends them so much that they are not allowed to see Kṛṣṇa's unmanifest form."[45] Kṛṣṇa also reiterates the subordination of Brahman to the Puruṣa, which we have already seen in the Upaniṣads: "Great Brahman is to Me a womb, in it I plant the seed: from this derives the origin of all contingent beings"; and "I am the base supporting Brahman. . . .[46] R. C. Zaehner states that Kṛṣṇa "transcends the immortal Brahman as much as He transcends the phenomenal world," and he suggests that another translation of *uttama puruṣa* (lit. "highest" person) is "superman."[47] But he chooses instead to use "superman" for *uttara puruṣa*, the "higher" person of the *Chāndogya Upaniṣad*.[48] To use "superman" for both would obscure an all important distinction between the Upaniṣadic supermen and Kṛṣṇa, the supreme Titan. As Zaehner states: "In arrogating this title (*uttama puruṣa*) exclusively to Himself Kṛṣṇa denies it to the liberated individual."[49] Stressing this distinction, both he and Robert S. Minor are determined to reject a nondualistic interpretation that would dissolve all selves into the one divine self.[50] What we have then is a relation of Kṛṣṇa to individual selves much like, with the major exception of *bhakti* intimacy, the relation of the Lord Īśvara and autonomous *puruṣas* of Sāṃkhya-Yoga.

The five types of Indian Titanism were partially inspired by Doniger O'Flaherty's "Three Stages of Alignment of Gods, Demons, and Men," which begins with "Vedic Sacrifice (God and Men versus Demons)" followed by a second stage of "Post-Vedic Antiascetic Orthodoxy."[51] She observes that the tensions within her second stage are resolved either by destroying "the ascetic power of the man or demon" (Brahmin Titanism), or by making "the ascetic man or demon into a god," which leads to Bhakti Titanism.[52] The origins of the Kṛṣṇa figure are obscure, but Kṛṣṇa as divinized ascetic or deified epic hero are two major options. (The earliest reference identifies him as a student of the guru Ghora Āngirasa.)[53] One could argue that Bhakti Titanism is actually a subcategory of the third or fourth forms, where the savior is a yogi or gnostic who has turned from selfish isolation to compassion for all creatures. On this interpretation, Kṛṣṇa would be an example of a "reverse" *avatāra*—like Jesus and Gautama (mortals made highest God)—who take on, in the imagination of their devotees, the salvation of both humans and gods alike. This transformation of Yoga Titanism into Bhakti Titanism is most evident in Mahāyāna Buddhism.

In this section we have covered the development of the Puruṣa motif from the *Ṛgveda* through the Upaniṣads to the *Bhagavad-gītā*. We have seen that there is a clear transformation of the Puruṣa as a sacrificial victim to a Titan of the universe, a view already implied in the *Ṛgveda*. We need to acknowledge, however, that the Sāṃkhya *puruṣa* is far less masculine than the Vedic *puruṣa*. The former, as we have seen, is impotent and passive as opposed to the active *prakṛti*. In the Sāṃkhya system, as C. Mackenzie Brown explains, the "Paursic ('manly') character of the cosmic [Vedic] Puruṣa loses any heroic, aggressive tendencies, becoming absorbed in the image of the quiescent witness."[54] We have also noted that in the *Gītā* Kṛṣṇa elevates himself as the ultimate Puruṣa, higher even than Brahman, and takes a position equivalent to that of Īśvara the Lord. In the next section we will discover that the theme of the Great Yogi continues in Purāṇic cosmogony as well.

The *Puruṣa* as Cosmic Yogi

Hindu accounts of the fall of human beings generally describe the gods as very anxious about the implications of such a great increase of evil in the world. The logic of Vedic religion is clear: wicked people would sacrifice less, thus the gods would have less power. But even more threatening to the gods (and to the priests who cultivated them) is the existence of human ascetics. Doniger observes that "a priest might legitimately emulate the gods, but an ascetic should not. An ambitious priest was like a god; an ambitious ascetic was like a demon."[55] The power of performing austerities (*tapas*) was one that the gods could not keep to themselves, as they did the soma sacrifice. Asuras and humans, therefore, had equal access to this powerful means of gaining merit and liberation.

The reformulation of the Puruṣa hymn in the Purāṇas demonstrates the power and significance of Yoga Titanism. Here the divinized male person is given the highest title—*puruṣottama*—and he is also called *mahāyogin*. Madeleine Biardeau contends that this identification of the Puruṣa as a yogi "is the most important aspect of the primal divinity, who is no longer a sacrificial victim: it is by an act of yoga that he will first set the universe in motion."[56] (It is important to note that all the Purāṇas share this new yogi-centered cosmogony.) Ironically, the Purāṇas, a voluminous literature devoted ostensibly to ritual and sacrifice, are subverted at their core by a creative agent, who not only represents the rejection of Vedic ritual but also hostility to the Hindu gods. Yoga Titanism is found at the heart of texts that inform the daily practice of hundreds of millions of Hindus.

In answer to her question "What does this cosmogony mean?" Biardeau answers:

> In the beginning was yoga, and no longer the sacrifice. The Absolute is that of the yogi . . . Yoga thus becomes the supreme value, and the Absolute is that of the yogi. . . . The starting point for everything, the ground zero of cosmogony, thus takes the form of a projection of the yogi into the absolute.[57]

It is significant to note that the Sāṃkhya system is firmly embedded in the Puranic cosmogony, so much so that some have called its primary form a remythologized Sāṃkhya.[58] One might also call it a remasculinized Sāṃkhya as well, for in some of the Purāṇas nature draws, contrary to original Sāṃkhya and to the Śākta Purāṇas, all of its being from the cosmic yogi.[59] This is the reason why Viṣṇu is now seen, as Kṛṣṇa is in the *Gītā*,[60] as the creator of both *puruṣa* and *prakṛti*. The presence of Sāṃkhya allows us, once again, to thwart an exclusively monistic interpretation, one that would dissolve all individuals into a divine unity. At the end of the cosmic cycle, *prakṛti* does return to its undifferentiated state, but one can assume that in most instances ordinary *puruṣas* remain separate from the *mahāyogin*.

Monism, Ecology, and Titanism

W. P. Mei claims that it is the Chinese, more than any "other major-world civilization, [which] has laid emphasis . . . on the cosmic importance of man."[61] In the foregoing we have demonstrated that the Indians have done this as well; but they have not, unfortunately, kept a proper balance, as have the Chinese, between humans, heaven, and earth. In a recent article, David Kinsley points to the fact that the Vedic tradition deified basic natural elements and made mountains and rivers into goddesses. He also mentions the organic, holistic worldview, based on internal rather than external relations, which is contained within Hinduism. By homologizing the cosmos to the human form, the Hindu sages, according to Kinsley, have given the cosmos great value. Using the Puruṣa hymn as an example of this organic view, Kinsley does not realize that *puruṣa* as human form preempts both heaven and earth. The latter cannot possibly have the intrinsic value that they do in Chinese philosophy. The ecological vision of organic harmony can come only from a worldview in which each member of the cosmic triad has its own independence and integrity. Even in Sāṃkhya-Yoga, where *prakṛti* does have its own nature, it devolves, once human *puruṣas* are free from it, into an inactive, valueless mass.

Referring to some of the same passages that we have used to support Hindu Titanism, Kinsley admits that "such hymns might be taken as evidence of spiritual megalomania, delusions of grandeur. However, in the context of Hindu philosophical thought, particularly in the context of the monistic vision of reality, it is clear that they represent redefinitions of 'I' and 'me'."[62] If Kinsley means the absolute monism of Advaita Vedānta, then the holistic and pluralistic web of existence we witness with our five senses is not such a rich fabric at all, but an undifferentiated One. Organic holism loses all of its conceptual power for ecology if it is interpreted in terms of pure nondualism.[63] Rāmānuja's panentheism—just like American process theology—is a much better philosophical model. There is a significant contrast between seeing the cosmos as a dreamlike appearance (Śaṅkara) and the cosmos as the very body of the Godhead (Rāmānuja).[64] The ultimate effect is that absolute monism desacralizes the universe, while panentheism resacralizes it. If by "monistic vision of reality" Kinsley means general Upaniṣadic monism, then he must acknowledge the undeniable presence of Sāṃkhya's influence in the Upaniṣads and in the *Gītā*. If the passages are interpreted from this perspective—individual selves are plural, real, and supreme—then it is difficult to avoid Kinsley's diagnosis of "spiritual megalomania." The passages that we have examined from the Upaniṣads and Gītā are not cosmocentric and not even theocentric if Puruṣa is a deified yogi.

In a provocative article criticizing the use of Advaita Vedānta for environmental ethics, Lance E. Nelson contends that Advaita Vedānta achieves its nonduality "exclusively not inclusively" such that disunity rather than unity with the world is the result. (John White makes the same point by distinguishing between the pantheistic unity of God and the world and Śaṅkara's "transcendental dualism" of Brahman and a world existing only for the ignorant. See *supra*, p. 52.) Citing Śaṅkara's writings directly, Nelson shows that the Advaitin, either before or after liberation, imputes no value whatsoever to the natural world. Interestingly enough, the Advaitins borrowed the Sāṃkhya word *kaivalya*, which emphasizes the isolation of the liberated one, and the result, according to Nelson, is "the same world alienation that we find in the Jaina, Sāṃkhya-Yoga, and early Buddhist traditions."[65] Furthermore, Nelson demonstrates that although Advaita Vedānta celebrates the one who is liberated while embodied (*jīvanmukta*), the preferred state is disembodied isolation. In this sense the *jīvanmukta* is superior to Īśvara, because the creator of the universe must always be connected to that universe. Nelson's conclusion is that Īśvara's "Godhood" limits "his true nature as Brahman,"[66] while only brahmin males (Śaṅkara's own restriction) are eligible for complete liberation. Spiritual Titanism is confirmed, as we once again see that these men are capable of a spiritual perfection higher than God himself.

Hindu and Christian Titanism appear to meet in Raimondo Panikkar, who suggests that "[man] is in some ways the successor of God, the agent of divinity . . . the destiny of God himself is in man's power. . . . Inasmuch as man is, God is not; insofar as God is, man is not; the one means the absence of the other. . . ."[67] In a related statement in his *Vedic Experience* he claims that "God without man is nothing, literally 'no-thing.'"[68] This passage taken alone might imply a theology that insists on an interdependence between God and the world, such that we find, for example, in process theology. But taken in context and together with the previous claim, the assumption appears to be a strong gods versus humans antagonism, based on the zero-sum power relation that we find in the Vedic relationship of gods, *asuras*, and human beings. There may even be hints of the atheism of the Reformation's *Jesuologie* and of Vivekananda's overthrowing of the Father by the Son. Even though Panikkar says that his view leads to an "all-embracing cosmotheandric reality," it is anthropomorphic through and through—the cosmos collapses into the human form. A philosophy that puts humans first, be it Euro-American or Indian, is simply not suited for an ecological vision of reality.

In conclusion let us think of Brahmā's advise to Divodāsa with new ecological meaning: "Enough of this asceticism, my son. By your dharma you have conquered all worlds, now you should protect the world, for there is no other dharma like that."[69]

6 The Yogi and the Goddess

Without you [Rādhā], I [Kṛṣṇa] am inert and am always powerless. You have all powers [*śakti*] as your own form; come into my presence.

—Brahmavaivarta Purāṇa[1]

You should consider who you are, and who nature is. . . . How could you transcend nature? What you hear, what you eat, what you see—it's all Nature. How could you be beyond Nature?

—Pāravatī to Śiva, *Skanda Purāṇa*[2]

Prologue: The Dancing Goddess

In the beginning there were disembodied spirits suspended in space, unmoving and fixed in trance. Enter a dancing Goddess, creating solid ground wherever she steps. Her dynamic gestures cause the spirits to stir and gradually, one by one, they begin to dance with the Goddess. As they dance, they take on bodies, and they, too, begin to feel ground beneath their moving feet. Only one spirit, Īśvara the Lord, remains fixed and undisturbed. The cosmic dance continues and becomes more complex, creative, and frenzied. Īśvara, however, begins to call the spirits back to their original state. He exhorts them to give up their embodied lives, which to him are sinful and degrading. One by one, the spirits disengage from the Goddess, throw off their bodies, and return to their static state of complete autonomy and isolation. Without dancing partners the Goddess also falls into inactivity. The cosmic dance is finished and the evolution of the world ceases.[3]

Introduction

This chapter entertains the thesis that Indian goddess worship serves to balance masculine views of individual autonomy and separation from the body and nature. As we have seen, Yoga Titanism emphasizes personal isolation and is similar to Western Titanism in that respect. The first section contrasts the passive and inert views of the material principle (primarily found in Greek thought) with the dynamic and creative views of Hinduism. The second section traces the philosophical origins of Śākta theology with a focus on some basic problems of Sāṃkhya's *puruṣa-prakṛti* dualism. The third section demonstrates the fact that Purāṇic writers appropriated the Sāṃkhya principle of *prakṛti* and the Vedāntist concept of *māyā* to establish a powerful goddess ontology, one that overcomes the alienation from nature and from other selves found in Sāṃkhya-Yoga philosophy. Hindu Tantrics used the concept of *śakti* to produce the same results. The fourth section draws on Stanley N. Kurtz's psychoanalytic study of Hindu goddesses and presents his reasons why goddess worship survived in the Indian subcontinent. The fifth section contains a critique of Kurtz's view and confirms a suspicion that traditional Śākta theology does not actually express a genuine female voice. If this is so, then this mitigates somewhat the thesis that Śākta theology is an answer to Titanism. Finally, some encouraging manifestations of Śākta theology among contemporary Indian women are discussed.

The Material Principle: East and West

Recall Rammurti Mishra's incredible claim about the yogi's nature in the previous chapter. Let us now rephrase these assertions in terms of nuclear physics, à la Edward Teller: "Deep inside the hydrogen atom lies hidden a tremendous force which will lead humans to omnipotence and omniscience." This is not totally fair—physical and spiritual power are being conflated—but the principal point is the conceptual convergence of Indian and Western forms of Titanism. Even though Yoga Titanism is a benign form of extreme humanism, it nevertheless uses the same language of hubris, power, and conquest as Western Titanism. Spiritual and technological Titanism meet at this very point.

Let us dwell for a moment on Edward Teller, the Titanism of cold war militarism, and the co-option of female creative power. The first atomic weapon was called Oppenheimer's baby and the hydrogen bomb was known as Teller's baby. There was some dispute over whether Teller was mother or father, because some argued that it was Stanislaw Ulam who came up with the original idea. On this account Father Ulam inseminated Teller with the idea and Mother Teller carried the fetus to term. Carol Cohn, who provides a fascinating analysis of this phenomenon of male creation, also finds it significant that all the bombs have male names. Therefore, nuclear scientists, in Cohn's words, have given "birth to male progeny with the ultimate power of violent domination over female Nature. The defense intellectuals' project is the creation of abstract formulations to control the forces the scientists discovered, and to participate thereby in their world-creating/destroying power."[4]

The desire to become father of oneself is one of the general features of the psychology of Titanism. By claiming the power of self-creation, the Hindu Titan is able to eliminate the female role and to manipulate ordinary reproduction to his own advantage. For example, the Vedic father re-creates himself in the mother's womb or womb substitute. This theme is most explicit in a late Upaniṣad, the *Yogatattva*: "He who was his father is now his son, and he who is his son will be again his father."[5] Prajāpati "placed the power to produce progeny in himself" and then proceeded to create the Devas and the Asuras out of his mouth.[6] In the *Kūrma Purāṇa* Viṣṇu directly enters Aditi's womb and is conceived as Vāmana, the dwarf incarnation.[7] In the *Bhāgavata* version of the story, Viṣṇu first "penetrates" Kaśyapa with his "ray" and then his semen his deposited in Aditi's womb.[8] Stories of the Buddha's conception in the *Mahāvastu* indicate clearly that the heavenly Bodhisattva is essentially placing a human version of himself in Māyā's womb.[9] Other womb substitutes appear in many stories where Promethean churning (the key root *manth* again) and giving issue from one's mind or thigh seem to be the most common form of male procreation. (Mind-born sons, the ten great sages, are sinless and nonprocreating.) The following sons are said to have been "thigh-born" of their fathers: Asuras from Brahmā's thigh, Vaiśyas from Prajāpati's, Kutsa from Indra's, a long-awaited son from King Yuvanāśva's, Anga (Vena's father) from Uru's, and Niṣāda from Vena's thigh. (Pṛthu, however, is "churned" from his father's right arm.) We also have the incredible example of Brahmā giving "birth" to thousands of sages from semen prematurely ejaculated at the sight of Pārvatī as bride. In the Hebrew tradition we find a rib-born Eve and Jacob's thigh-born sons; and in Greek mythology we of course have the thigh-born Zeus giving issue to Athene from his mind.

The co-option and exploitation of the creative energies of the female have a long history in Europe. Hesiod's *Theogony* still preserves the idea of primordial chaos and Gaia the earth goddess as the source of all things, but the power of the Greek Goddess was gradually coopted by male deities, starting with Zeus and his self-created daughter, as well as with priests and philosophers. Although there is an egalitarian human creation story in Gen. 1:26, in Gen. 2 Eve is made out of Adam's rib and the "mother of all the living" becomes his subordinate. We now know that many ancient Hebrews worshiped goddesses along with Yahweh, but this practice was of course never condoned by the priests or prophets. The last trace of the feminine in Hebrew scripture, a figure called Sophia (Yahweh's helpmate in Prov. 8:30), was replaced, except for the Gnostic sects, by the masculine Logos by Philo of Alexandria. For Philo the cosmos becomes the mind-born creation of God, whose Logos makes the world out of absolute nothing, not the feminine chaos implied in Gen. 1:1. The final banishment of the Goddess of watery chaos is implied in the declaration in Revelation that in the "new heaven and new earth . . . the sea [is] no more" (21:1). In the new creation, the writer is telling us, the irrational goddesses will not bother us anymore.

In pre-Socratic philosophy the idea of *phusis* (Lat. *natura*), although not identified as female, was a creative and dynamic material principle. This idea was replaced by inert atoms or by Aristotle's *hulē*, both passive and inactive material principles. Aristotle's idea that the female womb was simply a receptacle for self-contained male seed joined similar views of human reproduction in the ancient world. The father essentially recreates himself in the womb of the passive mother. There are, however, some significant exceptions to this view. While most Buddhists affirmed the passive role of the female, both the Jainas and the Tantrics thought that the menstrual blood served a purpose in human conception.[10] In the Jewish tradition there is a fascinating parallel to the Tantric idea of white and red "semen":

> There are three partners in man . . . his father supplies the semen of the white substance out of which are formed the child's bones, sinews, nails, and the white of his eyes. His mother supplies the semen of the red substance out of which is formed his skin, flesh, hair and black of his eye. God gives him the soul and breath, beauty of features, eyesight, hearing, speech, understanding, and discernment.[11]

Although sexist and theocentric, this Jewish view does give an active role to the female in the formation of the fetus. The Western esoteric tradition preserved the coequal partnership of male and female principles until, as Carolyn Merchant has shown,[12] witch-hunts and mechanistic science virtually eliminated the idea of dynamic nature and the feminine symbolism attached to it.

The Goddess in Indian Philosophy

While male patriarchs in India established a society that devalued women and severely restricted their autonomy, they consistently and openly acknowledged the feminine as the source of cosmic matter and energy. Although the Hindu Goddess tradition may go back as far as the Harrapan civilization, Tracy Pintchman's recent work has demonstrated that the Vedic tradition may have been a greater source than has previously been thought. Pintchman shows that the waters (*ap*), the earth goddess (Pṛthivī/Bhūmi), Aditi (mother of the gods), Virāj (coequal with Puruṣa), Vāc (the voice of the *mantra* and essential breath *ātman*), and Śacī/Indrānī (Indra's consort) all echo in later portrayals of the Goddess.[13] We have seen that the Sāṃkhya dualism of *puruṣa* and *prakṛti* constituted the metaphysical basis for yogic retreat and isolation, but some Purānic writers transformed *prakṛti* into a feminine power that sacralizes the body, the emotions, nature, and human relations. The Goddess as *prakṛti* was alternatively or simultaneously identified with the creative *māyā* of the Vedāntist tradition and with the powerful *śakti* of Tantrism. J. N. Tiwari states that the

> philosophical basis of the Great Goddess should be traced to a theistic adaptation of Upaniṣadic Vedāntism mixed with the Sāṃkhya conception of Prakṛti. As it is, the Goddess is imagined as the Supreme Principle in her own right, as eternally existing, as Supreme Knowledge, as the cause of the bondage and the final liberation of beings, etc.[14]

In the *Brahmavaivarta Purāṇa* Rādhā as *prakṛti* is identified with the energy of Brahman itself; she is the true form of Brahman, or sometimes superior to it.[15]

While early Sāṃkhya does not identify *prakṛti* as feminine, the later *Sāṃkhya-kārikā* contains a vivid metaphor of *prakṛti* as a seductive dancer who entices all the inactive *puruṣas* (save one Īśvara, who remains free and detached) to join in her creation of the world. The fall into the created world can be reversed only by breaking away from *prakṛti* using the spiritual discipline of Īśvara—the *ma-*

hāyogin—as a model for liberation. Successful yogic liberation would leave *prakṛti* without any dance partners and she then returns to an undifferentiated mass. "Says the indifferent one [*puruṣa*], 'I have seen her'; the other [*prakṛti*] ceases, saying 'I have been seen.'"[16] (As we shall see, the bashful *prakṛti*, whose action reflects the ideal Hindu wife, is dramatically transformed in the Śākta tradition.) *Puruṣas* not only attain complete separation from nature, but also from Īśvara as well. There is no union with ultimate reality as in Upaniṣadic monism: "With the cessation of *prakṛti* . . . the *puruṣa* . . . attains isolation (*kaivalya*) which is both certain and final."[17]

Kathleen M. Erndl acknowledges the influence of both Sāṃkhya and Vedānta on Śākta theology, but argues that the latter "differs from them in its relentless exaltation of the material world. It is more thoroughly 'world-affirming' than either of them."[18] We have seen that Sāṃkhya's *prakṛti* is more dynamic and creative than Greek ideas of matter, but Erndl notes that Sāṃkhya ultimately joins the Greek and Christian project of devaluing matter, and in turn of devaluing the female. (Even though *prakṛti* is the active power, the figurative language of the Sāṃkhya literature always subordinates it to *puruṣa*, usually as a servant/wife to master/husband.) As we have seen, *prakṛti* will, according to the original view, return to an inactive, undifferentiated mass, and the *puruṣas* will be free of its interference and distractions. In contrast to the near universal myth of the clash of sky father gods with earth or water goddesses, Sāṃkhya dualism contains little conflict or tension. Indeed, enlightened souls discover that nature's intellectual and spiritual qualities (*sattvaguṇa*) are their ultimate means of escape from her. The *Sāṃkhya-kārikā* is rich in powerful figures of speech: "As the unknowing milk functions for the sake of the nourishment of the calf; so the prakṛti functions for the sake of the release of the puruṣa."[19]

With regard to Vedāntist influence on the Śākta movement, both Erndl and Mackenzie Brown recognize that goddess philosophy generally avoids the strict nondualism of the Advaitins. In their enthusiasm for the goddess to preempt all previous ontological states, Śākta writers sometimes call Devī *nirguṇā* Brahman (transcending all qualities) as well as *saguṇā* Brahman (containing all qualities). Making the Goddess free of qualities does not mean that the phenomenal world then becomes an illusion, as it does in Advaita Vedānta. (As an example, only one major commentary on the *Devī-Māhātmya*, the one by Nāgoji Bhatta, describes the Goddess as static *nirguṇā* Brahman. Another commentary by Advaitin Bhāskarārāya emphasizes the fact that the Goddess as *nirguṇā*

Brahman is dynamic in nature and that the world she produces is real.)[20] In general Śākta theology is a thoroughgoing panentheism in which the Goddess is a divine matrix for all things (hence, she is not any one thing in particular) rather than an abstract unity transcending all qualities. Mackenzie Brown points out that "absolute identity would preclude any real relationship,"[21] and relations with people and nature are the real genius of the Goddess religion. Sāṃkhya's commitment to the plurality of souls serves as an important counter to the monistic impersonalism of Advaita Vedānta. If selves are actually unreal, then it is difficult to understand how there could be any intelligible basis for personal and social relations.

In Aldous Huxley's *After a Many Summer Dies the Swan*, the protagonist says: "The more power we have, the more intensely do we feel our solitude. I have enjoyed much power in my life."[22] In terms of the Śākta theology we have just discussed, this view of power, the power of the Titan, is an illusion. This view of power is not exclusive to the English Huxley, for Hindu yogis have claimed that, by their ascetic isolation, they have surpassed "the gods in the realm of divinity."[23] This claim is open to Pārvatī's rebuke (see the epigraph to this chapter) that no one escapes nature and the limitations of its cosmic web of relations, and even the Sāṃkhya philosophers held that *prakṛti* is the source of all power. Therefore, the completely autonomous soul, according to Śākta theology, is impotent and passive, unmasking the claim of "atomic" power by Rammurti Mishra as a vain and empty boast. The yogi is actually a false Titan: he claims powers and attributes that his own philosophy denies him. Catherine Keller prefers to see this act of self-deception in Freudian terms. The male ego isolates himself because of the fear of castration, but in effect he has castrated himself in the process. In the nuclear age this has led to a sustained attempt at self-transcendence in a "fail-proof phallus, the steel missile carrying the *nux* which cannot be castrated."[24]

Even if this Sāṃkhya-Śākta theory is wrong, most of us would agree that the power of Huxley's protagonist is ultimately destructive. *Śakti* power must be seen as shared power, for *prakṛti* gives power to all who dance with her. In the West the concept of shared power is expressed most clearly in feminist and process philosophies, which stand in opposition to the orthodox Christian view of divine omnicausality.[25] The power of the Titan is based on possession, competition, fear, and control, whereas a view of shared power requires openness and trust on the part of the participants. One could easily argue that isolation and possession actually diminishes any constructive use of personal power. John B. Cobb and David R. Griffin, two process philosophers, state that the persuasive power "to open the future and give freedom [to others] is a greater power than the supposed power of absolute control. . . ."[26]

Purāṇic Expressions of the Goddess

In the *Purāṇas* the creative powers of *prakṛti* are generally identified with each of the Hindu gods: *rajas* for Brahmā the creator; *sattva* for Viṣṇu the preserver; and *tamas* for Śiva the destroyer. (The more sectarian texts sometimes combine all the *guṇas* in either Śiva or Viṣṇu.) The *Purāṇas* that favor Devī, however, make it clear that these powers are essentially feminine in nature. Notice the explicit use of Sāṃkhya terminology in these hymns to Devī from the *Devī-Māhātmya*:

> You are the primordial material (*prakṛti*) of everything, manifesting the triad of constituent strands [of *guṇas*];
> (You are) the cause of all the worlds . . . the supreme, original, untransformed Prakṛti;
> O you, the eternal, who become the power of creation, sustenance, and destruction, abiding in the qualities [*guṇas*] of primordial matter [*prakṛti*], actually consisting of those qualities, O Nārāyanī, praise be to you![27]

The great Goddess, here associated with Viṣṇu's (=Nārāyana) *śakti*, has taken over all the powers traditionally associated with the male trinity. Indeed, the male gods are essentially impotent without their *śaktis*. In *Brahmavaivarta Purāṇa* Kṛṣṇa acknowledges this with regard to Rādhā: "Without you, I am inert and am always powerless. You have all powers (*śakti*) as your own form; come into my presence."[28] Even in the tradition of Caitanya, which in its Hari Krishna expression has become very anti-Goddess, we find that "Rādhā is the full *śakti* and Kṛṣṇa is the full *Śaktiman*,"[29] which means "container of *śakti*."

In his insightful article "Consort of None, Śakti of All: The Virsion of the *Devī* Māhātmya,"[30] Thomas B. Coburn makes two significant observations. First, the Devī of the *Devī-Māhātmya* is not specifically paired with either Śiva or Viṣṇu, making this one of the first truly Śākta Purāṇas; and second, many of the *śakti* names are original with this text. The author(s) obviously know that traditionally Indra's consort is Śacī; Viṣṇu's wife is Lakṣmī; and Śiva's mate is Satī, Umā, or Pārvatī. But they deliberately coin feminized versions of the male names—Aindrī for Indra, Vaiṣṇavī for Viṣṇu, and Māhaswarī for Śiva—so as to dissociate these feminine divinities from any previous mythological connections. The authors very much wish to stress the fact that these are not just wives of male deities; rather, they are very much their own power, or more precisely, Devī's *śakti*.

One critical moment in the narrative of the *Devī-Māhātmya* may be cause for some qualification to the current thesis. Knowing that Mahiṣasura cannot be defeated by man or beast, all the male gods combine their own energy (*tejas*) to create the Goddess. The passage, in Coburn's translation, is as follows:

> Then from Viṣṇu's face, which was filled with rage,
> Came forth a great fiery splendor (*tejas*),
> (and also from the faces) of Brahmā and Śiva.
> And from the bodies of the other gods, Indra and the others,
> Came forth a great fiery splendor,
> and it became unified in one place.
> An exceedingly fiery mass like a flaming mountain
> Did the gods see there, filling the firmament with flames.
> That peerless splendor, born from the bodies of all the gods,
> Unified and pervading the triple world with its lustre, became a woman.[31]

The fact that Devī is produced from the gods' *tejas* appears to mitigate the thesis that Devī is a cosmic power truly her own. Coburn has captured the meaning of *tejas* nicely by combining the ideas of brilliance and luminosity, and it has been variously defined as "fiery splendour, glory, fiery destructive power, energy."[32] *Tejas* can also mean "virile semen," which relates it to another word for male power—*vīrya*, meaning "manliness, heroism; male seed." For example, Agni's fiery seed (*tejas*), which later becomes Śiva's, the incredibly hot semen that cannot be contained by anything except the goddess Gaṅgā (as Pārvatī's substitute womb), gives rise to the war-god Skanda.

Interestingly enough, especially for those used to Judeo-Christian ideas of divinity, *tejas* is not a necessary attribute, that is, it is not inherent in the nature of the gods themselves. This explains why the *devas* and the *asuras* both need *soma* or *amṛta* to keep themselves "energized," and that is the reason why the *Manusmṛti* frequently refers to *tejas'* origin as the Veda and the rituals it contains.[33] In the same text the derivative nature of *tejas* is seen in the phrase "the brilliant energy of ultimate reality (*brahmā*)."[34] *Tejas* is not only an attribute of the gods and antigods, but it is also found in the Manus, sages, priests, kings, and ordinary men. The priest "takes on a physical form of brilliant energy (*tejas*) and attains the supreme condition . . ."; the king is "made from particles of these lords and gods, therefore he surpasses all living beings in brilliant energy (*tejas*)."[35] *Tejas* ebbs and flows, as can be seen in the man who breaks a vow of chastity, sheds his semen, and loses his *tejas* back to the gods.[36] Also significant is the case of the man who loses his *tejas* by having sex with a menstruating woman, and the priest who loses his vitality by looking at a woman "putting on her eye make-up, rubbing oil on herself, undressed, or giving birth.[37] Even in their misogyny the author(s) of the *Manusmṛti* give a backhanded compliment to the power of woman.

The verbal root *śak* gives rise to at least three words in the Vedas: Śakra (powerful one), a name for Indra; *śacī* (personalized as Indra's consort Śacī); and *śakti*. The latter two words have the general meaning of "ability, power, capacity," but until the Śākta Purāṇas they were not yet related to any notion of cosmic power as feminine. Returning to the *Devī-Māhātmya* let us look at a crucial passage: "Whatever and wherever anything exists. . . . O you who have everything as your very soul, of all that, you are the power (*śakti*). . . ."[38] We can see that the first Śākta theologians have drawn on the Vedic *śakti* to make a full-blown deity, separate from, and now fundamental to, the existence of all gods and goddesses. As Coburn phrases it: rather than being "quasi-independent of its possessor" (the Vedic view), *śakti* now "is not something that a deity has, but something that the Goddess *is*. . . ."[39] *Śakti* is something Devī has as a necessary attribute and, panentheistically, something that everything else in the universe has by virtue of Devī's omnipresence. Phrased metaphysically, *śakti* is always a substance, not an attribute, while the reverse is true of *tejas*, where even in Indian physics fire (*tejas*) is just one of the attributes, along with air and water, of a basic substance (*bhūta*).

Śākta theology appears to have broken the vicious cycle of the Vedic maxim, explained superbly by Brian K. Smith (supra, p. 100), that one gains power only at another's expense. The Vedic power game, as with most patriarchal concepts of power, is a zero-sum game. Those who control the sacrifice, either by hook or by crook (with the gods dominating in the "crook" department), control *tejas*.

So the result is constant battles between gods and antigods, gods and ascetics, priests and kings. The Śākta view is different: even though Mahiṣa loses his *tejas*—Devī teases him to show his "womanish" nature[40]—he still presumably has his own *śakti*, for this is a power that all beings have by virtue of their very existence.

If Devī has her own ontological status as supreme *prakṛti* and *śakti*, then we are compelled to read her "creation" out of the gods' *tejas* much differently than one might initially. In the context of Śākta ontology, it must mean that the gods were simply able to make her appear, or, as we shall see, to add attributes to a preexisting primordial power. It might also mean that the gods are now assigning, as a sign of deference (they give her all their weapons), their "brilliance" to Devī and become "dim" in the same way that Śiva becomes inert when Kālī dances upon him. Significant also is the fact that Devī calls on a god's *śakti*, not his *tejas*, to join in her fight against Mahiṣa. Equally significant is the fact that when Mahiṣa complains about being "ganged up on" by so many goddesses, Devī draws all the *śaktis* into herself and finishes the battle alone. Finally, even though the text refers back to the creation out of the gods' *tejas*—"born from the bodies of the gods"[41]—the very next verse states that the Goddess "was born from the body of Gaurī (=Pārvatī)," which essentially means that she is born out of herself, because, as Coburn sees it, Gaurī as a "supreme form of the Goddess."[42] Or to see the question even more fundamentally the author(s) clarifies Devī's "birth": "She is said to be born in the world, even though she is eternal."[43]

Our interpretation is confirmed by looking at the same event as portrayed in the *Devī-Bhāgavata Purāṇa*. Just as in the *Devī-Māhātmya*, the Goddess, here called Mahālakṣmī, appears out of the gods' *tejas*. However, in the detailed description that follows, it is clear that the gods are simply adding attributes to, or enhancing preexisting attributes of, a primordial deity. If Devī is nothing but the sum total of the gods' fiery energy, then the following statement makes no sense: "Even Brahmā, Viṣṇu, Maheṣa, and Indra are never competent enough to describe her form properly."[44] The Goddess is "constant, she is always existent; . . . She assumes different forms for the fulfillment of the deva's ends. . . ."[45] In a clear allusion to Sāṃkhya, the author(s) describes Devī as the actor and the gods as mere spectators. The Devī "comes out of that mass of celestial light,"[46] which suggests that she comes out on her own stage with the gods' *tejas* as its lighting.

The *Devī-Bhāgavata Purāṇa* combines Vedānta, Sāṃkhya, and Tantra in a marvelous synthesis. Devī is first and foremost Nirguṇā

Śakti or Mahāmāyā. In her *saguṇa* form the Goddess is the divine creatrix, and a combination of sattvic *śakti,* rajasic *śakti*, and tamasic *śakti* brings the world into existence. For this purpose she manifests herself as Mahālakṣmī (*sattvaguṇa*) making all intellectual and spiritual activity possible; as Mahāsarasvatī (*rajasguṇa*) empowering all human and animal activity; and as Mahākālī (*tamasguṇa*) giving us all things inert and death itself. (In other texts Mahālaksmī and Mahāsarasvatī switch *guṇas*.)[47] After creation Mahādevī reveals herself as the terrible Kālī and her consort Śiva; as Lakṣmī, goddess of wealth and wife of Viṣṇu; and finally as Sarasvatī, Brahmā's wife and the goddess of knowledge and wisdom.

It might appear that Kālī, the bloodthirsty goddess of death and destruction, presents a very negative image of women. As an alternative to the standard view that Kālī represents a projection of a fear of female sexuality,[48] Lina Gupta proposes that Kālī represents a revolt against patriarchy's rules about the proper dress and behavior of women. Instead of wearing a beautiful sari, Kālī is essentially nude; and rather than being adorned with jewels, she wears skulls, severed heads, and arms. In contrast to Pārvatī, Kālī is an independent "spouse" to Śiva; she does not perform any wifely duties, she has no children, and Śiva is constantly attempting to counter her unconventional activities. Violating Manu's laws, Kālī's "femininity belongs to her and not to her husband."[49] Even more provocative is Gupta's suggestion that Kālī's wrath may well be the expression of the anger of all of India's oppressed women. As Gupta states: "The dark goddess is perpetually present in the inner and outer struggles faced by women at all times. Her darkness represents those rejected and suppressed parts of female creativity, energy, and power that have not been given a chance to be actualized."[50]

The *Devī-Bhāgavata Purāṇa* presents an interesting feminist twist to the story of Brahmā's mind-born sons, who are, not surprisingly, sterile. Brahmā complains that they are more interested in meditating and performing austerities rather than in creating worlds. In earlier accounts Brahmā succeeds in producing a female partner with whom he can copulate and produce other creatures, but the *Devī-Bhāgavata* portrays Brahmā as incapable of making himself a consort and the gods are at a loss about how to create anything at all. The Goddess kidnaps them in her chariot and takes them to her "Jewel Island," whereupon she turns them into females so that they can discover the secrets of procreation. MacKenzie Brown shows how this account of the Devī's Jeweled Island populated with female deities is a direct counter to the *Mahābhārata's* account of Nārada's journey to the White Island, where the exclusively male residents are awaiting final union with the Lord.[51] These stories clearly display the tension between the world-denying asceticism of the yoga ideal and the world-affirming themes of Śākta theology that are at the focus of this chapter.

One of the most dramatic demonstrations of the Goddess as a necessary material cause is found in the Kedārakaṇḍa of the *Skanda Purāṇa*. Although not considered a Śākta Purāṇa, it has been described by Doniger O'Flaherty as containing a "primitive" and "cynical" feminism because its portrayal of strong, assertive women results in a "satire on Hindu misogyny."[52] One of the main myths of this work is the story of the birth of Śiva's son Skanda (=Kumāra=Kārttikeya), who is destined to kill the Asura Tāraka. In order for this prophecy to be fulfilled, the gods have to bring Śiva and Pārvatī together in sexual union. The gods persuade Himavān, god of the Himalayan mountains, to offer his daughter in marriage. When the two succeed in obtaining an audience with Śiva, the great god commands that Pārvatī be removed from his presence. Contrary to his wish, Pārvatī steps forward and engages him philosophically: "You should consider who you are, and who Nature [*prakṛti*] is." Expressing what can only be called a form of Yoga Titanism, Śiva declares to Pārvatī: "I will destroy Nature with my ultimate inner ascetic heat, and I will stay here without Nature." Pārvatī's answer is swift and to the point: "How could you transcend nature? What you hear, what you eat, what you see—it's all Nature. How could you be beyond Nature? You are enveloped in Nature, even though you don't know it."[53]

Pārvatī has adopted basic Sāṃkhya philosophy, but with a significant twist: without nature all souls are inert and lifeless, and yogic isolation from the world is no longer seen as a spiritual ideal. Pārvatī's rebuke also implies that for Indian philosophy nature now has intrinsic value. Prakṛti's dance is not temporary and is not just a means to an end: the liberation of *puruṣas* to their isolated *lokas*. Rather, Devī's dance—now performed by Śiva, her principal ally—is eternal and her message is clear: return to the earth, to the body, the passions, and to ordinary human relations. In contrast to the ascetic tradition, the Goddess supports all activities from worldly enjoyment (*bhukti*) to spiritual liberation (*mukti*). Not only are the two not incompatible, but they are now inseparable in Sākta thought.

The latter thesis is particularly well supported in our present text, wherein Pārvatī essentially becomes the embodiment of Kāma, even after Śiva has burned him to ashes with his third eye. The gods fall into despair and they beg Śiva to resuscitate the god of desire. The gods warn that the world cannot live without love and that it will be ruined as a result of his rash act. Śiva refuses to see the logic of this version of Pārvatī's argument—that isolated *puruṣas* are empty and impotent without the life-giving qualities of *prakṛti*. Śiva repeats his warning that desire is the cause of the downfall of all beings, including the gods. As a rejoinder, the gods, never known for their philosophical acumen, present a very subtle and effective argument. They remind Śiva that the universe was created by desire: "Indeed, the whole of it is in the form of *kāma*. That *kāma* is not killed."[54] The gods then lay the philosophical noose around the great god's neck: "It is from *kāma* that the fierce *krodha* (anger) takes origin. You yourself have been won over by *krodha*."[55] This response makes Śiva even more angry and he becomes "desirous of burning (everything) with his third eye."

In her *Asceticism and Eroticism in the Mythology of Śiva*, Wendy Doniger presents a thorough analysis of the Śiva-Kāma-Pārvatī relationship, and one of the most helpful references she found was a Buddhist poem, which reveals succinctly the fundamental problem of Hindu asceticism:

> Love and anger both are states
> hostile to self-control
> What then did Śiva hope to gain
> by slaying Love in anger?[56]

The anger of the gods and sages, and the alacrity by which they incinerate their opponents, represents a fatal flaw in their spiritual discipline. Rather than find a Golden Mean as the Buddha or Aristotle recommend, the Hindus are notorious for pursuing, as Doniger suggests,[57] the Golden Extremes of excessive eroticism on the one hand and excessive asceticism on the other—both filled with the pride and hubris of a Titan.

The *Skanda Purāṇa* presents Pārvatī (here called Girijā) as the "mother of the universe": it was she "who created the three worlds along with Brahmā and others. Making use of the qualities of *rajas*, *sattva*, and *tamas*, she caused the origin, sustenance, and annihilation (of the worlds)."[58] Pārvatī's plan for the seduction of Śiva does not follow Buddhist lines; rather, it is eminently Hindu—thoroughly excessive and thoroughly dialectical. (Her *tapas* is so great that it dialectically coincides with the heat of her desire to become Śiva's mate.) Pārvatī's penance produces a fire so great that it threatens the triple worlds. This leads to yet another embassy of the gods to Śiva, in this case led by Viṣṇu. This time Śiva relents, predicting that

Pārvatī will bring Kāma back to life. He still, however, warns about the dangers of desire, but at least now he concedes the winning point in the previous debate: "It is from it (*kāma*) that anger is produced."[59]

Śiva concedes much more in the scene in which the two lovers become engaged. While earlier praised as the "father, mother, and lord" of all the worlds, Śiva now proclaims Pārvatī to be the creatrix of the universe by means of her *māyā* and her *prakṛti*. The translator G. V. Tagare finds it odd that Śiva launches into a detailed exposition of Sāṃkhya cosmogony (with a bit of Vedānta mixed in), but it is both natural and particularly conducive to the thesis of this chapter. Śiva admits that Pārvatī as *prakṛti* is "capable of action continuously," while he as the *puruṣa* is totally inactive. (This gives Śiva the lame excuse that it must be Pārvatī who actually proposes marriage!) The crucial passage is the following: "The being devoid of *guṇa* has become enveloped by *guṇās*. . . . The independent one has become dependent. O goddess, a great thing has been achieved by you."[60] The great Goddess has persuaded a great, but reluctant Yogi that he must merge with *prakṛti*, which amounts to a total transformation of the Sāṃkhya philosophy. The alleged independence of the isolated *puruṣa* has been replaced by an interdependent relational self. Kāma has indeed been reborn, namely, in the *śakti* of the androgyne that is Śiva-Pārvatī—the Ardhanārīśvara. By means of a grand *coincidentia oppositorum* they have both reached a double goal: the fire of yogic *tapas* and the fire of *kāma*. In Śākta theology the possibility of both *mukti* and *bukti* has been combined in one deity.

Kurtz's Psychoanalytic Interpretation

A comparative study of the Goddess reveals an interesting puzzle: patriarchy succeeded in suppressing the Goddess in Europe, but millions of Hindus still celebrate her in India. We have already proposed one possible solution: female energy became passive and inert in Greek thought but remained creative and dynamic in Hinduism. In his book *All Mothers Are One*, Stanley N. Kurtz proposes a sociopsychological explanation for the survival of the Goddess in India. Kurtz's field studies of Santoṣi Mā, the most popular Goddess in India today, has led him to revise not only the traditional categories of Hindu goddesses, but also to offer a revised psychoanalytic understanding of child development in the Indian family.

In terms of classical Freudian theory, the typical Indian male appears to have failed to resolve the Oedipus complex. As a way to explain the demise of the Goddess in Europe and her continued presence in India, this theory has very negative implications for the Indian psyche. The Indian male's unresolved relation and therefore unhealthy attachment to his mother is reflected in his society's continued celebration of the Goddess, whose two traditional forms represent the bad, terrifying mother on the one hand (Kālī and Durgā) and the nurturing domesticated wife-mother on the other (Pārvatī, Lakṣmī, and Sarasvatī) on the other. Therefore, while the typical Western male frees himself from this ambivalent mother image and becomes an autonomous individual, the Indian male remains trapped in the Oedipal phase and suffers a lack of ego identity and self-esteem. The traditional psychoanalytic image of the Indian male is of a young boy, spoiled by an overindulgent mother, suddenly thrust into a male community that terrifies him and that offers him no constructive way of coping with the transition. Kurtz summarizes this position:

> [Traditional] analysts give us a Hindu child locked in the mother's embrace. In this traditional account, the mother's indulgent presence surrounds the child until around the age of five when the father's discipline intervenes traumatically. This juxtaposition of prolonged indulgence and sudden frustration is said to mark the Hindu adult with a hidden yearning for the idyllic past, a time when child and mother were one.[61]

In contrast the Western male does not remain "locked in the mother's embrace"; rather, he forms a successful relation with both his biological and spiritual father and leaves his mother and the Goddess behind. Cosmic power then is coopted by the male and masculinized, as we saw in the language of the defense intellectuals.

Kurtz tries to demonstrate how the evidence of Santoṣi Mā dissolves the traditional distinction between unmarried goddesses of terror and destruction on the one hand and married goddesses of domestic virtue on the other. In the movie about Santoṣi Mā, a daughter of the elephant god Gaṇeśa and hence a granddaughter of Pārvatī, she is portrayed as a benevolent virgin who is abused, both verbally and physically, by the married goddesses. Even before the rise of Santoṣi Mā, there were enough discrepancies in the traditional model to bring it into question. For example, the ferocious, blood-drinking Kālī standing on the body of her husband Śiva is a striking counterexample to this model. (The fact that Śiva eventually pacifies her does not entirely explain away the anomaly.) The traditional model has also been undermined by Lynn Bennett's field studies in Nepal, which show a tension between "dangerous" wives, especially when the young Hindu wife first enters her husband's family, and benevolent unmarried sisters.[62]

In his investigation of Santoṣi Mā, Kurtz was frustrated by the tendency of his respondents to redefine her in terms of the other goddesses, especially Durgā. His failure to discover the specific sociological origins of a "new" goddess led him to an even greater discovery: in India all goddesses are ultimately one. There are not two types of goddess, one malevolent and the other benevolent, but rather one Goddess who appears diverse because the typical Hindu child, growing up in an extended family, experiences a wide variety of women. A mother, heretofore perceived as completely benevolent, can now appear as malevolent when she gives the child over to another female family member for care. The child will forgive her mother when she returns safely to her, but will still continue to mistrust her and other women in the extended family. In an intricate new schema to explain the Hindu goddesses, Kurtz provides for a malevolent-benevolent range for all the goddesses as psychological projections of sisters, daughters, aunts, wives, mothers, or mothers-in-law.

Kurtz believes that many observers have misperceived the Indian mother as a *smother* mother, a term more appropriate for the isolated mother of Western nuclear families. Kurtz shows that the Indian mother, like mothers in other non-Western societies, does not show inordinate affection for her children. The conclusion that Kurtz draws is that the Indian child, far from being less able to cope in the wider world, is better equipped psychologically and emotionally to face the deepest issues of human life. This is especially true if this psychological development is continually reinforced by hearing and incorporating the stories of Hindu mythology. While the Western individual is left alone to resolve the basic issues of separation, sex, violence, and death, Hindu mythology provides the Indian with a public form of psychotherapy that is free and readily available.

Finally, to correct the misapplication of Freudian models to Indian culture, Kurtz claims that Indian males pass through a Durgā complex rather than an Oedipus complex. The Durgā complex resolves pre-Oedipal tensions between the child and his "mothers" in the formation of an "ego of the whole," a social, relational self that gives the child a sense that "he is whole and good in so far as he contains and is contained by the group."[63] On this account the isolated Western self or yogic *puruṣa* is the pathology, not the norm. (We need only recall Pārvatī's rebuke of Śiva to remind us of this truth.) Kurtz states that in "the Hindu case . . . the movement is not away from the mother toward individuation and bonding with other males. Rather, the movement is away from the biological mother toward a more mature immersion in a larger and fundamentally benevolent group of mothers. . . ."[64]

Instead of the Western rejection of the mother and a lifetime of uncertainty about how to deal with women, the Indian male achieves a healthier view of the role of women in his life. In ancient Europe the Goddess virtually disappeared from established religion, appearing unresolved in dreams, as witches in fairy tales, and as objects of ambivalent feelings for the insecure, defensive, and sometimes abusive male. In India, however, the Goddess continues her reign and millions of males worship her enthusiastically, without embarrassment, in all her forms. "In worshipping the Goddess," Kurtz concludes, "Hindus recapitulate and reinforce their successful developmental journey through the world of women."[65] Without something equivalent Kurtz's theory must imply that the Western male appears doomed to continue through life without a satisfactory way of relating to women.

Does the Goddess Speak with a Woman's Voice?

Our emphasis on a dynamic and creative material principle and on Kurtz's theory about Indian developmental psychology may help us understand the pervasive role that the Goddess plays in Hindu religious life. Sadly for the theoretician and philosopher, social realities do not always conveniently map onto metaphysical theories. The marriage of Śiva and Pārvatī—a union of *puruṣa* and *prakṛti*—did not end the strong ascetic tradition of yogic personal isolation and escape. If Kurtz is right about the Durgā Complex, how does he explain the widespread and time-honored "aberration" of the isolated yogi, one who has obviously failed to resolve pre-Oedipal tensions in his prescribed way? Obviously many Indian males have not experienced a "successful journey through the world of women." We need a better understanding of why Śiva thought that he could live without nature; or alternatively why males elsewhere have wished to conquer it with technology. In either view nature, and by implication the female, is devalued unnecessarily. Why is it that, even within Hindu Goddess worship, male priests are still largely in control of the ritual and access to Mahādevī? Why are some males, even in the Indian context, still so confused and defensive about female power? In India and elsewhere this male frustration has unfortunately turned into a cult of misogyny, whose tragic consequences are found everywhere in the physical and sexual abuse of women. Even after taking refuge in the Goddess, Śuka of the *Devī-Bhāgavata Puruna* viciously condemns ordinary women who "suck the blood out of persons like leeches" and "steal away the semen virile."[66]

Sometimes this misogyny is transferred to the Goddess herself. A "folk" Purāṇa in Kannada presents the goddess Ādiśakti in a particularly negative way. Ādiśakti, true to the Śākta theology, is the creator of the triple world, and as she attains puberty she exclaims: "Ahha, nothing in sight to satisfy my passion, to please my youth. I've to (be)get one myself."[67] She then creates Brahmā, who proves to be a paragon of virtue and who resists her advances. For his impudence he is burned to ashes. Ādiśakti creates Viṣṇu, who is also aghast at his mother's immorality, and he, too, is killed by the "eye of fire" in her palm. Her third son Śiva skillfully tricks his mother into giving him her *śakti* power, and then burns her to ashes. He resurrects his brothers and creates three gentle and obedient wives from the Goddess's ashes. Although there is clear recognition of the feminine origin of all cosmic power, this myth is obviously a patriarchal subversion of the positive aspects of Śākta theology. Particularly clear is the hypocritical focus on female sexuality and on the male need to control it.

During the celebration of Dashain in Nepal the text of the *Devī-Māhātmya* is read to men only and the ritual is performed only by initiated males. Lynn Bennett, whom Kurtz cites favorably, has observed that while Nepali men are much more involved in Durgā worship, Nepali women are exclusively involved in the cult of Pārvatī. Her explanation is that "Durgā reflects a predominantly male view, focused on the problematic woman, while Pārvatī presents Hindu women's own idealized perceptions of themselves and the problems they experience."[68] It is interesting to note that Durgā worship in Nepal was imported from South India rather than from the North, where Durgā's role as good daughter-wife is emphasized much more. In Calcutta, for example, the festival culminates in Durgā being welcomed into all homes as the returning daughter, far removed from in-laws where she was perceived as a threat.

More specific and sexist is the North Indian rule that a husband must pay for fourteen recitations of the *Devī-Māhātmya* in order to control an unruly wife, but he only has to pay for twelve recitations to defeat an enemy.[69] A recitation of the *Devī-Māhātmya* may also protect a Hindu male's genitals and semen and help him get a good wife. Therefore, it looks as if the Devī myth contains far more unresolved pre-Oedipal conflicts than Kurtz would like to admit. After all, Durgā is the king's goddess, and her cult is administered by him and by his priests. In the not too distant past these same men went to war with her blessings, and Hindu militants called on her before they destroyed the mosque in Adhyohya in December 1992. If Durgā is the leader of armies, then she is not so different from Yahweh the Warrior, Lord of Hosts (=armies).

These observations raise some problems for my thesis that Goddess worship serves as an answer to Hindu Titanism. If Durgā is primarily a projection of male desires to control the world, then Kurtz and I are in trouble. If Durgā is nothing but a female Titan, then my thesis is rejected, not supported. In this view the Goddess represents an uneasy fusion of the stereotypical compassionate mother and aggressive male-warrior. (Devotees are never lovers of Devī, as they are of Kṛṣṇa, but are children in her maternal embrace.) The maternal role is virtually absent in the *Devī-Māhātmya*, and the words *tejas* and *vīrya* (virile, heroic power) appear frequently.[70] But even in the *Devī-Bhāgavata*, where the maternal role is strong, anger, violence, and aggression are also present. Here her battle with Mahiṣa is portrayed as a contest between a real man (the Goddess) and a eunuch-demon, who has, as Doniger translates it, "no balls."[71] Devī reminds the demons that she has manliness (*pauruṣa*) as her "inherent nature," obviously referring to her *puruṣa* nature.[72] Although the final goal of the authors of the *Devī-Bhāgavata* is to present the Goddess as beyond gender, it is still significant to note that in her cosmic manifestation (*viśvarūpa*) she appears in a male form complete with male genitals.

It is also intriguing to note that one Indian artist has portrayed Indira Gandhi not as Sītā, nor Sarasvatī, but as Durgā riding on her tiger.[73] This particular deification of Indira Gandhi brings us back to one of the central themes of Hindu Titanism: the apotheosis of individual human beings. This divinization of human beings was usually focused on the male priest or on the male yogi, but could, especially as Śākta theology became popular, also be embodied in a woman as well. Both the humanization and feminization of God is seen in Vasudeva S. Agrawala's view where Brahman is both eternal man and eternal woman.[74] If Titanism is defining divinity in terms of humanity, here is a possible source for both male and female Titans in the Hindu tradition.

Another objection could be raised to the thesis that a dynamic material principle is a necessary condition for Goddess philosophy. One of the major philosophical shifts in Tantric Buddhism is that the powers of the male and female agents are reversed: the male is now active and creative and the female inactive and passive. (Hindu Tantrism preserves the original concept of dynamic femininity.) This Buddhist reversal may already be evident in the pre-Tantric stories of the Buddha's birth, where the Sanskrit word *māyā* is used to name the Buddha's mother, but her role is completely passive in nature. This objection, however, is based on misinterpreting the Buddhist *prajñā* and *upāya* as equivalents of the Hindu Śiva and Śakti.

Miranda Shaw's recent book on women and Tantric Buddhism also helps to clarify some basic issues. First, Shaw believes that the "confluence of Buddhism and Śāktism is such that Tantric Buddhism could properly be called 'Śākta Buddhism.'"[75] Second, her research has shown that women were highly valued in both Hindu and Buddhist Tantric schools, so that this revalorization of women had more to do with the Tantric subversion of conventional gender roles than with any attention to the nature of the material principle. Feminists may be inclined to praise Tantric Buddhism for the fact that it, especially in its Tibetan schools, produced a very large number of women spiritual masters. In the context of Yoga Titanism, however, one might question whether encouraging spiritual asceticism in women locks them into traditional male roles. In a provocative observation about Buddhist discipline, Rita M. Gross states: "Maybe [female ascetics] are simply the creations of patriarchs who use them to control life and distance themselves from others! Maybe that is why Buddhism sometimes seems to glorify aloneness and be deficient in its emphasis on relationship!"[76]

A mitigating factor here is that Tantric yogis and yoginis are much more world- and body-affirming than their non-Tantric counterparts. This means that Yoga Titanism, as we have defined it, may be significantly mitigated in Tantric philosophy and religion. This is especially true with regard to the concept of self in Tantric Buddhism. Shaw's rich description of this self contrasts significantly with the Sāṃkhya *puruṣa* or Jaina *jīva*: "Not a 'soul' in a 'body' but rather a multilayered mind-body continuum of corporeality, affectivity, cognitivity, and spirituality whose layers are subtly interwoven and mutually interactive."[77] As we have seen, the concept of an autonomous, nonmaterial self at odds with the body and nature is a distinctive feature of Spiritual Titanism.

Conclusions

Westerners in search of a Goddess in eclipse for nearly two thousand years have the principal advantage of starting fresh. Most women and men are in control of their own research and of the reconstruction of the myths they wish to live by. They are free to draw inspiration from a vast cross-cultural reservoir of spiritual resources. If they perceive that ancient Goddess worship has been compromised by too much male interference, then they can choose from myths selectively or create new ones of their own. Cynthia Humes's field research in Uttar Pradesh indicates that more Hindu women are now willing to reform their own tradition. Humes agrees that there is a fundamental residue of sexism and patriarchal subversion in traditional Devī worship: "[I]ronically, men may more closely express divinity than females, even when the Divine is viewed ultimately as the Goddess, for men are not 'permeated' with evils as women are. . . ."[78] Nevertheless, Humes has observed significant innovations. At the Vindhyachal temple near Mirzapur many women, having learned Sanskrit in school, are now reciting the *Devī-Māhātmya* by themselves. Other women sing praises to the Goddess in the vernacular, and one of the most famous singers is called *guru* by her own husband. Other women are "channeling" for the Goddess, or in a substantial break from tradition, are creating modern dances for her.

In the area of ecology one example is worthy of mention. In her book *Staying Alive: Women, Ecology, and Development* Vandana Shiva draws on the principles of Goddess philosophy and critiques the standard model of economic development in her own Indian subcontinent. She calls it "maldevelopment" and claims that it is the product of a partriarchal view of the world. Shiva describes this philosophy as one that

> ruptures the cooperative unity of masculine and feminine, and places man, shorn of the feminine principle, above nature and women, and separated from both. . . . Nature and women are turned into passive objects, to be used and exploited for the uncontrolled and uncontrollable desires of alienated man.[79]

Shiva's operative word for feminine power is *prakṛti*, and she believes that India's women (and the men who work with them in ecologically sound occupations) are the current embodiment of the

Goddess' dynamic, healing power. Shiva and the brave women she writes about are using Śākta theology to fight their battles over the forests, water, and food of India.

Before we discuss one last contemporary example, let us briefly look at one positive female model from the *Mahābhārata*, one that serves as a balance to Durgā the warrior. This is the story of Draupadī, common wife of the Pandava brothers and a goddess in her own right, at least in the Tamil tradition.[80] In the *Mahābhārata* Kṛṣṇa is not, contrary to his popular reputation, a god of peace and compassion, but a warrior-god who leads his own clan and his relatives into total destruction. One essential part of Kṛṣṇa's plan is that Yudhishthira, the eldest and most pacifist of the Pandava brothers, should lose a game of dice, which leads to the humiliation of Draupadī and to the exile of his brothers. In response Draupadī dares to condemn Kṛṣṇa:

> As a man splits log with log, stone with stone, iron with iron—things that [of themselves] can neither move nor think—so does the Lord God, the Self-subsistent, the primal Grandsire, hurt one creature by means of another, establishing for himself an alibi. Joining things together only to disjoin them again the Lord acts at his own good pleasure, playing with his creatures as children play with dolls. He does not treat his creatures as a father or a mother would but acts in raging anger; and since he acts so, others follow his example.[81]

Although Draupadī is not exactly an innocent agent in the high drama of this grand epic, her indictment of God is as severe as Job's. Yudhishthira is shocked at his wife's blasphemy and defends Kṛṣṇa in ways very similar to Job's friends. Finally, Gandharī, wife of the Kuru king Dhritarashtra, also curses Kṛṣṇa for the destruction that he has wrought, and predicts that his tribe will also be destroyed and that he will fall, Achilles-like, to the arrow of a hunter.[82]

Finally, let us feature Mallika Sarabhai, a Gujarati dancer and actress, most famous for her role as Draupadī in Peter Brook's *Mahābhārata*. In a recent interview in the *Deccan Herald*, Sarabhai tells how she fought for a rewriting of Draupadī's character. As she explains: "Despite researching the *Mahābhārata* for eleven years, they are white Anglo-Saxon men. To them, the whole concept of women as Shakti was unknown."[83] Since then she has gone on to choreograph and stage *Shakti* and *Sita's Daughters*, both powerful expressions of Śākta philosophy. The first piece is in English, and when women's groups encouraged her to translate it and to tour Indian villages, she realized that she had to produce something more appropriate for village women. The result was *Sita's Daughters*, which incorporated stories of rape and female infanticide from village women themselves. The rural performances take three times as long as the city ones, because the village women insist on interrupting the show and telling their own stories.

In this chapter we have addressed several related questions. The first was a quest for the reason why Devī worship thrives in India but died out in Europe. Even though social practices do not necessarily follow from a belief in metaphysical categories, Śākta theology must still have something to do with how Indians have conceived of the material principle. The worship of the Goddess appears to require that we view matter, as did the ancients and Indians today, as dynamic, organic, interrelated, and alive. We found that Kurtz's psychoanalytic hypothesis failed to explain the indomitable force and attraction of India's ascetic tradition and the spiritual Titanism that is manifest in its goals of personal isolation and in its illusions of spiritual power. (One has to admit, however, that some significant difference in socialization must account for the fact that Indian males worship the Goddess without embarrassment, while the majority of Western males would find it very difficult to do so.) Furthermore, we found that since males have written the scripture and still control the ritual, the Hindu Goddess does not always speak with a truly feminine voice. Finally, however, we have found hopeful signs of Indian women reclaiming the Śākta tradition as a means for constructive personal and social action. These women will surely succeed in giving the Hindu Goddess a distinctively female voice, and they will form a vanguard against the various liabilities of Hindu Titanism.

Epilogue: The Triumph of the Goddess

In the beginning there were disembodied spirits suspended in space, unmoving in their trance state. Enter a dancing Goddess, creating solid ground wherever she steps. Her dynamic gestures cause the spirits to stir and gradually, one by one, they dance with the Goddess. As they dance, they take on bodies, and they, too, begin to feel the ground beneath their moving feet. Only one spirit named Īśvara the Lord remains unmoved and undisturbed. The cosmic dance continues and becomes more complex, creative, and frenzied. The spirits call to Īśvara and encourage him to join them, but he resists saying that what they are doing is sinful and degrading. The dancing beings persist in their attempt to get the great Yogi to join the cosmic dance, and finally, but reluctantly, he agrees. His steps are awkward at first, but gradually he, too, is dancing eagerly like the rest of them. At times it appears as if the Goddess and the Yogi are a single, united body. The Goddess is well pleased and the cosmos continues and all embodied beings are blessed beyond measure.

7 Neo-Vedānta and Aurobindo's Superman

You have assumed a body; therefore enjoy God through His human forms.

—Ramakrishna[1]

It is the greatest of all lies that we are mere men; we are the God of the Universe. . . . In worshipping God we have been always worshipping our own hidden self.

—Vivekananda[2]

To fulfill God in life is man's manhood. He starts from the animal vitality and its activities, but a divine existence is his objective.

—Aurobindo[3]

But what is remarkable is that once we have had the experience of a single contact with the Divine . . . we shall know everything, and even more.

—The Mother[4]

Introduction

Both Ramakrishna and Aurobindo were considered *avatāras*, incarnations of the divine. Ramakrishna's divine nature (as Viṣṇu) was confirmed by several prominent Bengali holy men, and one of Aurobindo's followers has called him the "author of the universe."[5] As this divine status was self-attested as well as proclaimed by their disciples, it would seem that they are indeed very good candidates for spiritual Titanism. We shall see, however, that there are some important mitigating factors, most notably Tantric elements in which

Śākta philosophy offers its social, relational, and world-affirming qualities. Worship of the Mother was central to both Ramakrishna and Aurobindo and their philosophies are incomprehensible without acknowledging this fact. (Interestingly, both also marginalized their own wives in favor of Devī.) By all accounts Ramakrishna never became a full Tantric hero, but remained "Kālī's child," which is relevant to our Nietzschean heuristic of camel, lion (=hero=Titan), and child. In contrast Aurobindo's *śakti* is more masculine and assertive and he could be seen, especially because of his commitment to a chaste Śiva-Śakti, as a "right-handed" Tantric hero. In his rejection of Devī worship as "unmanly," Vivekananda, Ramakrishna's principal disciple, was definitely the lion-hero spiritual type. He was once described as a "Hindu Napolean bent upon the spiritual conquest of the world."[6]

Ramakrishna, Vivekananda, and Aurobindo have been labeled neo-Vedāntists (the latter called it realistic Advaita),[7] a view of Vedānta that rejects the Advaitins' idea that the world is illusory. As Aurobindo phrased it, philosophers need to move from "universal illusionism" to "universal realism,"[8] in the strict philosophical sense of assuming the world to be fully real. Ramakrishna and Aurobindo affirmed that the world is the primary locus of cosmic power as *śakti*. This allowed them to avoid absolute monism on the one hand and a Sāṃkhya-like dualism on the other. This means that the extremes of dissolution of the self and isolation of the self are eliminated. In this regard, Ramakrishna's rejection of yogic renunication and Aurobindo's emphasis on collective salvation are of paramount importance.

Ramakrishna: Kālī's Child

Ramakrishna did not style himself as a philosopher or theologian, nor did he leave a written record, and neither did he read any scholarly books. He captivated his disciples with brilliant parables, singing and dancing, and direct religious experience. The principal source of his views in English is *The Gospel of Ramakrishna*, which is a translation of the Bengali *Śrīśrīrāmakṛṣṇa-Kathāmṛta*. In his recent work *Kālī's Child* Jeffrey J. Kripal has shown that the translator, Swami Nikhilananda, was concerned not only with disguising the Tantric elements of Ramakrishna's vision but also with the specific homoerotic aspects that Kripal makes the focus of his book. The evidence is clear that Ramakrishna's Tantrism was a qualified "left-handed" sort and not the sublimated right-handed version we find in Aurobindo.

Ramakrishna's first spiritual teacher was a woman known as the Bhairavī Brāhmaṇī, who taught a mixture of Tantra and Bengali Vaishnavism. She worked with Ramakrishna for nearly four years, and she was the first to assure him that his fits of abnormal behavior were a sign of divine inspiration. She was also the first to recognize his divine nature and she adopted him as the baby Kṛṣṇa, just as village women had done during his childhood. The Brāhmaṇī's attempt to promote Ramakrishna from Tantric child to Tantric hero appears to have been a failure. Although he did succeed in many ways to dissolve the distinction between the pure and the impure, he was simply unable to perform some of the basic left-handed practices. He was ridiculed for his spiritual naïveté during a visit to a Tantric community, and he could not complete the test of the five *M*s that the Brāhmaṇī herself administered.

The five *M*s (*maṃsa, matsya, madya, mūdra,* and *maithuna*) have been mischievously translated by Wendy Doniger as the five *F*s—flesh, fish, fermented grapes, frumentum, and fornication.[9] There are two radically opposed camps of interpretation of Ramakrishna's experience with the five *M*s. On the one hand, there is Saradananda who claimed that Ramakrishna completely refused to participate, thereby legitimizing the view that being Kālī's child is spiritually superior to the decadent state of being her lover. On the other hand, Datta's belief, phrased by Kripal, was that Ramakrishna "easily performed all of these obscene and horrific rites with the Bhairavī."[10] Kripal believes that the truth lies somewhere in between because the *Kathāmṛta* indicates that the Bhairavī persuaded him to attempt the five *M*s and that he most likely balked at one, left out one (*mūdra*), achieved two, and fudged on one. Most surprisingly, Ramakrishna appears to have passed the first *M* in its most horrific form: eating rotten human flesh. Fulfilling the second *M* was not that difficult for Bengalis, for they have a great passion for fish, but Ramakrishna was able to eat it in the Tantric way—boiled in a human skull. Ramakrishna fudged on the third *M:* so great was his aversion to wine that he was only able to touch his tongue to a drop of it. The most notorious *M*—ritual intercourse—proved to be Ramakrishna's greatest problem. All that Ramakrishna could manage was to sit on the virgin's lap, crying out for the Mother, and falling into *samādhi*. Kripal's most controversial suggestion is that sexual abuse during childhood and also during his apprenticeship with the Advaitin Totapuri rendered him totally unable to relate to women in a mature manner. He remained Kālī's child, never her lover (nor any other woman's), and poured his sexual energies into intense emotional and physical relationships with his boy disciples.

It is a great irony that what Kripal takes to be a personally devastating encounter—the apprenticeship with Totapuri—the orthodox followers interpret as the philosophical turning point of Ramakrishna's life. Vivekananda and others maintain that Totapuri taught him that there was something higher and more ultimate than the Mother, namely, the *nirguṇa* Brahman of Advaita Vedānta. It is true that Ramakrishna quickly absorbed the teaching and he amazed his guru in experiencing nonduality in such a short time. Kripal, however, demonstrates very convincingly that it was Totapuri who was converted to S´a¯kta theology rather than Ramakrishna being transformed into an Advaitin. Even *The Gospel of Ramakrishna* records Totapuri's attempt to drown himself in the Ganges only to be saved by a vision of the Mother.[11]

In one crucial passage Ramakrishna refers to a sword of *gnosis* by which he was able to cut the world of name and form from the formless Absolute and to attain *samādhi* in the latter. Presumably, Ramakrishna was then able to leave the world of *prakṛti* behind. Kripal argues that this was only a temporary division, and that his dialectic, like Aurobindo's, was always "both-and synthetic" rather than the "neither/nor" of the Advaitin *neti, neti*. As Kripal states: "Moreover, within this dialectic, the goddess of the Many always is given preference over the god of the One. . . . In the end, her truths are more ultimate, more psychologically true, more mystically satisfying than those of . . . Vedānta."[12] One specific psychological truth mentioned here is the I-Thou experience of the *bhakta-śākta*, which requires a social, relational self not the totally dissolved self of the Advaitin. In a direct reference to the life of Kṛṣṇa,[13] Ramakrishna definitely sides with Kṛṣṇa's Gopīs, who even though they had an experience of the formless one, much preferred the I-Thou experience with their Lord.

Let us return to Ramakrishna's divine status and try to gain some clarification about these allegations. Ramakrishna's father Kshudiram was passionately devout and managed to accomplish several major pilgrimages during this lifetime. During a trip to Gayā in 1835 Viṣṇu appeared to him in a dream and declared that he would be born as his son. At the same time Ramakrishna's mother Chandra Devi also experienced an amazing dream: "It was as if a luminous god entered my bed and lay down."[14] Later, in broad daylight at the Śiva temple, she claimed that she was impregnated by a divine light that emanated from Śiva's "great limb." From the very beginning Ramakrishna's life was marked by the interplay of the erotic and the divine and by the powerful Bengali mixture of Vaishnava devotionalism and Śiva-Śākta sensualism.

After he was installed as the priest at Dakshineswar, he began having bizarre experiences, which both he and his associates thought was some severe mental disorder. As we have already seen, it was the Brāhmaṇī who declared that Ramakrishna was not insane but was in fact an incarnation of Viṣṇu. This claim was confirmed by two local spiritual leaders: Vaishnavacharan, an eminent Tantric teacher, and Pundit Gauri. Ever refusing to make an issue of it or to exploit it in any way, Ramakrishna was very nonchalant and modest about these attestations. He never, however, denied the truth of them and never rejected the implication that he was in a great line of men-gods—from Kṛṣṇa, Buddha, Christ, and down to Caitanya.

In many sayings Ramakrishna was inclined to speak of the incarnation of God in every person, good or evil. Ramakrishna's own interpretation of Nārāyāṇa, a name for Viṣṇu, was "man (*nara*) is in his essence God."[15] This doctrine appears to take on a very specific application after he dislocated his arm while "embracing the Lord Jagannath in the erotic state."[16] After this incident Ramakrishna committed himself almost exclusively to a view of total divine immanence in which social relations and the body took on new emphasis and value. Furthermore, as Kripal demonstrates, Ramakrishna's sayings about this crucial event are intimately connected to explicit exclamations of love for his male disciples: "I love them, I see Nārāyāṇa in them."[17] Therefore, this statement and others ("You have assumed a body; therefore enjoy God through His human forms")[18] have an undeniable homoerotic ring to them. Ramakrishna admitted that God manifests herself to a "greater degree in pure-souled devotees,"[19] namely, his young male disciples. By turning from "the Spirit-form of God" to particular human forms,[20] Ramakrishna may have been finally embracing a Tantric practice that he previously rejected. In Vaishnavacharan's Tantric community one was obliged to choose a ritual sex partner as one's own deity and then to "delight in God." If Kripal is correct, Ramakrishna's view of incarnation and human divinity is quite distant from the grand cosmic theories of divinization that we have found in other forms of Indian Titanism. Not only is the hubris and social isolation eliminated, but we now see that the act of celebrating God in the form of young boys is more emotional and psychological than theological and philosophical.

In using Nietzsche's metamorphosis of camel, to lion, to child we have assumed that the child state represents a complete reconciliation of the tensions and liabilities of the first two stages. Ramakrishna's story may compel us to reconsider the truth of this hypothesis. There is at least one interesting parallel between the lives of Ramakrishna and Nietzsche: their intense fear of women and their inability to relate to them in a normal way. It is true that Nietzsche's child is, as opposed to the Nay-saying lion, a Yea-sayer; and Kripal's thesis about Ramakrishna is intriguing: after the Jagannath incident, he fully affirmed the divinity of the world and the body. It is also important to determine the nature of the child that Ramakrishna affirms. It is definitely not the fetus in the womb, a position of total union with the mother that would have its philosophical equivalent in Advaita Vedānta. Rather, it is the toddler stage that suits Ramakrishna's views best. Here there is identity within unity—the I-Thou relation that Ramakrishna revels in—and, as Kripal (following Kadar) shows, he can enjoy a woman only at the mother's breasts or on her lap. Kripal also offers three other illuminating observations: (1) The toddler stage requires the social structure of the married householder, which Ramakrishna always rejected as "dangerous" and "dirty"; (2) the mother-child relationship is always potentially sexual ("even as a Mother, she insisted upon being a Lover");[21] and (3) this truth is played out when Ramakrishna takes on the mother's role in his relations with his male disciples.[22]

Ramakrishna's relationship with his young followers appears to have all the characteristics of what Freud called a polymorphous sexuality, a pregenital sexuality in which the whole body is sexually sensitive and alive. (Ramakrishna called it the Goddess's love-body.) Pandit Gauri taught Ramakrishna that every pore is a *yoni* and that every hair a *lingam*, and Ramakrishna declared that these hairs became erect at the sight of one of his boy disciples.[23] Ramakrishna was literally lovesick for these young men. Before their arrival at the temple he would cry for hours about his inability to attract disciples. Once they started to arrive he could not keep his hands off them. Narendra (later the famous Vivekananda) was especially put off by Ramakrishna's first approaches to him. The Master insisted that some of his favorite disciples give up their family and education and move in with him. Rakhal, one of Ramakrishna's most beloved, always appeared to have had his head in his lap and he said that Rakhal had "completely surrendered himself to me."[24]

William Blake balanced his "Songs of Innocence" with "Songs of Experience"; similarly, in his *Four Quartets* T. S. Eliot returned to the rose garden only after full immersion in the world of experience. A full dialectic of the sacred in which the pure is synthesized with the impure—in which infantile sexuality is replaced (but not lost) in genital sexuality—is not present in Ramakrishna. He is fully cognizant that such a commitment would involve a "fall" that he was not willing to experience:

> The Child is a very pure state. In the Tantras there is talk about the left-handed practice with a woman, but this is not good. It leads to a fall. . . . I performed the worship of the sixteen-year-old girl in the child state. I saw that her breasts were Mother's breasts, that her vagina was Mother's vagina. This is the child state—*the last word in mystical practice.*[25]

Ramakrishna, however, is emphatic about the fact that the purity of the child (and his boy disciples) should never be sullied by the impurities of the world; and in insisting that this is the ultimate in spiritual practice, he precludes the full operation of the dialectic of the sacred. In Norman O. Brown's neo-Freudian vision, "Love's Body" is not possible without full immersion in the world. The mature lover rediscovers the polymorphous sexual body in a process of returning to Eliot's garden and "knowing it for the first time." Eliot's development may be seen as fulfilling the threefold dialectic of premodern > modern > constructive postmodern, while Ramakrishna's position may be interpreted as one stuck in premodern notions of innocence and totality.

Vivekananda's "Manly" Neo-Vedānta

We have already discussed Vivekananda's claim that "God evolves out of man," and we now want to analyze his contention that "we are the God of the universe." The most important issue to settle first is the meaning of the word "God." For Judeo-Christian theists the best Sanskrit equivalent is Īśvara, and for an Indian to say "I am Īśvara"—namely, the creator of the universe and all beings in it—would indeed be blasphemy and would constitute spiritual Titanism. Interestingly enough, Śaṅkara twice declared that he was Īśvara,[26] even though this would be a false claim according to his own doctrine of *jīvanmukta*. While the embodied saint could claim the elimination of ignorance, he could not consistently claim Īśvara's principal attribute: eternal creation by his power of *māyā*. For Vivekananda

Īśvara is not only the Creator but includes all the sensible world as well (*saguṇa* Brahman), and he reminds us that this is the not the "God" with which we are identical:

> There is one thing to be remembered: that the assertion—I am God—cannot be made with regard to the sense-world. If you say in the sense-world that you are God, what is to prevent your doing wrong? So the affirmation of your divinity applies only to the noumenal.[27]

We are God only in the sense that our essence is *nirguṇa* Brahman or Ātman. (This is also Śaṅkara's position, because, as we have seen, humans are superior to Īśvara in that they can transcend *saguṇa* Brahman while the Creator cannot.) This is what Vivekananda means in the statement "the Real Man is God." The problem, however, is that both Śaṅkara and Vivekananda are still affirming spiritual Titanism in their implication that Īśvara, although worshiped as God, is not truly divine because he cannot transcend the phenomenal world. Only human beings—only male Brahmins for Śaṅkara—can attain the true Godhood of *nirguṇa* Brahman-Ātman. A further problem may also arise when Vivekananda states that "You and I are all Personal Gods." Strictly speaking the only personal God is Īśvara the Creator and this is, according to Vivekananda himself, blasphemous Titanism. If he means only that Ātman is our own personal "piece" of Brahman, then the problem is avoided.

In his book on Ramakrishna Kripal ably defends the traditional view that Vivekananda rejects his Master's Śākta philosophy, which, in this same view, Ramakrishna is also supposed to have given up. After his death the worship of Kālī, according to Kripal, recedes into the background:

> The meeting room of the young disciples is [now] called the "room of Śiva's demons [*gaṇas*]" in order to stress the "manly states" that would be practiced there and to distance its occupants from those effeminate men whom Narendra [Vivekananda] disdained as the "girlfriend class."[28]

Since his childhood days Ramakrishna enjoyed taking on female disguises and played the roles very convincingly, but Vivekananda rejects this practice as degenerate Vaishnavism: "Your Bhakti is sentimental nonsense, which makes one impotent."[29] Vivekananda also focuses on different scripture than did Ramakrishna: the latter preferred the Purāṇas and the Tantras, while the former liked the Gīta and the Upaniṣads, rejecting the Purāṇas as superstitious and the Tantras as obscene and poison to the mind. Vivekananda completely reverses the Tantric position of Kālī over Śiva. According to Kripal, he "brags that, in the end, Śiva reclaimed his rightful dominance over Śakti and made her a servant, and that Kṛṣṇa left the women of Vrindavana to become a mighty king in a distant city."[30] Therefore, Vivekananda rejects both the possibility of becoming either Kālī's child or lover, and returns the yogi to the nay-saying lion stage. He was in fact called "Narendra the Lion," who wished "to preach the virtues of spiritual manliness and renunciation."[31]

There is, however, evidence that shows Vivekananda much more favorably inclined to Śākta thought. It is not true that the Goddess completely recede into the background, because Vivekananda writes poems in honor of her, with one on Kālī that enthusiastically celebrates her destructive power.[32] While in the United States he taught classes on Mother worship, one in which he said that

> Mother is the first manifestation of power and is considered a higher idea than the father. With the name of Mother comes the idea of Shakti, Divine Energy and Omnipotence. . . . She is the sum total of the energy of the universe. . . . Power is power everywhere, whether in the form of evil or as Saviour of the world. . . . The first idea connoted by it [Mother worship] is that of energy—I am the power that is in all beings.[33]

Vivekananda also believed that Mother worship was the best way to solve the problem of evil and to express the idea of nonduality.[34] Most of Vivekananda's principal Western contacts were women and he spoke often about women's rights. (Significantly, however, he focused on the traditional view of chastity as the highest virtue.) In February of 1899 Vivekananda encouraged Nivedita (Margaret Noble), one of his most celebrated disciples, to deliver a speech on Kālī, and he took strong exception to the critical remarks about this made by Mahendralal Sarkar, Ramakrishna's doctor.[35]

Vivekananda's article "Modern India," published in a Bengali journal *Udbodhan* in March of 1899, ends with this prayer to Devī: "O Thou Lord of Gauri, O Thou Mother of the Universe, vouchsafe manliness unto me! O Thou Mother of Strength, take away my weakness, take away my unmanliness, and make me a Man!"[36] This prayer reminds one of ancient Hindu kings who called on Durgā before they went into war, and it is yet another example of the Goddess being exploited for specific male purposes. Vivekananda was obsessed with the idea of strength and virility, and he appropriates the idea of *śakti* for this purpose. In this passage he focuses on *ojas*, another term for "virility" and equivalent to *tejas*: "This *ojas* is the real man and in human beings alone is it possible for this storage of *ojas* to be accomplished."[37] As in traditional yoga practice all sexual energy must be converted to *ojas*, and only by this means can men become God. Therefore, Vivekananda's philosophy is, on balance, much more a "manly" neo-Vedānta rather than a feminist Śākta philosophy.

Supermind, Superman, and Supernature

The strongest case for spiritual Titanism in Aurobindo is found in his claim that he is the one who "brings down" the Supermind, the highest expression of divinity. Rāma established righteousness on earth and Kṛṣṇa was the embodiment of the Overmind (an immanent cosmic consciousness), but the third and most important *avatāra* would be the incarnation of the Supermind, a transcendental divine mind. Aurobindo declared that the Supermind descended in his person on 24 November 1926. "If Supermind exists, if it descends, if it becomes the ruling principle, all that seems impossible to mind becomes not only possible but inevitable."[38] Reducing God to a human form is one of the principal strategies of Indian Titanism, and the following anthropomorphic definition of God from an Aurobindo commentator confirms this: "God will be the theandric personality of the superman who partakes and communes with the Absolute and all the manifestations of the Absolute."[39] The Supermind will be the principal faculty of the Superman, who then will bring about Supernature. Rather than a trance state the descent of the Supermind will be a "waking union with the Divine."[40] The evolution of life to this point has been a "secret Yoga," but after the descent of the Supermind the principal secret will be revealed: all of Nature is being totally transformed by Spirit.[41] This is the true meaning of Integral Yoga, a comprehensive spiritual process that supercedes all previous forms of yoga.

Aurobindo claims a status higher than earlier saints and yogis, who were only *jīvanmuktas* not true Supermen. In their ascetic practices *jīvanmukti puruṣas* such as Mahāvīra and Buddha escaped not only the realm of desire but, as one commentator phrases it, also the "urge of evolution itself. Freed from the shackles of the body, [they stopped] short of the supreme effort to turn the body into a perfect image of the Divine. . . ."[42] Aurobindo always speaks of the descent of the divine not humans ascending to Godhood, but it is still not clear where he stands on Avatāravāda versus Uttāravāda. One reading would be that Rāma and Kṛṣṇa are *avatāras* but that he is a *jīvanmukta* who has corrected and expanded the work of earlier yogis. This means that the Superman is not an *avatāra* but, as L. Thomas O'Neill phrases it, "a man integrally transformed into divinity. A superman is the divine man and not the divine as man. . . . the Avatār[a] comes to lead evolution whereas the superman is the summit of evolution."[43]

Even though the *jīvanmukta* attains liberation while in the body, the body and nature as a whole are not completely transformed as they should be. As Aurobindo states: "For its perfect solution would be the material immortality of a fully organized mind-supporting animal body,"[44] which he claims would lead to a "practical omnipotence." Claims of human immortality and omnipotence are of course primary facets of spiritual Titanism, but this claim of bodily immortality presents further problems. Philosophers have long debated the intelligibility of human immortality without a body, but the claim of somatic immortality exacerbates those logical problems even more. Without attempting to solve them, Aurobindo alludes to those very problems: "To discover and realize the immortal life in a body subjected to death and constant mutation,—this is offered to us as the manifestation of God in Matter and the goal of Nature in her terrestrial evolution."[45] The Platonic and traditional Indian assumption of the soul's clean break with the finite world appears to be a far stronger philosophical basis from which to argue for the soul's immortality. This book is committed to an embodied self, one that recognizes its limits within the body and the world. Aurobindo's "both-and, synthetic" dialectic may work for some issues—most promisingly with regard to the reconciliation of *sat* (being) and *asat* (relative nonbeing)—but it cannot resolve the logical contradiction of an immortalized mortal.[46]

The Gnostic Titanism we found in Jainism also appears in Aurobindo and in the Mother, the latter claiming that even after only one experience of the Divine "we shall know everything, and even more."[47] The Mother may mean only that we know the unity of Divine and of other general attributes. But if the claim is anything like the Jaina position, then we definitely have a case of Gnostic Titanism. In *The Life Divine* Aurobindo speaks of a race of gnostic beings—omnipotent and omniscient—who not only embody a universal spirituality but also, because of their divine knowledge, "increase the power of instrumentation . . . on [their] surroundings and on the world of physical Nature."[48] This is the only allusion to technological Titanism that I have found in any Indian philosophical text.

Fundamental to Aurobindo's philosophy is a version of progressive evolution that goes far beyond Darwinian or neo-Darwinian ideas. Aurobindo expands the principle of the survival of the fittest in the following way: "The struggle for life is not only a struggle to survive, it is also a struggle for possession and perfection."[49] This idea of spiritual evolution informs New Age philosophy and it assumes that human beings are currently the highest manifestation of Spirit in Nature. (This view of course ignores the fact that human beings are contingent, not necessary, results of the evolutionary process.) Aurobindo and others give a very anthropocentric focus to evolution: "For Man is Nature's great term of transition in which she grows conscious of her aim; in him she looks up from the animal with open eyes towards her divine ideal."[50] Making humans the center of cosmic evolution is of course another major aspect of spiritual Titanism.

In a short work called *The Superman* Aurobindo carefully distances himself from Nietzsche's concept of *Übermensch*. Aurobindo has no sympathy for those who describe the Superman as the "deification of the rare or solitary ego,"[51] which, says Aurobindo, is unfortunately one valid interpretation of Nietzsche's "Overman." Accepting the cooriginality of Devas and Asuras, Aurobindo states: "For the deity within may confront us either as the God or the stern convulsed visage of the Titan. Nietzsche hymned the Olympian, but presented him with the aspect of the Asura."[52] Aurobindo attributes this distortion to Nietzsche's extreme animus against Christianity and to an inability to recognize the value of the concept of Christ as *avatāra*. Aurobindo presents the popular Purāṇic view of the Devas as beings of light and harmony and the Asuras as their angry and rebellious opposites. Aurobindo admits that it was unfair that the Asuras were cheated of their share of soma, but they, as the elder gods, thrive on "division and egoism" and therefore must always be suppressed as our current asuric tendencies. The Asuras are those whose wills are at odds with the divine will, while the true Superman is one whose will conforms to the "All-will." As Aurobindo states: "My free-will would become God-will and Fate [would] put off her mask."[53]

Using the work in chapter 3 as a guide, we must say that Aurobindo is unfair to both Hindu and Greek Asuras. More significantly, he also misinterprets Nietzsche's concept of *Übermensch*, which, as we have demonstrated in the introduction, manifests itself in the child stage, not in the second metamorphosis of the lion. Aurobindo, however, is so close to Nietzsche on one point that it appears that there must have been some influence. In *Thus Spake Zarathustra* Nietzsche claims that there will be just as much difference between current humanity and *Übermenschen* as there is between humans and apes.[54] Similarly, Aurobindo states that "man may develop his manhood into that true supermanhood which shall exceed our present state as much as this exceeds the animal state from which science tells us that we have issued."[55] Both thinkers, therefore, predict a future "overcoming" of humankind's present limitations.

As already indicated, the strongest mitigating factor in Aurobindo's Titanism is his commitment to Śākta philosophy. The Tantric influences are subtle but clear, complete with Tantric terms such as *sādhaka* (Tantric aspirant) and *sādhanā* (Tantric practice). The primordial being of Aurobindo's Śākta cosmogony is Mahāśakti, the transcendent Universal Mother, who "descends" as the Tantric polarity of Īśvara-Śakti, which expresses itself as the *puruṣa-prakṛti* dualism in the nescient world. The Sāṃkhya philosophers made the mistake of ontologizing the strict dualism of this low-level perception of the world. What they overlooked was the dialectical interpenetration of Īśvara-Śakti; furthermore, they neglected the fact that the originally passive *puruṣa* will finally dominate *prakṛti* rather than leaving her for his isolated realm of liberation. P. B. Saint-Hilaire phrases Aurobindo's view of *puruṣa* and *prakṛti* most aptly:

> Puruṣa and Prakṛti are separate powers, while Īśvara and Śakti are contained in each other. . . . Puruṣa is the true being . . . in ordinary man, he is covered by the ego and by the ignorant play of . . . Prakṛti, and remains veiled as a "witness" which upholds and observes the play of the Ignorance. When he emerges, he is perceived at first as a calm, immovable consciousness, detached from the play of Nature. Thereafter he gradually asserts himself as the sovereign Master of Prakṛti.[56]

Here is the evidence for what we earlier called Aurobindo's masculinized Śākta philosophy, a development similar to Vivekananda's. Aurobindo echoes the sexism of Francis Bacon when he declares that only the descent of the Supermind "can victoriously handle . . . physical Nature and annihilate its difficulties."[57] The supreme irony in this position is that the Supermind is essentially Mahāśakti, who is being called upon to tame a lower form of herself. It is no coincidence that Aurobindo's masculinized Śākta philosophy is coupled with a "right-handed" view of Tantra. Aurobindo would completely agree with Śaiva Siddhānta, one of whose texts reads: "Śiva generates Śakti, and Śakti generates Śiva. Both in their happy union produce the worlds and souls. Still Śiva is [ever] chaste and the sweet-speeched Śakti is [ever] a virgin."[58]

With some variations Aurobindo's Śākta cosmogony follows the schematic of *Devī-Bhāgavata Purāṇa* discussed in chapter 6. Aurobindo's Mahāśakti corresponds to Nirguṇa Śakti or Mahāmāyā, because Aurobindo distinguishes between a formless and formed absolute. (Aurobindo uses the original meaning of *māyā* as "creative power" rather than the Advaitin "illusion.") While Saguṇa Śakti emanates in three manifestations in the *Devī-Bhāgavata*, Aurobindo presents four "personalities" of the Goddess. First, there is Maheśvarī, whose qualities are "comprehending wisdom," "inexhaustible compassion," and "all-ruling greatness." Second, there is Mahākālī, whose attributes are "splendid strength," "overwhelming will," "impetuous swiftness and world-shaking force." The third, Mahālakṣmī, is known for her "beauty and harmony, her intricate and subtle opulence, her compelling attraction and captivating grace." Finally, the "youngest" Devī personality, Mahāsarasvatī, who is "equipped with her close and profound capacity of intimate knowledge and careful flawless work and quiet and exact perfection in all things."[59] In all her manifestations the Great Mother descends into the lowest levels of existence in order to transform all Nature into Supernature. In what looks like an obvious allusion to the Puruṣa hymn, Aurobindo asserts that the sacrifice of the Puruṣa is really the sacrifice of the Mother herself.[60]

We have described spiritual Titanism as the supreme exertion of human will to attain divinity and/or to displace the gods themselves. Aurobindo's emphasis on the grace of the Mother further distances him from spiritual Titanism. The Goddess will not automatically bestow her grace on a totally unenlightened humanity, so we must make some initial efforts to prepare ourselves. As Aurobindo states: "Supreme Grace will act only in the conditions of the Light and the Truth; it will not act in conditions laid upon it by . . . Falsehood and . . . Ignorance."[61] The preparatory stage requires total and complete surrender of self and all ego attachments. This must be a truly sattvic—that is, pure and active—surrender rather than an inert tamasic passivity where the assumption is that Devī will make all the effort. When the Mother does grant her favors the spiritual aspirant will enjoy her complete protection and will have no fears.

Through service and self-surrender we become children of the Mother and we become participants in her divine play (*līlā*). With self-surrender on both sides there is certainly no spiritual Titanism in this theology of grace. The "bringing down" of the Supermind turns out to be the selfless action of Devī rather than the self-centered initiative of a solitary individual. If the conditions of self-purification and self-surrender to the Mother are met, cosmic evolution, Aurobindo assures us, will come swiftly.[62]

Also contrary to the Yoga Titanism we have found in Sāṃkhya-Yoga is Aurobindo's focus on the community of *puruṣa* souls. The self for him is social and relational, not solitary and self-determining. Autonomous action is divisive and disunifying and therefore asuric. Instead of the individual divinity of Sāṃkhya-Yoga, Aurobindo's soul is "an individual being of the Divine, the Divine extended in multiplicity is the Self of all individual existences."[63] (All Indian philosophies related to Vedāntist pantheism will have this difference with Sāṃkhya's spiritual atomism.) The goal is "a life in the divine"[64] in all its manifestations rather than taking on a divine status apart from nature and other people.

If there is any problem for Aurobindo, it is the elimination of self-determination rather than its dominance. Although he warns that the community should never replace the individual, Aurobindo argues that our true will is the All-Will, and that we have to become "the instrument of God and to accept [our] Master."[65] This is the "positive" liberty of classical conservatism, in which freedom is defined as doing what we ought according to God's law rather than the "negative" liberty of doing what we want according to our wishes. In the negative view the primary obstacles to liberty are external (governmental regulations and the constraints of others), but the main obstacles for positive liberty are internal, namely, our base desires. As Aurobindo phrases it: "For a great liberty is this, to be delivered from the Animal and the Rakṣasa in ourselves, free to choose the right or be chosen by it."[66]

For Aurobindo the extension of the liberated soul is not only vertical (i.e., upward to Śakti) but also horizontal (outward to humanity and nature). The soul's

> unity with the transcendent one is incomplete without its unity with the cosmic many. And that lateral unity translates itself by multiplication, a reproduction of its own liberated state at other points in the multiplicity. . . . Therefore, whenever even a single soul is liberated, there is a tendency

> to an extension and even to an outburst of the same divine self-consciousness in other individual souls. . . .[67]

Although he confuses the Buddha's vow to preach with the Bodhisattva's vow of total self-surrender, Aurobindo acknowledges that this principle finds its best expression in the Bodhisattva's decision not to enter Nirvaṇa until all sentient beings are saved. Aurobindo's Integral Yoga, however, extends even beyond sentient beings, for all of nature will be redeemed. Even in Mahāyāna Buddhism the Bodhisattva and his community of saints will exit nature as we know it. In contrast, as O'Neil phrases it, "the Superman is liberated in nature, not from it."[68] Such a view obviously has significant ecological implications.

Along with Aurobindo's concept of social self comes an emphasis on the affective dimensions of the human person. He recognizes the fact that the use of pure reason is necessary to reach the heights of metaphysical knowledge, but this knowledge does not "fully satisfy the demand of our integral being."[69] An Integral Yoga requires a complete view of the human being as well as the involvement of all nature. Pure reason produces the abstract philosophy necessary to guide life, but it is the passions that really drive human action. "It is not our intellectual ideas that govern our action, but our nature and temperament—or, as the Greeks would have said, *thumos* and not *nous*."[70] As a result Aurobindo's works are filled with references to joy, delight, and bliss: "The joy of being to others; for their joy will be part of his own joy of existence. To be occupied with the good of all beings, to make the joy and grief of other one's own."[71] For Aurobindo gnostic being is replaced by bliss being, such that the heart supersedes the mind in "universal beauty and harmony."[72]

Aurobindo's commitment to Vedāntist philosophy allows him to counter the individualism and anthropocentrism found in the Jaina-Sāṃkhya-Yoga traditions. In this regard he retells the Mahābhārata story of the Asura Virochana and Indra to explain the correct way to see the relationship of self and God. Virochana looked at himself in the mirror and concluded that he was God. "He gave full rein to the sense of individuality in himself which he mistook for the deity." Indra looked in the mirror, but he was still not clear on the matter. He returned to the Devas' priest Bṛhaspati and found out that "he was God only because all things were God, since nothing existed but the One. If he was the one God, so was his enemy, the very feelings of separateness and enmity were not permanent reality but transient phenomena."[73] This story demonstrates yet another way to distinguish between the self-deification of spiritual Titanism on the one hand and the surrender of the self to the One in pantheistic and monistic traditions.

Conclusions

One is struck by some affinities between Aurobindo's vision and that of Buddhism, a connection he himself acknowledged. From the standpoint of constructive postmodernism, the conceptual framework of this study, Buddhist philosophy is still preferred over Aurobindo's neo-Vedānta. Even though his dynamic Śakti is a clear advance over Śaṅkara's static Brahman, Aurobindo is still wedded to a substance metaphysics, one that prefers permanence over impermanence.[74] Furthermore, Aurobindo maintains that the goal of evolution is already prefigured in its beginning: "This teleology does not bring in any factor which does not belong to the totality; it proposes only the realisation of the totality in the part."[75] This is definitely a premodern totalism rather than a modern version of evolution. This makes Aurobindo very different from Whitehead and other emergent evolutionists, who believe that real novelty comes into the world.[76] Aurobindo's solutions to the problems of the One and the Many and the self and others also have a ring of premodernism. (The apparent fusion of human will with the All-Will is especially problematic.) Therefore, we will now turn to Buddhism and Chinese philosophy as the most appropriate ancient precursors of constructive postmodernism and as the most promising answers to spiritual Titanism.

8 Buddhism, Humanism, and Titanism

This process by which a historical individual is deified is one of exaggeration and exaggerated reverence. It is essentially a process of falsification, the creation of a massive delusion.

—Paul Williams[1]

To remain merely in your own tranquility is the inferior way. You should work for the benefit of living beings.

—The Siddha Kāṇḥapa[2]

The passions are the Buddha nature.

—Myokyo-ni[3]

Introduction

In this chapter we shall investigate the hypothesis that some aspects of Buddhism represent a form of Titanism. At the end of chapter 2 we saw how the Buddha's philosophy might be conceived as an anticipation of constructive postmodernism. We have also seen that Nāgārjuna's masterful dialectic undermines any unwarranted knowledge claims as well as thoroughly refuting any notion of a substantial self, Buddha, or world. Pure Land Buddhism avoids extreme humanism in the same way that Christianity does, namely, by denying the basis for humanism in the first place. Shinran's rejection of "self-power" in favor of the "other" power of the Amitābha Buddha undercuts the axiom that humans can establish virtue or liberate themselves under their own power. On this point Pure Land Buddhism joins the Abrahamic religions and leaves the gnostic religions of Asia.

In chapter 3 we demonstrated that Asura Titanism was the weakest form of Indian Titanism. It is even weaker in Buddhism, because the conflict between the *devas* and the *asuras* found in Hinduism is not present in Buddhism. In Buddhist mythology the *devas* are portrayed as completely devoted to the Buddha—a typical Titanistic reversal—so the Hindu tension between the gods and humans is also virtually absent in Buddhism. The Buddha rejected the Vedic sacrifice and priestly prerogatives, so Brahmin Titanism is obviously not an issue. One might, however, be able to discern expressions of the other forms of Titanism—namely, the Buddha as master yogi, as perfect knower, and as savior. We shall investigate the first two issues in this chapter.

The first section defends the thesis that Buddhism is a form of humanism that does not lead to Titanism. The second section contains a discussion of a passage that might indicate that the Buddha claimed an ontological status beyond the six realms of existence. Section three is an analysis of the term *mahāpurisa* (lit. "great person"), the Pāli equivalent of the Sanskrit *mahāpuruṣa* and a frequent title of the Buddha. The fourth section discusses the Puruṣa hymn, its connection to the *viśvarūpa*—the cosmic body of Viṣṇu, and how this became the basis for the "cosmological Buddha" in some Mahāyāna schools. As later Buddhists did indeed deify their master, the issue of Titanism becomes a relevant one. We find, for example, that in the *Mahāvastu* the Buddha attributes the term *mahāpuruṣa* to himself and elevates himself far above what is found in the Pāli scriptures. In the fifth section the Buddhist Siddhas are discussed as possible spiritual Titans; and in the last section Zen is offered as the best Buddhist answer to spiritual Titanism.

Buddhist Humanism

In an unpublished paper entitled "Buddhism and Chinese Humanism," David J. Kalupahana contends that it is Buddhism, not Confucianism, which should be promoted as the true humanism of Asia. He claims that Gautama's rejection of transcendental knowledge, his declaration of moral freedom in the midst of karmic determinants, and his refusal to go beyond immediate experience all converge with major elements of Western humanism. Based on knowledge gained from experience and induction, a Buddhist, says Kalupahana, can use an evaluative knowledge called *anumana*, a mode of moral reflection that allows her to complete the eightfold path and to become an *uttamapurisa*, an "ultimate" person. This ideal person is one who acts with a clear goal in view and who harms neither herself nor others. Although Kalupahana translates *uttamapurisa* as "superman," this obviously does not represent a Buddhist Titan, as it may have in Hinduism or as it does in the later Buddhist *Mahāvastu*. The *uttamapurisa* simply acts "with a clear goal in view and does not waver when faced with obstacles. He is one who has attained freedom from the suffering and unhappiness in the world. . . . Such a person . . . is not only happy by himself, but also makes other people happy by being pleasant and helpful to them."[4] This Buddhist saint sounds very much like a Confucian sage rather than a spiritual Titan.

Kalupahana sums up his view of Buddhist humanism in this way:

> The philosophy of early Buddhism. . . undoubtedly represents one of the most comprehensive and systematic forms of humanism. It is based on naturalistic metaphysics, with causal dependence as its central theme. Rejecting any form of transcendentalism, determinism, or fatalism, it emphasizes its ultimate faith in man and recognizes his power or potentiality in solving his problems through reliance primarily upon empirical knowledge, reason and scientific method applied with courage and vision. It believes in the freedom of man, not in a transcendental sphere, but here and now. The highest goal it offers is not other-worldly but this-worldly.[5]

Kalupahana concedes that Western humanists would not be sympathetic to the Buddhist belief in transmigration, but he counters that the Buddhist version of reincarnation does not undermine human freedom in the way that he believes that Hindu or Jaina views do.

Two other objections to Kalupahana's thesis should be mentioned. First, Buddhist monks claim that the capacity of retrocognition, clairvoyance, and telepathy aids them in apprehending the twelvefold chain of causal dependence. Contemporary Western humanists, especially those associated with a leading humanist journal *Free Inquiry*, have consistently rejected claims of ESP and other claims of paranormal experience. Second, these same critics might also respond negatively to Buddhism's "soft" determinism, claiming that true humanism must be based on a theory of genuine self-determination. If freedom of this sort is a requirement for humanistic philosophy, then none of the classical Asian philosophies, including Confucianism, qualifies as such. Ironically, contemporary Western humanists cannot consistently hold to this criterion of freedom either. The Humanist Pantheon, comprised of historical humanists chosen by the editors of *Free Inquiry*, is filled with determinists such as Lucretius, Epictetus, Spinoza, Hume, Mill, and Freud.[6] Their Academy of Humanism also contains the sociobiologist Edward O. Wilson and other prominent scientists who subscribe to the theory of universal determinism. It is clear that ancient and contemporary humanists support moral and social freedom, but do not agree on the issue of free will and an internal self-determining agent. Furthermore, we have seen that too much emphasis on self-determination can lead to Titanism.

Spiritual goals are present in both Buddhism and Confucianism, so again we must reject the proposals of those who insist that true humanism must be thoroughly secular. In chapter 10 we shall see how Confucian humanism recognizes a finely tuned balance between humans, heaven, and earth. Although it is more anthropocentric than Confucianism, early Buddhist humanism never exaggerates the human position as much as Sāṃkhya, Jainism, or technological Titanism. Without falling into Titanism Buddhists agreed with the Jainas that human beings can achieve liberation under their own power and with their own efforts—without divine aid, prayer, or sacrifice. With all these qualifications in mind, Kalupahana's thesis that Pāli Buddhism contains "a very enlightened form of humanism"[7] is a very well supported.

Japan's Soka Gakkai is one of the current Mahāyāna schools that continues the tradition of Buddhist humanism. Their leader, Daisaku Ikeda, although a controversial political figure, has written a very fine biography of the Buddha that strongly emphasizes the humanity of the Buddha,[8] and thus avoids the docetism that characterizes many other Mahāyāna schools. Ikeda follows the medieval monk Nichiren, whom he paraphrases as saying: "The Buddha is an ordinary human being; ordinary human beings are the Buddha."[9] The interpretation of the second phrase is essential to formulating Buddhist humanism correctly. If it means that all of us have the potential to understand the Four Noble Truths and to overcome craving in our lives, then we have done justice to Pāli Buddhist philosophy. If it means that all of us somehow possess a Buddha-nature metaphysically equivalent to the *dharmakāya*, the cosmic "body" of the Buddha, then we have strayed from Buddhist humanism. The monism of this position, namely, the implication that all individuals are essentially one, undermines a central tenet of humanism: the individual integrity of each human being. The individualism of humanism has been seen as its greatest flaw, and it certainly is if the individual is conceived as a social atom externally related to other isolated selves. But if the individual is interpreted as the relational and social self of Buddhism and Confucianism, then we have an idea of self that avoids the two extremes of monistic dissolution and social atomism. This means that any Titanism found in Mahāyāna Buddhism will be mitigated considerably, as it is in Vedānta, by monistic tendencies that merge all selves into one; and this point is maintained even in those Mahāyāna schools that are consistently nonsubstantialist in their monism. (In other words, the self can dissolve just as well into *śūnyatā* as it can into a divine substance.) On the other hand, Titanism is exacerbated in the spiritual atomism of Jainism and Sāṃkhya-Yoga.

The Buddha Is just the Buddha

In the Pāli scriptures there is a famous exchange between the Buddha and a brahmin named Dona that seems to imply that the Buddha was a spiritual Titan. Dona asked the Buddha what sort of being he was, and Gautama answered that he was he was neither a god nor a *gandhabba* (heavenly being) nor a *yakkha* (demon) nor a human.[10] The apparent meaning of this statement is that the Buddha was not a member of any of the six realms of existence, that is, those for hellish beings, animals, hungry ghosts, humans, *asuras*, and gods. For some Mahāyāna Buddhists this passage is positive proof that the Buddha definitely claimed to have a transcendental existence and could legitimately be called a god beyond the gods (*devatīdeva*).

Of all the realms of existence the *deva-loka* is an especially difficult one to leave: the gods are enjoying blessedness, but they are accruing karma because of their indulgence in heavenly bliss. This view is found in a wide variety of Buddhist schools. In *the Bardo Thödol* it is clear that being a god does not mean that one is liberated. A commentator on this famous text describes divine existence as a "realm of pride," complete self-absorption, and "intoxication with the existence of the ego."[11] In Buddhaghosa's eschatology, the gods are expelled from their realm by a cycle of cosmic destruction that forces them to take on human incarnations.[12] This preference for human existence, the embodied existence where true enlightenment can take place, does display the anthropocentrism of a Titanistic worldview.

One of the signs of Titanism is the belief that we can transcend our own human setting and limitations and be changed into "new beings," roughly similar to the ontological change, for example, which some Christians find in Paul's theology. There is, however, a significant difference between Christian and Indian views: in most forms of Buddhism, Jainism, and Hinduism, humans transform themselves on their own power, a central claim in all forms of humanism. Or, in Jainism, as we have seen, it is more accurate to say that the saint discovers a divine nature that is already there, so no actual transformation is necessary. In Christianity, by contrast, it is God who affects this fundamental change. In Christianity God is elevated and preserved in his transcendent splendor, while in these Indian views the gods are demoted and criticized. In Indian religion such a procedure reverses the status of divinity and humanity and privileges human existence as the sole mode of liberation. The Buddha, however, seems to go further: he appears to claim a transcendental existence separate from all the karmic realms.

Kalupahana contends that this interpretation of the exchange between Gautama and Dona is incorrect.[13] Rather than a self-attribution of *devatīdeva* or of some other transcendental nature, Kalupahana interprets this claim as the logical implication of a central Buddhist doctrine: human beings, under their own power, can reduce their karmic debt to zero and will not be born again in any realm. The Buddha's final words to Dona support Kalupahana's reading: "Those *āsavas* [defiling tendencies] whereby, if they were not abandoned, I should become a *gandhabba,* a *yakkha*, a human being,—those *āsavas* in me are abandoned . . . not to arise again in future time."[14] The Buddha goes on to compare his state with a lotus blossom untainted by dirty water, and finally reveals that his nature is neither merely human nor divine; rather, he is a Buddha, a perfected human being beyond all defiling tendencies.

We can now propose that the Buddha's "Middle Way" offers a compelling answer to Indian Titanism. According to the Buddha, there is just as much craving in the yogis' desire for absolute mastery of themselves and of the spiritual universe as there is in those who indulge in sensual pleasures and worldly domination. "Craving for views" is another urge that must be quelled, and in texts such as Sūtra 63 of the *Majjhima Nikāya* the Buddha is steadfast in his refusal to consider metaphysical questions that go beyond what can be known and that can only frustrate those who ask them. In his refusal to dignify Māluṅkyāputta's questions about the status of the saint after death, the Buddha is implying that there is simply no state to either perceive or know. This undermines any metaphysical speculation about beings beyond the six realms, especially a transcendental Buddha as an eternal substance supporting all existence.

The Buddha as *Mahāpurisa*

In his study of the *mahāpurisa* concept in early Buddhism, Bellanwila Wimalaratana focuses on the thirty-two marks (*lakṣaṇa*) of the ideal man. Wimalaratana demonstrates that these marks of perfection were part of an ancient art of prognostication. In Buddhism they applied to both the perfect ruler (*cakravartin*) and the Buddha, except the latter had eighty additional distinctive marks, the "minor" *lakṣaṇa* as they are called. The *dharma* king would be able to conquer the physical world, whereas the Buddha would conquer the spiritual world. At his birth brahmin priests announced that Siddhartha Gautama could have chosen either destiny.

In the earliest sūtras Gautama did not himself say that he had the *lakṣaṇa*, but he never discouraged those who attributed them to him. Gautama said that earlier sages did not realize that the marks were signs of merit accrued in previous lives. As he states: "Seers not of our communion, brethren, are acquainted with these marks, but they know not for what deeds done any one of the marks is acquired."[15] Therefore, early Buddhists took the marks, whose Hindu meanings were exclusively prognostic, and grafted them onto their moral theory. For example, the Buddha's perfectly even fingers meant that he was completely free of grasping; and his smooth skin, which can collect no dust, represents freedom from defilement. Lustful people are fated to have arches, so there will always be an empty space in their footprints. The Buddha, being free from lust, had perfectly flat feet and left no space in his footprint; furthermore, he leveled out the ground as he walked.[16] (In the Christian's "new earth" there will be no sea [Rev. 21:1], but in the Buddha's new world there will be no mountains!) In addition to the *lakṣaṇa*, the Buddha manifested other unique characteristics: "If the revered Gotama is walking he leads off with his right foot; he does not put the foot too far (forward), he does not place the foot too short; he does not walk too quickly; he does not walk too slowly. . . ."[17]

Wimalaratana contends that commentators such as the Rhys Davids were wrong in thinking that the Buddhist *mahāpurisa* concept was based on the Puruṣa hymn.[18] This hymn, which was analyzed in chapter 5, describes the Puruṣa as creating the universe out of his body, something the early Buddhist texts do not maintain. Furthermore, in the Puruṣa hymn there is no mention of any "prediction of personality . . . from physiognomical characteristics,"[19] even though this was part of pre-Buddhist Indian tradition. None of the Hindu gods are said to have the *lakṣaṇa*, so they are not, at this stage in the history of Buddhism, signs of a divine being. Therefore, the attribution of the *lakṣaṇa* to the Buddha indicates an elevation of his humanity not a transformation into divinity. In other words, early Buddhists were drawing on physical marks that distinguished superior human beings and not attributes generally given to the gods. Wimalaratana sums up his argument this way: ". . . The marks belong neither to Viṣṇu, Nārāyana, or Śiva in their origin, nor are they signs of deification. Possession of these attributes does not invalidate the Buddha's humanity in any way. Yet it indicates that in him humanity has become perfected."[20] The fact that Rāma was said to have the same long arms as the Buddha is a minor exception to this rule. The Hindu deities also used the power of the third eye (*ūrnā*), but from the Buddha's *ūrnā* came rays of compassion and wisdom, not destruction.

The Cosmological Buddha of Mahāyāna

Wimalaratana's thesis that the Puruṣa hymn was not an influence on the early Buddhist concept of *mahāpurisa* appears convincing. We have also seen here and in chapter 4 that although the Buddha adapts yogic practices, he does not become either a Gnostic Titan or a Yoga Titan. There is, however, very good evidence that the Puruṣa motif entered Mahāyāna Buddhism through the concept of Viṣṇu's cosmic body (*viśvarūpa*). The most dramatic and well-known presentation of this concept is in chapter 11 of the *Bhagavad-gītā*, where Arjuna, heretofore engaging Kṛṣṇa in his human form (*manusarūpa*), asks him to reveal his divine form (*viśvarūpa*). Consistent with the Puruṣa hymn, Kṛṣṇa's transfiguration shows that he is coextensive with heaven and all worlds, and that he is active in all actions, both good and evil.

In the fourth part of the *Dirghāgama* (sometimes called the *Sūtra of Cosmology*) the *dharmakāya* is described as the *viśvarūpa*: "All the common multitude, in the three thousandfold world, *devas*, men, *asuras*, the [denizens] of hell, demons, and animals. . . appear without exception in his body."[21] Angela F. Howard speculates that Buddhist artists chose not to give the cosmological Buddha many hands and many arms so as to preserve some differences between the Hindu and Buddhist *viśvarūpa*.[22] One successful Hindu response to the challenge of Buddhism was to absorb the Buddha as an *avatāra* of Viṣṇu. Not only did the Mahāyānists not object, but they obviously drew on this connection for their ideas about the Buddha's nature. According to J. R. Haldar, the Buddha was given all the Hindu deities' attributes except the power of creation.[23] One of the Buddha's powers in particular—*nārāyana-bala*—links him directly to Viṣṇu.[24] In the *Lalitavistara* the sage Asita discovered this in the infant Buddha and observed that it was more powerful than a thunderbolt, the equivalent to ten Chaddanta elephants.

The power of Hindu seers was such that they were said not only to have created all beings—gods, demons, and humans alike—but themselves as well—for instance, both Puruṣa and Manu were considered self-created. As we have seen, the desire to become father of oneself is one of the general features of the psychology of Titanism, and humans creating both themselves and the gods has to be the ultimate expression of this extreme humanism. Mahāyāna Buddhism is no exception, for it appropriated the word Svāyambhū (the self-existent) as a Buddha name, consistent with the authors of the *Mahāvastu* making the Buddha self-born, like the Hindu Manus.[25] One of most striking Buddhist temple complexes in Kathmandu is Svāyambhūnath, dedicated to the Buddha as the Self-Existent-One.

As early as the fourth century B.C.E. the Mahasanghikas began to move the locus of the Buddha's nature from the mundane to the supramundane. We can find later evidence of this in the Pāli *Questions of Milinda* where the Buddha is called *uttamapurisa*, "the supernal person of the world," mounted on top of the cosmic pillar.[26] This development culminated in the *trikāya* doctrine, where the real Buddha was the *dharmakāya*, and the thrity-two marks were usually said to reside in the *sambhogakāya* not in the *nirmāṇakāya* of the historical Buddha. Wimalaratana states that the "Mahasanghikas and their offshoots so universalized the Buddha as almost to eclipse his historical personality. They identified him in his essential essence with the universal Buddhahood that in time became identified with the Universe."[27] Buddhist docetism was already well under way.

Buddhist mythology and iconography began to portray the Buddha as a heavenly Bodhisattva, witnessing and enacting his own birth as the infant Siddhartha. (In one common depiction of Kṛṣṇa's birth, Viṣṇu is present in the same fashion. An illustrated life of the

Buddha I bought in China features an Indian artist who uses the iconography of Kṛṣṇa to depict the Buddha and his family.) During the Buddha's conception the Bodhisattva is symbolized as an elephant (or the Bodhisattva is riding on an elephant), who literally enters the womb of Queen Māyā and deposits a copy of himself there. In the *Mahāvastu* the gods declare that she will give birth to the *mahāpuruṣa*. At his birth he surveys the universe, and finding no being superior to him, proclaims: "I shall become the Supreme of Men, all-knowing and all-seeing."[28] The thirty-two *lakṣaṇas* are found on his body and the infant Buddha declares that this would be his last life.

A Buddhist form of docetism, which we have already discussed in connection with Christ and Mahāvīra, naturally followed this transformation of the Buddha's nature. According to the *Mahāvastu*, the Buddha did not need to wash, but did so to "appear" as a normal human being. For the same reason, the Buddha ate food even though he did not need it. (In the *Lankāvatāra Sūtra* the Buddha's food is not flesh food but the Dharma itself.)[29] The Buddha made use of medicines even though he was never sick; he seemed to sleep but was always in meditation; and he appeared to age and to die, but his death was an illusion. In striking contrast are the Pāli works, where the Buddha, even with the *lakṣaṇa*, is subject to all the needs and ills of the mortal body. In the *Mahā-Sakuludāyisutta*, for example, the Buddha, in a rather anti-ascetic mood, declares that sometimes he eats a full bowl of food while his monks only eat a half bowl.[30]

One could argue that Buddhist docetism is much more extreme than that found in Christianity. Mahāyāna scholastics of the first centuries of the Common Era used the *via negativa* in ways that made being a Buddha wholly different from anything else in our experience. The result is that the Buddha as he appeared in his *nirmāṇakāya* is not at all as the Buddha nature is in the true reality of the *dharmakāya*. (In chap. 4 we have already seen the implications this has for the Buddha-mind and for the nature of omniscience.) By contrast the Pāli scriptures are resolutely empiricist in dissolving the distinction between reality and appearance. It is Paul Griffiths who proposes the most disturbing result for Mahāyāna docetism: all the propositions about the life and teachings of Siddhartha Gautama are, strictly speaking, false.[31] The Three Refuges (the Buddha, the Dharma, and the Saṅgha) now have no meaning and the Four Noble Truths are also false. From the standpoint of true reality there is no transitoriness or suffering; there is no craving and no cause of suffering; there is no death and rebirth; and there is no eightfold path to lead us through the obstacles of Saṃsara. Rather than Nāgārjuna's dialectic coincidence of Nirvaṇa and Saṃsara, which may allow us to understand how one can be free while actually being embodied, Asaṅga and Vasubandhu's position appears to be that Nirvaṇa is the pure reality of the *dharmakāya*. If the Buddha anticipates a constructive postmodernism, as we have argued in chapter 2, it appears that Asaṅga and his associates support either a premodern totality or a reactive form of modernist monism (also discussed in chap. 2) in which the self-world split is resolutely and unequivocally dissolved. Consonant with premodern cosmologies, "Buddha does nothing new"[32] because time, history, and progress are only illusions.

The Siddhas: Buddha's Lions

One might suppose that the strongest case for spiritual Titanism in Buddhism can be found in the Tantric cult of Hevajra and in the eighty-four Siddhas of Tibetan Buddhism. Indeed, James B. Robinson describes the Buddhist Tantric as one who "can take on all the power and freedom of divinity by one's own spiritual effort."[33] Lord Hevajra contains all the Buddhas within him and his "essence of the deity."[34] Sometimes called sole hero yoga, the Tantric yogi, like Nietzsche's second metamorphosis, is fearless and "wanders like a lion"; but like the third metamorphosis he learns to accept "whatever demon [that] should appear before him" as an integral part of himself.[35] Although the complementary female is a definite part of Tantric practice, Buddhist Tantrism reverses the Śākta view of active female and passive male. As *prakṛti* the Goddess was primordial cause, but in the *Hevajra Tantra* the "*yogin* is Means and Compassion (*upāya*), and the *yoginī* [is] Wisdom (*prajñā*) and Voidness for she is deprived of causation."[36]

Deity Yoga is one practice that is inspired by the *Hevajra Tantra* and others such as the *Vajrapanjara Tantra*. The latter text begins with a critique of Nāgārjuna's doctrine of emptiness:

> If emptiness were the method, then
> Buddhahood could not be. Since other
> Than this cause there would be no other fruit,
> The method is not emptiness.[37]

The text explains that *śūnyatā* has a limited scope: it is intended only as propaedeutic to clear away all false conceptions of the self and substance. The point appears to be that one cannot become a Buddha by simply meditating on the nonsubstantiality of things. Furthermore, Nāgārjuna certainly could not have meant that becoming a Buddha was not possible. The real method of Buddhist liberation is the "circle of a mandala" or Deity Yoga in which the aspirant merges with one of the principal Buddhas. (The Buddhas of the mandala are Vairocana [the center], Ratnasambhava [south], Amoghasiddhi [north], Amitābha [west], and Akṣobhya [east].) The mandala is the "residence" of the Buddha and by a ritualized presence in the mandala, the aspirant attains the Buddha's "Form" body, another translation of the Sambhogakāya. The yogi takes on the thirty-two *lakṣaṇas* and the eighty minor marks and thereby takes on "the Teacher's [Buddha's] form."[38] Actually, in taking on the Sambhogakāya the lama also takes on the Dharmakāya, because ontologically they are ultimately indistinguishable.

Another passage in the *Vajrapanjara Tantra* indicates that the virtue of pride is somehow associated with Deity Yoga: "Through the yoga of Buddha pride/Buddhahood will not be distant."[39] The commentator Devakulamahamati explains that this Buddha pride is simply "being free from the pride of ordinariness," and "will not be distant" means that one can become a Buddha in this life.[40] One could say, however, that this practice does express the hubris of Yoga Titanism, particularly when Deity Yoga is described as "a method for the supreme achievement" and as a way of attaining "omniscient wisdom."[41] A dissatisfaction with Nāgārjuna's dialectic method may indicate that some Tibetan Buddhists do not fully appreciate the humility that comes from the fallibility of all knowledge claims, including those about the Trikāya doctrine.

Spiritual Titanism, therefore, does appear to be present here, but some mitigating factors should be acknowledged. The Yoga Titanism we have found in the Jaina-Sāṃkhya-Yoga systems involves the total isolation of a substantial spiritual self. The movement in Deity Yoga appears to be just the opposite: the giving up of self and merging with a Buddha. In the former, one is discovering one's divinity and abiding alone in it, but in the latter one is being transformed into a divine Buddha. Furthermore, the main purpose of "omniscient wisdom" is to aid in the liberation of all sentient beings, a soteriological view of omniscience that we found in the Pāli scriptures; and, we must add, a moral imperative in the Jaina-Sāṃkhya-Yoga traditions. Finally, we will see that embodiment and the valorization of the body are important for the Tantric tradition, but they were not for most of the other spiritual ways of India. The centrality of the body is seen in the fact that the *rūpa skandha* is associated with the Vairocana Buddha, the Buddha at the very center of the Tibetan mandala.

Let us now look at the eighty-four Siddhas, whose gurus initiated them by means of the *Hevajra Tantra*. The powers of *siddhi* were recognized and practiced by the earliest Buddhist monks. Here is a description from a Pāli text:

> [The monk] becomes many or having become many, becomes one again; he becomes visible or invisible; he goes feeling no obstruction to the further side of a wall or rampart or hill as if through air; he penetrates up and down through solid ground as if through water; he walks on water without breaking through as if on solid ground; he travels cross-legged in the sky like the birds on the wind; even the sun and the moon, so potent, so mighty though they be, he touches and feels with his hand; he reaches in the very body even up to the heaven of Brahman.[42]

The Buddha himself practiced *siddhi* powers. He and his disciples were said to have flown to Sri Lanka for missionary work; and the famous thousand Buddha art motif comes from a incident in which the Buddha, in order to avoid capture, became "many [i.e., 1,000] [but] one again." The Buddha, however, was persistent in his warning that *siddhis* could easily corrupt their practitioners and that they alone could not promote liberation from the cycles of rebirth. Even the Buddhist Tantrics held that the yogi who remained attached to the "minor" *siddhis* could not be saved, for only the higher *siddhis*, developed by compassionate outreach, could do that. As Robinson states: "By allowing himself to be beguiled by lesser powers, the siddha prevents himself from taking that one step further to total liberation."[43] To place this within our Nietzschean heuristic, one could say that the yogi of the minor *siddhis* is still trapped in the lion stage, where the freedom and pride of having power over ordinary constraints prevent one from further spiritual development.

We will generally focus on those Siddhas whose lives offer evidence against the charge of spiritual Titanism. First, however, let us look at a Siddha who expresses the greatest temptation of yogic powers. There is the story of Kāṇḥapa who deluded himself into believing that he was more powerful than his guru. In a fit of anger he killed a young girl with his yogic powers. For his crime he was rebuked by the girl's people: "Those who call themselves Buddhists have great compassion. Yogins do not kill."[44] With the aid of a *ḍākinī* named Bandhe, Kāṇhapa finally learned his lesson; and, interestingly enough, he was one of the few Siddhas who did not take their body with them to the Ḍākas realm.

Nonviolence (*ahiṃsā*) is the theme of several of the stories, including the life of the hunter Śavaripa who, after instruction from Avalokiteśvara, gave up his career of killing animals and eating their flesh. Truer to the Tantric way, however, many Siddhas eat flesh in a way that does not harm them and/or in a way that the animals killed are resuscitated. The philosophical basis for this phenomenon is the Yogacārā doctrine that all things are one, or at least that all distinctions are overcome, in the Buddha-mind. Several passages from the Siddha stories reveal the extreme view that all distinctions are illusions. Śāntideva enlightened the Siddha Bhusuku with the following verse:

> These animals which I killed
> in the beginning did not come from anywhere.
> In the duration, they did not stay anywhere.
> In the end, they were not destroyed into anything.
> From the outset, existing things are not real,
> so how can the killing and the killed be real?[45]

We have already seen that monistic metaphysics dissolves all the differences (particularly the distinction between self and others) that make spiritual Titanism problematic. It is important to note, however, that monistic illusionism was not part of the original Tantra, which affirms the reality of a completely differentiated world.[46]

Although the feminine principle is passive, it still plays an essential role in Buddhist Tantrism. It represents *śūnyatā* and this principle allows one to achieve the important goal of overcoming all distinctions. Aided by a *ḍākinī* disguised as a barmaid, Prince Lūyipa learned the truth of the total equality of all things: he was forced to reject the distinction between good and bad food and demonstrated this by eating fish entrails. Not only do many of the Siddhas receive instruction from *ḍākinīs*, but some of the Siddhas are themselves women. Even as a young woman, Lakṣmīnkarā was a Tantric adept, and when she was married she refused to live with her violent Sri Lankan prince. After becoming a Siddha herself, she then arranged for the conversion of her husband. The most powerful Siddha story dealing with women is the tale of two sisters—Mekhalā and Kanakhalā—whose guru demanded their heads as payment for his instruction. The two immediately decapitated themselves with the "sharp sword of knowledge," and the two *yoginīs* were praised by their guru for their fierce dedication and were rewarded by the reunion of their heads with their bodies.

Just as women find their way to liberation through Tantra, so do the lower castes. Both Camaripa the shoemaker and Kaṃparipa the smith had given up all hope of spiritual initiation because of their low social status, but they were saved by Tantric yogis who accepted them. This unconditional affirmation of the world is grounded in the Mahāyāna insight that Saṃsāra is Nirvāṇa and that Nirvāṇa is Saṃsāra. Such a doctrine allows Buddhist Tantrism and other Mahāyānist schools to validate the body and all of its affections. As N. N. Bhattacharyya states: "Liberation is not of the soul. It is of [the] body which can be attained within the span of a human life."[47] It is therefore significant that, after a life of love and compassion, most of the Siddhas leave earth with their bodies intact. Buddhist Tantrism has overcome one of the main failings of Yoga Titanism: its mind-body dualism and its attendant antisocial isolationism. In his praise of the two sister Siddhas, Kāṇḥapa explains that "to remain merely in your own tranquility is the inferior way. You should work for the benefit of living beings."[48]

Zen, the Body, and Society

Zen Buddhism's commitment to the Mahāyānist identity of Nirvāṇa and Saṃsāra is enhanced considerably by its association with Chinese naturalism and its refusal to separate mind and body. The great Zen master Dōgen (1200–1253) wrote:

> In Buddhism one can naturally learn the Buddha Way both through the body and through the mind. But if one strives with the mind alone, one will never in all eternity attain the Buddha Way. It can be attained only if one gives up all egotistical knowing, thinking, interpreting, and understanding. . . . The Buddha Way is therefore to be attained above all through the body.[49]

Dōgen realized that the ascetic tradition, including his own Buddhism, assumes that the mind should control the body; but he deliberately reversed this traditional priority. Paradoxically, it is in the state of prolonged sitting meditation (*zazen*) that the Zen monk is able transform the old mental self into a new "body-mind." The practice of *zazen* forces the mind to stop thinking and this state of "no-mind" will allow monks to reunite with their body and nature as whole. As Arifuku Kōgaku phrases it: "It is nothing other than the human being's becoming through the body a thing of nature."[50]

Kōgaku finds that Dōgen's doctrine of body-mind compares very favorably to Nietzsche's idea of the body as a "great reason." Like Dōgen Zarathustra proposes that the "small reason" they call spirit should be a servant to the body, for "I am body entirely, and nothing beside; and soul is only a word for something about the body."[51] In a general way Kōgaku conceives the practice of *zazen* as "the formation of an 'overhuman' (*übermenschlich*) body by means of the human body."[52] In a bold inversion of the Cartesian method, Nietzsche persuasively justifies the somatic approach: the body is "by far the richer phenomenon, affording clearer observation" and "it is therefore methodologically permissible to take the *richer* phenomenon as a key to the understanding of the poorer."[53] (Given the fact that the Japanese *mi* can mean both "self" and "body," one should add that the East Asian languages are far richer in their ability to express these basic truths.) Kōgaku concludes his insightful article with the observation that both Dōgen and Nietzsche extend the notion of body into nature, so that the "whole earth is the true body of the Buddha" and that Zarathustra's motto "Be true to the earth" is also an expression of the *Übermensch*'s new body-self.

Moving from the Sōtō Zen to Rinzai Zen, we will, with the aid of Graham Parkes, continue the comparative analysis of Zen and Nietzsche. Parkes's focus is on the cultivation of the emotions, and he wishes to destroy the stereotypical view of "the Nietzschean *Übermensch* overflowing with unbridled Dionysiac passion and . . . the serene Zen master sitting in dispassionate contemplation, unperturbed by a single affect."[54] Contrary to popular conception, Nietzsche is just as critical of an undisciplined life of passion as any Indian ascetic. Taking the Rinzai monk Hakuin as his point of comparison, Parkes proceeds to argue that both he and Nietzsche have a very similar program of spiritualizing the emotions. Hakuin warns that "a person who fanatically avoids the object of the senses and dreads the eight winds that stimulate the passions . . . never will be able to achieve the Buddha Way."[55] Parkes speculates that Daoist influence—the idea that the sage has ordinary emotions but is not ensnared by them—may well have led to the positive view of the passions that we find in Rinzai or Linji Chan, as the southern school of instant enlightenment is called in China.

Parkes begins with *The Platform Sūtra of the Sixth Patriarch*, and finds metaphors of discipline and enlightenment that are also found in Nietzsche. Images of flowing water are used to described the emotions. For Nietzsche the wild torrent of the passions should not be made to dry up, because their source is life itself, which is, as we shall see in chapter 11, the real meaning of Nietzsche's will to power. In the *Platform Sūtra* all "passions and troubles" are "like a great sea which gathers all the flowing streams and merges together the small waters and the large waters into one."[56] Rather than reject them outright, Zen and Nietzsche wish to harness the power of the passions for a spiritual end. As the Sixth Patriarch Huineng says: "Good friends, the very passions themselves are enlightenment."[57] and Nietzsche agrees: "To sow the seed of good spiritual works on the soil of the vanquished passions is the next and most urgent task."[58]

In *The Twilight of the Idols* Parkes finds the most instructive passages about the cultivation of the passions. Nietzsche proposes a three-stage dialectical progression in which the first stage is described as "unspiritual" and "vulgar commonness." Here the person is unable "to resist a stimulus—one *must* react, one follows every impulse." The second stage initiates the "schooling for spirituality: not to react at once to a stimulus, but to gain control of all the inhibiting, excluding the instincts." At this point the person has a "strong will," but paradoxically its "essential feature is precisely *not* to 'will'—to *be able* to suspend decision."[59]

The achievement of the third stage requires that one give up the illusion of an ego will—recognizing the will to power as the flow of life itself—and here Nietzsche merges with Dao and Zen freedom and spontaneity. His model is, however, more vigorous and assertive (or "Teutonic," as Parkes says), but still consonant with the Chinese, especially in its "essential feature": the "ease of metamorphosis [and] the inability *not* to react," living fully with the emotions without being ensnared by them. In Nietzsche's Dionysian state "the whole affective system is excited and enhanced"—perhaps too much so for Daoist tastes—"so that it discharges all its means of expression at once and drives forth simultaneously the power of representation, imitation, transfiguration, transformation, and every kind of mimicking and acting."[60] In *The Will to Power* Nietzsche says that one must take the passions "into service, which involves tyrannizing them for a long time [second stage]. . . . Eventually one gives them back their freedom with confidence: they love us like good servants and ultimately go where our best interest inclines."[61] This is obviously not a Daoist or Zennist means, but the end of spiritualizing the passions is the same.

With the foregoing in mind we should not be surprised to learn that it was a Linji monk who added the last two pictures to the famous *Ten Oxherding Pictures*. Earlier versions of these poignant metaphors of the spiritual life consisted of five, six, or eight black-and-white ink drawings ending with a totally white circle. A Linji monk by the name of Guoan Shiyuan (ca. 1150) added a ninth drawing "Returning to the Origin" (a natural landscape with no humans) and a tenth "Entering the Marketplace with Helping Hands" (showing the pilgrim engaging a Buddha). The obvious point of these last pictures is the one that the Siddha Kāṇḥapa just made: "To remain merely in your own tranquility is the inferior way. You should work for the benefit of living beings." In other words, one is not to remain in the nonduality of *śūnyatā*, but is to returned purified and transformed for action in the world.

The transitional quality of the eighth picture can be seen in terms of Han dynasty bronze mirrors, which had mountains, trees, and wild animals engraved on their backs. In addition to the Zen idea of the enlightened self as a perfectly polished mirror *reflecting* nature as it is, these bronze mirrors offer an equally powerful Daoist notion of looking *through* the mirror at the true nature of reality.[62] This is an introspective look that turns out to have an exterospective result; or, better yet, we have proved that there is no insurmountable gap between the inner and the outer. Notice that neither metaphor assumes that reality is an undifferentiated unity. Finally, the tenth ox-herding picture takes us from the many wonders of nature to the plurality of social relations—a plurality in an organic natural and social whole, but a plurality nonetheless.

Let us now look at Ueda Shizuteru's interpretation of the *Ten Oxherding Pictures*. Ueda believes that they reveal a "threefold negative dialectic," one that has similarities to the dialectic of constructive postmodernism discussed in chapter 2. The first seven drawings represent the first thesis of the dialectic: a self struggling for enlightenment within the framework of a substance metaphysics. The eighth picture of the void represents *śūnyatā* (as in all interpretations), "which empties the self of all substantiality"; and this represents the first negation of the dialectic. Steve Odin then explains the rest:

> Ueda emphasizes that this Zen Buddhist Nothingness that desubstantializes the ego-self must not be adhered to as a

> Nothingness but must itself be emptied through a deeper realization of the Nothingness of Nothingness. The ninth and tenth stages depict the true self in the locus of absolute Nothingness, the middle way of emptiness between eternalism and nihilism.[63]

The concept of absolute Nothingness is very obscure and problematic. Parmenides seems to be correct in his argument that absolute nonbeing (*ouk on*) is unthinkable, whereas in *The Sophist* Plato proposed that "relative" nonbeing (*me on*), produced by the Form of Difference, is eminently intelligible.[64] The same result can be achieved less obscurely by the triadic formulas that were presented in chapter 2. Mapping it on to the *Ten Oxherding Pictures* we would have the substantial self (1-7) > no substantial self (8) > relational process self (9–10). This would follow the general triadic model of metaphysics, deconstruction, and constructive postmodernism.

In his monumental work *The Social Self in Zen and American Pragmatism* (published in this same Constructive Postmodern Thought series), Steven Odin has studied in great detail the "social turn" in twentieth-century Japanese philosophy. As he explains:

> Whereas earlier Japanese models of selfhood tended to articulate human nature in negative terms as *muga* (Sk. *anātman*) or "no-self," the models formulated by 20th Century Japanese thinkers have underscored the dialectical relation between the individual and social aspects of personhood.[65]

The Japanese word for person (*ningen*) serves this philosophical purpose just as well as the Chinese word *ren*, which has the same fully relational meaning. (See chap. 9 for a more in-depth discussion on *ren*.) *Ningen* is composed of two Chinese characters, one meaning individual and the other meaning society. Developing a *ningen* model of selfhood, Watsuji Tetsurō contends that even Heidegger's *Mitsein* has not overcome the anthropocentric bias of Western philosophy.

Building on Watsuji and others of the Kyoto school Odin makes a thorough and convincing case for substantial parallels between twentieth-century Zen philosophy and American pragmatism. Rejecting at least a half dozen previous interpretations of *śūnyatā* in Zen philosophy, he settles on the choice of "social" for *śūnya* and "sociality" for *śūnyatā*. Focusing his study on George Herbert Mead, Odin discovers that "both Mead and Zen have thus converged upon the same fundamental insight: that the self and all events are a function of reality."[66]

Using also Dorinne Kondo's work *Crafting Selves*, Odin offers a model for self creation that follows our dialectic of reconstruction: people "learn to deconstruct their separate ego selves and to reconstruct new contextual selves which are *relationally defined* as social, decentered, multiple, fluid, open, shifting, and ever-changing."[67] Vigorously rejecting deconstructive postmodernism, Odin retains all the value of postmodernism without the negatives of the French deconstructionists: "While [they] shatter all self-identity into a multiple play of differences with no unity, Mead instead shows how the multiple self arises by taking on the social roles of others in the community at the Me pole while having a source of unity and individuality at the I pole."[68] In chapters 9 and 10 we shall see that Confucianism provides a similar view of the constitution of selfhood.

Conclusions

Let us now conclude with a summary of our discoveries. The Buddha's Middle Way and his rejection of all craving—yogic as well as sensual—represents one of the most effective responses to Indian Titanism. Although the Buddha adopted many of the techniques of the yogis, he did not accept their ontology of self nor their specific spiritual goals. Therefore, there is no evidence for any Yoga Titanism. In chapter 4 Gnostic Titanism was also eliminated when we discovered that the Buddha's knowledge claims were so qualified that the term *omniscience* is probably inappropriate. We also found that the Pāli Buddhist use of the term *mahāpurisa* is not connected with the Puruṣa hymn of the *Ṛgveda*, one of the primary sources for Hindu Titanism. In the early texts *mahāpurisa* means perfect man, but it does not mean that the Buddha was God. We did find, however, some evidence of Buddhist Titanism in the *Mahāvastu*, the concept of Svāyambhū, the *trikāya* doctrine, the appropriation of the *viś-varūpa* concept in the cosmological Buddha, and Tantric Deity Yoga. The Siddhas' remarkable feats, on the other hand, were overshadowed by an emphasis on their playfulness and on their ultimate commitment to compassion and social outreach. Finally, we have presented Zen, with its commitment to the body and a social self, as the most compelling Buddhist answer to spiritual Titanism.

9 On the Deification of Confucius

It is fair to say that Confucius never ceased to be the object of the cult he had wanted: . . . [celebrating] the wisdom that causes men to turn away from mystical practices and theories, from magic and prayer, from doctrines of personal power and salvation.

—Marcel Granet[1]

It is most interesting that [the] educated elite resisted all efforts to deify their Master and that in a land where it was commonplace to turn men into gods, Confucius remained a human figure. Perhaps he could most aptly be called the spiritual ancestor of the literati.

—Laurence G. Thompson[2]

[Confucius] was surely no deity figure, but a humanist and a scholar. . . . It is interesting that later generations nearly made him a god, but actually made him a king . . . to highlight his wisdom [and] his moral claims to rulership.

—Julia Ching[3]

Introduction

Except for a miraculous birth story, Confucius was not elevated in the same way as Jesus, Kṛṣṇa, or Gautama. The deification of Jesus and Gautama happened fairly soon after their deaths, but the glorification of Confucius by Chinese culture did not happen for five hundred years. An analysis of the ways in which Confucius was regarded by Chinese culture reveals instructive differences between him and the other saviors. Mahāyāna Buddhist and orthodox Christian philosophers rejected many popular notions about their respective saviors, but most accepted them as gods. For the purposes of our thesis, it is significant that most Confucian philosophers never viewed Confucius as a deity. Furthermore, popular notions of Confucius as a perfect sage differ very much from the modes of deification we have seen so far. In summary terms, Confucius was not divinized as a savior; rather, he was canonized as the saint of the literati.

In this chapter we will investigate the development of ideas about the nature of Confucius' person. First, we will review the relevant historical facts about how he was regarded in Chinese culture and politics. Second, we will analyze two crucial texts that some claim support the divinity of the sage. Here we will take issue with recent attempts by Roger T. Ames, David L. Hall, and Edward Machle to deify Confucius and the Confucian sage in general. Finally, we will propose Confucianism as one of the most constructive Asian answers to spiritual Titanism.

The History of Confucius' Elevation

The first phase of the cult of Confucius was the regular sacrifice made by his own family at Chufu in Shandong province. In 59 C.E. Emperor Mingdi initiated the second phase by making the ritual obligatory for all Confucian scholars. In 72 C.E. Mingdi traveled to Chufu and offered sacrifices at its temple.[4] The aim of these sacrifices, following the dictates of the *Liji*, was to honor the deeds of a great man, not to propitiate a god. James Legge explains the nature of Chinese sacrifices: "There is not, and never was, any idea of propitiation or expiation in them. They are the tributes of duty and gratitude, accompanied with petitions and thanksgivings."[5]

The movement to glorify Confucius reached its peak at the beginning of the later Han dynasty, but, as Fung Yu-lan observes, "with the rise of the Old Text School . . . this literature gradually fell into disfavor and the position of Confucius reverted from that of a semi-divine being back once more to that of a teacher."[6] The literature to which Fung refers includes an amazing tale about a sexual liaison between Confucius' mother and the Black Emperor and her confinement in a hollow mulberry tree. This material also portrays Confucius as an uncrowned king, a savior of the world, and a sage who could foretell the future.

It is a significant fact that the Tartars of the Wei dynasty (220–65 C.E.) forbade barren women from praying to Confucius to alleviate their condition.[7] During the Tang dynasty, however, the pendulum swung back in the direction of glorification. In 630 C.E., on the recommendation of Fang Xuanling, prime minister of Emperor Taizong, all districts had temples erected to Confucius. His title was "The Late Sage" and Yen Hui, his favorite disciple, was called "The Late Teacher."

The Tang era saw the third phase of the development of the cult of Confucius: its incorporation into the state religion. During this period Confucius joined Laozi in the Daoist pantheon, which was headed by the Tang emperor himself. The emperor also ruled over many other subordinate deities, including the kitchen god of every Chinese household. (One might imagine that this religious system kept the masses in line far better than any actual spy network.) Marcel Granet explains this system: "It had been so from antiquity in the case of the Heroes linked to the cult of a Holy Power. Under the Empire, the gods themselves were promoted, demoted, or cashiered; they were merely the officials of a state religion whose true deity was the Emperor. His will alone endowed all other gods with being."[8] Although the emperor called himself "Heaven's humble servant," it is clear that he made himself a Titan by taking over divine prerogatives in this hierarchical system. In the preface of his translation of Wu Chengen's *Monkey*, Arthur Waley observes that, of all people, the Chinese are most transparent in confirming the "theory that a people's gods are the replica of its earthly rulers. . . . Heaven is simply the whole bureaucratic system transferred to the empyrean."[9] Confucius appears only once in this delightful tale, which involves practically every Buddhist, Daoist, and nature deity in Chinese religious history, and in this one appearance he is portrayed as a human teacher of virtue.[10]

After the uncertain years of the Tang dynasty, Confucianism regained its preeminent position during the Song dynasty. This was due primarily to the brilliance of the neo-Confucian philosophers of this period, and none of these thinkers saw Confucius as anything other than a great sage. For example, Anne D. Birdwhistell observes that for Shao Yong "the sage does not possess any unique existence that excludes him from the class of humans. He is not a deity or a spirit."[11] The state cult of Confucius, however, continued. Emperor Taizu (960–976 C.E.) sacrificed to him on a regular basis. In 1008 C.E. records indicate that Emperor Chenzong (997–1022 C.E.), who claimed to have had frequent heavenly visitations, set a precedent by kowtowing to Confucius at the temple in Lu.[12] In 1012 C.E. Chenzong bestowed on him the title "Most Perfect Sage."

It was not until the reigns of Renzong and Shenzong (1023–1086 C.E.) that neo-Confucian influence was powerful enough to moderate the excesses of the cult. In 1074 C.E. some officials proposed that Confucius be called *di* (God), but the Confucians of the Hanlin Academy and the Board of Rites rejected the proposal. The official reason given was that *di* was not a title that Zhou officials ever used for nobility, but John K. Shryock suspects that "the real reason was [that] the idea of divinity associated with the word . . . would have been obnoxious to the neo-Confucians."[13] As an obvious but instructive contrast, just think of the undisputed doctrine of Christ's divinity in the medieval church.

The Mongol emperors mandated that the spirit tablets of Zhuxi and of other neo-Confucian masters be placed alongside those of Yen Hui, Zengzi, Zisi, and Mencius. (Other Confucian scholars were installed, and sometimes removed, over the centuries, with two added as recent as 1919.) In his detailed description of the Confucian temple at Anjing, Shryock hesitates to translate the word *shen* as "god(s)" for the reason that the Chinese could not possibly have considered all these men, including Confucius, as gods. Significantly, the word *di* is used to describe Guangong, the "god" of war, and currently the most popular god in Hong Kong. Shryock concludes that the "positions of Confucius and Guangong are different. The former is usually considered as the perfect man, while the latter is a god in full standing."[14] Reflecting this distinction in recent centuries, Confucian temples have been called *wen miao*, rendered most appropriately as "civil temple," not sacred temple. As Laurence G. Thompson states: "The entire complex was thus a memorial hall rather than a palace of gods."[15]

In 1530 C.E. further attempts to discourage the deification of Confucius were made. It was decided that Confucius would no longer be called prince and that the buildings erected in his honor would not be called temples, but simply halls. (Under the Manchus, however, the title "prince" was not only restored, but also applied to Confucius' ancestors.) Furthermore, images of Confucius and his disciples, installed under Buddhist influence during the reign of Xuanzong (712–756 C.E.), were replaced by spirit tablets. Because of this switch, the Jesuits, who arrived at the end of the sixteenth century, had no reason to call Confucianism an idolatrous religion.

The coming of the Jesuits offers some significant insights about how the Ming Chinese viewed Jesus vis-à-vis Confucius. It is obvious that the Chinese, however much they elevated Confucius, definitely did not see his nature in terms of anything like the Christian Incarnation. Surveying passages of anti-Christian polemics from studies of the Jesuit-Confucian encounter, one is struck by the surprise and incredulity caused by the claim that the Christian God became a man.[16] A paraphrase of a recurring question found among these critics would be: "Who is minding Heaven while God is walking around as this carpenter's son turned religious fanatic and criminal?" When Confucius is mentioned in this material, he is not a god, but simply a sage who knew what Heaven was. The Chinese sages had a clear sense of the proper place and function of Heaven, Earth, and human beings. God's place is in Heaven and the human task is to establish the virtues and cultivate social harmony on earth. These anti-Christian comments, combined with the previous evidence, lead to the conclusion that the elevation of Confucius cannot possibly be conceived as the presence of God in a human being.

In 1700 Jesuit priests asked the emperor Kangxi whether the veneration of Confucius was a religious act, and his answer was that it was not.[17] Kangxi explained the cult of Confucius in the following terms:

> The sage, by the doctrine of the five human relationships, the virtues of Tao, and the cardinal principles of (the relationship between) ruler and minister, father and son, had handed down such eternal truths which inculcate in people the duties of honoring their superiors and ancestors. This is why the sage should be worshipped. You Westerners also have saints, and honor them because of their deeds.[18]

Confucius is "worshipped" not because of his divine nature, but because of his actions and thoughts. Note, also, that Confucius is not compared to Christ, but to the Christian saints.

With this perspective in mind, let us look at the standard emperor's "prayer" to Confucius:

> Great art thou, O thou of perfect wisdom. Full is thy virtue, thy doctrine complete. Mortals have never known thine equal. All kings honor thee. Thine ordinances and laws have come down to us in glory. Thou art the model from the school of emperors. With profound reverence the vessels of worship and sacrifice have been placed here. Filled with awe we clash our cymbals and strike our bells.[19]

These words celebrate Confucius' unequaled moral virtue, but it no way implies that he is a god. This constitutes the veneration of a saint-sage, not a deity.

Let us now look at the accompanying mandarin's benediction:

> I sacrifice to the philosopher K'ung, the old teacher, the perfect sage, and say: "O Teacher, like to Heaven and Earth in virtue, whose doctrine embraces past, and present, thou didst gather and put forth the Six Classics, and produced teachings for all generations . . . I present in reverential obedience to the ancient ordinances sacrifices chosen with care—animal offerings, silks, wines, and fruits. With thee are united the philosopher Yen Hui, the continuer of thy work; the philosopher Tseng-tzu, the interpreter of thy basic teachings; the philosopher Tzu-ssu, thine own mediator; and the philosopher Meng [Mencius] next in dignity after thee. Mayst thou be pleased with our offerings![20]

Confucius is called a perfect sage, and his virtue is compared to Heaven, but he is not identified with Heaven. The fact that sacrifices are also given for his favorite disciple, his grandson, and two other Confucian philosophers indicates that humans are being celebrated, not gods.

During the Qing dynasty, Confucius was elevated to the second rank of official deities, determined of course by the emperor himself. The first rank in the pantheon was reserved for Heaven, Earth, and the guardian spirits of land and harvests. In addition to the sun and the moon, Confucius joined all preceding emperors and kings, the patron saint of agriculture, and the planet Jupiter. The third rank of divinities was crowded with the patron saint of medicine, the god of war, a separate god of artillery, the North Star, the East Peak, the city god of Beijing, the dragons of the Jade Fountain (near Beijing) and Kunming lake, and a host of other luminaries.[21] Again it is clear that we are dealing with a very different concept of deity than is found in the Abrahamic religions.

In 1907 Confucius was promoted to the first rank of divinity, making him equal to Heaven and Earth. Here is part of the Empress Dowager's decree:

> In view of the supreme excellence of the great Sage Confucius, whose virtues equal Heaven and Earth, and make him worthy of the adoration of a myriad ages, it is the desire of

> Her Imperial Majesty, the Empress Dowager, Tzu-hsi, etc., that the great Sage shall in future be accorded the same sacrificial ceremonies of worship as are accorded to Heaven and Earth when sacrifice is paid by the Emperor.[22]

In a desperate attempt to thwart republican reformism, all mandarins were commanded to worship in Confucius' temple twice a month, rather than the previous monthly rite.

The rites at the Confucian temples were discontinued during the 1911 revolution, but in 1914 Yuan Shikai, war-lord president of the new Republic, declared that they should resume. Harboring imperial ambitions, he performed the ceremony on 23 December 1914, but he merely bowed at the altar rather than kowtowing and only parts of a bullock were sacrificed.[23] Nevertheless, when asked if this meant that the Republic was now supporting a state religion, Yuan's answer was very much like Emperor Kangxi's response to the Jesuits: the worship of Confucius was not a religious rite. Some eminent Confucian scholars—Kang Yuwei, Chen Huanzhang, and Yan Fu—did orchestrate an ill-fated move to make Confucianism the state religion and Confucius its spiritual head. At the Constitutional Convention of 1915 the Kang group presented its bold proposal, but all it got, after much heated debate, was wording praising the moral superiority of Confucianism.

Kang revived the New Text School of the early Han dynasty to support the spiritual nature of Confucius (e.g., Kang retold the story of his miraculous birth), and he reintroduced the idea of the Three Ages, but now with a distinctively evolutionary and progressive meaning. Yet even Kang stops short of deification:

> But there was one in whom was concentrated the excellence of all the other philosophers, and whose surpassing god-like sageness was such that all men rallied around him, so that he bound them into one great unity, this way becoming the model for a myriad ages.[24]

In the next section we will argue that there is a subtle, but important difference between a person having godlike qualities and actually being divine.

In arguing that China should have a state religion like Japan's Shintoism or Italy's Roman Catholicism, Kang made a telling distinction between his Confucian *ren daojiao* and a Christian *shen daojiao*. The former would be humanistic and civil, and the latter was theocentric and sacred. Kang argued that Confucianism is superior because it eliminates divine authority, for a *ren daojiao* society would be ruled by a human king not by a divine one.[25] What we see in Yuan's rejection of a Confucian religion and Kang's quasi-scientific humanism is essentially a fulfillment of the Confucian view of, as Herbert Fingarette so aptly phrased it in a book title, the "secular as sacred." On such a view, where the idea of a transcendent deity is not functional, the word "deification" has no meaning at all.

Is the Sage God?

In their excellent book, *Thinking Through Confucius*, David L. Hall and Roger T. Ames reformulate Confucius' genius in a brilliant way, especially with regard to the issue of aesthetic ordering. But it is both disappointing and puzzling to read that Hall and Ames want to deify Confucius, something most Confucian philosophers, as we have seen, always resisted. Their argument is not taken from Confucius himself, where obviously no argument can be found, but from Mencius and the *Doctrine of the Mean*.[26] From the *Mencius* 7b25, Ames translates the following: "Being sage, to be unfathomable, is called 'divinity' (*shen*)." Ames may have mistranslated this passage, for it is clear that the character *shen* is predicative not substantive. If *shen* is predicative, then a standard Chinese-English dictionary dictates that the sage is "wonderful, marvelous, miraculous," *not* divine.[27] In his annotated *Mencius* Yang Buojun lists five instances of the character *shen*—three substantive and two predicative, and 7b25 is definitely one of the latter.[28]

Tu Wei-ming quotes this passage from the Lau translation ("to be a sage . . . is called 'divine'"), but qualifies it by observing that "the idea of spiritual in this connection by no means signifies a 'spiritual being' (*shen ren*) which rises above the sage."[29] Even if Mencius actually meant to divinize the sage, this is clearly not the original position of Confucius. It is consistent with his position to call the sage goodness itself, but neither the *Analects* nor the other early literature support the deification of the sage.

Hall and Ames's use of the *Doctrine of the Mean* is also problematic. They quote the famous passage: "So earnest and sincere—he is humanity! How deep and unfathomable—he is abyss! How vast and great—he is Heaven (*tian*). Who can know him except he who really has quickness of apprehension, intelligence, sageliness, and wisdom, and understands [the] character of Heaven?"[30] Hall and Ames's interpretation goes wrong for at least two reasons: (1) they ignore the obviously figurative nature of this passage; and (2) they do not read the passage in its own context or in the context of traditional and contemporary commentary. On the first point, Hall and Ames overlook the nature of the text's language. Just as we are not to believe that the sage is actually an abyss—he is only "deep and unfathomable" *as* an abyss—we are not to think that the sage is literally Heaven. Charles Muller's translation does not even hint at the sage's divinity: "So sincere is his *ren*, so unfathomable is his depth, so vast is his spaciousness."[31]

On the second point, chap. 31 describes the sage in human, not in divine terms: "Only the perfect sage . . . has quickness of apprehension, intelligence, insight, and wisdom, which enable him to rule all men. . . . All embracing and extensive as Heaven and deep and unceasingly springing as an abyss! He appears and all people respect him, speaks and all people believe him, acts and all people are pleased with him. . . . Therefore we say that he is a counterpart of Heaven." The attributes of the entire passage are elevated and exaggerated, but they are not to be taken as divine. Furthermore, we see the source of the similes with Heaven and the abyss. Finally, we see that the sage is the counterpart of Heaven, not identical to Heaven. This passage reinforces the Chinese view of the Cosmic Triad, in which each member maintains its own place, role, and integrity.

Tu Wei-ming, even though cited favorably by Hall and Ames, offers a less monistic, less pantheistic view of the cosmic triad of Heaven, Earth, and human beings. For Tu human beings constitute a trinity with Heaven and Earth, in which they "form a coincidence with Heaven," but they maintain a "conceptual separation" within "an unbreakable organismic continuum."[32] This has to be the correct view of the Cosmic Triad. "Coincidence" and "conceptual separation" clearly do not indicate identity of any kind. Hall and Ames even quote Tu's warning that the *Doctrine of the Mean* "does not mean to suggest that Confucius is, in a sense, being 'deified.'"[33] Nevertheless, Hall and Ames, going against the texts and the tradition, claim that "the fact is, however, that Confucius is deified, or rather deifies himself."[34] Ironically, Hall and Ames fight gallantly against the Christian idea of transcendence all throughout their book; but then, by raising the issue of deification, which makes sense only within a view of divine transcendence (or human transcendence in the case of Yoga Titanism), they undercut their otherwise innovative reinterpretation of Confucius.

Hall and Ames's deification of Confucius is especially baffling because they argue persuasively that *tian* should be defined in a completely naturalistic way. *Tian* is "the cosmological whole"; or it is "a general designation for the phenomenal world as it emerges of its own accord."[35] On this view a person aspires to become *tian* by extending the self into nature, not by identifying the self with a god. Within the context of Hall and Ames's own rendering of *tian*, the verb "deify" is totally inappropriate. If *tian* is not a deity, then there can be no discussion about deification.

Hall and Ames's insightful analysis of *de* leads us to the same conclusion. For them "accumulating *de*" allows us to integrate ourselves with our environment so that we act effortlessly and harmoniously with nature and society. They quote the *Yi Jing* on this point: "The greatest person is one whose *de* is coincident with the heavens and earth, whose brilliance is coincident with the sun and moon, whose ordering is coincident with the four seasons. . . ."[36] Again there is modeling, complementarity, and interpenetration, but there is not identity or deification. In the *Analects* Confucius says: "It is Heaven that is great and it was Yao who modeled himself upon it."[37]

If not interpreted too monistically or mystically, Hall and Ames correctly define the Confucian religion as one that attempts to achieve "a quality of integration in the world which dissolves the distinction between part and whole, and makes of one a peculiar focus of meaning and value in the field of existing things," but then they reiterate their claim that *tian ren* means "the human being becomes 'deity.'"[38] At least they qualify "deity" with quotation marks, but their choice of words is still wrong. Except for the mystical traditions a central message of the world religions has been to respect the qualitative difference between Creator and creature, between ground of Being and beings themselves. The Confucian tradition maintains this distinction in a more acceptable way, using what I call a doctrine of relative transcendence, while the Abrahamic tradition makes the distinction problematic with its view of radical transcendence.

Even so, we can learn a lesson from the prophet Isaiah. When he describes the Messiah as "mighty God" (*'el gibbor*),[39] he is not deifying him; rather, he is only saying that the Messiah will act with the power of God. The Hebrew word *'el* (God) is some times used to make superlatives, such as *harere'el*—"towering mountains" not divine mountains—and *'arze'el*—the "towering cedars" of Lebanon. Just as the Confucian sage is great *like* Heaven, so too will the Messiah be mighty *like* God. Hall and Ames are making the same mistake as Christian commentators do, when they claim that the Hebrew prophets spoke of a divine Messiah. Most Confucian philosophers have resisted the deification of Confucius with the same fervor that the Jews have rejected the divinity of Jesus, and we should do the same.

Edward Machle's innovative rereading of Xunzi (discussed in the next chapter) is also marred by his view that the sage is a supernatural being: "The sages may thus justly be considered gods—and greater gods than most, since a sage is 'equal to Tian and Earth.'"[40] Machle claims that "such an apotheosis of human into godhead is, of course, no great problem for Chinese culture,"[41] but in the previous section we have seen that there was a general waxing and waning of the elevation of Confucius and of the other sages. Most important, however, is that the philosophers themselves, except for Kang Youwei, Chen Huan Chang, and Yen Fu early in this century, resisted the deification of Confucius. Not one of the medieval Confucian scholars, as we shall see in the next chapter, supported such a notion. Buddhist and Christian philosophers appeared to have no problem with the deification of their respective figures, but Confucian philosophers obviously did. On this issue especially it is important to keep Chinese popular culture and religion separate from Confucian philosophy.

Machle shows that previous commentators have underplayed the use of the words *shen* and *shenming* in the text of the *Xunzi*. As a result they end up overemphasizing Xunzi's naturalism. The *shen* or "divinity of Tian" is shown only indirectly in the cycles of the heavens and the seasons. As the *Xunzi* states: "It is to be called *shen* because though we do not see its workings, we see its effectiveness."[42] As we shall see, this is how Machle is able to distinguish between Tian and nature: Tian is the invisible spiritual force behind nature. As there is no plural in Chinese, *shen* can be seen as both the singular divinity Tian and the plurality of its spiritual effects. "Not seeing the actual workings, we see the effects, and for this reason [the agents] are properly called spirits (*shen*)."[43] But surely we are not to call these spiritual effects either God or gods. If we are to use the word God, we should reserve it exclusively for Tian, which according to Machle is at the "top of the cosmic hierarchy, as perfect *yang* and as preeminent *shen*."[44]

As in the Hebrew uses of *ruah* (spirit) and *nephesh* (lit. "breath"), the Chinese soul can also be called *shen*, this time "human spirit" not a divine being. (Machle correctly relates this usage to the Greek *psychē*.) Therefore, Xunzi has no problem celebrating departed *shen*, but he does reject superstitions about ghosts (*gui*). It is clear that in stating that the natural effects of Tian, including the actions of the sage, are *shen*, Xunzi is in no way saying that they are divine beings. This conclusion is consistent with Machle's insistence, in a dispute with Robert Eno,[45] that Tian and the sage kings must be seen as distinct beings. This criticism also applies to Hall's and Ames's monistic tendencies to identify or merge Tian and the sage.

The parallel to the Hebrews and the Greeks is instructive: neither human *nephesh* nor *psychē* can be called a divine being. A Christian parallel is also appropriate: Confucians are born with the *shen* of Tian in the same way that Christians are created in the image of God. Tian gives humans mind (*xin*), sensibilities, and feelings, and the Christian God bestows reason, conscience, and righteousness, but the resultant beings are not gods, even if they are saints or sages. (The Christians are closer to Mencius on the presence of conscience in the human soul.) Sages then become "host[s] of a divine manifestation (*shenming*)"[46] so they can do Tian's work on earth. (Consistent with Confucian humanism, they do this by learning, not by original divine endowment or by grace.) But in neither Christianity nor Confucianism does the knowledge of God-Tian result in becoming God, especially since, in both traditions, complete knowledge of God is impossible.

A grammatical analysis of the *Xunzi* also supports my position, and Machle himself supplies the data. In Xunzi's usage of *shen*, it "is often more adjectival in force (eight times) or part of an adjectival or adverbial phrase (eight times); twice, as a noun, it refers to one's vital functionings. The rest of the time it clearly indicates 'supernatural' beings or forces. . . ."[47] We have already discussed Mencius's use of *shen* as a predicate adjective, so we should use the meanings "wonderful, marvelous, miraculous"—not "divine"—for the adjectival uses that Machle finds in the *Xunzi*.

If Tian's natural effects are *shen*, then that means that its effects and the sage's actions are "spiritual," just as "Tian in us" or the "image of God" might be called our spiritual natures. Therefore, the claim that the sage is "the equal of Tian and Earth" is not to say that she is same as Heaven; rather, it means that each of the members of the cosmic triad are equally valuable, although Heaven and Earth can claim supremacy in the fact that they both produce human beings. On the other hand, Heaven and Earth cannot be truly fulfilled without the sage. "Tian-and-Earth produce the *junzi* . . . (who) is the 'general manager' (*ling*) of the myriad things."[48] Even Xunzi's "perfect man" (*zhi ren*) does not "compete with Tian" by encroaching on "Tian's province."[49]

Although we can understand his reasons for using the first two terms, we must reject as misleading Machle's characterization of the sage as "unnatural, artificial, and indeed, supernatural."[50] Machle's defense of Xunzi against Mencius and his later Confucian supporters is a compelling one. Mencius believed that the sage was a natural development from innate potentials in human nature. Xunzi rejected this potential goodness, and his critics were justified in asking about how the sage could ever come about. Machle, after presenting the deficiencies of the Mencian position,[51] believes that the answer to this question is implied but obvious: the Confucian sages learned virtue from the great sage-kings. This, then, is the reason for the two misleading terms unnatural and artificial to describe the sage's education. Machle believes that the sage is "supernatural" in part because "Xun[zi]'s idea of the sage's 'transforming like a god' goes far beyond mere model-emulation."[52] Machle does not give references for either "transforming like a god" or "as if he were a god,"[53] so we were unable to check the context, but the simile obviously weakens the attribution of divinity in the same way that it does in the passage from the *Doctrine of the Mean* that was just discussed. Furthermore, when Machle indicates that "nothing is more divine than to be transformed according to the Dao,"[54] the adjective *shen* would be better translated as "wonderful, marvelous, or miraculous." Finally, with such weak evidence for the divinity of the sage, we must stand by the "model-emulation" as the essential foundation of Chinese virtue ethics.

The Sage as a Great Person

The Confucian sages Yao and Shun were not gods, they were great humans, who ordered themselves according to the seasons, shone like the heavens, and attuned themselves with the cosmic harmonies. They were mighty *like* Heaven, not Heaven themselves. In the *Doctrine of Mean* we read that "the highest integrity is 'god-like'. . . . Integrity is not simply completing oneself, it is the means of completing things and events."[55] Again great persons are not gods, but simply leaders who have wisdom, the perspicacity to get things done, and to expand their influence in the world. This is the meaning of Mencius' profound remark that "everything is complete here in me. Can there be any greater joy than in plumbing oneself and finding oneself true."[56] What Mencius means is that all of us in our original natures have the potential of "completing things and events"; we all have the potential of becoming sages, but not gods. Confucius is "cosmic" only in the sense of the extent of his influence, not because of any special divine nature. The lives of the sages are, like nature, expansive and productive, and this is a key to understanding a crucial text in the *Analects*: "It is the person who extends the Dao, not Dao that extends the person."[57] As we have seen, this passage sums up succinctly the nature of Confucian humanism.

Without ever approaching anything like the Christian idea of transcendence, Confucian philosophers nevertheless recognize a qualitative difference between humans and the divine. Therefore, Confucian thinkers do not humanize God nor do they divinize human beings. Even the ancient sage kings, although great, were not considered gods. Confucius, himself humble about his own achievements, clearly recognized the necessity of balance, of accepting limitations, and of concentrating on an earthly moral life. Even though they are mediators between heaven and earth, the Confucian sages are still rooted firmly in the earth, in their physical selves, and in the body of society.

Confucius offers the best answer to spiritual Titanism for the following reasons: (1) he rejects the distinction between theory and practice as well as the bifurcation of heart and mind; (2) he believes that the main purpose of knowledge is not for power or control, but for edification and pure joy; (3) he has no concept of rational autonomy, a dominant idea in Western humanism, but operates with a relational, social self; and (4) he proposes an aesthetic, rather than rational, ordering of human lives. Like an artist, the Confucian sage seeks harmony among human selves and attunement with natural things. This contrasts significantly with mere agreement, or what is worse, with bureaucratic enforcement of rules and short-sighted exploitation of the environment. Like an expert performer, the Confucian participates in the holy rites of *li* and is thereby humanized, not divinized, by them.

10 Xunzi and Neoconfucianism

> Promethean defiance and Faustian restlessness are not at all compatible with the cherished value of harmony . . . in east Asian thought . . . According to [Confucian] thinking, to be fully human requires the courage and wisdom of constantly harmonizing oneself with an ever-enlarging network of relationships, which necessitates . . . going beyond the restrictions of anthropocentrism.
>
> —Tu Wei-ming[1]

Introduction

In this chapter we will expand the argument that Confucian philosophy offers the most constructive answer to Titanism. In the first section we will analyze Xunzi's view of the Cosmic Triad, drawing on the recent contributions of Edward Machle. The deification of the sage is a sure sign of Titanism, but Xunzi's perfect man (*zhi ren*) does not "compete with Tian" by encroaching on "Tian's province." However, the traditional reading of Xunzi as a thoroughgoing naturalist and prototechnologist appears to undermine the thesis that Xunzi offers an answer to Titanism. In the second section, we discuss the traditional interpretation, and in the third, Machle's answer to this view is presented. In the final section we show how the neo-Confucian philosophers generally avoid Titanism's mistakes. We will also show that some elements of twentieth-century Western philosophy are consonant with the Confucian view of human nature and reality in general. This will constitute an extension of the earlier discussion of the self and of constructive postmodernism.

Xunzi, Tian, and the Cosmic Triad

In was Xunzi who introduced the doctrine of the Cosmic Triad, which asserts that human beings are equal partners with Heaven and Earth. In the history of Chinese philosophy it is rare to find the roles of these constituents confused in the way we find in the cosmotheandric hymns of the Vedas, Sāṃkhya-Yoga, or Hindu and Christian incarnational theologies. The Chinese phrase for the Heaven-Earth-human alliance is *san cai*, which means "three powers, three forces, three origins."[2] Each partner in the Cosmic Triad is able to maintain its integrity because each is equiprimordial. While all three are essentially interdependent, none is created by the other. The contrast with other worldviews is striking. In orthodox Christianity the universe is created out of nothing, and after being used as an instrument for God's self-glorification, it returns to nothing. Nature has no intrinsic value in the Indian religious tradition either. The earth, other worlds, and the body are also mere instruments for spiritual liberation. In the mystical systems the human form and body disappear completely in a grand theocentric or cosmocentric totality. It is not surprising then that we find technological Titanism in Euro-America and spiritual Titanism, except for its monistic systems, in India.

Of all Confucian philosophers it is Xunzi who appears most intent on preserving the integrity of each partner in the Cosmic Triad. Modern commentators have assumed that Xunzi was the most naturalistic of the early Confucian philosophers and that whenever he used the word *tian* we should usually read "nature." Edward Machle's recent book *Nature and Heaven in "The Xunzi,"* a new translation and commentary on chapter 17 of the *Xunzi*, represents a challenge to the traditional view. Machle believes that Xunzi is closer to the ancient Zhou belief in Tian as a providential deity, separate but in no way completely distinct from the constancies of the heavens and the seasons. Xunzi's Tian, therefore, is God of the heavens, a demythologized sky father god and the *yang* consort of the *yin* earth. Using Schleiermacher's principle of absolute dependence and drawing on Otto's *mysterium tremendum*, Machle argues that Tian can be conceived, with the qualifications that were just described, as a bona fide Confucian God. As Machle states: "Tian performs the functons of a god, but has no anthropomorphizing stories."[3] The last point is unique and essential to the Confucian answer to Titanism.

Machle demonstrates his view in his translation as well as in his commentary. For example, at the beginning of chap. 17, where Wing-tsit Chan tends to merge Heaven and Nature by stating that Tian "operates with constant regularity," Machle subtly separates Tian and Nature's regularities with that fact that "Tian maintains constant routines for the heavenly bodies"; and he comments that "Tian is thus distinguishable from nature both by its primacy and its functions. . . ."[4] Machle of course agrees that Tian's providence is "general" rather than "specific," so Tian does not favor one person or society over another. Even though the barbarians may have their customs, Xunzi maintains that only the Chinese have Li, the correct rules of human behavior. (We will now follow Machle's convention of leaving *li* as the Chinese *logos* in italics and always indicating the ritual *li* as Li.) This is due, however, to the keen perception of Chinese sages and not to any special action on the part of Tian.

Xunzi believes that Tian rules only in the higher levels of the cosmic hierarchy and that humans should always expect irregularities in their immediate lives and environment. Separating those that might be signs of Tian (eclipses and falling stars) from those that are not (floods, drought, etc.) is an important duty of the sage and of the wise administrator. Only the superstitious person thinks that the latter are acts of divine retribution. "As for the falling of stars and the groaning of trees, they are but [passing] changes in Tian and Earth, mutations of *yin* and *yang* or deviant emergents among things. It is appropriate to think them weird, but dreading them is an error."[5]

Returning now to the ideal balance in the Cosmic Triad, Xunzi tells that we are not to compete with Heaven, for each member of the triad has its own distinct role to play. "Heaven has its seasons, Earth has its wealth [resources], and man has his government [culture]. This is how they are able to form a triad (*can*)."[6] Machle's translation of the last sentence draws on another use of *can* as describing the alignment of the three stars in Orion's belt. Here, then, is Machle's translation of this passage: "Tian has its season, Earth has its productiveness, and [the] man has [an ability] to set things in order. It is this situation that constitutes their potential to be harmoniously aligned."[7] Machle inserts the definite article before "man" to emphasize the hierarchical thinking that pervades all of Confucianism. It is not just any person who can align himself with Heaven and Earth; it is only the sage, the "perfect man." Only he "who understands the distinctive functions of Heaven . . . may be called a perfect man (*zhi ren*)."[8]

The literal meaning of *zhi ren*, according to Machle, is "he who has arrived" or the "ultimate man." (Zhuangzi's *zhi ren*, most likely the source of Xunzi's use of the term, will be discussed in chap. 11.)

This suggests parallels to both Buddhism and Hinduism. The Buddha is called the Tatāgatha—literally the one who has arrived at Nirvāṇa with nothing else to do or will. Pāli Buddhism agrees with Confucianism that this "perfect" person (Pāli *uttamapurisa*) is in no way a deity. The second translation of *zhi ren* as "ultimate person" can be contrasted to Kṛṣṇa as *uttamapuruṣa*, a "superman" superior even to Brahman the Godhead. The Pāli *uttamapurisa* is simply a perfected human being rather than a Vedic cosmic man (*puruṣa*). As we have seen, this Hindu Titan does not appear in Buddhism until the Buddha is called *mahāpuruṣa* in the *Mahāvastu*.[9]

The sage models himself on Heaven, which performs its "office" without any action or effort. The emperor also follows the sage's lead: he is to center himself on the pole star, face south, do nothing, and let his ministers run the state.[10] This is where Daoist *wu wei* and Confucian sagehood converge in stark contrast to Western and Indian forms of extreme humanism, where the Titan, by a supreme act of willpower, overcomes the constraints of body and natural environment and attempts to isolate himself from both. Machle reminds us that for the Chinese an assertion of will reveals an imperfect state rather than the ideal: "Where we hold 'will' to be one of the perfections of a person, the Chinese idea would suggest that it is rather a mark of an imperfection, either in the person or in his or her situation, an imperfection that requires will or effort to deal with."[11] This means that Tian also has no will and this fact has allowed Westerners and even many Chinese to mistranslate Tian as nature. This negative view of the will also strengthens the position of Chinese philosophy (including Chinese Buddhism) as an answer to Titanism. As we shall see in chap. 11, Nietzsche's will to power is a natural impulse rather than an intentional will, a fact that establishes a close affinity between him and the Chinese.

Xunzi believes that people should order their lives on natural harmonies and regularities, but, contrary to Mencius and the neo-Confucians, he says that they should not "deliberate" or "devote any effort" to the "deep" and "invisible" processes of Heaven's hidden spirit. This would constitute hubris on their part and tend to upset the balance of the Cosmic Triad. Xunzi's caution here is completely compatible with Confucius' own diffidence about all things spiritual and his exhortations that we should concentrate on human affairs. Therefore, the superior person (*junzi*), one step lower than the sage (*sheng ren*) or the perfect person (*zhi ren*), is content with knowing Heaven's distinctive functions, but remains ignorant and silent about the inner secrets of Heaven. "The superior man is serious about what lies in himself and does not desire what comes from Heaven. The inferior man neglects what is in himself and desires what comes from Heaven [i.e., a misdirected desire for good fortune]."[12] True Confucian humanists stay within themselves and their society and do not aspire to Heaven or have Nietzsche's "otherworldly hopes."

Is Xunzi a Technological Titan?

Xunzi's cosmology seems to be just the right response to Titanism, but the traditional interpretation of him as a thoroughgoing naturalist and prototechnologist appears to undermine this thesis. In some passages he seems to say that we should control nature and harness its energies. The following poem, translated by Chan, contains the most explicit evidence for Xunzi's call for human exploitation:

> Instead of regarding Heaven as great and admiring it,
> Why not foster it as a thing and regulate it?
> Instead of obeying Heaven and singing praise to it,
> Why not control the mandate of Heaven and use it?
> Instead of looking on the seasons and waiting for them,
> Why not respond to them and make use of them?
> Instead of letting things multiply by themselves,
> Why not exercise your ability to transform [and increase] them?
> Instead of thinking about things as things,
> Why not attend to them so you won't lose them?
> Instead of admiring how things come into being,
> Why not do something to bring them to full development.[13]

Chan comments that "nowhere else in the history of Chinese thought is the idea of controlling nature so definite and so strong. It is a pity that this did not lead to a development of natural science." Chan expresses disappointment that the Han Chinese did not follow through with Xunzi's program for applied science, and he blames this failure on orthodox Confucians and Daoists who overemphasized the harmony between human beings and nature. In the context of the current study, a very different response suggests itself. In this text we seem to have a recipe for technological domination and control, even (in lines 5-6) a plan for climate control and (in lines 7-8) a premonition of genetic manipulation of biological species. An alternative judgment is that the Han leaders were wise to reject what modern commentators have interpreted as Xunzi's utilitarianism and incipient technologism.

We began by praising Xunzi's insights about the relationship among humans, Heaven, and Earth. Such a cosmology should be superior to other worldviews in which human beings have exercised overreaching self-aggrandizement at the expense of nature and the spiritual. Confucian cosmology should then serve as an effective answer to Titanism. Could it be that Xunzi's alleged naturalism is too excessive and upsets the balance of the Cosmic Triad, such that there is insufficient respect for the integrity of Heaven and Earth? With Machle now tempering a view of strict naturalism, this definitely cannot be the reason. Furthermore, the neo-Confucians naturalize Heaven more thoroughly and consistently than Xunzi does, even with the traditional interpretation of his naturalism.

Is it then due to Xunzi's view that human nature is originally evil? We entertain this hypothesis only because commentators have said that the rise of technology in Europe has gone hand-in-hand with a Calvinist doctrine of human depravity. But we all know that it is simply wrong to cast Xunzi as a Confucian Calvinist. Although he disagrees with Mencius about original human nature, he is just as confident as Mencius is about the capacity for people to establish virtue on their own power. Not only is he just as confident, but some recent commentators believe that his theory of human virtue is more philosophically sound than Mencius'.[14] Finally, it is perhaps incorrect to say that Xunzi believes that human nature is evil. Like all Confucians he believes that human nature (*xing*) comes from Tian, but he disagrees with Mencius that we have inherent tendencies to the good. For Xunzi proper inclinations to virtue can come only from moral education.

Perhaps the clue to why Xunzi may be a prototechnologist can be found in his concept of *xin*. Usually translated as "heart/mind" or simply "heart," Xunzi's *xin* is more properly translated as "mind" in a cognitive sense. When heart and mind are separated, the latter tends to become a calculating, objectifying, even manipulative faculty. Xunzi speaks often of *xin* as the "ruler" of the body and how it is to produce order where Tian is unable to. Furthermore, Xunzi's approach to the rectification of names is almost exclusively logical, rather than social and moral, and this focus may again be attributed to his concept of *xin*.

But it cannot be Xunzi's concept of mind that leads him astray, because even Mencius warns us that if the mind is not in control, then the senses may well distract us from virtue.[15] Furthermore, many neo-

Confucians separate the cognitive and affective parts of the soul just as Xunzi does, yet they generally maintain a balanced view of the Cosmic Triad and do not recommend the exploitation of nature. But even with some separation of mind, feelings, and senses, we must remind ourselves that Confucian philosophy never entertained a complete subject/object split, which led to the egocentric predicament and to other serious problems associated with modern Western philosophy.[16]

Some might say that the solution to the problem lies in Xunzi's difference with Mencius. By rejecting the Mencian view that Heaven is in everyone of us, Xunzi literally cuts the heart out of Confucian philosophy. The result is that he is unable to express the essential interrelation of the partners of the Cosmic Triad. Just as important as the integrity of each is the holistic view of their interpenetration, a pervasive theme, as we shall see, in neo-Confucianism. On this view, Heaven and Earth, for Xunzi, are not internally, but externally related to one another and to human beings. This would explain why in this passage both Heaven and Earth are described as primarily objects for human use. Thomé H. Fang is a supporter of this view:

> [Xunzi] was the only one who seemed to be "fed up" with the value-centric conception of Heaven. Just for this reason, he wanted to set up the supremacy of man apart from unnecessary complication with Nature, which is nothing more than a neutral order with physical energies in store for human utilization.[17]

Without mentioning Xunzi specifically, the neo-Confucian Zhangzai, centuries later, diagnosed this problem succinctly:

> When the Way of Heaven and the nature of man function separately, there cannot be sincerity. When there is a difference between the knowledge obtained by following Heaven and that obtained by following man, there cannot be perfect enlightenment. . . . And when the nature of man and the Way of Heaven are united in harmony, they will be preserved and abide in sincerity.[18]

Xunzi's critics would argue that he overreacted to Mencius by strictly separating the elements of the Cosmic Triad. As a result he did not fully appreciate the moral and aesthetic powers of Heaven and Earth nor did he completely understand their interactive harmonies. Returning to the poetic lines just quoted, we should, contrary to Xunzi's apparent advice to regulate it, simply admire Heaven as great; instead of genetic engineering, we should allow species to "multiply by themselves"; we should stand in awe of Heaven and Earth rather than exploiting them for our own use. The cosmic trinity can be sustained, as the *Doctrine of the Mean* says, only if human beings "assist in the transforming and nourishing process of Heaven and Earth."[19]

In order to avoid the anthropomorphism he found in Mencius, Xunzi's critics claim that he still preserves an anthropocentrism that leads him to treat Heaven and Earth more like objects rather than subjects in their own right. This is contrary to the Confucian tradition, as Tu Wei-ming maintains:

> Confucian humanism is therefore fundamentally different from anthropocentrism because it professes the unity of man and Heaven rather than the imposition of the human will on nature. In fact, the anthropocentric assumption that man is put on earth to pursue knowledge and, as knowledge expands, so does man's domination over earth, is quite different from the Confucian perception of the pursuit of knowledge as an integral part of one's self-cultivation.[20]

Note that, technological exploitation aside, the spiritual Titans of India might be said to have the same agenda. Earth and our bodies are viewed as not ends in themselves, but as means to a liberation that exceeds even the realm of the gods. Neither Heaven, especially in Buddhaghosa's doctrine of celestial destruction where the gods are forced into the human realm,[21] nor Earth can maintain their integrity or value in such a view.

Benjamin Schwartz sums up this traditional view of Xunzi by claiming that he represents a "paradigm of the positivist-technological orientation" and is the best Chinese example of the "scientific humanism" of Europe.[22] Since Xunzi lacks an appreciation of basic theoretical investigation, he is more like Francis Bacon than Galileo Galilei. There is more than a hint of Bacon's "knowledge is power" in the Chan translation of Xunzi's poetic lines. Tu Wei-Ming essentially agrees with this assessment of Xunzi, but he does add an important caveat at the end of this insightful passage:

> To be sure, the belief that knowledge implies power is not totally absent in the Confucian tradition. Xunzi, for example, strongly advocates the position that since culture is manmade, the human transformation of nature is not only nec-

> essary but also highly desirable. Yet, what Xunzi proposes is hardly a form of aggressive scientism. Indeed, he is so painfully aware of the principle of scarcity that his general attitude towards natural resources is not manipulative but conservationist.[23]

In this regard Chan observes that whereas Mencius idolized sage kings Yao and Shun, Xunzi preferred Yu, who was famous for his engineering feats, specifically the diversion of nine rivers to prevent flooding.[24] Tu, however, is correct in observing that this does not necessarily constitute an exploitive view of nature.

Machle: Xunzi not a Titan

Machle believes that the view of Xunzi as a prototechnologist is not supported either by his famous poem or in his philosophy as a whole. Let us first present his translation of this passage and then we will summarize his rebuttal.

> When "magnifying Tian," which is better:
> (merely) to contemplate it,
> or to turn things into wealth by nurturing them?
> When "following Tian," which is better:
> to sing its praises, or
> to make use of what occurs by conforming it to a pattern?
> When "attending to the seasons," which is better:
> (merely) to await them, or
> to employ them productively by responding to them?
> When "harmonizing with things," which is better:
> (merely) to prize them, or
> to transform them by manifesting their potential?
> When "thinking about things," which is better:
> (merely) to notice what they are on their own, or to avoid
> losing them, by
> making them conform to their underlying rationale (*li*)?
> (In short) which is better: to direct your concern toward that
> which gives birth to things, or to assist what brings existing things to full completion.

The most controversial phrase in the beginning of this poem is "*zhi tian ming er yong zhi*," which Chan translates as to "control the

Mandate of Heaven and use it" and Hu renders as "control Nature's course and use it." Since Xunzi does not use the phrase *tian ming* and because the line has one too many words, Machle believes that *tian* is an editorial insertion. Machle justifies his own translation by noting the contextual use of *tian* in the same chapter and in chap. 22 of the *Xunzi*. Machle's translation is "make use of what occurs by conforming it to a pattern." The final *zhi* in the phrase, according to Xunzi's normal usage, indicates that we should use what occurs naturally as a "pattern" for cultural institutions. Machle concludes that "Xunzi's aim is not 'to control nature's course' but 'to assist things in finding their place,' so as not 'to lose their essence.'"[25]

Before and after the poetic lines the prose passages dealing with government and Li definitely suggest that the transformation Xunzi calls for is not technological but spiritual and cultural. Machle has it just right:

> Order at the bottom of the cosmic hierarchy is not only not by nature, but is attainable only through highly cultivated humans. It is not brought about by purely technological means, for Xun[zi] admits that the farmer knows more about farming than does the *junzi*—any technologist knows more about his specialty than does the *junzi*—but it is still the *junzi*, following the sage, who sets things in order.[26]

Xunzi's warning not to "to neglect human effort and admire Heaven" (right after the poetic lines) is not a call for the control or exploitation of nature, but an exhortation for the *junzi* to fulfill a spiritual obligation. This is what Confucius meant by his cryptic saying that "the *junzi* is not an implement."[27] Likewise, Xunzi is saying that nature is not a mere instrument either. We do not use Heaven and Earth for our own ends (the rites are not propitiatory; prayers are not petitionary), but we celebrate and fulfill them for their own sake and value.

The human function in the Cosmic Triad is to complete the work of Tian, which "produces" but "cannot order." Tian produces a cosmos that has "veins" of *li*, like the veins of a piece of jade. One is reminded of Plato's *logos*, which he analogizes as the joints of a carcass. The true dialectician is like the expert butcher who knows exactly where to cut up the body of reality.[28] Similarly, the Confucian sage is like the master carver who knows that not to follow the veins is to destroy a good piece of stone. Therefore, as opposed to the Daoist sage, the Confucian sage is activist and exploitive in the good sense.

The sage has a sacred duty to transform Tian's natural constancies (*xing*) into patterns of culture (*wen*), not necessarily machines or factories. In short, the sages transform cosmic *li* (Machle's "underlying rationale") into cultural Li.

If we take a closer look at Xunzi's view that the mind (*xin*) is the "ruler" of the body, we find that this phrase has been misinterpreted. The human mind, located in the "central cavity" and still close to the heart, is produced by Tian to rule the five senses ("sensibilities" in Machle's translation). (By correlation the emperor's job, as the "son" and "mind" of Tian, is to rule the people's sensibilities.) Xunzi's concept of mind is obviously not separated from a person's affective or moral dimensions, because for him our moral faculties (*yi*) are found in our *xin*.[29] Xunzi believes that the sage's mind enables him to understand the Dao, and this mind is anything but manipulative and calculative. The sagely mind understands the Dao by its "emptiness, unity, and stillness,"[30] another possible Daoist influence on Xunzi. Xunzi's activism appears to begin in Daoist passivity, not in a desire for exploitation.

Neo-Confucianism and Titanism

One could say that what Confucian philosophy has that Western science lacks is the concept of a unifying force or principle. The concept of energy does not suffice in contemporary science because it is devoid of moral and aesthetic components. Henri Bergson solved this with his concept of *élan vital* and A. N. Whitehead offered his principle of creativity. In neo-Confucianism the major unifying principles are *qi* (cosmic energy) and *li*, both as a single cosmic principle and as multiple "essences" for all things. One can say that this is simply a metaphysical elaboration of Mencius's proposition that the *junzi* "is in the same stream as Heaven above and Earth below."[31]

One might say that Hindu and Buddhist metaphysics also have strong unifying principles, such as Ātman-Brahman or the Dharmakāya. In some schools, however, the integrity of individual things is dissolved in Brahman and in the Buddha's cosmic body. In contrast, neo-Confucianism maintains its famous principle: *li* is one, but its manifestations are many. (Significantly, some scholars believe that this principle has a Buddhist origin, going back perhaps as far as Dao Sheng.) With this axiom neo-Confucianism is able to chart a middle course between the deficiency of unity we find in Western science and the overwhelming unity of Indian monism. This is the primary way in which Confucians have preserved a proper balance among humans, Heaven, and Earth.

The metaphors of unity in neo-Confucianism manifest some anthropomorphism and anthropopathism, but their rhetorical and explanatory power far outweigh their occasional excesses. Because all things share *li*, human beings can be said to form one body with Heaven and Earth. The neo-Confucians avoid extreme humanism, because this body is never described in human terms, which is the case, however, with the Indian cosmic body. As some commentators are now arguing,[32] the concept of the universe as a living body is a powerful ecological metaphor. Just as we take care not to harm our own bodies, this image serves as a constant reminder that we should exercise the same care with nature.

Similar moral lessons are drawn from Zhangzai's famous statement that "Heaven is my father and Earth is my mother." In addition to the message that we should respect Heaven and Earth as we do our parents, there is also a subtler meaning of reciprocity and mutuality. Our parents need us just as much as we need them. In fact, as Heaven and Earth have no mind or sense organs of their own,[33] our special endowments are used to make the Dao known in sayings and rites and thereby expand the Dao. As Tu Wei-ming states: "The uniqueness of being human is the intrinsic capacity of the mind to 'embody' (*ti*) the cosmos in its conscience and consciousness. Through this embodying, the mind realizes its own sensitivity, manifests true humanity and assists in the cosmic transformation of Heaven and Earth."[34]

I disagree, however, with Tu's assessment that this concept invest humans with "a kind of godlike creativity."[35] As an integral partner in the Cosmic Triad, human beings are unique in consciously expressing morality in language and other specific human activity. This can be "godlike creativity" only if Heaven is described in uniquely human terms. The Abrahamic religions do this consistently, but Confucianism, to its credit, generally does not. For example, the Hebrew God appears to his prophets and speaks his Word, but the Confucian Heaven, as Mencius says, "does not speak but reveals itself by its acts and deeds."[36] Ultimately, the Christian God, especially under the influence of Greek substance metaphysics, does everything and we do nothing. In contrast the Confucian emphasis is on mutuality and reciprocity. As Mencius quotes from the *Taishi*: "Heaven sees with the eyes of its people. Heaven hears with the ears of its people."[37] Similar notions are found in process theology, where in a real sense God comes to know as human beings come to know. God and the world are internally related, rather than the external relations demanded by orthodox Christian transcendence.

If Confucianism is "neither theocentric nor anthropocentric," as Tu Wei-ming astutely observes in his book on the *Zhong Yong*, then it is misleading to say that "humanity is Heaven's form of self-disclosure, self-expression, and self-realization."[38] By indicating that humanity is a form of Heaven, such theocentric language tends to undermine the integrity of humanity in the Cosmic Triad. Since Tu himself insists that the Confucian Heaven is not humanized, it would be better to say that transcendent principles are revealed through human consciousness. Tu is also correct in claiming that there are no grounds for Promethean hubris in Confucian cosmology. But in saying that the sage and Heaven comprise an "indivisibly single oneness,"[39] the balance of the cosmic trinity is again put at risk. We prefer Tu's general tendency to interpret the coincidence of Heaven, Earth, and humanity in terms of interpenetrating coexistence rather than monistic identity.

As Heaven and Earth have no mind of their own, human consciousness then serves as the "cosmic mind." This locution raises the critical response that both neo-Confucianism and process philosophy express an unacceptable panpsychism. For example, Whitehead's doctrine of prehension holds that every actual occasion "prehends" or feels every other actual occasion. Similarly, Neo-Confucianism uses specifically human terms such as *cheng* (sincerity) and *ren* (benevolence) in a metaphysical sense, and now we see that the human mind is the mind of Heaven and Earth. There is no question that both Whitehead and the neo-Confucians have stretched the ordinary meaning of words. But in his defense, Whitehead makes it clear that prehension is simply a nonconscious "taking account" of another presence. Similarly, the neo-Confucians explain that Heaven is "sincere" and "faithful" only because it never fails in its regularity and impartiality. Any being can be "sincere" simply by being "true" to itself, which is much easier for natural things than for human beings.

For Zhuxi the cosmic meaning of "mind" is simply "to produce things" and he distinguished the metaphysical "substance" of *ren* from its specific "function" as human love.[40] Therefore, to say that persons are the mind of Heaven and Earth does not mean that humans have become God; it only means that they are playing their proper role in the universe. Earth provides the resources; Heaven provides impartial rules and regulations; and people provide the eyes, ears, and mind to make this known. Humans are transformed by the "sincerity" and "integrity" of Heaven and Earth, while the latter are transformed by the unique contributions of human culture.

The foregoing definitely does not solve the problems of panpsychism and anthropomorphism in neo-Confucianism. Indeed, there are thinkers in this school who tend to undermine the delicate balance in the Cosmic Triad. In India we found that it was the realistic systems of Sāṃkhya-Yoga and Jainism that represented the strongest forms of Titanism, but ironically it is the idealistic schools of neo-Confucianism that appear to threaten the balance of the Cosmic Triad. Neo-Confucian idealism reaches its zenith in Wang Yangming, who claims that it is mind that "produces Heaven, Earth, spiritual beings, and the Lord." He believes that "wherever the will is directed there is a thing."[41] Another idealist Lu Xiangshan affirms that "man and Heaven and Earth coexist as three ultimates," and goes on to insist on a specific *dao* for each.[42] Lu holds that this is the "basis [for] Confucian doctrines," but it is difficult to understand how this foundation can stand if Wang is correct that the mind produces the Cosmic Triad. "Even Heaven and Earth," says Wang, "cannot exist without the innate knowledge that is inherent in man."[43] In the following passage, however, Wang does reaffirm the interdependence of the basic elements:

> My clear intelligence is the master of Heaven and Earth and spiritual beings. . . . Separated from my clear intelligence, there will be no Heaven, Earth, spiritual beings, or myriad things, and separated from these, there will not be my clear intelligence. Thus they are all permeated with one material force. How can they be separated? I asked further, "Heaven, Earth, spiritual beings, and the myriad things have existed from great antiquity. Why should it be that if my clear intelligence is gone, they will all cease to exist?"[44]

Here at least Wang implies that Heaven, Earth, and mind are internally related—one cannot stand without the other—and that *qi* is the unifying force among them. One also assumes that while humans serve as "the mind of Heaven and Earth," the latter also contribute their equal shares, as Confucian tradition dictates. But, within the context of the current study, one might still be concerned about the mind as "master" and the idealism that is implied in such statements.

Self, Body, and Society

In stark contrast to Greek philosophy, Confucian discussions of human nature rarely ever mention reason as the essence of persons and never describe the self as autonomous. Instead, the focus is on a balance between the cognitive and the affective dimensions of human activity. Two Chinese terms are particularly important on this count: *xin* (heart-mind) and *ren* (human heartedness). The meaning of the two elements of the graph *ren* is "two peopleness" (a perfect Chinese equivalent of Buber's *Mitmenschlichkeit*), so the concept of *ren* manifests a strong relational and social view of the self. While Aristotle maintains that "reason more than anything else *is* man,"[45] Confucius would say that heart is the center of personhood and that relating to people according to Li is the essence of being human. Hall and Ames phrase the Confucian view aptly: "The very notion of 'individual' in the strictest sense is suspect from the Confucian perspective. 'Sociality' is at the very root of existence."[46]

After two thousand years Western philosophy has finally discovered the relational self. Thinkers as diverse as Karl Marx, Martin Heidegger, George Herbert Mead, Maurice Merleau-Ponty, Gabriel Marcel, and Martin Buber have taught us that the self is the product of interpersonal and societal relations. The Confucian vision of human beings compares more favorably to Marcel and Buber's, primarily because they believe that the self also has a transcendent dimension. For them persons have a divine grounding, as well as the sociological setting that serves to express the Heaven that is already in us. In this twentieth-century context Xunzi is more like Marx and Mead, namely, the self is exclusively a social product. Unlike Marx and Mead, Xunzi believes that Heaven exists, but its function is separate, even though our basic natures come from it. As this basic nature has no inclination to the good, the function of society is to tame selfish desires and to form the virtuous person from raw material. Whereas Xunzi thought that we had to struggle with our natures, Mencius thought, just as Aristotle did, that people take to virtue with joy and ease rather than with difficulty. This means, as the *Analects* relates, that the *junzi* expresses these same feelings in nature: "The wise find joy in water; the benevolent find joy in mountains."[47] In both Daoism and Confucianism we have an ecological sensitivity that we do not find in any other Asian philosophy.

With the discovery of the relational self in the West there has also come the insight that the self is fully "somatic." Taking a strong stand against Cartesian dualism, Merleau-Ponty, for example, makes especially important contributions here with his notion that the self is essentially coextensive with the body. (This means, as we have mentioned previously, that the body is constitutive of personal identity, most powerfully so in affective dimensions of human experience.) The self is fully embodied, not only in the immediate physical sense, but in the wider world as well. For the Confucian moral learning is literally an education of the entire body. Ritual, music, and the martial arts harmonize both body and soul such that they become attuned to the laws of Heaven and Earth. In Christian theology the image of God is a spiritual gift separate from the body, but for the Confucian one's heavenly endowment is expressed, as Tu Wei-ming observes, in organic terms such as "physical form" (*xing*) or a "bodily design" brought about by "germination" of moral seeds.[48] Mencius calls the original heart the "great body" and it is what animates and cultivates the physical form (the "small body"). The result is a veritable fusion of the inner and the outer such that the virtues, while "rooted in [the] heart," are also manifested clearly in the face, limbs, and back.[49] This means that sages literally "image" the virtue in their bodies. Is this perhaps the ethical implication of Wittgenstein's famous statement that "meaning is a physiognomy"?[50] In contrast to some recent interpretations, I maintain that Wittgenstein joins the dialogical existentialists and Whitehead in a constructive postmodernism that merges nicely with both Confucianism and Buddhism.[51]

11 Laozi, Zhuangzi, and Nietzsche

Daoism protests not so much against gods who transcend the world as against humans masquerading as gods.

—Ellen Chen[1]

There are two limiting cases, the child and the saint, where this pawning of one's liberty . . . does not take place.

—Gabriel Marcel[2]

La vérité sort de la bouche des enfants et des fous.

—Old French saying

Time spent laughing is time spent with the gods.

—Japanese proverb

Introduction

It should be an uncontroversial thesis that the *wu wei* of Daoism stands as the very opposite of the overassertive claims of spiritual Titanism. Affirming the same integrated self as Zen Buddhism and Confucianism, Daoism rejects the dualism of matter and spirit that one finds in Jainism, Sāṃkhya-Yoga, and the Abrahamic religions. We shall find, however, that, as opposed to the social self of Confucianism, Zhuangzi's philosophy appears to join Yoga Titanism in affirming an antisocial self, which although living in the world, remains disengaged from it. On the other hand, Laozi's Daoism expresses a distinct preference for the feminine, which, as we have seen in Śākta theology, offers a necessary corrective to typical male ideas of isolation and autonomy. We have observed that spiritual Titanism can be found not only in the deification of humans beings, but also in the closely related claim of human immortality. Religious Daoism makes claims in the latter area and also transforms Laozi into a cosmic man, and the *Zhuangzi* also appears to deify the sage. These three issues, plus the question of postmodernism and Nietzsche's relation to Zhuangzi, will be discussed in this final chapter.

The first section will compare and contrast the Vedic Puruṣa and the Chinese cosmic man Panku. We shall discover that the Chinese myth has its own origins; and if there was Indo-Iranian influence, it was late and it could have made the Panku myth more anthropocentric. The second section deals with the concept of personal immortality and the "immortals" in religious Daoism and the basis that some commentators see for this idea in the *Daodejing*. The third section discusses Zhuangzi's alleged anticipation of postmodernism. We will side with those commentators who see significant differences between him and the French deconstructionists. In the fourth section we shall analyze Zhuangzi's concepts of the perfect person (*zhi ren*) and the true person (*zhen ren*). The descriptions of these remarkable characters might at first glance lead us to call them Titans, but we will argue that this would be a mistaken interpretation. In the fifth section we will look at some similarities between Zhuangzi and Nietzsche, but we will also find some important differences. (In a word, Nietzsche is ultimately more Tantric than he is Daoist.) Nevertheless, the comparative analysis with Daoism allows us to get a better idea of the childlike spontaneity and freedom that Nietzsche attributes to his *Übermensch*. In the concluding section we return to the Confucian sage as the most satisfactory answer to the spiritual Titanism.

Puruṣa and Panku

We have seen that the psychology of Titanism extends male power everywhere it can, including the act of conception itself. The story of Laozi's birth may contain a significant exception to the Indian model of the father placing a copy of himself in the womb. As Kristofer Schipper states:

> The body of the Dao is first a woman, then a child, whereas the father is entirely absent from this genesis. . . . It is the Mother in whom and through whom this transformation is accomplished. The Dao has taken form in her. Through her the Dao has been revealed.[3]

Schipper does admit that some texts indicate that an "Old Lord" (Laojun) transforms the mother's womb, but he says that *jun* doesn't necessarily mean male, because the mythological use of the word usually indicates a goddess not a god. But Schipper does allow the interpretation that the "Old Lord" is Laozi himself before his conception, so it could be that this story is not entirely different from the Indian model of the savior becoming the father of himself. If Schipper is correct, however, this is completely consistent with the Daoist (except for Zhuangzi) preference for the feminine and for the "soft" virtues. This preference did not lead to any appreciable change in women's inequality or lack of power, but it did produce at least two notable advances for Chinese women, one specific and temporary and the other more general and significant. First, in the second century C.E. religious Daoists throughout China instituted a practice of having equal numbers of male and female masters at their temples. Second, Schipper points out that China was the only ancient society where women were in control of the sexual education of their husbands.[4]

An imperial inscription of 165 C.E. indicates that Laozi had been elevated to the highest possible cosmic level: he is declared to be coeternal with the sun, moon, and the stars. If Kṛṣṇa and the Buddha could take on the *viśvarūpa* of the Puruṣa, then it was only natural that religious Daoists would also identify Laozi with Panku, the cosmic man:

> [Laozi's] left eye became the sun; his right eye, the moon; his head became mount Kunlun; his beard, the planets and constellations; his bones, dragons; his flesh, four-footed creatures; his intestines, snakes; his stomach, the sea; his fingers, the Five Peaks; his hair, trees and grasses [etc.]. . . .[5]

The Daoist philosophical texts, on the other hand, do not contain any evidence of the cosmicization of the sage. As we shall see, the Daoist sages, rather than becoming Panku, return to a state resembling primordial chaos (*hundun*). It is an act of merging and not one of anthropomorphic projection. Therefore, just as we have seen with regard to Confucius, the deification and cosmicization of Laozi happened in the religious tradition and not in the philosophical texts.

The Chinese myth of the cosmic man Panku appears to have some similarities with the Puruṣa hymn of the Ṛgveda, particularly with regard to the theme of dismemberment:

> After the death of Panku, his breath became the wind and clouds, his voice the thunder, his left and right eyes the sun and moon, his four limbs and the five "bodies" (fingers) the four quarters of the earth and five great mountains, his blood the rivers, his muscles and veins the strata of earth, his flesh the soil, his hair and beard the constellations, his skin and body-hair the plants and trees, his teeth and bone the metals and stones, his marrow gold and precious stones, and his sweat the rain.[6]

The most striking difference between the two myths is that no living beings or artifacts come directly from the Chinese giant's body, whereas creations from the Puruṣa's body include such things as gods, animals, scripture, and humans arranged according to caste. More important is the fact that in the Chinese view Heaven and Earth already exist, having both arisen out of chaos (*hundun*), and it is Panku's job to open up a space between the two so that a natural and cultural world can evolve. In the Puruṣa hymn the cosmic man encompasses the entire universe: he is three quarters Heaven and one quarter Earth. Only in the later versions of the Chinese myth does Panku also create Heaven and Earth, and this more anthropocentric version could have been the result of a Chinese adaptation of the Puruṣa theme as the cosmological body of Buddha. Therefore, in the original Chinese view the balance of the Cosmic Triad is preserved whereas the integrity of Heaven and Earth is compromised in both the Puruṣa hymn and in the later Chinese version.

The Panku myth is intimately connected to a totemic dog-deity named Panhu, who was worshiped by the Man tribes in South China. Besides their linguistic affinity, the two are also closely connected with primordial chaos (*hundun*) and, alternatively, creation out of a calabash gourd (*hulu*) or cosmic egg. (Prajāpati and Puruṣa are also said to have come out of a golden embryo [*hiraṇyagarbha*].) The connection to Panhu may explain why Panku has animal as well as human characteristics: "two horns projected from his head, and two tusks from his upper jaw. His body was thickly covered with hair."[7] Although the Indian tradition has its share of theriomorphic deities, all are of Purāṇic and therefore late derivation. (The intriguing exception of course is the horned figure of the Harrapans whom some take to be a proto-Śiva.) No such animal characteristics are attached to the Puruṣa—hence a more anthropomorphic figure—and who, as we have seen, becomes identified as a cosmic yogi in the

Purāṇas. Therefore, scholars are justified in holding to an independent Chinese origin of the Panku myth.

It is also important to note the pivotal role that a goddess plays in the Panku and Panhu myths. Just as a feminine principle Virāj is present in the Puruṣa hymn so does Panku appear to be androgynous, combining both the *yin* and the *yang*. The principal goddess is called Nugua and her origins, like Panhu's, are theriomorphic: she is most closely associated with snakes, snails, and frogs. She is most often paired with Fuxi the "ox-tamer" and is credited with repairing the damage of the Great Deluge. She is also associated with a time in China when people knew "their mothers rather than their fathers," and also significant is the masculinization of Nugua in later patriarchal ages.[8] After the Great Deluge she is said to have given birth to a son, a "queer thing" called *hundun* with no anus or urinary opening. After pondering the matter for a while, Nugua and her husband decided to cut up their child and the pieces became the people of the world.

Whereas the *Daodejing* frequently speaks of origins in the Mother and the feminine, the primordial ground of the *Zhuangzi* appears to be gender neutral. (In several passages Zhuangzi reverses the traditional qualities of the *yin* and the *yang*;[9] but, if this is a deliberate privileging of the feminine, it does not at all effect the general antisocial attitude of his sage.) While the dismemberment of Panku gives us the natural world, the "boring" of Hundun in the *Zhuangzi* (end of chap. 7) produces, as it does in the Nugua story, the human world. This elegant and concise parable tells the story of three emperors: Shu of the South Sea (symbolizing *yin*), Hu of the North Sea (representing *yang*), and Hundun of the Center. Shu and Hu met Hundun in the Center and their host treated them very graciously. Wanting to repay Hundun for his hospitality and noticing that Hundun did not have the seven human orfices, Shu and Hu proceeded to create an opening for Hundun on each successive day. Their kindness was very ill conceived and Hundun died on the seventh day. Max Kaltenmark captures the Daoist moral of this story: "An untimely zeal [of Hu and Shu] would wish to make it [Hundun] like everybody else, and initiate it into civilized life by giving it the sense organs that destroy its unity. The myth is a perfect symbol of the Founding Kings' original sin."[10]

For the Daoist true kindness and reciprocity need no acknowledgment; indeed, Shu and Hu's gesture, just like any human moral response, is always bound to have elements of self-interest and insincerity. For the Daoist destructive chaos is made by humans, who are always too "hurried" and "hasty" (Victor Mair's translation of Shu and Hu). This agitated chaos is different from the natural chaos of Hundun, who is just right (*ziran*) as it is. Most importantly, the original sin in this story is anthropocentricism, a fault that Zhuangzi continually attempts to rectify by constant reference to the nonhuman realm and nonhuman values.

There is a direct connection between the "uncarved block" (*pu*) of the *Daodejing* and the unbored Hundun. The *Zhuangzi* is populated with sages who have returned to this self-contained state. There is the *zhen ren* of chapter 6 who breathes from his heels rather than from the nose and mouth. Later in the same chapter Confucius says that the sages "forget liver and gall, cast aside ears and eyes. . . ."[11] Near the end of this chapter we find that Yierhzi has been tattooed with *ren* and *yi*, the moral equivalent of the boring of the senses. Pierced as he is with these marks, Yierzi cannot wander free like the sage. Only after these moral tattoos have been "wipe[d] away" will Yierzi be liberated and be like Hundun again. Right at the end of chap. 6 Yen Hui describes "sitting" and "forgetting" in terms of letting his "organs and members drop away [and] dismiss[ing] eyesight and hearing." In chap. 11 Big Concealment (Hungmeng) says to Cloud Chief: "Smash your form and body, spit out hearing and eyesight. . . . and you may join in a great unity with deep and boundless . . . dark and undifferentiated chaos (*hundun*). . . ."[12] Only then can Cloud Chief be a Great Person (*da ren*) and "a true friend of Heaven and Earth."[13] In Hinduism and Christianity the creation of order out of chaos is good and redemptive. Daoism sees it very differently.

Immortality and the Immortals

There is one line in the *Daodejing* that some commentators and translators believe are grounds for a belief in personal immortality. The last line of chap. 33 is translated by Henry Wei as: "He who dies but yet does not perish becomes immortal."[14] Most other translations do not support Wei's meaning, which may be influenced by the eternalist beliefs of his publishers, the Theosophical Society. The Wangbi text literally reads: "One who dies without being forgotten has longevity."[15] This has led some to conjecture that the Daoist belief is very close to the Confucian (or even the Hebrew) view that one's "immortality" lies in being remembered for one's deeds and virtues.

Ellen Chen rejects this interpretation as inconsistent with the self-effacing Dao and Daoists who are supposed to model the Dao. Instead she takes her lead from Wangbi's commentary, which reads: "Whoever dies, but whose Dao by which he lived does not perish, completes his longevity. The body is gone, but the Dao still exists."[16] People are "immortal" only insofar as they are one with the Dao. Furthermore, the phrases "immortal Dao" or "eternal Dao" may also be misleading, giving the false impression of Indian or Christian ideas of immutable spiritual substance. The character *chang* very often qualifies the Dao, and the rendering "eternal" should be replaced by something like "constant" or "steady." For example, in chap. 16 Wing-tsit Chan proposes that one becomes "everlasting" by being in accord with an "eternal" Dao, while Michael LaFargue says that "one lasts very long" following the "steady" Dao.[17]

Other passages in the *Daodejing* also allude to a human state that may appear deathless or eternal, but we should call these people balanced and invulnerable rather than immortal or eternal. Those who are immune to weapons and to the attacks of wild animals because they have no "death spot"[18] have stayed, as the first stanza implies, in tune with the Dao. Proposing a life-death dialectic, the poet tells us that the "thirteen body parts" (four limbs and nine orifices) are both "life-givers" and "death-bringers." (The myth of piercing the Hundun is obviously in the background here.) Thus, those who have "lived life . . . lavishly" have dissipated their *de*, but those who have preserved their *de*—the abundant *de* of the child—will not die prematurely. Like the Hundun, people should "stop the apertures, close the doors,"[19] and then they can save their life (*shen*). With "accumulated *de*" people can, just like Nietzsche's *Übermenschen*, become "all overcoming" and "have long life and enduring vision."[20]

The immortals (*xian*) of religious Daoism should be interpreted much in the same way as these sages from the *Daodejing*. They are more fantastic and eccentric, more like Zhuangzi's fabulous characters, but there are fundamental similarities. There are innumerable immortals, so we will touch on only some of the most notable. At the time of his story Zhongli Chuan was six hundred years old and a master of the art of inner alchemy. He inducted Lu Dungbin as a fellow immortal by a simple test of character. Zhongli required that Lu do many good deeds, and he offered him some false gold to expedite the process of helping poor people become rich. Lu refused to use alchemy to achieve his goal, proved that he had a good heart, and immediately entered into Zhongli's instruction. The immortals, however, were not paragons of conventional virtue, for Lu seduced a maiden Ho Xiengu

(White Peony) and his powerful semen made her one of the immortals. Lan Caiho was a musician of indeterminate sex, who exclaimed "I'm pregnant all year long" and who could mediate easily between the *yin* and the *yang*; Cao Guojin was a drunken geomancer; Zhang Guolao was a former minister who rode a mule backward; and every night Li Tieguai returned to a gourd to sleep, reenacting the Daoist return to the Hundun. In addition to their eccentric behavior the immortals are known primarily, just as the Buddhist Siddhas are, for their humanitarian aid to the poor and oppressed.[21]

The translation of *xian* as "immortal" is misleading (Victor Mair would rather call them transcendents), because these beings are not gods even in the sense of the popular Chinese religion. The character *xian* is composed of two glyphs—human being and mountain—and if we use these as a guide to the meaning of *xian* we would get "people of the mountains" or even "human mountain." Phonologically, *xian* is related to such meanings as "to change," "to evolve," and "to dance," which provides another link to the self-transforming sages of philosophical Daoism. Although they are known to help the harvests in the plains, they do not themselves eat grains. They also "protect the land,"[22] perhaps an indirect recognition of the importance of mountain watersheds. (Zhuangzi's *shen ren* "keeps creatures free from plagues and makes the grain ripen every year.")[23] In contrast to the gods of the cities, who command formal worship and sacrifice, the immortals are not bound by religious rite, philosophical doctrine, or political administration. This is entirely consistent with their natures, which are completely free and spontaneous, providing the people of the plains with symbols of personal liberation, play, and boundless joy.

We now take an abrupt comparative leap to the "immortals" of Herman Hesse's *Steppenwolf*. (Actually, as a devoted Nietzschean Hesse's place in this chapter is very appropriate.) At the beginning of the novel the protagonist Harry Haller is trapped in a dualistic wolf-man persona, which is gradually replaced with a view of the "onion" self, a thousand layered self that Hesse drew either from Asian or Nietzschean sources (or both). Hesse's immortals symbolize the free self-transformation that is possible if one embraces this idea of the soul. Harry encounters Goethe in a dream and he chides this immortal for taking himself so seriously and for betraying the spirit of Romanticism. Harry contrasts Goethe to Mozart, who "did not make pretensions in his own life to the enduring and the orderly and to exalted dignity as you did. He did not think himself so important! He sang his divine melodies and died [young]."[24] (The movie *Amadeus* portrays Mozart exactly in this way.) Goethe's response is a veritable act of Daoist self-transformation: he changes into Mozart, then to Schubert, and the once stiff old figure begins to dance. (Hesse's immortals also have a laughter that is, as Nietzsche once said, "no human laughter," but a cosmic laughter that flows naturally from a recognition of the fluidity and absurdity of the universe.) Harry also learns how to dance and his teacher is a lovely creature of indeterminate sex—Hermine/Herman—who compels him to follow both the bliss and the chaos of his thousand selves.

There are at least three conclusions to be drawn from this section. First, those who claim that the *Daodejing* contains a doctrine of personal immortality are misguided. Second, the immortals of religious Daoism and *Steppenwolf* are definitely not Titans. They do not take on divine attributes or prerogatives; in fact, they would hold up to ridicule and howl with laughter at anyone who would. Third, Hesse's allusions to the self returning to the Mother, then the dualistic wolf-man self, and finally the onion self suggest a dialectical progression from premodern unity, through modern duality, to the fragmented self of postmodernism.

Zhuangzi and Postmodernism

Because of his skepticism, relativism, and extreme distrust of language, some writers have proposed that Zhuangzi is the ancient Chinese equivalent of Jacques Derrida. Zhuangzi subtly attacks the logocentrism of the Mohists: their argumentative confidence, their firm belief that reason can alter human behavior, and their ethical universalism. Although Confucius and Mencius have nothing equivalent to the Greek idea of *logos*, Zhuangzi nevertheless criticizes Confucius' rectification of names and Mencius' concept of innate ethical dispositions. In the playful dialogues of the *Zhuangzi* Confucius is made to turn on his own doctrines and to assure his favorite disciple Yen Hui that it is not necessary that names and things correspond to one another. After observing that Mengsun was "mourning" without doing the requisite actions prescribed by *Li*, Yen Hui despaired that he had "no words to name them."[25] Later Confucius is made to concede that people have been crippled by *ren* and *yi*, and that the Daoist sages have completely transcended the constraints of Confucian morality. In this exchange at the end of chap. 6 the roles are reversed, and Yen Hui, who already in the *Analects* appears inclined to Daoism, shocks his master by admitting that he has forgotten not only *ren* and *yi*, but also *Li* and music. It is clear that Zhuangzi has "deconstructed" both Mohist theories (closest to the Greeks of any Chinese philosophy) and the Confucian codification of Zhou traditions.

David Loy proposes that both Nāgārjuna and Zhuangzi express the method of French deconstruction in several seminal ways.[26] First, there is the deconstruction of the self, which is part of a larger project of demonstrating, at least in Buddhism, that no thing whatever has self-existence. Second, there is the complete subversion of all distinctions: the finite/infinite, appearance/reality, true/false, good/evil, and even life/death. For Nāgārjuna this is usually accomplished with a neither/nor dialectic, while Zhuangzi synthesizes the opposites in a both-and dialectic. The resolution of these distinctions is based on a basic axiom common to both Buddhism and Daoism: that things are internally, not externally related to one another. Derrida's concept of *différance* performs the same function, namely, showing how things, if pressed enough, turn into their opposites, vindicating the Daoist dictum that "reversal is the action of the Dao."[27] When Zhuangzi asks us to consider the fact that very big things from one perspective might be very small from another, then "we have perceived the laws of difference."[28]

Mark Berkson points out a third similarity between Derrida and Zhaungzi: they both believe in the complete arbitrariness of signifiers. As Zhuangzi states: "Things are so because they are called so"; and "a name is only a guest of reality,"[29] undermining the connection between words and things at the heart of Confucian philosophy. Because "speech has no constancy,"[30] Zhuangzi might even have agreed with Derrida that once a word is spoken it can never have the same meaning in any of its successive uses. Zhuangzi and Derrida realize that they may be subject to the criticism that they, too, are attempting to use language to communicate their linguistic skepticism; but both of them, according to Berkson, meet this criticism with an apophatic (from the Greek *apophasis*=denial) use of language. Zhuangzi is especially clever in the use of this strategy. For example, he is constantly warning his readers of the completely vulnerable nature of what is he saying: "I'm going to try speaking some reckless words and I want you to listen to them recklessly."[31] As Berkson states: "The [apophatic] writer often begins with an apology that says, in effect, although I have no choice but to use language here, I won't be using it in *that* way, and please don't take it as such."[32] Derrida typically warns his readers by saying that some words are being written "under erasure." Borrowing a technique from the later Heidegger, Derrida will place an "X" on a word so as to call its fixed meaning into question. These procedures lead to the creation of texts that are extremely playful and also very obscure.

If the basis for clear distinction and differentiation is subverted, then judgments about true/false or good/evil are ultimately groundless. Skepticism about knowledge claims and moral relativism, so argues the deconstructionist, follow necessarily. Zhuangzi, however, has another solution. Behind the infinite play of signifiers, there is the Dao, and Zhuangzi never rejects its existence and never denies that conforming to the Dao is what we ought to do. Whereas it is arguable whether Nāgārjuna accepts or rejects an ultimate reality—the subtlety of his dialectic is consummate—the text of the *Zhuangzi* is unequivocal about the existence of the Dao and our access to it through "illumination." "The sage . . . opens things up to the light of Heaven."[33] "Wherever we walk, how can the Way be absent?" he says, and its linguistic equivalent is "whatever the standpoint, how can saying be unallowable?"[34] The literal meaning of *dao*, after all, is "track" or "road," and any road is walkable and even rough ones are at least climbable. Therefore, the Way is walkable, and if we are careful with our language, it is talkable, too. At least the figurative language of the *Daodejing* and the *Zhuangzi* is acceptable talk about the Dao. At most, by another interpretation of this passage, we can say that all language gets at the Dao (words and things could not exist without it), but only partially and only indirectly. Zhuangzi never gives up on words, for he even wants to have "a word" with the man "who has forgotten words."[35] Berkson's image of someone turning on the lights in a dark room full of people groping around with flashlights is a brilliant analogy to explain Zhuangzi's idea of illumination and to show that he ultimately parts company with French deconstruction.[36] Derrida believes that we are producing ever increasing polyvalent meanings, while Zhuangzi believes that the sage discovers a univocal, transcendent meaning of the Dao whose worldly meanings are irreducibly polyvalent.

Returning to the comparison between Zhuangzi and Nāgārjuna, Loy's claim that both philosophers point to a nondual reality beyond language may not be correct. While Kalupahana's rejection of the traditional absolutist interpretation of Nāgārjuna is still much in dispute (it is enough to confirm Kalupahana's point that this was certainly not the Buddha's view), we should side with Berkson's view that what the sage discovers is the equality of all perspectives, not their complete identity. The monistic interpretation is supported by passages such as the one at the beginning of chap. 4: "The Way doesn't want things mixed with it. When it becomes a mixture, it becomes many ways; with many ways, there is a bustle; and where there is a lot of bustle, there is trouble—trouble that has no remedy!"[37] This passage expresses the odd implication that competing linguistic and cultural worlds are completely alien to the Dao, which, if the Dao is the source of all perspectives, cannot be correct. In any case the passage does not imply that these worlds are illusory; their existence and the trouble they cause are very real. Furthermore, this passage once again supports the Dao as the norm, a view that undermines a deconstructionist interpretation of Zhuangzi.

That Zhuangzi's vision is more pluralistic than monistic is supported by many texts. Heaven blows "on the ten thousand things in a different way, so that each can be itself—all take what they want for themselves. . . ."[38] Ordinary people forget who the great piper is and claim absolute truth for their own perspectives, whereas the sage acknowledges the relative truth of all of them. (Here the gap between Derrida and Zhuangzi is greatest: Derrida recognizes the relative truth of all perspectives, but would never commit himself to an ontological source for them.) As Berkson states: "Each individual is unique and sounds different (will have a different viewpoint and nature), but underlying all is the sound of Heaven; behind all of the differences, there is an all-encompassing, underlying Dao."[39] Knowledge is indeed possible—it is, in Kwang-ming Wu's incredibly playful translation, "huge" and it "widens, widens"—while perspectival knowledge is "small" and it is "picky, picky"; "huge words burn, burn; small words chat, chat."[40]

If the Dao exists and if we are exhorted to conform to its norms, then Zhuangzi is not the skeptic or relativist that many have taken him to be. Recently a number of scholars have constructed cogent arguments against both of these claims. Philip J. Ivanhoe looks at Zhuangzi from the standpoints of four types on skepticism: sense, ethical, epistemological, and language skepticism, and concludes that Zhuangzi can only be called a language skeptic and a qualified epistemological skeptic.[41] ("Great Understanding" as intuitive knowledge of the Dao is available to the sage or to the "knack" master.) As we have just seen, being skeptical about discursive speech to capture the Dao does not undermine either Zhuangzi's commitment to the Dao nor his belief that there is a correct way to follow it. Paul Kjellberg argues that Zhuangzi's skepticism is very much like the Greek's; it is a therapeutic method designed to effect an *epoché*, a suspension of judgment about conventions that distort reality and confine the human spirit. With regard to relativism, it holds only among various language games and not the Heaven's eye perspective of the sage, similar to the "bird's eye" (*guan*) view of the *Daodejing*.[42]

If Zhuangzi is not a desconstructive postmodernist, can he be construed as a constructive postmodernist? Daoism joins Buddhism in offering a basic process philosophy that informs much of contemporary constructive postmodernism. One might say, however, that the Dao represents a premodern totality from which all things arise, to which all things must conform, and to which all things must eventually return. The fact that the Daoist sage must model the Hundun, a primordial unity without openings, appears distinctively premodern. A premodernist interpretation of Daoism is much better grounded in the *Daodejing*, but it probably does not do justice to Zhuangzi's philosophical brilliance and innovation. As we have just seen, Zhuangzi's view of reality is not simply monistic, but a rather sophisticated idea of plural linguistic worlds.

Paul Kjellberg takes a view opposite to Loy by locating language's difficulty not in the fact that its constant categorizing fails in the face of an undifferentiated reality; rather, it fails because reality is far more subtly differentiated than we can ever imagine or language could ever express. (*The Tao of Physics* notwithstanding, contemporary physics appears to confirm this as well as today's forms of process pluralism.) If ultimate reality were totally unstructured, then Zhuangzi's "knack" masters, who most commentators see as on par with the sage, could not possibly operate. We must assume that the "natural veins" (*tian li*, like veins of jade says Fung Yulan)[43] that Cook Ding follow are very real and, by analogy, mark off real divisions of the Dao, divisions that ordinary conventions and language always obscure. According to A. C. Graham's translation of *tian li*, Cook Ding is following "Heaven's structuring," just as Woodcarver Qing "matches Heaven with Heaven," and just as Plato's dialectical butcher is following the *logos*.[44] If Dao has a *logos*, then Zhuangzi is definitely not a deconsturctionist. Finally, we should remember that Lord Wenhui acknowledges the moral implications of Cook Ding's skill. He praises him not for his butchering expertise, but because the amazing cook teaches Wenhui "how to nurture life."[45]

David L. Hall offers a pluralist interpretation of Daoism that might go too far. Hall shows that contemporary postmodernism is driven by perceptions of difference, and he is correct in his assumption that Derrida's *différance* is related to Heidegger's principle of the ontological *Differenz* between Being and beings. From my own work on Heidegger's *Differenz*, I have concluded that Being is best interpreted in terms of Kant's transcendental conditions for the possibility of experience, rather than the more traditional idea of the ground of being. (If I am correct about Heidegger, he, at least in his early period, stands among the constructive postmodernists and not among the deconstructionists.) Drawing out the implications of Hall's ideas, one could say that the premodern vision privileges Being as the ground of existence and conceives of beings in a holistic relationship with Being. Hall suggests that Parmenides gave the first philosophical expression to this position by arguing that only Being exists and that existence of plural beings is self-contradictory.

Modernism produced an array of responses to this, ranging from removing Being=God to a transcendent realm to reducing Being to the matter of scientific materialism. The postmodern revolution of Derrida of course attempts to eliminate all vestiges of this metaphysics of presence. As Hall explains: "It is feasible . . . to ask after the differences among beings without admitting the possibility of any ontological contrast. On such a reading there is no ontological ground."[46] Hall's proposal that philosophical Daoism embodies this position is not at all supported by the texts. As just argued, the *Daodejing* most likely represents a premodern position, while the *Zhuangzi* anticipates a constructive postmodernism that validates multiple perspectives without rejecting the idea of an ontological ground or even ontological structure. Hall argues that in the *Daodejing* the dialectical relation of *you* and *wu* is found in individual beings and their negations, such that the former are the "named" and the latter are the "nameless." Hall's thesis stands as a weak third to the two principal views of the use of these terms in the first chapter of the *Daodejing*. The "modern" interpretation holds that the Dao can be named as non-Being (not Hall's non-being), while the "traditional" interpretation insists that the Dao as Being cannot be named at all.[47] With regard to Zhuangzi, Hall's interpretation would make impossible his "Great Knowledge"—the illumination that comes in seeing all perspectives from the standpoint of the Dao.

Zhuangzi clearly recognized the fatal flaws in what we now call the modernist distinctions of fact/value and is/ought; and, in his anticipation of Derridian *différance*, he offers a distinctively postmodernist, rather than premodernist, solution. His concept of self is the most difficult to articulate. Neither Confucians nor Daoists ever posit the autonomous self that we have found in Jainism and Sāṃkhya-Yoga, but the social-relational Confucian self, which melds with constructive postmodernism, is rejected in the *Zhuangzi*. (The sage's self is distinctively nonsocial, in terms of the necessity of relating to other human beings; but, ironically, it is fully relational in terms of its connection to all natural things.) As we have already seen, the Buddha deconstructed the self, but that did not mean that the self was thereby completely "decentered," as Derrida would hold. The Buddhist self is still very much a locus of agency and moral responsibility. However we decide to describe the Daoist self, there is one thing that we can say for sure: Zhuangzi's sages, even in all their many self-transformations, are definitely more centered than the Derridean fragmented self. We shall now see if the Daoist sage is like the Confucian sage with regard to the attribute of "divinity."

Zhuangzi and the Perfect Person

In this section we shall investigate the meanings of several Daoist ideal persons and compare them with the spiritual Titans of previous chapters. The phrasing differs, but it appears that they all refer to the same spiritual person. Throughout the chapters of the *Zhuangzi,* he or she is called perfect person (*zhi ren*), true person (*zhen ren*), spirit person (*shen ren*), great person (*da ren*), complete person (*cheng ren*), the sage (*sheng*), and person of virtue (*de ren*). (Occasionally one appears higher than the other, and, as Graham observes, the great man of the Outer Chapters is uncharacteristically intellectual.)[48] The Zhuangzi of the Inner Chapters tends to describe the sage in hyperbolic terms. The following passage, in Watson's translation, is typical:

> The Perfect Man is godlike. Though the great swamps blaze, they cannot burn him; though the great rivers freeze, they cannot chill him; though swift lightning splits the hills and howling gales shake the sea, they cannot frighten him. A man like this rides the clouds and mist, straddles the sun and moon, and wanders beyond the four seas. Even life and death have no effect on him, much less the rules of profit and loss.[49]

Throughout the entire *Zhuangzi* the perfect person is portrayed as immune to the exigencies of the world, but the sages in the Outer Chapters do not undertake great transcendent journeys. (In this respect they are more like the sages of the *Daodejing*.) The only exception is Confucius' description of Laozi as a dragon "riding on the breath of the clouds, feeding on the yin and yang."[50]

Regarding the "perfect man" passage, there are at least two problems that need to be addressed: (1) are perfect persons being deified; and (2) what are we to make of their fantastic trips? Let us look at five translations of the phrase *zhi ren shen*:

> Burton Watson: "The Perfect Man is godlike."
> Wing-tsit Chan: "The perfect man is a spiritual being."
> A. C. Graham: "The utmost man is daemonic."
> Fung Yulan: "The perfect man is mysterious."
> Kwang-ming Wu: "The ultimately arrived man is spirit-filled."[51]

Following our analysis of Mencius' use of *shen* in chap. 9, we note once again that *shen* is standing as a predicate adjective and its meaning then should be "wonderful, marvelous, miraculous." Linking the sage with the knackmasters, Wu agrees with this line of thinking: the *zhi ren* is "daemonically marvelous, skillful, versatile."[52] Noting three interrelated meanings of *shen*, Wu proposes a cosmic sense in which *qi* and *shen* are functionally equivalent, a psychological meaning of human vitality (the Greek *pyschē*), and a special instance in which the sage or the knackmaster, because of their openness to the Dao, receive an extra charge of cosmic *shen*. They become veritable geniuses in their chosen tasks. As Wu states: "This is almost like the Socratic daemon, though without its nagging foreboding, forbidding connotations."[53] We can safely conclude that the *zhi ren* are not divine beings as we have defined them in the introduction; they are not "godlike" but they are definitely "spirit-filled." Although Xunzi's sage becomes a *zhi ren* because of his virtuous actions, his idea of *shenming*, as a divine enhancement, is comparable to Wu's third meaning of *shen*.

Now, how are we to take the descriptions of the incredible journeys of the *zhi ren*? Are they just part of what Lee Yearly calls Zhuangzi's "rhetoric of exaggeration"; or shall we see them as examples of the incredible hubris of the Indian yogis, who also flew through the heavens and claimed the power of a thousand gods? One hypothesis could be that these heavenly journeys are descriptions of shamanistic visions, but Zhuangzi always condemns the shaman and elevates his *zhi ren* instead. For example, the shaman considers pigs inauspicious, but the perfect person finds them auspicious. However, the fact that Daoist sages considers them so does not necessarily mean that they would find any other animal inauspicious. Instead, they would reject completely the conventional distinction between the two. We should, however, not dismiss outright the possibility that shamanism was the origin of these fantastic images.[54] Robert Eno phrases the issue this way:

> The shamanic universe of the *Zhuangzi* relentlessly reflects a fundamental duality between the empowered and the non-empowered: those whose focus allows them to manipulate this protean Nature and transcend the limits it initially seems to place on human life, and those who remain imprisoned within those limits.[55]

If shamanism is defined in this more general way, then Eno is correct in associating Zhuangzi with it.

Chapter 7 of the *Zhuangzi* contains a detailed story about the shaman Jixian, who is characterized as *shen*, rendered "daemonic" by Graham, a "shaman of the gods" by Watson, and a "wonderful wizard" by Fung.[56] The Daoist Liezi, a student of Huzi, has been momentarily captivated by Jixian, who "could tell whether men would live or die, survive or perish, be fortunate or unfortunate, live a long time or die young, and he would predict the year, month, week, and day as though he were a god himself."[57] Huzi asks Liezi to bring the shaman to him, and Huzi proceeds to baffle and befuddle the wizard on successive visits. It is clear that Zhuangzi sees the shaman as completely entrenched in the conventions and superstitions of his society. Whereas the shaman has a predictable form, Jixian fails "to physiognomize" Huzi, who, like the Dao, transforms himself on each visit. On the final visit Jixian runs off before he meets the sage, presumably out of fear that he too will lose his form.

The perfect persons do not divine nor do they prognosticate; they do breathe from their heels—suggesting a distinction between a yogi and a shaman—but the clear indication is that Daoist sages transcend any possible categorization whatever. Just after the story of Huzi and the shaman, Zhuangzi describes the perfect person as one like a mirror, someone who reflects the self-transformations of the Dao rather than imposing linguistic and cultural forms on it. The sage and the knackmaster both have mirrorlike selves such that Cook Ding can follow "Heaven's structuring" or Woodcarver Qing can match "Heaven with Heaven."[58] Graham's rendering of "what is Heaven's" and the appearance of *shen* immediately thereafter demonstrates that the knackmaster is joining his *shen*, which is of Heaven, with the *shen* of Heaven.

Except for Laozi flying like a dragon on the wind in chap. 14, hyperbolic descriptions of the sage are contained in the Inner Chapters, where we are also introduced to monsters, cripples, and other odd creatures. This suggests that they join the flying sages as part of Zhuangzi's rhetorical strategy to jolt us out of the conventional world and to express the complete freedom of the sage. Just as we are not to take the man with his organs jumbled up literally, so are we not to believe that the Daoist sages actually fly through the air. Zhuangzi introduces one of these descriptions with an "apophatic" warning:

> I'm going to try speaking some reckless words and I want you to listen to them recklessly. How will that be? The sage leans on the sun and moon, tucks the universe under his arm, merges himself with things, leaves the confusion and muddle as it is, and looks on slaves as exalted.[59]

As a language skeptic Zhuangzi never wants us to take him literally, and through this hyperbolic language he expresses indirectly the total freedom of the spiritual person.

There is another reason why the Daoist sage is not a spiritual Titan. The extreme humanism of Titanism, in which human agency is exaggerated, is inverted in Daoism by the fact that it is Heaven/Nature (*tian*) that works through the perfect person. Using the technique of "fasting of the mind," the Daoist sage empties himself of everything, including any notion of self. In chapter 4 of the *Zhuangzi* Confucius teaches Yen Hui the specific techniques: first he listens with his ear and then listens with his heart/mind (*xin*), but then he must leave both of these to tap into the energy (*qi*) of the universe. As Graham states:

> Then the self dissolves, energies strange to him and higher than his own (the "daemonic" [*shen*]) enter from the outside, the agent of his actions is no longer the man but Heaven working through him, yet paradoxically . . . in discovering a deeper self he becomes for the first time truly the agent.[60]

In most passages Zhuangzi favors Heaven/Nature over the human, and only occasionally does he invert this priority, probably to make sure that we do not take this as a conceptualized dichotomy. In the *zhi ren* Heaven and the human are fully integrated, but, as we have just argued, not unified without differentiation.

Yet another reason why the Daoist sage is not a Titan is the fact that she is portrayed not as a Nietzschean lion but as a Nietzschean child. In chapter 6 of the *Zhuangzi* we meet an old Woman "Crookback" (Watson's translation), who, after hearing the Dao, now has the look of a child. The idea that a physical old person has the "look" of a child is a clue that the child image is a symbol for something more than just an infant or a juvenile. In chapter 23 of the *Zhuangzi*, Laozi draws on some of the positive qualities of the infant:

> Can you be rude and unwitting? Can you be a little baby? The baby howls all day, yet its throat never gets hoarse—harmony at its height! The baby makes fists all day, yet its fingers never get cramped—virtue [*de*] is all it holds to. The baby stares all day without blinking its eyes—it has no preferences in the world of externals.[61]

The sentence about the baby crying all day also appears in chapter 55 of the *Daodejing*, which says that the child possesses its full allotment of *de* and the "perfection of its life-force (*jing*)."[62] The third stanza, however, speaks of the use of heart/mind (*xin*) to direct creative energy (*qi*), which suggests a conscious effort to conform to the Dao. The quoted passage from the *Zhuangzi* suggests that learning from the child is only preparatory to becoming a *zhi ren*. Modeling the fist that never cramps and the throat that never gets hoarse allows "the freeing of the ice-bound, the thawing of the frozen."[63] Unlike the ordinary child, the perfect person, like the person in the tenth ox-herding picture, returns to society, leads an ordinary life, may even become a ruler, but never becomes entangled in human affairs. The perfect person may be as old and deformed as the hunchbacked woman, but she now has the look and qualities of a child.

In chapter 4 of the *Zhuangzi* Yenhui says that while being "outwardly compliant" one must be "inwardly direct." Only then can one be a "companion of Heaven" and be equal to the Son of Heaven. One will then be, as Graham translates it, "excused by others as childlike."[64] But you should ignore those who dismiss you like this, because by being merely outwardly compliant they are only "companion[s] of men." The meaning here appears to be that what is most important is being inwardly in tune with the Dao, a state that returns us to the condition of a child. For the *Daodejing* this state represents the fullness of *de*, the original power that each of us has by virtue of being part of the Dao. As children we all had full possession of life force that is the Dao—full possession of what Nietzsche called the will to power.

Zhuangzi and Nietzsche

With regard to the will to power contemporary Nietzsche scholarship has corrected yet another major misunderstanding of Nietzsche's philosophy, and it has given us yet another reason to reject the thesis that Nietzsche proposes some form of spiritual Titanism. The will to power is not an individual, egoistic will but it is the life force itself, described by Graham Parkes as "the matrix of forces that animate all sentient beings."[65] This interpretation is supported by Nietzsche's statement that the will to power is not simply the self's "desiring" or "commanding," but nature's "fundamental will stands revealed" in its "total organic process."[66] He makes the provocative charge that the "will of psychology. . . . does not exist at all,"[67] and that our grammar has seduced us into thinking that there must be a subject to the will in itself. If the will to power is the life force, then the grammatical mistake is clear when we ask the absurd question: does life itself have a will to live?

With this interpretation of the will to power before us, comparisons to Chinese philosophy are much more apt and instructive. Roger T. Ames has done one of the most insightful studies, focusing on the Daoist *de* and on the will to power. Ames proposes that the relationship of *de* and *dao* is one in which the Dao is like a field of creative energy out of which its particular manifestations arise as many *de*.[68] An instructive parallel would be Whitehead's actual occasions arising out of what he called creativity. Ames's description of Daoist ontology as hylozoistic is also compatible with Whitehead's view that actual occasions are psychophysical unities. Nietzsche and the Daoists, however, are metaphysically closer, because they reject the idea that there are universals (Whitehead calls them eternal objects) by which the creative field is structured and ordered. (A focus on Zhuangzi's *tian li*—Heaven's structuring—may bring him closer to Whitehead.) This ontological pluralism supports the perspectivism that we find in Nietzsche and Zhuangzi. The principal difference is that the Daoist sage can, as we have seen, transcend all perspectives and attain a state of illumination of the Dao as a whole. The Daoist would disagree with Zarathustra's "Daoism": "'This is *my* way; where is yours?' thus I answered those who asked me 'the way.' For *the* way—that does not exist."[69] Both the Confucians and the Daoists believe in *the* way, a single, broad path that has, as Herbert Fingarette has astutely observed, no crossroads.[70]

While Ames overlooks this significant difference, he nevertheless succeeds with his most insightful point: the creative potential in both *de* and the will to power allows the Daoists and Nietzsche to see person-making and self-transformation as a creative art form. As Ames explains: "The weight of the Daoist discussion tends to be cosmological, not in the abstract sense of 'a science of first principles,' but in the aesthetic sense of *ars contextualis*, 'the art of contextualization' or 'composition.'"[71] Ames observes that the Confucians share this aesthetic cosmology and we will argue later that their version of it should be preferred.

Daoist and Nietzschean self-transformation requires a world in which all substances—including an immutable soul and an eternal God—are eliminated. The Daoists would agree with Zarathustra's claim that "it is of time and becoming that the best parables should speak: let them be a praise and a justification of all impermanence."[72] (Permanent substance, says Nietzsche, is an empty fiction, invented by pure reason.)[73] This radical process philosophy allows for the actualization of innumerable identities (recall that Huzi had a new "self" every time Jixian visited), which Nietzsche described as "a multiplicity of subjects, whose interaction and struggle is the basis of our thought and our consciousness in general."[74] In *The Twilight of the Idols* the Dionysian is described as being able to enter "into any skin, into any affect: he constantly transforms himself."[75]

Zarathustra also proclaims: "I overcame myself, the sufferer; I carried my own ashes to the mountains; I invented a brighter flame for myself. And behold, then this ghost fled from me."[76] Self-overcoming is of course self-transformation, and Zarathustra has carried to the mountains the ashes of the conventional self that he has destroyed. There he has fashioned a new self: "How could you want to become new without first becoming ashes."[77] Like the Daoist sage whose self has become "daemonic," so has Zarathustra's self attained a "brighter flame" for itself. (This is the closest the *Übermensch* comes to divinity: just as the Daoist sage is filled with *shen* so is the Overman the supreme embodiment of the will to power.) And just as the Daoist sage rejects the superstitions of *gui*, so too is Zarathustra freed from the ghosts of popular religion.

Much of Daoist imagery and mythology is based on life in mountain wildernesses far from the cities and farms of the plains. The dog-deity Panhu once helped Emperor Gauxin win a military victory and Gauxin gave him his youngest daughter in marriage. Panhu took her to the mountains where she gave birth to twelve children, who learned the language of animals and who "disliked level land."[78] One of course is reminded of Zarathustra's missionary failures in the villages of the plain—they found him "wild and strange"—and his preference for his mountain cave and his animal friends, particularly the eagle and serpent, with whom he feels more safe than with humankind.

The mountains are also a place where one can accumulate one's *de*—one's will to power—so that one can recapture the fullness of *de* one had as a child. (Those who live in the mountains do not eat the five grains, a diet that dissipates *de* rather than preserves it.) The way of the sage is also crooked like a mountain path rather than straight like a city street, a moral code, or a Mohist argument. In chapter 4 of the *Zhuangzi* the madman of Chu yells out to Confucius: "Leave off, leave off—this teaching men virtue! Dangerous, dangerous—to mark off the ground and run! Fool, fool—don't spoil my walking! I walk a crooked way—don't step on my feet."[79] Zarathustra also says that "all good things approach their goal crookedly . . . all good things laugh."[80] One of the higher men says that Zarathustra is evidence for the truth that the sage walks "on the most crooked ways."[81]

In one of Nietzsche's most powerful parables—"The Vision and the Riddle"—we find Zarathustra walking a mountain path with a crippled dwarf riding on his shoulder. Our initial impression of the dwarf is a negative one: he is "the spirit of gravity" and he is Zarathustra's "devil and archenemy." He is "half dwarf, half mole, making lame, dripping lead into [Zarathustra's] ear."[82] Earlier in the book Zarathustra says that his "devil" is a serious and solemn "spirit of gravity"; and this spirit is opposed to his dancing god and to his newly found power to fly. Zarathustra's powers are very similar to Zhuangzi's *zhi ren*: "Now I am light, now I fly, . . . now a god dances through me."[83] (Zarathustra's bright flame and his power to fly is the Nietzschean equivalent of the spiritual enhancement [*shenming*] of the Daoist sage.) The spirit of gravity also "orders" that our children be taught self-loathing so that they then become camels of slave morality—loaded down with "too many alien grave words and values."[84] The person who has discovered herself says: "This is *my* good and evil," but the "mole and dwarf," representing the spirit of gravity, counters with moral universalism: "Good for all, evil for all."[85]

Returning to "The Vision and the Riddle," Zarathustra finally challenges the dwarf: "Stop, dwarf! It is I or you! But I am the stronger of us two: you do not know my abysmal thought. *That* you could not bear!"[86] Zarathustra then presents the dwarf with a vision of eternal recurrence, but, curiously and surprisingly, the dwarf is not only able to bear this terrible truth but he also appears to know all about it and its implications. Speaking like a Daoist sage he declares: "All that is straight lies. . . . All truth is crooked; time itself is a circle."[87] (Laurence Lampert's cannot possibly be correct in claiming that the dwarf is somehow the spirit of rationalism.[88] The rationalist prefers a "straight" idea of truth and a linear view of time.) In *The Joyful Wisdom* it is a demon who brings the news of eternal recurrence, but those strong enough to accept the message will declare:

"You are a god, and never have I heard anything more godly."[89] Zarathustra's devil-dwarf may have a more positive role to play than we first thought.

Earlier in the story the dwarf offers other sagely advise: "O Zarathustra . . . you philosopher's stone! You threw yourself up high, but every stone that is thrown must fall."[90] Is it possible that Zarathustra by climbing too high and by presuming to fly needs to be reminded by this alter ego dwarf of his own motto "Be true to the earth"? Commentators have identified several alter egos in *Zarathustra*, so it is quite possible that the dwarf is yet another one of Zarathustra's multiple selves. We should always remember that all overcoming is *self*-overcoming, and that even Overmen will have "overdragons" who are worthy of them.[91] Zarathustra goes on to advise the higher men that they should not fear the devil, and that they should not be so obtuse as to call the Overman a devil, as surely the people of the plains will do.

Could it be that the dwarf is a symbol of Zarathustra's most abysmal thought that he has always "carried"?[92] After all, the motto "What goes up must come down" is simply the vertical version of "What goes around comes around." Earlier in "The Way of the Creator" Zarathustra warned his "brothers" that "lusting for the heights" is "so many convulsions of the ambitious."[93] The dwarf's point is confirmed in the section "The Spirit of Gravity," which reminds us that even when humans learn to fly "the boundary stones themselves will fly up into the air before [them], and [they] will rebaptize the earth—'the light one.'"[94] Even those who fly should remain true to the earth; for all those who fly, Johnathan Livingston Seagull and Zhuangzi's Peng bird notwithstanding, will eventually have to make a landing.

"The Vision and the Riddle" ends with a shocking scene where Zarathustra comes upon a shepherd with a snake in his throat. The snake—"the heaviest and the blackest"—could symbolize the choking effects of the slave morality, and, as my students have suggested, the snake's head, which Zarathustra exhorts the shepherd to bite off, could represent the Christian God himself. At the passionate urging of Zarathustra, the shepherd does decapitate the snake and is immediately transformed: "No longer shepherd, no longer human—one changed, radiant, laughing . . . a laughter that was no human laughter."[95] After the death of God, there is only eternal recurrence, and this "cosmic" laughter of Hesse's immortals is the only proper emotional response to such a meaningless existence. As Graham Parkes says: "laughter [is] an often necessary concomitant of insight into the way things are."[96] Eternal recurrence is meaningless only in the sense of being nonteleological, not in the sense that humans cannot create meaning from it, as Nietzsche's *Übermensch* and even as Camus's absurdist heroes must do. Only the Daoist sage must repress the urge of value creation.

Cosmic laughter is different from the laughter of the child who is the only being capable of loving herself and embracing every moment without any awareness of the terror of the inevitable return of many similar moments. Cosmic laughter is instead the "Olympian laughter" of the "deeply wounded,"[97] those, like Nietzsche, who have suffered greatly, who know eternal recurrence as an "abysmal thought," but who still realize that they must embrace it with a child's acceptance. It is the laughter of the lion, who has come home to Zarathustra's mountain retreat resigned to the futility of all his Nay-saying and protesting—in short, a reformed Titan.[98] It is also the laughter of the Daoist sage or Zen master who says "Yes" to anything and everything in the universe, even though at its core it is a faceless *hundun*. (The *hundun* as belly; Nietzsche's "belly of being speaks";[99] the mountain sages beat on their bellies; the belly laugh.) As the *Daodejing* says: "When the inferior person hears the Dao, he roars. If Dao were not laughed at, it would not be Dao."[100]

Contrary to the Mahāyāna scholastics who claim that a true Buddha would never "laugh a great afflicted laugh, openly showing his grinning teeth,"[101] the Tantric Buddhist would revel in such behavior. We are also reminded of the pagan gods who laughed themselves to death, both because the Christian God took himself so seriously and because the gods of course knew the truth of eternal recurrence all along.[102] Finally, there is the Goddess and her laughter. There is the Gnostic Goddess Sophia, who ridicules Yahweh for being blind and selfish; Durgā, who emits bloodcurdling laughter at the impudence of the Asuras and at the presumption of Mahiṣasura, especially his feeble attempts to seduce her; and Ramakrishna's Goddess, who laughs at human beings for their possessiveness and for their futile strategies to beat death.[103] Ramakrishna also believed that in the Kaliyuga one does not hear God's voice "except through the mouth of a child or a madman or some such person."[104]

Even with this new interpretation of the dwarf's identity, his negative attributes may still outweigh his positive ones. In *Thus Spake Zarathustra* the camel is the one who accepts the lie that "life is a grave burden," and this is a load that the camel carries "faithfully . . . on hard shoulders and over rough mountains."[105] Is the dwarf crippled because of the slave morality, or is he more like

Zhuangzi's sage-cripples? Recall that the hesitant and fearful tightrope walker in the town of Motley Cow is called lamefoot by the jester, who taunts the man for his lack of courage and knocks him off the rope. (Zarathustra promises to give the mortally wounded man a proper burial but leaves his body in the crook of a tree!)[106] Nevertheless, as with all things Nietzschean, we must interpret the dwarf dialectically not dualistically. The latter view, expressed by Lampert, sees the confrontation between Zarathustra and the dwarf in a Manichean way: "To club the Dwarf to death is to club to death the whole rational, Socratic tradition, . . ."[107] which is seen as an evil that must be completely destroyed. We have already objected to seeing the dwarf as a rationalist, and we now must question whether the dwarf's disappearance actually means that he has been annihilated. Nietzsche hated dualism just as much as he did rationalism, so the best solution is that the dwarf dissolves into the dialectical unity/difference that is Zarathustra's character.

One way to see this dialectical interpretation is the Tantric one, expressed most appropriately in the *Hevajra Tantra*: "whatever demon should appear before him" is an integral part of himself.[108] The eschatological pilgrims in the *Bardo Thödol* are told to take the wrathful deities that threaten them as simply psychological projections of their own evil deeds. (Even in dualistic Zoroastrianism the soul sees his good and evil deeds projected as a lovely maiden and an ugly hag, respectively.)[109] As Zarathustra is beyond good and evil, the dwarf is an alter ego projection of his most abysmal thoughts; or he is, as suggested earlier, a counter to his attempts to climb ever higher and to ignore the truth of "What goes up must come down."

Yet another dialectical reading rests on the recognition that the cripple, the monster, the fool, the madman, and the child are all allies in the spiritual instruction of the convention-bound and the unenlightened. ("Truth comes from the mouth of babes and fools," as the French say.) In his analysis of the deformed and monstrous in the *Zhuangzi*, Robert E. Allinson states: "The higher realization . . . is [that] monsters . . . are our greatest blessing and without them we could neither progress in a spiritual direction nor would we have a constant reminder and embodiment of that progress."[110] As with the Daoist and Hesse's immortals, the monster, the fool, and the child's greatest value is their spontaneity and freedom; and as such they can speak the truth when society's conventions have either obscured it or prohibited its proclamation. (In taking her jester's advise the queen was allowed to go against convention and tradition.) Allinson sees the effect of this liberating speech and behavior very incisively:

> In the clear-cut separation between form and content (monster and true speech), there is the greatest chance for the cancellation of the analytical judgment at the same moment as the engagement of the receptive, intuitive function. . . . The acceptance of the monster as a brother takes social and philosophical courage.[111]

Thus we celebrate Beauty's courage in her acceptance of the Beast. While we are shocked and puzzled by Zhuangzi's strange creatures (particularly master Yu with his internal organs on top his head), we also learn from the people of Wei, who accept their ugly man (even encourage their daughters to marry him) and want him as their ruler.[112] Not only do we learn that monstrous appearances deceive, but they can also preserve and protect. Zhuangzi gives the examples of the deformed youth who does not have to work or go to war and the gnarled tree that is never cut. For the Daoist what each of these have in common is that they have kept their power and their virtue (*de*) whole.

The first card in the Tarot deck is the Fool. Representing the number zero, the symbolic referent could be the Buddhist *śūnyatā*, the Goddess in her *nirguṇa* form, the *hundun*, or the Dao itself. In Vicki Noble's feminist recreation of the Tarot, the fool is a child walking on her hands in a stream filled with lotus flowers and sacred mushrooms (*amanita muscaria*) growing on its banks. There is a mountain in the background and the Fool is accompanied by a cat, a vulture, and a crocodile. The Fool represents psychic wholeness, so one is reminded of the Daoist sage who preserves his childlike *de* and who is not bothered by wild animals.

We might also think of Zarathustra himself in his mountain retreat surrounded by his animal friends and Parkes's description of the Third Metamorphosis as childlike innocence "joined with the archaic wisdom of the animals."[113] Recall Nietzsche's enigmatic description of the child as an "innocence and forgetting, a new beginning, a game [of creation], a self-propelled wheel, a first movement, a sacred Yes." Noble's comments are illuminatingly parallel: "the Fool is perpetually young, always starting fresh, like the sunrise. It represents innocence, without ideas of sin or transgression."[114] The Fool also represents the openness and daring that is required in all creative enterprises, so we have chosen to interpret the child metamorphosis as one that goes beyond innocence to experience as well. Recall the sagely crone appears as a Woman Crookback. She is asked how it is that she has the face of a child. Representing the marriage of innocence and experience, she responds that she has simply heard (not learned) the Dao.[115]

The Triumph of the Confucian Sage

One image of self-cultivation in early Chinese thought is the carving of a raw stone. At birth we are like uncut gems, and we have an obligation to shape and polish our potential in the most unique and beautiful ways possible. The *Book of Songs* proclaims: "Elegant is the *junzi*; he is as if cut, as if filed; as if chiseled, as if polished; how freshly bright; how refined. . . ."[116] The Daoists of course rejected this metaphor insisting that we remain as uncarved blocks (*pu*), and Liezi is one of the best examples: "From the carved gem he returned to the unhewn block/Unique, in his own shape, he took his stand."[117] Nietzsche, however, agreed with the Confucians that self-cultivation was an artistic undertaking, but his images are much more assertive, even violent. Nietzsche's famous idea of philosophizing with a hammer has aesthetic roots. The "beauty of the *Übermensch*" sleeps as an "image of [all] images" in stone and one must take a hammer to break it out: "Alas, that it must sleep in the hardest, the ugliest stone! Now my hammer rages cruelly against its prison. Pieces of rock rain from the stone: what is that to me? I want to perfect it. . . ."[118] Centuries of slave morality have made humans hard as rock, just as bad faith has given Sartre's anti-Semite the durability of stone.

(Parkes attempts to defuse a possible protofascist interpretation here—namely, totalitarian social engineering for a new society—by insisting that Nietzsche used the hammer on himself first, which indicates that his program is always self-creation rather than other-creation.[119] Unfortunately, Parkes's point is not always supported, especially when we read about the "conquering race" who shapes the "raw material of people and semianimals" with a "frightening artist-egoism that looks like bronze and knows itself to be justified for all eternity in its 'work,' as a mother in her child.")[120]

Nietzsche's conception of self-creation is significantly different from the Chinese conceptions. We are reminded of Mencius' response to Gaozi's analogy of making cups and bowls from wood and the *reductio* involved in implying that anything good can come from an act of violence. (The only Chinese thinker who approaches Nietzsche's assertiveness is Xunzi, whose images of straightening crooked wood and sharpening blunt metal appears to support Gaozi.) The activism of Mencius' view comes with his notion that we must carefully tend and fertilize the moral sprouts that we are given at birth. The Daoists countered Confucian self-cultivation with the image of the uncarved block (*pu*) and the infant who has yet to smile, or the person who conforms most closely to the Hundun.

In an article on Nietzsche and Rinzai Zen discussed in chapter 8, Parkes proposes that Nietzsche's self-cultivation is not assertive at all but corresponds more closely with the Rinzai and Daoist idea of discovering a natural human core, a *homo natura* who is not carved out of stone but simply freed from culture's petrifications.[121] He goes on to suggest that Nietzsche also has his own version of Daoist illumination (*ming*) in which all things are seen simply as they really are. If Nietzsche's *homo natura* is like the Daoist *pu*, then it would be unnecessary for him to say that it needs to be perfected. There is only an image in Nietzsche's ugly stone, one that needs to be actively sculpted and formed. And if Nietzsche does indeed believe in something like the Daoist *ming* (we should be wary of the truth of this hypothesis), then he is not the deconstructive postmodernist that many have taken him to be.

Even Parkes has to conclude that despite the basic similarities among the Rinzai monk, the Daoist sage, and Zarathustra—the spiritualizing of the emotions is fundamental—he admits to a "striking difference in the *modi operandi*."[122] Parkes sees the Rinzai monk as engaged with his fellow monks and the world while Nietzsche was much more solitary, even more so than the antisocial Daoist sage. (Nietzsche also places much more emphasis on pain, suffering, despair, and tragedy, while the Daoist sage is immune to these.) The Zen monk and Daoist sage will be indistinguishable from the herd, while the *Übermensch* will be a new aristocrat, "a master of the earth" and "a master over all men."[123] Finally, as Roger Ames sees it, the many *de* ideally blend and harmonize, while the many wills to power in Nietzsche compete with one another. Ames cites two illustrative texts, one that points out the equivalent Nietzschean *de* ontology and the other that demonstrates the difference with Daoism:

> Every center of force adopts a perspective toward the entire remainder, i.e., its own particular valuation, mode of action, and mode of resistance . . . life itself is essentially appropriation, injury, overpowering of what is alien and the weaker; suppression, hardness, imposition of one's own forms, incorporation and at least, at its mildest, exploitation.[124]

Nietzsche's language is one of competition and dominance rather than Daoist submission and integration. Zhuangzi's antisociality is noncompetitive, as can be seen from his suggestion that the ideal state is like fish swimming together but distinctly apart. Unnatural expressions of human love, which are always insincere, are like fish who have been forced, because their lake has dried up, to rub up against one another, flopping and gasping mindlessly together. Like fish swimming deep, Daoist sages live "forgetful of each other for ever and ever."[125]

In his insightful study of Nietzsche and Zhuangzi, Chen Guying observes that both these thinkers create "an enormous gap between the individual and society."[126] They also share the provocative view that self-consciousness developed only because of society; and that rulers, priests, and moralists are able to manipulate people simply by allowing their rules and mores to reflect back on self-conscious selves.[127] (This leads to the unexpected result, thoroughly postmodern in nature, that rather than preserving individual integrity, self-consciousness actually undermines it.) Zhuangzi's Confucius admits that he is "sentenced by Heaven" to live in society and he, too, has been crippled by *ren* and *yi*. He explains to Yen Hui that the Daoist sages roam "beyond the guidelines," while he roams within them and that "beyond and within have nothing in common."[128] This means that the Daoist sage retreats to the mountains and eventually becomes like Hundun, and Zarathustra also returns to his mountain cave where he rejects his disciples and embraces his animal friends.

One might counter that there is some outward reach in the knackmasters—Cook Ding's *de* becomes one with the ox and Woodcarver Qing's *de* becomes one with the wood, but this seems to have limited social and political meaning. It is significant that "motherly love" (*ci*), one of the three "treasures" of the *Daodejing*, is found only four times in the entire *Zhuangzi* and not once in the Inner Chapters.[129] With regard to the virtue of compassion, the follower of the Dao will tend not to harm others, but Zhuangzi, according to Ivanhoe, "does not seem to argue that we possess any natural active feelings of concern for others."[130]

Confucian sages produce "an ever-expanding circle of human relatedness,"[131] while Zhuangzi's sages explicitly reject this Heideggerian *Mitsein*: "Which of us can be *with* where there is no being with, be *for* where there is no being for."[132] In stark contrast Confucian sages broaden themselves by means of *yi* as "self-assertive and meaning bestowing" and its homophone *yi** as "self-sacrificing and meaning-deriving."[133] (In a very striking comparison Merleau-Ponty would call *yi* centrifugal *Sinngebung* and *yi** would be the centripetal forces of the social, historical, and cultural world.) By enlarging themselves the sages can also enlarge others, and by doing this they can "extend the Dao" and "form a trinity with Heaven and Earth."[134] Even with such achievements, Confucian sages still remain earth-bound humans with limitations, for even Yao and Shun had "found it difficult to accomplish *ren*."[135] In the *Doctrine of the Mean*, where sages are especially elevated, the author(s) admits that "there is something which even the sage does not know . . . [and] is not able to put into practice."[136] The Chinese sages are definitely not Titans. Titans assert their self-sufficiency and egoistic wills; they stand as solitary rebels against society and nature; and they claim knowledge of things that they cannot possibly know. China's sages, on the other hand, are corporate personalities; they claim to know little; they blend in and harmonize; they find joy in nature; and they preserve their childlike hearts.

Notes

Preface

1. Mircea Eliade, *Patanjali and Yoga*, trans. Charles L. Markmann (New York: Schocken, 1975), p. 50.

2. *Empirical Research into the Phenomenon of Kundalini* (New Delhi: Kundalini Research Association International, n.d.), p. 13.

3. R. C. Zaehner, *Our Savage God* (London: Collins, 1974), p. 263.

4. See C. S. Lewis's affirmation of humanism in *The Abolition of Man* (New York: Macmillan, 1947), p. 30; Nicholas F. Gier, "Religious Liberalism and the Founding Fathers," in *Two Centuries of Philosophy in America*, ed. Peter Caws (Oxford: Blackwell, 1980), pp. 22–45; and Gier, *God, Reason, and the Evangelicals* (Lanham, MD: University Press of America, 1987), chap. 9.

5. Edward Said, *Orientalism* (New York: Pantheon, 1978), p. 3.

6. Ibid., p. 204.

7. See, for example, Bhiku Parekh, *Gandhi's Political Philosophy* (London: Macmillan, 1989).

8. Quoted in David E. Shaner, "The Japanese Experience of Nature," in *Nature in Asian Traditions of Thought*, eds. J. B. Callicott and R. T. Ames (Albany: SUNY Press, 1989), p. 181.

9. M. K. Gandhi, *Harijan* 7 (August 19, 1939), p. 237.

10. See my article "The Color of Sin/The Color of Skin: Ancient Color Blindness and the Philosophical Origins of Modern Racism," *Journal of Religious Thought* 46:1 (Summer-Fall 1989), pp. 42–52. One could counter that the Indian caste system is evidence against this thesis, but this system was racist only in its original form. As intermarriage between Aryan and non-Aryan did eventually occur on a wide scale, an Aryan apartheid never developed and the caste system became a source of social, not racial, discrimination.

11. For an argument that Wittgenstein does not go the way of French deconstruction, see my review of Gertrude Conway's book *Wittgenstein on*

Foundations in *International Philosophical Quarterly* 32:1 (March 1992), pp. 119–25; and my article "Wittgenstein and Deconstruction" (unpublished).

12. Nicholas F. Gier, "Wittgenstein and Forms of Life," *Philosophy of the Social Sciences* 10 (1980), pp. 241–58.

13. See Gier, *Wittgenstein and Phenomenology: A Comparative Study of the Later Wittgenstein, Husserl, Heidegger, and Merleau-Ponty* (Albany: SUNY Press, 1981), pp. 128–30.

14. *Analects* 6.23. Translations of the *Analects* and the *Mencius* are from D. C. Lau unless otherwise noted. In abbreviated references to Chinese works translators will always be indicated in parentheses.

Introduction

1. Karl H. Potter, *Presuppositions of India's Philosophies* (Westport, CT: Greenwood, 1963), p. 3.

2. Heinrich Zimmer, *Philosophies of India,* ed. Joseph Campell (Cleveland, OH: World Publishing, 1956), p. 232.

3. Quoted in Freeman Dyson, "The Race Is Over," *New York Review of Books* (March 6, 1997), p. 4.

4. *Chāndogya Upaniṣad* 3.17.6.

5. *Mark* 10:18.

6. *Swami Vivekananda's Speeches and Writings* (Madras, India: G. A. Natesan, 6th ed., 1922), p. 47.

7. Zimmer, *Philosophies of India,* pp. 231–32.

8. Hesoid, *Works & Days and Theogony*, trans. Stanley Lombardo (Indianapolis, IN: Hackett Publishing, 1993); *Theogony* 209.

9. From the "Prometheus" fragment of 1816, quoted in Joseph C. McLelland, *Prometheus Rebound: The Irony of Atheism* (Waterloo, Ontario: Wilfrid Laurier University Press, 1988), p. 112. I am indebted to McLelland for several references on the use of the Prometheus myth in Western culture.

10. Percy Bysshe Shelley, *Prometheus Unbound*, ed. L. J. Zillman (Seattle: University of Washington Press, 1959), p. 121.

11. Quoted in McLelland, *Prometheus Rebound,* p. 116.

12. "Prometheus," trans. Michael Hamburger, in *Goethe's Collected Works: Selected Poems*, ed. Christopher Middleton (New York: Suhrkamp, 1983), vol. 1, p. 29.

13. Ibid., p. 31.

14. Fragments of Goethe's *Prometheus*, trans. Frank Ryder, in *Goethe's Collected Works: Eary Verse Drama and Prose Plays*, vol. 7, p. 242.

15. Ibid, pp. 242, 245.

16. From the preface of Elizabeth Barrett Browning's translation of *Prometheus Bound* (1835), quoted in McLelland, *Prometheus Rebound,* pp. 37, 86.

17. *Adv. Marcion* 1.1.247, quoted in McLelland, *Prometheus Rebound,* p. 3.

18. Simone Weil, *The Intuitions of the Pre-Christians*, pp. 105ff; quoted in McLelland, *Prometheus Rebound,* p. 38.

19. A. L. Basham, *The Wonder that Was India* (London: Sidgwick & Jackson, 3rd ed., 1967), p. 88.

20. Mary Boyce, *Zoroastrians* (London: Routledge & Kegan Paul, 1979), pp. 8ff; see also her book *A History of Zoroastrianism* (Leiden, Netherlands: Brill, 1975), vol. 1. For the best work on Zoroaster's dates see Gherardo Gnoli, *Zoroaster's Time and Homeland* (Naples: Instituto Universitario Orientale, 1980).

21. *Jaiminīya Brāhmaṇa* 1.97–98.

22. Wendy Doniger O'Flaherty, *Women, Androgynes, and Other Mythical Beasts* (Chicago: University of Chicago Press, 1980), p. 96. Doniger observes, citing the research of Gananath Obeyesekere, that Sri Lankan Buddhists had no problems with the divine-human interaction in their adaptations of the stories of the goddess Pattini, but the Hindu Tamils were forced to make "a number of adjustments in the myth and ritual" because of what I call the Indo-Iranian theistic principle. Presumably non-Aryan indigenous ideas on Sri Lanka contained no strong prohibitions about the mixing of the divine and the human.

23. Quoted in Doniger O'Flaherty, *The Origins of Evil in Hindu Mythology* (New Delhi: Motilal Banarsidass, 1976), pp. 91–92. It is not clear what scripture Doniger is quoting here.

24. *Skanda Puraṇa* 1.2.29.14; trans. G. V. Tagare in *Ancient Indian Tradition and Mythology*, eds. G. P. Bhatt and J. L. Shastri (New Delhi: Motilal Banarsidass, 1993), vol. 50, p. 237.

25. *The Śrīmad Devī Bhāgavatam* (*Devī-Bhāgavata Purāṇa*), trans. Swami Vijnananada (New Delhi: Manoharlal, 1921–23), 5.2.9, p. 357.

26. Although he does not make the distinction as strong as it could be, here is Franklin Edgerton's comment on the Gītā's view: "Even though . . . the Gītā regards God as immanent in all beings, and its author hopes for ultimate union with Him, still he seems to shrink from the bold assertion "I am God," which requires more courage than the Upaniṣadic "I am Brah-

man," simply because Brahman is impersonal and the Gītā's God is definitely personal" (Edgerton, trans., *The Bhagavad Gītā* [New York: Harper, 1944), p. 139.

27. An unnamed Jaina monk comes to Vena and declares: "I am most adored by the gods. . . . [my faith is] Arhats are the gods . . . [and] the best worship is that of a Jaina mendicant." Vena learns quickly from his new teacher: "I alone am the highest (form of) religion; I alone deserve to be worshipped; I am eternal; . . . I am the ancient, very holy, Jaina religion" (*Padma Purāṇa* 2.37.13, 17, 20; 2.38.18; trans. N. A. Deshpande in *Ancient Indian Tradition and Mythology*, vol. 41, pp. 1038, 1043.)

28. Ibid., 2.28.35, vol. 41, p. 1003.

29. Padmanabh S. Jaini, "On the *Sarvajñatva* (Omniscience) of Mahāvīra and the Buddha," in *Buddhist Studies in Honour of I. B. Horner*, eds. L. Cousins et al. (Dordrecht, Netherlands: Reidel, 1974), p. 72.

30. Ibid.

31. Potter, *Presuppositions of India's Philosophies,* p. 153; Zimmer, *Philosophies of India,* p. 400fn.

32. Potter, *Presuppositions of India's Philosophies,* p. 3.

33. S. K. Maitra, "The Gita's Conception of Freedom as Compared to Kant," in *Radhakrishnan: Comparative Studies in Philosophy*, eds. W. R. Inge et al. (New York: Humanities Press, 1951), pp. 348–61.

34. Potter, *Presuppositions of India's Philosophies,* p. 95. One reader has condemned Potter's remarks as "Orientialist," but it seems that this is the reverse of what has usually be taken to be the Orientalist bias. Euro-Americans have viewed Asian peoples as passive and impotent, not as power hungry individuals. The Orientalist sees Asians as different and "Other," not in terms of the common humanity that Potter and I do.

35. *The Complete Works of Swami Vivekananda* (Calcutta: Advaita Ashrama, 1970), vol. 8, p. 190. On this same page he also states: "'He that hath seen the son hath seen the Father,' and without seeing the Son, you *cannot* see the Father."

36. Vivekananda, *Karma-Yoga and Bhakti-Yoga* (New York: Ramakrishna-Vivekananda Center, rev. ed., 1973), p. 148.

37. Lance E. Nelson, "Living Liberation in Śaṇkara and Classical Advaita," in *Living Liberation in Hindu Thought*, eds. A. O. Fort and P. Y. Mumme (Albany: SUNY Press, 1996), p. 39.

38. In the Tantric Śaivism of Kashmir there is a focus on physicality involving "an alchemical transmutation leading to the divinization of the body itself" (Paul E. Muller-Ortega, "Aspects of Jīvanmukti in the Tantric Śaivism

of Kashmir," in *Living Liberation in Hindu Thought*, p. 198). Muller-Ortega also observes that for one Kashmiri Tantric "the primary characteristic of *jīvanmukti* involves not a Sāṃkhya-like introvertive *kaivalya*, but an extrovertive and open-eyed *samādhi*. . . ." (p. 195).

39. Jean-Paul Sartre, *Existentialism and Human Emotions* (New York: Philosophical Library, 1957), p. 63.

40. Martin Heidegger, "Letter on Humanism," in *Basic Writings*, ed. David F. Krell (San Francisco: Harper Collins, 1977), p. 223.

41. Steven Odin, *The Social Self in Zen and American Pragmatism*(Albany: SUNY Press, 1996). For a comparative study of Confucianism and pragmatism, see Warren G. Frisina, "Heaven's Partners or Nietzschean Free Spirits," *Philosophy East & West* 45:1 (January 1995), pp. 29–60.

42. See Padmanabh S. Jaini, "Karma and the Problem of Rebirth in Jainism," in *Karma and Rebirth in Classical Indian Tradition*, ed. Doniger O'Flaherty (Berkeley: University of California Press, 1980), p. 224. Jaini shows that the Buddhists—at least the Sautrāntikas—condemned Gośāla for the same reason.

43. Vijay Bhuvanbhanusuri, *The Essentials of Bhagavān Mahāvīr's Philosophy: Gaṇadharavāda*, trans. K. Ramappa (New Delhi: Motilal Banarsidass, 1989), p. 145.

44. A. C. Graham, *Chuang-tzu: The Inner Chapters* (London: Unwin Paperbacks, 1986), p. 47.

45. Friedrich Nietzsche, *Thus Spake Zarathustra,* in *The Portable Nietzsche*, trans. and ed. Walter Kaufmann (New York: Viking, 1954), p. 139.

46. Ibid., p. 125.

47. Ibid., p. 126.

48. Graham Parkes, *Composing the Soul: Reaches of Nietzsche's Psychology* (Chicago: University of Chicago Press, 1994), pp. 219–20.

49. Nietzsche, *Thus Spake Zarathustra*, p. 127.

50. Ibid., p. 125. Parkes is especially keen on presenting Nietzsche as an ecological philosopher. See his article "Human/Nature in Nietzsche and Taoism," in *Nature in Asian Traditions of Thought*, eds. J. B. Callicot and R. T. Ames (Albany: SUNY Press, 1989), pp. 79–97.

51. Parkes, "The Wandering Dance: Chuang Tzu and Zarathustra," *Philosophy East and West* 33:3 (July 1983), p. 245.

52. Quoted in Richard Valantasis, "Constructions of Power in Asceticism," *Journal of the American Academy of Religion* 63:4 (Summer 1995), p. 775.

53. Parkes, "Wandering Dance," p. 246.

54. Watson, *Complete Works of Chuang Tzu,* p. 198.

55. Nietzsche, *The Gay Science*, trans. Walter Kaufmann (New York: Random House, 1974), §109, p. 169.

56. Bernd Magnus, "Nietzsche's Philosophy in 1888: *The Will to Power* and the *Übermensch*," *Journal of the History of Philosophy* 24:1 (1986), p. 93.

57. Ibid., p. 83.

58. Ibid., p. 95.

59. Nietzsche, *Portable Nietzsche*, pp. 249–50.

60. Ibid., p. 143.

Chapter One: Spiritual Titanism in the West

1. *Analects* 15:28.

2. Aristotle, *Nicomachean Ethics*, trans. W. D. Ross, *The Works of Aristotle*, ed. W. D. Ross (Oxford: Clarendon Press, 1925), vol. 9, bk. 10, pp. 1178a6–7.

3. *Māndūkya Upaniṣad*, verse 11. All translations (unless otherwise noted) of the Vedas, Upaniṣads, and Bhagavad-gītā are cited from R. C. Zaehner, *Hindu Scriptures* (London: J. M. Dent & Sons, 1966).

4. *Taittīya Upaniṣad* 1.6.

5. *Kauṣītaki Upaniṣad* 1.4.

6. Quoted in J. E. Cirlot, *The Dictionary of Symbols*, trans. Jack Sage (New York: Philosophical Library, 2nd ed., 1971), p. 19.

7. Robert Grosseteste, "Man Is a Smaller World," printed together with Giovanni Pico della Mirandola's *Very Elegant Speech on the Dignity of Man*, trans. C. G. Wallis (Annapolis, MD: St. John's College Press, 1949), p. 25.

8. Quoted in Zimmer, *Philosophies of India*, p. 246.

9. Feodor Dostoevsky, *The Devils,* trans. David Magarshack (Harmondsworth, England: Penguin Books, 1971), p. 612.

10. Ibid., p. 613.

11. Jean-Paul Sartre, *No Exit and Other Plays*, trans. Stuart Gilbert (New York: Vintage Books, 1946), pp. 103–4.

12. Ibid., p. 126.

13. Sartre, *Existentialism and Human Emotions*, pp. 22, 53.

14. Ibid., p. 63.

15. Ibid., p. 40.

16. See Alphonso Lingus's comment on Taylor in "On Deconstructing Theology: A Symposium on *Erring: A Postmodern A / Theology*," *Journal of the American Academy of Religion* 54:3 (Fall, 1986), p. 529.

17. Catherine Keller, "Warriors, Women, and the Nuclear Complex," in *Sacred Interconnections: Postmodern Spirituality, Political Economy, and Art*, ed. David R. Griffin (Albany: SUNY Press, 1990), p. 72.

18. Thomas Aquinas, *de Veritate* 22.4.

19. Aristotle, *Nichomachean Ethics*, 1177a30.

20. Sartre, *Existentialism and Human Emotions*, p. 40.

21. Walter Bruggemann, *In Man We Trust: The Neglected Side of Biblical Faith* (Atlanta, GA: John Knox Press, 1972).

22. Athanasius, *De Incarnatione*, 54.3, in *The Library of Christian Classics*, ed. Edward R. Hardy (Philadelphia: Westminster Press, 1954), vol. 3, p. 107.

23. Etienne Gilson, *The Christian Philosophy of St. Thomas Aquinas*, trans. L. K. Shook (New York: Random, 1956), p. 349.

24. Phillipians 2:7 (RSV).

25. Quoted in Michael Green, ed., *The Truth of God Incarnate* (Grand Rapids, MI: Eerdmans, 1977), p. 135.

26. Ibid., p. 136.

27. Ibid.

28. *Incarnation and Myth: The Debate Continued*, Michael Goulder, ed. (Grand Rapids, MI: Eerdmans, 1979), pp. 189–90.

29. Don Cupitt, "The Christ of Christendom," in *The Myth of God Incarnate*, ed. John Hick (Philadephia: Westminster Press, 1977), pp. 142–43. Cupitt repeats his points in the later debate: "Mr. Hebblethwaite wishes to speak of God in glory as suffering and human, and in so doing breaks with monotheism and produces a theology which Feuerbach's celebrated analysis fits perfectly. . . . Why does Mr. Hebblethwaite go so far into anthropomorphism? The answer is clear. A historically-minded age can no longer claim to perceive two distinct compresent natures in Jesus. Jesus is simply human. So if divinity is to be predicated of Jesus, it must be predicated of his humanity. A man is God, God is a man. So Mr. Hebblethwaite's theory only con-

firms my own conviction that those who continue today to affirm a strong doctrine of the incarnation risk destroying belief in God" (*Incarnation and Myth*, pp. 44–45).

30. See Ronald H. Nash, *The Word of God and the Mind of Man* (Grand Rapids, MI: Zondervan, 1982); and Gordon H. Clark, *In Defense of Theology* (Milford, MI: Mott Media, 1984). For a discussion of the term *evangelical rationalism* see my book *God, Reason, and the Evangelicals* (Lanham, MD: University Press of America, 1987); chap. 1.

31. Stuart C. Hackett, "Personal Immortality and Human Nature: A Philosophical Case," a paper presented at the Advanced Seminar on Eschatology and the Second Coming, New Ecumenical Research Association, San Juan, Puerto Rico, February, 1984.

32. *Acts and Facts* (August 1976), p. 4.

33. See Alfred Bloom, *Shinran's Gospel of Pure Grace* (Tucson: University of Arizona Press, 1965).

34. Hackett, "Personal Immortality and Human Nature."

35. Gilson, *Christian Philosophy of St. Thomas Aquinas.*

36. *Śvetāśtavara Upaniṣad* 6.20; Isa. 34:3.

37. John B. Cobb and David R. Griffin, *Process Theology: An Introductory Exposition* (Philadelphia: Westminster Press, 1976), p. 8.

38. See my article "Three Types of Divine Power," *Process Studies* 20:4 (Winter 1991), pp. 221–32.

39. Gabriel Marcel, *Being and Having*, trans. Katharine Farrer (London: Dacre Press, 1949), p. 174.

40. Quoted in John W. Yolton, *John Locke: Problems and Perspectives* (Cambridge: Cambridge University Press, 1969), p. 6.

41. Sartre, *Existentialism and Human Emotions*, p. 36.

42. Ibid., p. 38.

43. Sartre, "An Interview" (1970), reprinted in Robert C. Solomon, *Phenomenology and Existentialism* (New York: Harper, 1972), p. 511–18.

44. Camus, *Carnets II*, January, 1942-March, 1951 (Paris: Gallimard, 1964), p. 42.

45. Camus, *The Myth of Sisyphus*, trans. Justin O'Brien (New York: Vintage Books, 1955), p. 91.

46. Ibid., p. 47.

47. Dostoevsky, *Crime and Punishment*, trans. Jessie Coulson (New York: Norton, 1964), pp. 523–24.

Chapter Two: The Self and Constructive Postmodernism

1. J. L. Jaini, Commentary on Kundakundācharya's Samayasara, in *The Sacred Books of the Jainas*, ed. Jaini (New York: AMS Press, 1974), vol. 8, p. 43.

2. *Portable Nietzsche*, p. 146.

3. Richard Rorty, A review of Ray Monk's *Bertrand Russell: The Spirit of Solitude, 1872–1921,* in *The New Republic* (December 2, 1996), p. 46.

4. David J. Kalupahana, *A History of Buddhist Philosophy: Continuities and Discontinuities* (Honolulu: University of Hawaii Press, 1992), pp. 116, 157, 176, 178, 187, 192, 222, 224, 233–34.

5. David L. Hall and Roger T. Ames, *Thinking Through Confucius* (Albany: SUNY Press, 1987). Hall and Ames call their method "cross-cultural anachronism," because the postmodern pragmatic and process categories they use might not have been in Confucius' mind as such (p. 7).

6. For example, Som Raj Gupta proposes that "when, following Śaṇkara, a student analyzes the Upaniṣadic statements about reality he finds that they cancel each other, that whatever they proclaim about reality they subsequently disclaim, that Upaniṣadic statements too are, in the final analysis, false fabrications. . . ." (*The Word Speaks to Faustian Man* [New Delhi: Motilal Banarsidass, 1991], pp. x–xi). Gupta seems to be suggesting that Śaṇkara holds something like the Buddhist dialectical identification of Saṃsara and Nirvāṇa, a doctrine that Nāgārjuna formulates in terms that do anticipate postmodern thought. Because Buddhism is more clearly antisubstance and antiessentialist, a postmodern interpretation of Buddhism has a much better chance of succeeding. See Kalupahana, *Nāgārjuna: Philosophy of the Middle Way* (Albany: SUNY Press, 1986); and Ian W. Mabbett, "Nāgārjuna and Deconstruction," *Philosophy East & West* 45:2 (April 1995), pp. 203–26. Kalupahana's interpretation is "constructive" postmodernism while Mabbett's reading is à la Derrida.

7. David R. Griffin, ed., *The Reenchantment of Science: Postmodern Proposals* (Albany: SUNY Press, 1988).

8. Recently A. L. Herman has made such an attempt in his "Karma, Saviors, and Communities," a paper presented at the Eight International Vedanta Congress, Miami University, October 1996.

9. John Kekes, "Shame and Moral Progress," in *Midwest Studies in Philosophy: Ethical Theory: Character and Virtue*, ed. Peter A. French et al. (Notre Dame, IN: University of Notre Dame, 1988), pp. 282–96.

10. Hall and Ames, *Thinking Through Confucius,* pp. 95–106.

11. Aristotle, *Nicomachean Ethics* 1106b36.

12. Aśvaghosa, *The Awakening of Faith in the Mahāyāna*, trans. Teitaro Suzuki (Chicago: Open Court Publishing, 1900), p. 66. See also Richard King, *Early Advaita Vedānta and Buddhism* (Albany: SUNY Press, 1995).

13. Parkes, *Composing the Soul*, p. 332.

14. For more on "synthetic" reason see chapter 9 of my book *Wittgenstein and Phenomenology*.

15. See my article "Gandhi: Premodern, Modern, or Postmodern?" *Gandhi Marg* 17:3 (October-December 1996), pp. 261–81.

16. Suzi Gablick, "The Reenchantment of Art: Reflections on the Two Postmodernisms," in *Sacred Interconnections: Postmodern Spirituality, Political Economy, and Art*, ed. David R. Griffin (Albany: SUNY Press, 1990), pp. 179–80.

17. Peter Ochs, "Charles Sanders Peirce," in *Founders of Constructive Postmodern Philosophy: Pierce, James, Bergson, Whitehead, and Hartshorne*, ed. David R. Griffin (Albany: SUNY Press, 1993), p. 72.

18. See Peter Harvey, "The Mind-Body Relationship in Pāli Buddhism: A Philosophical Investigation," *Asian Philosophy* 3:1 (1993), p. 34. On the Hebrew view of heart (*leb*) see J. Robert Nelson, *Human Life* (Philadelphia: Fortress Press, 1984), pp. 72–3.

19. Harvey, "Mind-Body Relationship in Pāli Buddhism"; Kalupahana, *The Principles of Buddhist Psychology* (Albany: SUNY Press, 1987).

20. For the best comparative studies of the Buddha and Hume, see L. Stafford Betty, "The Buddhist-Humean Parallels: Postmortem," *Philosophy East and West* 21:3 (July 1971), pp. 237–54; and James Giles, "The No-Self Theory: Hume, Buddhism, and Personal Identity," *Philosophy East and West* 43:2 (April 1993), pp. 175–200.

21. Kalupahana, *Principles of Buddhist Psychology*, pp. 20–21. Kalupahana's Pāli has been changed to Sanskrit.

22. Harvey, "Mind-Body Relationship in Pāli Buddhism," p. 31.

23. Kalupahana, *Nāgārjuna: The Philosophy of the Middle Way* (Albany: SUNY Press, 1986), p. 18. Kalupahana believes that professional intellectuals are far more prone to reify the self than their lay counterparts (*History of Buddhist Philosophy*, p. 224.)

24. See Suwanda H. J. Sugunasiri, "The Whole Body, Not Heart, as 'Seat of Consciousness': The Buddha's View," *Philosophy East & West* 45:3 (July 1995), pp. 409–30.

25. M. G. Dhadphale, "Some Off-Shoots of *Ahimsa* as Implied in the Jain Philosophy," in *The Contribution of Jainism to Indian Culture*, ed. R. C. Divivedi (New Delhi: Motilal Banarsidass, 1975), p. 131.

26. See Phyllis Granhoff, "The Violence of Non-Violence: A Study of Some Jain Responses to Non-Jain Religious Practices," *Journal of the International Association of Buddhist Studies* 15:1 (1992).

27. Gerald J. Larson, "The Philosophy of Sāṃkhya," in *Encyclopedia of Indian Philosophies*, eds. Larson and R. S. Bhattacharya (New Delhi: Motilal Banarsidass, 1987), vol. 4, p. 77.

28. George Kotturan, *Ahiṃsā: Gautama to Gandhi* (New Delhi: Sterling Publishers, 1973), p. 73.

29. Ibid.

30. John D. White, "God and the World from the Viewpoint of Advaita Vedānta: A Critical Assessment," *International Philosophical Quarterly* 30:2 (June 1981), pp. 185–93.

31. Steven Odin, *Process Metaphysics and Hua-Yen Buddhism* (Albany: SUNY Press, 1982).

32. If A and B are related by the *relatum* R, then there must be a *relatum* R_1 that relates R with A; furthermore, there must yet another R_2 that relates R with B. According to Bradley, the result is a vicious regress of relations (an R_3 that relates R_1 to R, *ad infinitum*), which proves, to Bradley's satisfaction, that A and B cannot be distinguished in the first place. See F. H. Bradley, *Appearance and Reality* (Oxford: Oxford University Press, 1930), p. 18.

33. Aristotle, *Nicomachean Ethics* 1096a21–22.

34. See Kalupahana, *History of Buddhist Philosophy*, p. 156; and *Vajracchedikā Prajñāpāramitā*, trans. Edward Conze (Rome: Serie Orientale Roma, 1957), §19, p. 86. Kalupahana rejects the transcendentalist interpretation of this passage that concludes that talk about karma is ineffable.

35. *Vajracchedikā* §21b, Conze trans., p. 87.

36. Ibid., §14, p. 77.

Chapter Three: Prometheus East: Greek and Hindu Titans

1. *Padma Purāṇa* 2.28.18, trans. Deshpande, *Ancient Indian Tradition and Mythology*, eds. G. P. Bhatt and J. L. Shastri (New Delhi: Motilal Banarsidass, 1981), vol. 41, p. 1043.

2. Quoted in Wendy Doniger O'Flaherty, *The Origins of Evil in Hindu Mythology* (New Delhi: Motilal Banarsidass, 1976), pp. 91–92. It is not clear what scripture Doniger is quoting here.

3. A. K. Coomaraswamy, "Angels and Titans: An Essay on Vedic Ontology," *Journal of the American Oriental Society* 55:5 (1935), p. 374.

4. Plato, *Laws* 701c.

5. *Śatapatha Brāhmaṇa* 2.1.6.8, trans. Doniger O'Flaherty, *Hindu Myths* (London: Penguin Books, 1975), p. 271.

6. *Bhāgavata Purāṇa* 7.1.8; G. V. Tagare, trans., *Ancient Indian Tradition and Mythology*, vol. 9, p. 886.

7. *Śatapatha Brāhmaṇa*, 9.5.1.12–13, trans. in Doniger, *Hindu Myths*, p. 272.

8. *Yasna* 30.5, trans. Jacques Duchesne-Guillemin, *The Hymns of Zarathustra*, trans. M. Henning (Boston: Beacon, 1963), p. 105. Even this free choice model is qualified by the following implication about "nature": "Now in the beginning the twin spirits have declared their nature, the better and the evil, in thought word and deed" (*Yasna* 30.3).

9. *Ṛgeda*, I.24.14.

10. Coomaraswamy, "Angels and Titans," pp. 373–74.

11. See Ganesh Vasudeo Tagare, trans., *Kūrma-Purāṇa,* in *Ancient Indian Tradition and Mythology* (New Delhi: Motilal Banarsidass, 1981), vol. 20, p. 174 fn.

12. The gods came to Śiva complaining about how his grace had led to severe overcrowding in heaven. Śiva insisted that he could do nothing about it, but Pārvatī created Gaṇeśa as a "maker of obstacles" so that humans would now go to hell. See *Skanda Purāṇa* 7.1.38.1–34.

13. See J. R. Haldar, *Early Buddhist Mythology* (New Delhi: Manohar, 1977), p. 149.

14. Ibid., p. 152.

15. Ibid., p. 150.

16. Wash Edward Hale, *Asura in Early Vedic Religion* (New Delhi: Motilal Banarsidass, 1986), p. 52.

17. Doniger O'Flaherty, *Origins of Evil in Hindu Mythology*, 1976), p. 333. In terms of equivalent proper names, there is a Pramanthu mentioned in the *Bhāgavata-Purāṇa* (5.15.5), but other than being descendent from the famous Mahārāja Gaya and having a brother Manthu, nothing else is known about him. Robert Graves suggests that these two brothers may be the prototypes for Prometheus and Epimetheus, but this seems unlikely given their minor status in the *Bhāgavata-Purāṇa*. Neither of them rate an entry in the massively thorough *Purāṇic Encyclopedia*. See Graves, *The Greek Myths* (New York: Braziller, 1957), vol. 1, p. 148.

18. Sukumari Bhattacharji, *The Indian Theogony* (Cambridge: Cambridge University Press, 1970), p. 134. See also Adalbert Kuhn, *Mythologishe Studien I: Die Herabkunft des Feuers und des Göttertranks* (Gütersloh: Verlag von C. Bertelsmann, 1886), pp. 15–17; 218–23.

19. See Margaret Stutley and James Stutley, *Harper's Dictionary of Hinduism* (New York: Harper, 1977), p. 231.

20. *Devī-Bhāgavata Purāṇa* 5.2.28; Vijanananda trans., p. 358.

21. *Saura Purāṇa* 49.7–143; discussed in Doniger O'Flaherty, *Origins of Evil in Hindu Mythology*, pp. 86–87.

22. *Bhāgavata Purāṇa* 2.7.18; G. V. Tagare, trans., *Ancient Indian Tradition and Mythology*, vol. 7, p. 191.

23. *Vāmana Purāṇa* 74; cited in *Purāṇic Encyclopedia* (New Delhi: Motilal Banarsidass, 1975), p. 103.

24. See Susan Wadley, *Shakti: Power in the Conceptual Structure of Karimpur Religion* (Chicago: University of Chicago Department of Anthropology, 1975), pp. 130–31.

25. *Padma Purāṇa* 6.3.1–6.18.120. See the other version at 6.96.1–6.104.29, in which after being decapitated Jalandhara's lustre (*tejas*) merges with Śiva's, which reminds us that Jalandhara was after all created from a portion of the great god.

26. *Mahābhārata* 12.160.29, trans. by Doniger O'Flaherty, *Origins of Evil in Hindu Mythology*, p. 71. As equal sons of Kaśyapa, see *Bhāgavata Purāṇa* 8.17.23.

27. I am again indebted to Doniger for these points (*Origins of Evil in Hindu Mythology*, p. 62).

28. Doniger O'Flaherty, *Hindu Myths* (London: Penguin Books, 1975), p. 280.

29. *Śatapatha Brāhmaṇa* 2.5.2.1–3 and 5.2.4.1–2; trans. by Doniger O'Flaherty, *Origins of Evil in Hindu Mythology*, p. 22.

30. *Padma Purāṇa* 2.28.30, trans. Deshpande, *Ancient Indian Tradition and Mythology*, vol. 41, p. 1003.

31. Ibid., 2.38.18, vol. 41, p. 1043.

32. Ibid., 2.28.52, vol. 41, p. 1005.

33. Ibid., 2.28.118, vol. 41, p. 1008.

34. Doniger O'Flaherty, *Origins of Evil in Hindu Mythology*, p. 332.

35. See *Ṛg-veda* 8.9.24; *Atharva-veda* 10.10.26.

36. See *Padma Purāṇa* 4.8.8–12.

37. Lama Anagarika Govinda, *Foundations of Tibetan Mysticism* (London: Rider, 1959), p. 19.

38. *The Laws of Manu*, trans. Doniger (New Delhi: Penguin Books, 1991), 1. 6.

39. Tagare, *Kūrma-Purana*, p. 173 fn.

40. *Bhāgavata Purāṇa* 8.17.19 (Tagare), vol. 9, p. 1086.

41. *Mahābrārata* 12.311, trans. Doniger, "Echoes of the *Mahābrārata,*" in *Purāṇa Perennis*, ed. Doniger (Albany: SUNY Press, 1993), p. 40.

42. *Devī-Bhāgavata Purāṇa* 1.14; Vijnanananda trans., p. 47.

43. *Mahābrārata* 12.319, trans. by Doniger in "Echoes of the *Mahābrārata*, p. 48.

44. C. Mackenzie Brown, "Modes of Perfected Living in the *Mahābhārata* and the *Purāṇas*," in *Living Liberation in Hindu Thought*, eds. A. O. Fort and P. Y. Mumme (Albany: SUNY Press, 1996), p. 170.

45. *Devī-Bhāgavata Purāṇa* 1.19; Vijnanananda trans., p. 72.

46. Aeschylus, *Three Greek Plays: Prometheus Bound, Agamemnon, the Trojan Women*, trans. Edith Hamilton (New York: Norton, 1937), pp. 30, 123.

47. See Don Handelman and David D. Shulman, *God Inside and Out: Śiva's Game of Dice* (Oxford: Oxford University Press, 1997), p. 56.

48. C. Kerényi, *Prometheus: Archetypal Image of Human Existence*, trans. Ralph Manheim (New York: Pantheon, 1963), p. 45. I am indebted to Kerényi for both references and insights.

49. Ibid., p. 61. Kerényi's comment is curious in light of the fact that Titans and Titanesses (in seven pairs) were intimately connected to a seven-day week, thirteen-month lunar calender. See Robert Graves, *Greek Myths*, vol. 1, pp. 27–29.

50. Ovid, *Metamorphoses* i–ii.

51. Homer, *Iliad* 14.258.

52. Impregnation by swallowing is common in ancient mythology. The precedent for the reproductive mechanics of this story about Zeus may be the Hittite account of Kumarbi (=Kronos) who bites off and swallows the penis of Anu (=Uranus) and gives birth to a Zeus-like storm god. See G. S. Kirk and J. E. Raven, *The Presocratic Philosophers* (London: Cambridge University Press, 1957), p. 36.

53. See the *Kathāmṛta* 5.68; cited in Jeffrey J. Kripal, *Kālī's Child* (Chicago: University of Chicago Press, 1995), p. 276.

54. Hesoid, *Works & Days and Theogony*, trans. Stanley Lombardo (Indianapolis, IN: Hackett Publishing, 1993); *Theogony*, 897–98.

55. Ibid., 932–33.

56. Aeschylus, *Prometheus Bound*, trans. Philip Vellacott (London: Penguin Books, 1961), 376.

57. Ibid., 977.

58. Ibid., 1001–4.

59. Ibid., 176–78.

60. Ibid., 982.

61. Doniger O'Flaherty, *Asceticism and Eroticism in the Mythology of Śiva* (Oxford: Oxford University Press, 1973), p. 82.

62. See Aristotle's *Meterologica* 4.11.389a28.

63. Graves, *Greek Myths*, vol. 1, p. 32.

64. Quoted in Kerényi, *Prometheus*, pp. 70, 71.

Chapter Four: Jaina Superhumanism and Gnostic Titanism

1 Jyoti Prasad Jain, *The Essence of Jainism* (Varanasi, India: Shuchita Publications, n.d.), p. 6.

2. Medhāvin, *Śrāvakācāra Dharma-saṃgraha-Śrāvakācāra* (Benares, India, 1910), iv. 29, quoted in R. Williams, *Jaina Yoga: A Survey of the Mediaeval Śrāvakācāras* (New Delhi: Motilal Banarsidass, 1983), p. xxii.

3. Padmanabh S. Jaini, *The Jaina Path of Purification* (New Delhi: Motilal Barnasidass, 1979), p. 266.

4. Umāsvati, *Tattvārtha Sūtra* (That Which Is), trans. Nathmal Tatia (New York: HarperCollins Publishers, 1994), p. 258.

5. Ibid., p. 285. This comes from the translator's appendix 4.

6. Zimmer, *Philosophies of India*, pp. 211–12.

7. *Tattvārtha Sūtra*, p. 285.

8. Ibid., p. 69. An alternative explanation of this very stylized figure (the outline might appear to some as a dress pattern) is "compared to three vases stacked on top of each other with the bottom and top vases turned upside-down" (ibid.).

9. See the *Tattvārtha Sūtra* 2.29 (and diagrams in Tatia's translation, p. 49) for the zigzag routes of the less perfect souls.

10. Mohan Lal Mehta, *Jaina Culture* (Varanasi, India: P. V. Research Institute, 1969), p. 105.

11. "Generally the Āryas are better born, better behaved, better spoken and more highly developed, both physically and spiritually, than the Mlecchas [the non-Aryans]" (*Tattvārtha Sūtra* 3.15, p. 85). The Digambara sect

also developed a caste system, but the presence of Brahmin Jainas did not prevent Jainas from performing their own worship at Jaina temples.

12. Hemacandra, *Yogaśastra* 2.4–5; cited in Paul Dundas, *The Jains* (London: Routledge, 1992), p. 201.

13. Jyoti Prasad Jain, *Essence of Jainism*, p. 11.

14. Jaini, *Jaina Path of Purification*, pp. 162–63.

15. Medhāvin, *Śrāvakācāra Dharma-samgraha-Śrāvakācāra*.

16. See P. S. Jaini, *Jaina Path of Puridication*, p. 194.

17. Bhuvanbhanusuri, *Essentials of Bhagavān Mahāvīr's Philosophy*, pp. 120, 122. The author also states that one can eliminate sin by venerating Mahāvīra (p. 71).

18. Ibid., p. 121.

19. See Devendra Muni, *Jaina Religion and Philosophy: An Introduction*, trans. Kewal Krishan Mitall (Daipur, India: Śrī Tārak Guru Jain Granthālya, 1985), p. 10.

20. Prem Suman Jain, "The Ethics of Jainism," in *World Religions and Global Ethics*, ed. S. Cromwell Crawford (New York: Paragon House, 1989), p. 71. Jyoti Prasad Jain uses the language of transformation, but it is clear that this is not a metaphysical change: "This transformation of man into god is the realistic end of religious pursuit in Jainism for a sincere aspirant of the Truth. . . . Each soul, when completely free from karmic influences, becomes 'itself' and transforms into 'divinity.'. . . Each liberated soul is a full and perfect divinity in itself and by itself" (*Essence of Jainism*, pp. 8, 10).

21. Jyoti Prasad Jain, *Essence of Jainism*, p. 8.

22. Krishna Prem and Madhava Ashish, *Man: The Measure of All Things* (Wheaton, IL: Theosophical Publishing House, 1969), pp. 187–88, 336. The Sāṃkhya tradition also makes humankind the end of all evolution: "From Brahmā down to a stock, the creation is for sake of Puruṣa, till there be discrimination" (*Sāṃkhya-pravacana-sūtra* 3.47, trans. Nandall Sinha, *The Sāṃkhya Philosophy*, in *Sacred Books of the Hindus*, ed. B. D. Basu [New York: AMS Press, 1974], vol. 11, p. 324).

23. *Māndūkya Upaniṣad* 1.1, trans. R. E. Hume, *The Thirteen Princpal Upanishads* (London: Oxford University Press, 2nd ed. rev., 1931).

24. See Jaini, *Jaina Path of Purification*, pp. 162–64.

25. Quoted in Sartre, *Existentialism and Human Emotions*, pp. 29–30.

26. See Bhuvanbhanusuri, *Essentials of Bhagavān Mahāvīr's Philosophy*, p. 35. "The Lord [Mahāvīra] had appeared here only to destroy his internal enemy namely . . . illusion" (p. 45).

27. M. G. Dhadphale, "Some Off-Shoots of *Ahiṃsā* as Implied in the Jain Philosophy" in *The Contribution of Jainism to Indian Culture*, ed. R. C. Divivedi (New Delhi: Motilal Banarsidass, 1975), p. 130.

28. Jyoti Prasad Jain, *Essence of Jainism*, p. 31.

29. *Kalpasūtra*, trans. K. C. Lalwani (New Delhi: Motilal Banarsidass, 1979), pp. 68–9.

30. "(The subject matter) of perfect knowledge (is) all the substances (and all their) modifications" (*Tattvārthadhigama-sūtra* 1.29, trans. and ed. J. L. Jaini in *The Sacred Books of the Jainas*, vol. 2, p. 43.)

31. P. S. Jaini, *Jaina Path of Purification*, p. 266.

32. Kundakundāchārya, *Pañchāstikāyasāra*, ed. and trans. A. Chakravartinayanar, in *The Sacred Book of the Jainas*, vol. 3, p. 159.

33. The *Cūḷa-sakuludāyisutta*, in the *Mijjhima-Nikāya* II, 31; *The Middle Length Sayings*, trans. I. B. Horner (London: Luzac, 1970), vol. 2, p. 229.

34. Kalupahana, *History of Buddhist Philosophy*, p. 130.

35. Paul J. Griffiths, *On Being Buddha: The Classical Doctrine of Buddhahood* (Albany: SUNY Press, 1994), pp. 191–92.

36. See D. C. Lau, "On Mencius' Use of the Method of Analogy in Argument," *Asia Major* 10 (1963); reprinted in Lau's translation of the *Mencius* as appendix 5.

37. A Tibetan scholastic "digest" cited in Griffiths, *On Being Buddha*, p. 171.

38. Quoted in Nick Herbert, *Quantum Reality: Beyond the New Physics* (New York: Doubleday Anchor, 1987), p. 173.

39. P. S. Jaini, "On the *Sarvajñatva* (*Omniscience*) of Mahāvīra and the Buddha," in *Buddhist Studies in Honour of I. B. Horner* (Dortrecht, Netherlands: Reidel, 1974), p. 79.

40. The *Kaṇṇakatthalasutta*, in the *Majjhima-Nikāya* II, 127; *The Middle Length Sayings*, vol. 2, pp. 309–10. Emphasis added.

41. *Mahāparinibbāna suttana* in the *Digha-Nikāya*, xvi.1.16; *Dialogues of the Buddha*, trans. T. W. Rhys Davids and C. A. F. Rhys Davids (London: Luzac, 1971), vol. 3, p. 87.

42. Nathan Katz, *Buddhist Images of Human Perfection* (New Delhi: Motilal Banarsidass, 1980), p. 134.

43. The *Tivijja-Vacchagottasutta* in the *Majjhima-Nikāya* I, 482; *The Middle Length Sayings*, vol. 2, p. 160.

44. Kalupahana, *Nāgārjuna: Philosophy of the Middle Way*, p. 92.

45. Nathmal Tatia's commentary on the *Tattvārtha Sūtra*, p. 281. Tatia acknowledges that the saint's omniscience is a major exception to *anekāntavāda* (p. xvii).

46. See P. S. Jaini, *Jaina Path of Purification*, p. 142.

47. Śri Nemichara Siddhānta Chakravarti, *Gommaṭsāra Jīva-Kanda*, trans. J. L. Jaini in *Sacred Books of the Jainas*, vol. 5, p. 289.

48. Ibid., p. 308.

49. Gandhi, *Young India* 8 (January 21, 1926), p. 30.

50. P. S. Jaini, *The Jaina Path in Purification*, p. 96.

51. Christopher Key Chapple, *Nonviolence to Animals, Earth, and Self in Asian Traditions* (Albany: SUNY Press, 1993), chap. 5.

52. See the *Tattvārtha Sūtra* 5.31, pp. 139–40.

53. Quoted in Kotturan, *Ahiṃsā,* p. 13. "No matter whether he is Śvetambara, or Digambara, a Buddhist or follower of any other creed, one who looks on all creatures as his own self, attains salvation" (quoted in ibid., p. 12).

54. See A. Siddhatissa, *Buddhist Ethics: Essence of Buddhism* (London: Allen & Unwin, 1970), p. 88; *Bhagavada Purāṇa* 3.29.28–32. Jainism does allow that if one cannot uphold the vow of noninjury to immobile beings, then one must at least maintain it for mobile beings.

55. N. D. Bhargava, "Some Chief Characteristics of the Jain Concept of Nonviolence," in *Contribution of Jainism to Indian Culture*, p. 124.

56. For more discussion see my article "Gandhi, Ahimsa, and the Self," *Gandhi Marg* 15:1(April-June 1993), pp. 24–38.

57. Ibid., p. 122. To be fair, Bhargava does insist that the use of the negative formulation does not mean that we should not love, but his rejection of interrelationship does not give strong motivation to do so.

58. See my article "The Virtue of Non-Violence: A Buddhist Perspective," *Seikyo Times* (February 1994), pp. 28–36.

59. See P. S. Jaini, "Karma and the Problem of Rebirth in Jainism," pp. 219ff.

60. See Tatia's translation of the *Tattvārtha Sūtra*, p. 285.

61. Ibid., 5.16, p. 127.

62. Ibid., p. 219.

63. Bhuvanbhanusuri, *Essentials of Bhagavān Mahāvīr's Philosophy*, pp. 23, 22.

64. Ibid., p. 22.

65. J. L. Jaini enthusiastically supports the radical dualism of Kundakundācharya in this passage: "God versus Satan becomes Pure Soul versus Matter. God is Pure Soul. Satan is Pure Matter, the tempter, seducer, deluder and Jailor of the Soul" (*Samayasara*, in *Sacred Books of the Jainas*, vol. 8, p. 43).

66. See the *Gommaṭsāra Jīva-Kanda*, *Sacred Books of the Jainas*, vol. 5, p. 144.

67. A. Chakravartinayanar, A philosophical introduction to *Pañchāstikāyasāra,* in *Sacred Books of the Jainas*, vol. 3, p. xxix.

Chapter Five: Hindu Titanism

1. Rammurti S. Mishra, *Yoga Sutras: The Textbook of Yoga Psychology* (New York: Doubleday Anchor, 1973), p. vi.

2. Madeleine Biardeau, "Purāṇic Cosmogony," in *Mythologies*, eds. Yves Bonnefoy et al., and trans. Wendy Doniger et al., (Chicago: University of Chicago Press, 1991), vol. 2, p. 818.

3. Quoted in Doniger O'Flaherty, *Origins of Evil in Hindu Mythology*, p. 195.

4. Brian K. Smith, "Eaters, Food, and Social Hierarchy in Ancient India," *Journal of the American Academy of Religion* 58:2 (Summer 1990), pp. 177, 178.

5. *Laws of Manu*, 9.317, 319; *Śatapatha Brāhmaṇa* 2.2.2.6; quoted in Doniger O'Flaherty, *Origins of Evil in Hindu Mythology*, p. 80. In the latter work the priest is given a mantra by which he is able to transform himself into a superman or *ati-manusa*. See Georg Feuerstein and Jeanine Miller, *Yoga and Beyond* (New York: Schocken, 1972), p. 18 fn. 45.

6. *Manusmṛti* 9.317–319; Doniger trans., p. 231.

7. See *The Indian Theogony*, pp. 334–36. Puruṣa can be see as the forerunner of Brahman, because the tenth book of the *Ṛgeda* is a precursor to the *Brāhmaṇas*, where Prajāpati takes the place of Puruṣa. He, Puruṣa, and Brahman can be seen as divinized human forms.

8. See *Maitrī Upaniṣad* 7.10 for the marvelous story about the gods and demons wishing to be instructed about Ātman. This also amounts to a powerful denigration of the former kings of heaven.

9. Doniger O'Flaherty, *Origins of Evil in Hindu Mythology*, p. 80.

10 Christopher Key Chapple, "Living Liberation in Sāṃkhya and Yoga," in *Living Liberation in Hindu Thought*, ed. Andrew O. Fort and Patricia Y. Mumme (Albany: SUNY Press, 1996), p. 127.

11. See, for example, the *Katha Upaniṣad* 3.11.

12. *Chāndogya Upaniṣad* 8.12.3. Chapple uses this passage as a concluding vision of a very different dialectical process. In a concise and brilliant interpretation of the Mahābhārata he sees the self-division of Vyāsa as an emanation of being (*sat*) out of nonbeing (*asat*) and a return to that undifferentiated source (*Nonviolence to Animals, Earth, and Self in Asian Traditions*, p. 82). In the context of the religion of Kṛṣṇa I would see this vision as holistic but with the differentiation of personal interaction.

13. See Eliade, *Yoga: Freedom, and Immortality* (Princeton, NJ: Princeton University Press, 2nd ed. 1969), p. 307.

14. See Gerald J. Larson, "The Philosophy of Sāṃkhya," in *Encyclopedia of Indian Philosophies*, vol. 4, p. 627n8.

15. Eliade, *Patanjali and Yoga*, pp. 53–54.

16. Eliade, *Yoga: Freedom, and Immortality*, p. 98.

17. *The Sāṃkhya-kārikā*, trans. Gerald Larson, *Classical Sāṃkhya* (New Delhi: Motilal Banarsidass, 2nd ed., 1979), §17.

18. *Sāṃkhya-pravacana-sūtra* 3.47, trans. Nandall Sinha, *The Sāṃkhya Philosophy* in *Sacred Books of the Hindus*, ed. B. D. Basu (New York: AMS Press, 1974), vol. 11, p. 324. I have given Eliade's alternative translations (*Patanjali and Yoga*, p. 20).

19. Mishra, *Yoga Sutras*, p. vi.

20. *Tattvārtha Sūtra* 10.1, p. 253.

21. See Vasudeva S. Agrawala, "Puruṣa-Sūkta," *Dr. Mirashi Felicitation Volume* (Nagpur, India: Vidarbha Samshodhan Mandal, 1965), pp. 7, 8.

22. See Raimondo Panikkar, *The Vedic Experience* (Berkeley: University of California Press, 1977), p. 73; and Chapple, *Nonviolence to Animals, Earth, and Self in Asian Traditions*, p. 50. I would reverse the following observation by Chapple: "The human order is seen as an extension of and utterly reliant on the natural order" (p. 52).

23. *Ṛgeda* 10.90.2.

24. *Atharva-veda* 10.2.4.

25. Ibid., v. 14.

26. Ibid., v. 21.

27. Ibid., v. 28.

28. Ibid., v. 33. "Now that Golden Person who is seen within the sun has a golden beard and golden hair. He is exceedingly brilliant, all, even to the fingernail tips. . . . His name is High. He is raised high above all evils. Verily, he who knows this rises high above all evils. . . . He is the lord of the

worlds which are beyond yonder sun, and also of the gods' desires." *Chāndogya Upaniṣad* 1.6.6–8. Cited from Robert E. Hume, *The Thirteen Principal Upanishads* (London: Oxford University Press, 2nd ed. revised, 1930).

29. *Bṛhadāraṇyaka Upaniṣad* 1.4.1.

30. Ibid., v. 10.

31. Ibid.

32. Ibid., 2.1.2 (Hume).

33. *Śvetāśvatāra Upaniṣad* 3.8, 9.

34. Ibid., 6.11.

35. *Muṇḍaka* 2.1.2; *Chāndogya* 4.15.5; 5.10.1; *Bṛhadāraṇyaka* 1.1–2.

36. *Śvetāśvatāra Upaniṣad* 6.11.

37. *Maitrī Upaniṣad* 2.7.

38. Ibid., 6.21, 22.

39. *Kauśītaki* 1.5, 6.

40. *Taittirīya* 1.6; 2.8.

41. *Maitrī* 4.4.

42. *Śvetāśvatāra* 6.20.

43. *Taittirīya* 3.5.

44. *Bhagavad-gītā* 15.15, 18.

45. Ibid., 11.13; 10.2; 11.52.

46. Ibid., 14.3, 27.

47. *The Bhagavad-gītā*, commentary and trans. R. C. Zaehner (New York: Oxford University Press, 1973), p. 368.

48. *Chāndogya Upaniṣad* 8.12.3.

49. Ibid., p. 367.

50. See Robert S. Minor, *An Exegetical Commentary of the "Bhagavad-gītā"* (New Delhi: Heritage Publishers, 1982), p. 429. Minor also does the best job of sorting out the three different uses of *puruṣa* in these verses.

51. Doniger O'Flaherty, *Origins of Evil in Hindu Mythology,* pp. 78ff.

52. Ibid., p. 82.

53. *Chāndogya* 3.17.6

54. C. Mackenzie Brown, *The Triumph of the Goddess* (Albany: SUNY Press, 1990), pp. 128–29.

55. Ibid., p. 89.

56. Biardeau, "Purānic Cosmogony," vol. 2, p. 818.

57. Ibid., p. 819.

58. A good example is *Viṣṇu Purāṇa* I.2. See J. A. B. van Buitenen, "Studies in Sankhya (II)," *Journal of the American Oriental Society* 77 (1957), pp. 15–25. For a reconsideration of this view see Hans H. Penner, "Cosmogony as Myth in the Viṣṇu Purāṇa," *History of Religions* 5:2 (Winter, 1966), pp. 283–99.

59. Biardeau, "Purānic Cosmogony," p. 818.

60. *Bhagavad-gītā* 7.12; 9.5ff.

61. W. P. Mei, "The Basis of Social, Ethical, and Spiritual Values in Chinese Philosophy," in *The Chinese Mind*, ed. Charles A. Moore (Honolulu: University of Hawaii Press, 1967), p. 324.

62. David Kinsley, "Reflections on Ecological Themes in Hinduism," *Journal of Dharma* 16:3 (July-September 1991), p. 241.

63. Other commentators have also taken issue with Advaita Vedānta's alleged strength for environmental philosophy. See, for example, Lance E. Nelson, "Reverence for Nature or the Irrelevance of Nature? Advaita Vedānta and Ecological Concern," *Journal of Dharma* 16:3 (July-September 1991), pp. 282–301; and "Living Liberation in Śaṇkara and Advaita Vedānta," in *Living Liberation in Hindu Thought*, pp. 17–62.

64. Klaus K. Klostermaier sketches an ecological theology based on Ramānuja in "Bhakti, *Ahiṃsā*, and Ecology," *Journal of Dharma* 16:3 (July-September 1991), pp. 251–252.

65. Nelson, "Reverence for Nature or the Irrelevance of Nature?" p. 299.

66. Nelson, "Living Liberation in Śaṇkara and Classical Advaita," p. 44.

67. Raimondo Panikkar, *Myth, Faith, and Hermeneutics* (New York: Paulist Press, 1979), p. 83.

68. Panikkar, *Vedic Experience*, p. 73.

69. Quoted in Doniger O'Flaherty, *Origins of Evil in Hindu Mythology*, p. 195.

Chapter Six: The Yogi and the Goddess

1. *Brahmavaivarta Purāṇa,* Rakṛti-Khanda 55.87, trans. Tracy Pintchman, *The Rise of the Goddess in the Hindu Tradition* (Albany: SUNY Press, 1994), p. 164.

2. The Kedārakhaṇḍa of the *Skanda Purāṇa,* 1.1.20.15–26. This is Doniger's translation in "The Scrapbook of Undeserved Salvation: The Kedārakhaṇḍa of the *Skanda Purāṇa*" in *Purāṇa Perennis,* p. 78.

3. This story, with an alternate ending in the epilogue, is a free adaptation of themes drawn from Sāṃkhya-Yoga and Śākta philosophies. It was first performed as a dance-story by Sunday School children in the Unitarian Universalist Church of the Palouse in April 1994.

4. See Carol Cohn, "Sex, Death, and the Rational World of Defense Intellectuals," in *Peace: Meanings, Policies, and Strategies* ed. Linda R. Forcey (New York: Praeger, 1989), p. 49.

5. Cited in Doniger O'Flaherty, *Women, Androgynes, and Other Mythical Beasts*, p. 105. Elsewhere Doniger observes: "In the Indian view the son is made out of the father's self, or actually is that self, and is therefore essentially indistinguishable from him" (*Tales of Sex and Violence* [Chicago: University of Chicago Press, 1985], p. 75).

6. *Śatapatha Brāhmaṇa* 2.1.6.7, trans. Doniger O'Flaherty, *Hindu Myths,* p. 271.

7. *Kūrma Purāṇa* 1.17.25–27.

8. *Bhāgavata Purāṇa* 8.17.23, Tagare trans., vol. 9, p. 1086.

9. The *Mahāvastu,* trans. J. J. Jones (London: Routledge Kegan & Paul, 1976), vol. 2, p. 3 (§2). Even though the Bodhisattva chooses Śuddhodana as a "worthy" father, he plays no role at all in the self-conception of the Buddha.

10. In *Questions of Milinda,* for example, the placenta is simply a passive receptacle for the semen, germinating as a seed does in the earth (trans. I. B. Horner [London: Luzac, 1969], vol. 1, p. 174.) For the Jaina and Tantric views see the *Tattvārthagdhigama-sūtra* 2.31 in *Sacred Books of the Jainas*, vol. 2, p. 70; and Daniel Cozort, *Highest Yoga Tantra* (Ithaca, NY: Snow Lion Publication, 1986), p. 72.

11. *Niddah* 31a; quoted in David Feldman, *Birth Control in Jewish Law* (New York: New York University Press, 1968), pp. 132–33.

12. Carolyn Merchant, *The Death of Nature: Women Ecology, and the Scientific Revolution* (San Francisco: Harper, 1980).

13. Tracy Pintchman, *The Rise of the Goddess in the Hindu Tradition* (Albany: SUNY Press, 1994), chap. 1.

14. J. N. Tiwari, *Goddess Cults in Ancient India* (New Delhi: Sundeep Prakashan, 1985), p. 65.

15. See Mackenzie Brown, *God as Mother: A Feminine Theology of India* (Hartford, CT: Claude Stark, 1974), pp. 126, 134. Śiva makes the same

point in his praise for Durgā: "Through *māyā*, you assume manhood (*purusatva*), and thorough *māyā* you are Prakṛti herself / You are beyond both, eternal, supporting the Supreme Brahman / O Goddess, you have the form of a woman; you are the excellent Puruṣa; and you are a eunuch" (quoted in ibid., p. 136).

16. The *Sāṃkhya-kārikā*, Larson trans, §66.

17. Ibid., §68.

18. Kathleen M. Erndl, *Victory to the Mother* (New York: Oxford University Press, 1993), p. 31.

19. *Sāṃkhya-kārikā*, §57.

20. See Thomas B. Coburn, *Encountering the Goddess* (Albany: SUNY Press, 1991), pp. 134, 145. This book contains a complete translation of the *Devī-Māhātmya* and this will be the translation cited in the next section.

21. Brown, *God as Mother*, p. 128.

22. Aldous Huxley, *After Many a Summer Dies the Swan* (London: Chatto and Windus, 1939), p. 175.

23. *Maitrī Upaniṣad* 4.4.

24. Catherine Keller, "Warriors, Women, and the Nuclear Complex," in *Sacred Interconnections: Postmodern Spirituality, Political Economy, and Art*, ed. David R. Griffin (Albany. SUNY Press, 1990), p. 72.

25. See my article "Three Types of Divine Power," *Process Studies* 20:4 (Winter 1991), pp. 221–32.

26. Cobb and Griffin, *Process Theology*, p. 119.

27. *Devī-Māhātmya* 1.59; 4.6; 11.10.

28. *Brahmavaivarta Purāṇa, Rakṛti-Khanda* 55.87; Pintchman trans., p. 164.

29. Kṛṣṇadāsa Kavirāja, *Caitanya-caritāmṛta* 1.4.83; cited in Edward C. Dimock Jr., "Līlā," *History of Religions* 29:2 (November 1989), p. 162.

30. Thomas B. Coburn, "Consort of None, *Śakti* of All: the Vision of the *Devī-Māhātmya*," in *The Divine Consort: Rādhā and the Goddess of India* (New Delhi: Motilal Banarsidass, 1984).

31. *Devī-Māhātmya* 2.9–12.

32. See Doniger O'Flaherty, *Asceticism and Eroticism in the Mythology of Śiva*, p. 325.

33. *The Laws of Manu*, Doniger trans., 4.186; 11.122, 247.

34. Ibid., 7.14.

35. Ibid., 3.93; 7.5.

36. Ibid., 11.122.

37. Ibid., 4:41, 44.

38. *Devī-Māhātmya* 1.63.

39. Coburn, *Devī-Māhātmya: The Crystallization of the Goddess Tradition* (New Delhi: Motilal Banarsidass, 1984), p. 147.

40. *Skanda Purāṇa* 1.3.1.10.

41. *Devī-Māhātmya* 4.34.

42. Coburn, *Devī-Māhātmya*, p. 154.

43. *Devī-Māhātmya* 1.48.

44. *Sri Mad Devi Bhagavatam* (*Devī-Bhāgavata Purāṇa*), trans. Swami Vijnanananda (New Delhi: Manoharlal, 1921–23), 5.8.55, p. 379.

45. Ibid., 5.8.57.

46. Ibid., 5.8.61.

47. See the *Varāha Purāṇa* 90.29–33.

48. See Sarah Caldwell, "Bhagavati: Ball of Fire," in *Devi: Hindu Goddesses*, eds. Hawley and Wulff (Berkeley: University of California Press, 1996), pp. 195–226.

49. Lina Gupta, "Kālī the Savior," in *After Patriarchy: Feminist Transformations of the World Religions*, eds. Paula M. Cooey, William R. Eakin, and Jay B. McDaniel (Maryknoll, NY: Orbis Books, 1993), p. 36.

50. Ibid., p. 37.

51. See Brown, *The Triumph of the Goddess* (Albany: SUNY Press, 1990), pp. 138–39; 206–12.

52. Doniger, "The Scrapbook of Undeserved Salvation: The Kedārakhanda of the *Skanda Purāna*," in *Purāna Perennis*, pp. 61, 73.

53. The Kedārakhaṇḍa of the *Skanda Purāṇa*, 1.1.20.15–26. This is Doniger's translation in ibid., p. 78.

54. *Skanda Purāṇa* 1.1.21.91, trans. G. V. Tagare in *Ancient Indian Tradition and Mythology*, eds. G. P. Bhatt (New Delhi: Motilal Banarsidass, 1992), vol. 49, p. 189.

55. Ibid., 1.1.21.95 (Tagare).

56. Quoted in Doniger O'Flaherty, *Asceticism and Eroticism in the Mythology of Śiva*, p. 150.

57. Ibid., p. 82.

58. *Skanda Purāṇa* 1.1.21.62.

59. Ibid., 1.1.22.26.

60. Ibid., 1.1.22.95–96.

61. Stanley N. Kurtz, *All Mothers Are One* (New York: Columbia University Press, 1992), p. 31.

62. Lynn Bennett, *Dangerous Wives and Sacred Sisters* (New York: Columbia University Press, 1983).

63. Kurtz, *All Mothers Are One*, p. 143.

64. Ibid., p. 93.

65. Ibid., p. 174.

66. *Devī-Bhāgavata Purāṇa* 1.15; Vijnanananda trans., pp. 52–53.

67. A. K. Ramanujan, "On Folk Mythologies and Folk Purāṇas," in *Purāṇa Perennis*, p. 107.

68. Bennett, *Dangerous Wives and Sacred Sisters*, p. 278.

69. Coburn, *Encountering the Goddess*, p. 222 fn. Coburn is drawing on Cynthia Humes's field research in Uttar Pradesh.

70. See the *Devī-Māhātmya* 3.38; see also *Skanda Purāṇa* 1.3.1.10.68.

71. *Devī-Bhāgavata* 5.10.32–34; Doniger O'Flaherty, *Women, Androgynes, and Other Mythical Beasts*, p. 82.

72. Brown, however, reminds us that the Sāṃkhya *puruṣa* is far less masculine than the Vedic *puruṣa*. The former, as we have seen, is impotent and passive as opposed to the active *prakṛti*. In the Sāṃkhya system, as Brown explains, the "Paursic ('manly') character of the cosmic [Vedic] Puruṣa loses any heroic, aggressive tendencies, becoming absorbed in the image of the quiescent witness. On the other hand, the feminine traits of Prakṛti, at least as they appear in the *Devī-Bhāgavata*, are primarily maternal and nonerotic, lenient rather than lustful. As Prakṛti and Puruṣa fuse in the higher nature of the Devī, she combines the ideal of the dispassionate witness and the compassionate mother" (*Triumph of the Goddess,* pp. 128–29). Brown also observes that there is an important contrast between the Goddess as primarily a warrior in the *Devī-Māhātyma* and her more maternal role in the *Devī-Bhāgavata*.

73. Susan S. Wadley, "Women and the Hindu Tradition," in *Women in India: Two Perspectives*, eds. Doranne Jacobson and Susan S. Wadley (Columbia, MO: South Asia Books, 1977), p. 132; cited in Tracy Pintchman, *The Rise of the Goddess in the Hindu Tradition* (Albany: SUNY Press, 1994), p. 211.

74. Vasudeva S. Agrawala, *The Glorification of the Great Goddess* (Varanasi, India: All-India Kashirag Trust, 1963), pp. 3, 4; cited in Coburn, *Encountering the Goddess*, p. 157.

75. Miranda Shaw, *Passionate Enlightenment: Women in Tantric Buddhism* (Princeton, NJ: Princeton University Press, 1994), p. 33.

76. Rita M. Gross, "Buddhism after Patriarchy?" in *After Patriarchy*, p. 33.

77. Shaw, *Passionate Enlightenment*, p. 11.

78. Cynthia Humes, "Glorifying the Great Goddess or Great Woman? Hindu Women's Experience in Ritual Recitation of the *Devī-Māhātmya*," in *Women and Goddess Traditions*, eds. Karen L. King and Karen Torjesen, (Philadelphia: Fortress Press, 1997), p. 52.

79. Vandana Shiva, *Staying Alive: Women, Ecology, and Development* (London: Zed Books, 1988), p. 6.

80. Alf Hiltebeitel has argued that a Tamil goddess cult of Draupadī is really the original basis of the *Mahābhārata* (*The Cult of Draupadī I* [Chicago: University of Chicago Press, 1988]).

81. *Mahābhārata* 3.31.34–7, trans. R. C. Zaehner, *Concordant Discord* (Oxford: Clarendon Press, 1970), p. 177.

82. *Mahābhārata* 11.25.40–1 in ibid., p. 183.

83. Aditi De, "Draupadi's Daughter," *Deccan Herald* (December 17, 1995), "Articulations" sec., p. 1.

Chapter Seven: Neo-Vedānta and Aurobindo's Superman

1. *The Gospel of Ramakrishna*, trans. and ed. Nikhilananda (New York: Ramakrishna-Vivekananda Center, 1942), p. 432; *Śrīśrīrāmakṛṣṇa-Kathāmṛta* 5.122.

2. Vivekananda, "The Real and the Apparent," in *The Complete Works of Swami Vivekananda* (Calcutta: Advaita Ashrama, 1970), vol. 2, p. 279.

3. Aurobindo, *The Life Divine* (Pondicherry, India: Sri Aurobindo Ashram Trust, 1970), p. 36.

4. *Collected Works of the Mother* (Pondicherry, India: Sri Aurobindo Ashram Trust, 1979), vol. 10, p. 34.

5. K. D. Sethna, *The Spirituality of the Future* (East Brunswick, NJ: Association of University Presses, 1981), p. 72. The full sentence is: "Many a reader of Sri Aurobindo's *Life Divine* has felt on putting it down that the author of this book must be the author of the universe!"

6. Niranjan Dhar, *Vedanta and the Bengal Renasissance* (Columbia, MO: South Asian Books, 1977), p. 143.

7. *Sri Aurobindo Birth Centenary Library* (Pondicherry, India: Sri Aurobindo Ashram Trust, 1970), vol. 12, p. 44.

8. Aurobindo, *Life Divine*, p. 416.

9. Wendy Doniger O'Fhaherty, foreword in Edward C. Dimock Jr., *The Place of the Hidden Moon* (Chicago: University of Chicago Press, 1989), p. xiii; cited in Kripal, *Kālī's Child*, p. 117.

10. Kripal, *Kālī's Child*, p. 118.

11. *The Gospel of Ramakrishna*, p. 31. The many passages that do appear to support the illusory nature of the world and a formless Brahman must be seen as a sign of deference to the many disciples who came from the Brāhmo Samāj.

12. Kripal, *Kāli's Child*, p. 146.

13. See ibid., p. 191.

14. *Śrīśrīrāmakṛṣṇa-Līlāprasaṇga* 1.4.7; trans. Kripal, p. 55.

15. Cited in Kripal, *Kāli's Child*, p. 227.

16. *Kathāmṛta* 4.227 (Kripal).

17. Ibid., 4.143.

18. *Gospel of Ramakrishna*, p. 432; *Kathāmaṛta* 5.122.

19. *Gospel of Ramakrishna*, p. 405.

20. Ibid., p. 432.

21. Kripal, p. 138.

22. Ibid., pp. 140–42.

23. *Kathāmaṛta* 4.36.

24. *Gospel of Ramakrishna* (condensed version), p. 326.

25. *Kathāmṛta* 2.62;5.140–41 (Kripal); see *Gospel of Ramakrishna*, p. 701.

26. *Upadeśasāhasrī* 2.3.1; 2.10.8; cited in Nelson, "Śaṅkara and Classical Advaita," in *Living Liberation in Hindu Thought*, p. 39.

27. Vivekananda, "On the Vedanta Philosophy," in *Complete Works*, vol. 5, p. 282.

28. Kripal, *Kāli's Child*, p. 26. Phrases cited from the *Līlāprasaṇga* 5.12.3.11.

29. Quoted in Narasingha P. Sil, "Vivekānada's Rāmakṛṣṇa: An Untold Story of Mythmaking and Propaganda," *Numen* 40 (1993), p. 46; quoted in Kripal, *Kāli's Child*, p. 26.

30. Kripal, *Kālī's Child*, p. 27. He cites the *Kathāmṛta* (4.296) as evidence.

31. Ibid., p. 26. Narendra was a "lion among men" (*Līlāprasaṅga* 5.12. 3.11).

32. Vivekananda, *Complete Works*, vol. 4, p. 384; vol. 5, p. 439. He was surprised that the temple priests allowed him to "worship the Mother to [his] heart's content," even though he had allegedly been spiritually polluted by traveling Europe and America (vol. 7, p. 239).

33. Ibid., vol. 7, p. 26; vol. 6, p. 147.

34. Ibid., vol. 6, pp. 145–50; vol. 8, p. 253.

35. See Dhar, *Vendanta and the Bengal Renaissance*, p. 126.

36. Vivekananda, "Modern India," in *Complete Works*, vol. 4, p. 480.

37. Ibid., vol. 8, p. 46.

38. Aurobindo, *Mind of Light*, p. 106

39. L. Thomas O'Neil, *Toward the Life Divine: Sri Aurobindo's Vision* (New Delhi: Manohar, 1979), p. 20. "Anthropomorphism is an imaged recognition of the truth that man is what he is because God is what He is and that there is one soul and body of things, humanity even in its incompleteness the most complete manifestation yet achieved here and divinity the perfection of what in man is imperfect. That he sees himself everywhere and worships that as a God is also true" (*Life Divine,* p. 699).

40. Quoted in A. K. Sarkar, *Sri Aurobindo's Vision of the Supermind* (New Delhi: South Asian Publishers, 1989), p. 23.

41. Aurobindo, *Synthesis of Yoga*, p. 591.

42. Haridas Chaudhuri, "Sri Aurobindo's Vision of Supermanhood," *Sri Aurobindo Circle No. 1* (Bombay: Bazar Printing Press, 1944), p. 71; cited in O'Neil, *Toward the Life Divine*, p. 76.

43. O'Neill, *Toward the Life Divine*, p. 75.

44. Aurobindo, *Life Divine*, p. 2.

45. Ibid.

46. See Aurobindo, *Life Divine,* p. 34; see also Nicholas F. Gier, "Dialectic: East and West," *Indian Philosophical Quarterly* 10 (January 1983), pp. 207–18.

47. *Collected Works of the Mother*, vol. 10, p. 34.

48. Aurobindo, *Life Divine*, p. 980.

49. Aurobindo, *Birth Centenary Library*, vol. 18, p. 71.

50. Aurobindo, *The Superman* (Pondicherry, India: Sri Aurobindo Ashram, 1991), p. 6. First published as three separate essays in 1915.

51. Ibid., p. 1.

52. Ibid., p. 2.

53. Ibid., p. 15.

54. Nietzsche, *Thus Spake Zarathustra*, in *The Portable Nietzsche*, p. 124.

55. Aurobindo, *Arya* (August 15, 1915), p. 9.

56. P. B. Saint-Hilaire, *The Future Evolution of Man* (Pondicherry, India: All India Press, 1963), p. 148.

57. Aurobindo, *The Mother* (Pondicherry, India: Sri Aurobindo Ashram, 1928), p. 2. Francis Bacon claimed that science does "not merely exert a gentle guidance over nature's course; [it has] the power to conquer and subdue her, to shake her to her foundations" (*The Works of Bacon*, eds. J. Sedding et al. [Stuttgart: F. F. Verlag, 1963], vol. 5, p. 506.

58. P. Nallaswami, *Śivajñana Siddiyār* 3.2.77; cited in R. C. Zaehner, *Evolution in Religion: A Study in Sri Aurobindo and Pierre Teilhard de Chardin* (Oxford: Clarendon Press, 1971), p. 104.

59. Aurobindo, *Mother*, pp. 36–37.

60. Ibid., p. 35.

61. Ibid., p. 1.

62. Aurobindo, *Life Divine*, p. 922.

63. Aurobindo, *Birth Centenary Library*, vol. 19, p. 960.

64. Aurobindo, *Life Divine*, p. 1067.

65. Aurobindo, *Superman*, p. 16.

66. Ibid., p. 15.

67. Aurobindo, *Life Divine*, p. 40.

68. O'Neil, *Toward the Life Divine*, p. 76.

69. Aurobindo, *Life Divine*, p. 61.

70. Aurobindo, *Superman*, p. 12.

71. Aurobindo, *Life Divine*, p. 976.

72. Ibid., p. 991.

73. Aurobindo, *Notes on the Mahabharat* (Pondicherry, India: Sri Aurobindo Ashram, 1956), p. 57.

74. "World-existence is the ecstatic dance of Śiva which multiplies the body of . . . God numberlessly to the view: it leaves that white substance pre-

cisely where and what it was, ever is and ever will be. . . ." (Aurobindo, *Life Divine*, p. 78).

75. Aurobindo, Śri Aurobindo *Birth Centenary Library*, vol. 19, p. 834.

76. "It is not true to say, as Whitehead does, that God goes on evolving with the evolution of the world, but evolution only exhibits different facets of the multiple nature of God" (S. K. Maitra, *The Meeting of East and West in Sri Aurobindo's Philosophy* [Pondicherry, India: Sri Aurobindo Ashram Press, 1956], p. 431). See also Sarkar's *Śri Aurobindo's Vision of the Supermind* for more Whitehead-Aurobindo comparative work. Unfortunately, both of these studies contain major errors in interpretating Whitehead's philosophy.

Chapter Eight: Buddhism, Humanism, and Titanism

1. Paul Williams, *Mahayana Buddhism: Doctrinal Foundations* (London: Routledge, 1989), p. 169.

2. James B. Robinson, ed. and trans., *Buddha's Lions: The Lives of the Eighty-four Siddhas* (Berkeley, CA: Dharma Publishing, 1979), p. 213.

3. Myokyo-ni, *Gentling the Bull* (London: Zen Centre, n.d.), p. 9.

4. David J. Kalupahana, "Buddhism and Chinese Humanism," p. 11. This paper was presented at a Symposium on Chinese Humanism, sponsored by the Society for Asian and Comparative Philosophy during a special session of the American Philosophical Association, March 25, 1977.

5. Ibid., p. 12.

6. See *Free Inquiry* 3:4 (Fall 1983), p. 7. The members of the Humanist Pantheon and the Academy of Humanism appears on the back cover of every recent issue.

7. Kalupahana, "Buddhism and Chinese Humanism," p. 1.

8. Daisaku Ikeda, *The Living Buddha: An Interpretative Biography*, trans. Burton Watson (New York: Weatherhill, 1976).

9. Soka Gakkai's *World Tribune* (June 6, 1994), p. 3.

10. *Anguttara-nikāya* 4.6.36; *The Book of Gradual Sayings*, trans. F. L. Woodward (London: Routledge and Kegan Paul, 1982), vol. 2, p. 44.

11. *The Tibetan Book of the Dead*, trans. Francesca Fremantle and Chögyam Trungpa (Boulder, CO: Shambala Publications, 1975), p. 10.

12. Buddhaghosa, *Visuddhimagga*, 414ff; *The Path of Purity*, trans. Pe Maung Tin (London: Luzac, 1971), pp. 480ff.

13. Kalupahana, *Buddhist Philosophy: A Historical Analysis* (Hon-

olulu: University of Hawaii Press, 1976), p. 112. See also his *History of Buddhist Philosophy*, pp. 122–23.

14. *Anguttara-nikāya* 4.6.36; *Book of Gradual Sayings*, vol. 2, p. 44.

15. *The Lakkhaṇa Suttanta* in *Dialogues of the Buddha*, trans. T. W. and C. A. F. Rhys David (Oxford: Oxford University Press, 1921), part 1, p. 139.

16. Bellanwila Wimalaratana, "A Study of the Concept of the *Mahāpurisa* in Buddhist Literature and Iconography" (University of Lancaster diss., 1980), pp. 274–75.

17. *Brahmāyusutta* in the *Majjhima Nikāya* II,137; *Middle Length Sayings*, vol. 2, p. 322.

18. See Rhys Davids' introduction to the *Lakkhaṇa Suttanta*, pp. 135–36.

19. Wimalaratana, "Study of the Concept of the Mahāpurisa in Buddhist Literature and Iconography," p. 267.

20. Ibid., p. 269.

21. Cited in Angela F. Howard, *The Imagery of the Cosmological Buddha* (Leiden, Netherlands: Brill, 1986), frontispiece in Chinese with translation. "The concept of a superior form of the divinity, as opposed to the common form, may have been a Buddhist borrowing from Hindu thought" (p. 58).

22. Ibid., p. 61.

23. J. R. Haldar, *Early Buddhist Mythology* (New Delhi: Manohar, 1977), p. 131.

24. See Wimalaratana, "Study of the Concept of the *Mahāpurisa* in Buddhist Literature and Iconography," p. 59.

25. *The Mahāvastu*, trans. J. J. Jones (London: Routledge Kegan Paul, 1976), vol. 2, pp. 3–8.

26. *Questions of Milinda*, trans. I. B. Horner (London: Luzar, 1969), vol. 1, p. 219.

27. Wimalaratana, "Study of the Concept of the Mahāpurisa in Buddhist Literature and Iconography," p. 56.

28. *Mahāvastu*, vol. 2, pp. 19–21.

29. "Mahāmati, the food for my Śrāvakas, Pratyekabuddhas, and Bodhisattvas is the Dharma and not flesh-food; how much more the Tathāgatha! The Tathagatha is the Dharmakāya, Mahāmati; he abides in the Dharma as food; he is not a body feeding on flesh. . . ." (*The Lankāvatāra Sūtra*, trans. D. T. Suzuki [London: Routledge and Kegan Paul, 1932], p. 219).

30. *Majjhima-Nikāya* II, 6; *Middle Length Sayings*, vol. 2, p. 207.

31. Griffiths, *On Being Buddha*, pp. 198ff.

32. Ibid., p. 93.

33. Robinson, *Buddha's Lions*, p. 6.

34. *The Concealed Essence of the Hevajra Tantra*, trans. G. W. Farrow and I. Menon (New Delhi: Motilal Banarsiddas, 1992), 10.2, p. 119.

35. On this and the next passage cited, I prefer D. L. Snellgrove's translation as excerpted in *The World of the Buddha*, ed. Lucian Stryk (New York: Grove, 1968), p. 309.

36. Ibid., p. 311.

37. Cited in Tsong-Karpa, *Tantra in Tibet* (London: Allen & Unwin, 1977), p. 117.

38. Ibid.

39. Ibid.

40. Ibid., p. 121. Daniel Cozort acknowledges that this pride might appear to be contrary to Buddhist selflessness, but he proposes that this "divine pride can actually serve as an *antidote* to the ordinary conception of I and the afflictive pride based on that" (*Highest Yoga Tantra* [Ithaca, NY: Snow Lion Publications, 1986], p. 57). Walt Anderson explains that "this is not the pride of the personal ego, but a sense of awe and respect for the enormous evolutionary force" (*Open Secrets: A Western Guide to Tibetan Buddhism*[Harmondsworth: Penguin Books, 1979], p. 72).

41. Tsong-Karpa, *Tantra in Tibet*, p. 122.

42. *Sāmañña-phala-sutta* 87.88; quoted in Robinson, *Buddha's Lions*, p. 8.

43. Robinson, *Buddha's Lions*, p. 7.

44. Ibid., p. 84.

45. Ibid., p. 149.

46. See N. N. Bhattacharya, *The History of the Tantric Religion* (New Delhi: Manohar Publications, 1982), p. 9.

47. Ibid., p. 282.

48. Robinson, *Buddha's Lions*, p. 213.

49. *Zuimonki* II, 26; quoted in Arifuku Kōgaku, "The Problem of the Body in Nietzsche and Dōgen," in *Nietzsche and Asian Thought*, ed. Graham Parkes (Chicago: University of Chicago Press, 1991), p. 220.

50. Kōgaku, "Problem of the Body in Nietzsche and Dōgen," in *Nietzsche and Asian Thought*, p. 219.

51. *Portable Nietzsche*, p. 146.

52. Kōgaku, "Problem of the Body in Nietzsche and Dōgen," in *Nietzsche and Asian Thought*," p. 219.

53. Quoted in ibid., p. 221.

54. Graham Parkes, "Nietzsche and Zen Master Hakuin on the Roles of Emotion and Passion," in *Emotions in Asian Thought*, eds. Roger Ames and Joel Marks (Albany: SUNY Press, 1995), p. 213.

55. Quoted in ibid., p. 223. No primary citation given.

56. *The Platform Scripture of the Sixth Patriarch*, ed. and trans. Philip B. Yampolsky (New York: Columbia University Press, 1967), §29, p. 150.

57. Ibid. §26, p. 148.

58. Nietzsche, *Human All-Too-Human*, trans. Paul V. Cohn, *The Complete Works of Friedrich Nietzsche*, ed. Oscar Levy (New York: Russell & Russell, 1964), vol. 7, p. 225.

59. *Portable Nietzsche*, p. 511. I have added to Graham's original points on this passage.

60. Ibid., p. 519.

61. *The Will to Power*, trans. Walter Kaufmann and R. J. Hollingdale (New York: Vintage Books, 1968), §384.

62. See Kristofer Schipper, *The Taoist Body*, trans. Karen C. Duval (Berkeley: University of California Press, 1993), p. 172.

63. Steven Odin, *The Social Self in Zen and American Pragmatism* (Albany: SUNY Press, 1996), p. 97.

64. It is Paul Tillich, not Plato, who makes this specific distinction between *ouk on* and *me on*. See his book *Systematic Theology* (Chicago: University of Chicago Press, 1951), vol. 1, p. 188.

65. Odin, *Social Self in Zen and American Pragmatism*, p. 33.

66. Ibid., p. 24.

67. Ibid., p. 61.

68. Ibid., p. 266.

Chapter Nine: The Deification of Confucius

1. Marcel Granet, *The Religion of the Chinese People* (Oxford: Basil Blackwell, 1975), p. 118.

2. Laurence G. Thompson, *Chinese Religion: An Introduction* (Belmont, CA: Wadsworth, 3rd ed., 1979), p. 78.

3. Julia Ching, "Who Were the Ancient Sages?" in Julia Ching and R. W. L. Guisso, eds., *Sages and Filial Sons* (Hong Kong: Chinese University of Hong Kong Press, 1991), p. 17.

4. See D. Howard Smith, *Confucius* (New York: Scribner's, 1973), p. 124.

5. Quoted in ibid., p. 176.

6. Fung Yu-lan, *A History of Chinese Philosophy* (Princeton, NJ: Princeton University Press, 1953), vol. 2, p. 168.

7. E. H. Parker, *Studies in Chinese Religion* (London: Chapman and Hall, 1910), p. 221.

8. Granet, *Religion of the Chinese People*, pp. 110–11.

9. Wu Chengen, *Monkey*, trans. Arthur Waley (New York: John Day, 1943), pp. 7–8.

10. See ibid., p. 284.

11. Anne D. Birdwhistell, *Transition to Neo-Confucianism* (Palo Alto, CA: Stanford University Press, 1989), p. 168. In her excellent study of sagehood, Julia Ching states: "The word 'sage' clearly refers to a great and superior being: not necessarily a god, but a human being whose understanding and virtue may be described as god-like." Ching adds that there were deity symbols in the sage-king tradition, but these were demythologized by Confucian philosophers. See Ching, "Who Were the Ancient Sages," in *Sages and Filial Sons*, p. 17.

12. See Raymond Dawson, *Imperial China* (London: Hutchinson, 1972), p. 141.

13. John K. Shryock, *The Origin and Development of the State Cult of Confucius* (New York: Century Co., 1932), p. 155.

14. Shryock, *The Temples of Anking and their Cults* (New York: AMS Press, 1973), p. 55.

15. See Thompson, *Chinese Religion*, p. 78.

16. See John D. Young, *Confucianism and Christianity: The First Encounter* (Hong Kong: Hong Kong University Press, 1983); and Jacques Gernet, *China and the Christian Impact: A Conflict of Cultures*, trans. Janet Lloyd (New York: Cambridge University Press, 1985).

17. See Shyrock, *Temples of Anking and Their Cults*, p. 57.

18. Translated by Young, *Confucianism and Christianity*, p. 121.

19. Quoted in K. L. Reichelt, *Religion in Chinese Garment*, trans. Joseph Tetlie (London: Lutterworth Press, 1951), p. 55.

20. Ibid., p. 56. Another version of this benediction contains the phrase "the efficacy of the Master matches that of Heaven and Earth," but this is the only allusion that might imply that Confucius has divine powers.

21. E. T. Williams, "The State Religion of China During the Manchu Dynasty," *Journal of the North China Branch, Royal Asiatic Society* 44 (1913), p. 151; quoted in ibid., p. 75.

22. Quoted in Friedrich Starr, *Confucianism: Ethics, Philosophy, Religion* (New York: Covici Friede, 1930), p. 232.

23. Quoted in ibid., pp. 233–34.

24. Kang Yu-wei, *Confucius as a Reformer* 2.1–2, quoted in Fung Yulan, *History of Chinese Philosophy*, vol. 2, p. 678.

25. Ch'u Chai and Winberg Chai, eds., *Confucianism* (Woodbury, NY: Baron's Educational Series, 1973), p. 162.

26. David L. Hall and Roger T. Ames, *Thinking Through Confucius* (Albany: SUNY Press, 1987), pp. 242–43.

27. *A Chinese-English Dictionary* (Beijing: Commercial Press, 1980), p. 608. I am grateful to Chen Lai of Beijing University and Tang Yi of Beijing's Institute of World Religions for making me aware of this mistranslation.

28. Yang Buojun, *Mengze Yi Zhu* (*Mencius* Annotated and Translated into Modern Chinese) (Beijing: Zhong Hua Press, 1984), p. 417. This means that every translator of 7b25 that I consulted has missed this predicative meaning of *shen*. Lionel Giles: "A sage who is beyond our comprehension may be called a divine man"; James Ware: "What remains unknown despite the fact that one is a sage is called divine"; Wing-Tsit Chan: "When a sage is beyond our knowledge, he is called a man of spirit"; and D. C. Lau: "To be sage and to transcend the understanding is called 'divine.'"

29. Tu Wei-ming, *Confucian Thought: Selfhood as Creative Transformation* (Albany: SUNY Press, 1985), p. 152. Tu calls on the authority of Zhuxi on this point. Tu also uses another unidentified translation of this passage that does not deify the sage: "He whose sageliness is beyond our comprehension is called spiritual" (p. 96).

30. *Doctrine of the Mean*, chap. 32 (Chan).

31. Charles Muller, *The Doctrine of the Mean* at www.acmuller.gol.com/contao/docofmean.htm.

32. Tu Wei-Ming, *Confucian Thought*, p. 129. In his commentary on the *Doctrine of the Mean*, Tu makes it clear that "this godlike creativity of Confucius must not conceived as the demonstration of some superhuman quality inherent in his nature. Far from being superhuman, what Confucius was able to manifest can be characterized as a 'refinement' of his humanity"

(*Centrality and Commonality: An Essay on Chung-Yung* [Albany: SUNY Press, 1985], p. 86).

33. Tu, *Confucian Thought*, p. 135.

34. Hall and Ames, *Thinking Through Confucius*, p. 243.

35. Ibid., p. 207.

36. *Yi Jing* 3.1

37. *Analects* 8.19.

38. Ibid., p. 243.

39. Isa. 9:6.

40. Edward Machle, *Nature and Heaven in "The Xunzi"* (Albany: SUNY Press, 1993), p. 162.

41. Ibid., p. 163.

42. *Xunzi*, chap. xvii, quoted in ibid., p. 168.

43. Ibid., p. 92. In a letter to me Philip J. Ivanhoe contends that Machle is overplaying divine agency in this passage. Graciously accepting my rendering of *shen,* he would translate the last phrase as "and for this reason we regard this as marvelous."

44. Ibid., p. 152.

45. Ibid., p. 21.

46. *Xunzi*, chap. xxi (Machle).

47. Machle, *Nature and Heaven in "The Xunzi,"* p. 168.

48. *Xunzi*, chap. ix; Machle trans., pp. 150–51.

49. *Xunzi*, chap. xvii; Machle trans., p. 86.

50. Machle, *Nature and Heaven in "The Xunzi,"* p. 155.

51. Ibid., pp. 185–87.

52. Ibid., p. 103.

53. Ibid., p. 133. In a personal communication Machle mentioned several more phrases like this in chapters 10, 11, 14, 16, 18, 22, 24, and 26.

54. *Xunzi*, chap. i; Machle trans., p. 161.

55. *Doctrine of the Mean*, chap. 24 (Ames).

56. *Mencius* 7a4 (Ames).

57. *Analects* 15.29. This is Ames's translation as found in his "Nietzsche's 'Will to Power' and Chinese 'Virtuality (*De*)'" in *Nietzsche and Asian*

Thought, ed. Graham Parkes (Chicago: Universtiy of Chicago Press, 1991), p. 139.

Chapter Ten: Xunzi and Neoconfucianism

1. Tu Wei-Ming, *Confucian Thought*, p. 21.

2. Y. P. Mei, "The Basis of Social, Ethical, and Spiritual Values in Chinese Philosophy" in *The Chinese Mind*, p. 324.

3. Machle, *Nature and Heaven in "The Xunzi,"* p. 176.

4. Ibid., p. 155.

5. *Xunzi*, chap. vii; Machle trans., p. 111.

6. *Xunzi*, chapter xvii, in *A Source Book in Chinese Philosophy* (hereafter *Source Book)*, trans. and ed. Wing-tsit Chan (Princeton, NJ: Princeton University Press, 1963), pp. 117, 119. Fung Yu-lan's alternative translations are in brackets. See Fung, *A Short History of Chinese Philosophy* (New York: Free Press, 1966), p. 144.

7. Machle, *Nature and Heaven in "The Xunzi,"* p. 86.

8. *Source Book*, p. 117.

9. See the *Mahāvastu*, trans. J. J. Jones, vol. 2, pp. 19–21.

10. See *Analects* 15:4.

11. Machle, *Nature and Heaven in "The Xunzi,"* p. 138.

12. Ibid., p. 120.

13. *Source Book*, p. 122. Chan's commentary is integrated in the text, so I choose not to footnote it. Burton Watson's translation does not differ in any significant respect from Chan's. See *Hsün Tzu: Basic Writings*, trans. Watson (New York: Columbia University Press, 1963), p. 86.

14. See Machle, *Nature and Heaven in "The Xunzi,"* pp. 185–87; and Ivanhoe, "Human Nature and Moral Understanding in Xunzi," *International Philosophical Quarterly* 34:2 (June, 1994), pp. 167–76.

15. *Mencius* 6a15.

16. T'ang Chün-i implies that the Chinese language itself forestalled such difficulties. "The Chinese translation of the words 'subject' and 'object' of Indian and Western philosophy are '*chu*' and '*pin*.'. . . Originally '*chu*' means host, and '*pin*' means guest. . . . It is quite clear that there is no dualism between host and guest. This metaphor is the best symbol for Chinese thought about the relation of the subjective individual and the objective world as mutually immanent and transcendent in an ultimate harmony" ("The Individual and the World in Chinese Methodology," in *The Chinese Mind*, p. 281).

17. Thomé H. Fang, "The World and the Individual in Chinese Metaphysics," in *The Chinese Mind*, p. 242.

18. *Source Book*, p. 507.

19. *Doctrine of the Mean* §22 (Chan).

20. Tu Wei-Ming, *Confucian Thought*, p. 75.

21. Buddhaghosa, *Path of Purity*, pp. 480ff.

22. Benjamin Schwartz, *The World of Thought in Ancient China* (Cambridge: Harvard University Press, 1985), p. 310. Schwartz qualifies Xunzi's utilitarianism as a method dictated primarily by the exigencies of his period. Under better conditions, argues Schwartz, Xunzi would agree with Confucius and Mencius that the virtuous person should be internally motivated rather than be guided by external reward or punishment. Xunzi is especially emphatic about pursuing music and the holy rites as ends in themselves.

23. Tu Wei-ming, *Confucian Thought*, p. 75.

24. *Source Book*, p. 134.

25. Machle, *Nature and Heaven in "The Xunzi,"* p. 127.

26. Ibid., pp. 148–49.

27. *Analects* 2:12.

28. See Plato's *Protagoras* 333.

29. See chapter 9 of the *Xunzi*.

30. *Xunzi*, chap. 21; Machle trans., p. 151.

31. *Mencius* 7a13.

32. See, for example, Sallie McFague, *Models of God: Theology for an Ecological, Nuclear Age* (Philadelphia: Fortress Press, 1987).

33. See Cheng Hao, *Source Book*, p. 525; and *Doctrine of the Mean*, §33.

34. Tu Wei-ming, *Confucian Thought*, p. 132.

35. Ibid.

36. *Mencius* 5a5.

37. Ibid.

38. Tu Wei-ming, *Centrality and Commonality*, pp. 9, 102. Also curious is Tu's comment that the Greek *homo mensura* is not humanistic enough (p. 102), presumably implying that Heaven ought to be humanized as well as Earth. Tu's phraseology is better when he states that the human project is "Heaven's self-consciousness in its own ultimate transformation" (p. 108).

39. Ibid., p. 84.

40. Zhuxi (Chu hsi), *Source Book*, pp. 593–94.

41. Wang Yang-Ming, *Source Book*, pp. 656, 673.

42. Lu Xiangshan (Lu Hsiang-Shan), *Source Book*, p. 575.

43. Wang Yang-ming, *Source Book*, p. 685.

44. Ibid., pp. 690–91.

45. Aristotle, *Nichomachean Ethics*, 1178a6–7.

46. Hall and Ames, *Thinking Through Confucius*, p. 153.

47. *Analects* 6.23.

48. Tu Wei-ming, *Confucian Thought*, pp. 23, 70. Most of the insights in this paragraph come from this outstanding book.

49. *Mencius* 7a21.

50. Ludwig Wittgenstein, *Philosophical Investigations*, trans. G. E. M. Anscombe (Oxford: Blackwell, 1958), §568.

51. See my article "Wittgenstein and Deconstruction" (unpublished) and also my book *Wittgenstein and Phenomenology*.

Chapter Eleven: Laozi, Zhuangzi, and Nietzsche

1. Ellen Chen, *The Tao Te Ching: A New Translation and Commentary* (New York: Paragon House, 1989), p. 41.

2. Gabriel Marcel, *Being and Having*, trans. James Collins (New York: Harper, 1965), p. 70.

3. Schipper, *Taoist Body*, pp. 124, 125.

4. Ibid., p. 126.

5. Quoted in ibid., p. 114.

6. Quoted in N. J. Girardot, *Myth and Meaning in Early Taoism* (Berkeley: University of California Press, 1983), p. 194.

7. J. C. Ferguson, "Chinese Mythology," in *The Mythology of All Races*, ed. J. McCulloch (Boston: Marshall Jones, 1928), p. 57; quoted in ibid., p. 192.

8. See Girardot, *Myth and Meaning in Early Taoism*, p. 177.

9. Watson, *Complete Works of Chuang Tzu*, p. 225.

10. Max Kaltenmark, *Lao Tzu and Taoism*, trans. Roger Greaves (Stanford: Stanford University Press, 1969), p. 101; quoted in Girardot, *Myth and Meaning in Early Taoism*, p. 94.

11. Watson, *Complete works of Chuang Tzu*, p. 87; Graham, *Chuang-tzu*, p. 89.

12. Watson, *Complete works of Chuang Tzu*, p. 122.

13. Ibid., p. 124.

14. Henry Wei, trans., *The Guiding Light of Lao Tzu* (Wheaton, IL: Theosophical Publishing House, 1982), p. 170.

15. Chen, *Tao Te Ching*, p. 137.

16. Ibid. Fung Yulan claims that Zhuangzi's position is the same as the *Daodejing*. The Dao continues to exist but one's *xin* ceases when the body dies. See Fung Yulan, *A Taoist Classic: Chuang-tzu* (Beijing: Foreign Languages Press, 1989), p. 62.

17. Wing-tsit Chan, *The Way of Lao-tzu* (Indianapolis, IN: Library of Liberal Arts, 1963), p. 128; Michael LaFargue, *The Tao of the Tao Te Ching* (Albany: SUNY Press, 1992), p. 62.

18. *Daodejing*, chap. 50 (LaFargue).

19. Ibid.

20. *Daodejing*, chap. 59 (Chen).

21. I am indebted to Schipper, *Taoist Body* (pp. 160–67) for this material on the immortals.

22. Ibid., p. 172.

23. Graham, *Chuang-tzu*, p. 46; Watson, *Complete Works of Chuang Tzu*, p. 33.

24. Herman Hesse, *Steppenwolf*, trans. Basil Creighton (New York: Bantam Books, 1969), p. 110. Nietzsche believes that Goethe was the *Übermensch* of the eighteenth century: "A kind of self-overcoming on the part of that century. He bore its strongest instincts within himself. . . . What he wanted was totality; he fought the mutual extraneousness of reason, senses, feeling, and will . . . he disciplined himself to wholeness, he created himself" (*Portable Nietzsche*, p. 554).

25. Watson, *Complete Works of Chuang Tzu*, p. 86; Graham, *Chuang-tzu*, p. 89.

26. David Loy, "Zhuangzi and Nāgārjuna on the Truth of No Truth" in *Essays on Skepticism, Relativism, and Ethics in the "Zhuangzi,"* eds. P. J. Ivanhoe and Paul Kjellberg (Albany: SUNY Press, 1995), pp. 50–67.

27. *Daodejing*, chap. 40 (Chan).

28. Watson, *Complete Works of Chuang Tzu*, p. 179.

29. Watson, *Complete Works of Chuang Tzu*, pp. 32, 40; Graham, *Chuang-tzu*, pp. 45, 53.

30. Watson, *Complete Works of Chuang Tzu*, p. 43; Graham, *Chuang-tzu*, p. 57.

31. Watson, *Complete Works of Chuang Tzu*, p. 47; Graham, *Chuang-tzu*, p. 59.

32. Mark Berkson, "Language: The Guest of Reality—Zhuangzi and Derrida on Language, Reality, and Skillfulness " in *Essay in Skepticism, Relativism, and Ethics in the "Zhuangzi,"* p. 110.

33. Graham, *Chuang-tzu*, p. 52; Watson, *Complete Works of Chuang Tzu*, p. 40.

34. Ibid.

35. Watson, *Complete Works of Chuang Tzu*, p. 302; Graham, *Chuang-tzu*, p. 190.

36. Berkson, "Language," p. 108.

37. Watson, *Complete Works of Chuang Tzu*, p. 54; Graham, *Chuang-tzu*, p. 66.

38. Watson, *Complete Works of Chuang Tzu*, p. 37; Graham, *Chuang-tzu*, p. 49.

39. Berkson, "Language," p. 108.

40. Kwang-ming Wu, *The Butterfly as Companion: Meditations on the First Three Chapters of the "Chuang-tzu"* (Albany: SUNY Press, 1990), p. 136: Watson, *Complete Works of Chuang Tzu*, p. 37; Graham, *Chuang-tzu*, p. 50.

41. Philip J. Ivanhoe, "Zhuangzi on Skepticism, Skill, and the Ineffable *Dao*," *Journal of the American Academy of Religion* 51:4 (Winter, 1993), pp. 639–54.

42. This is Chen's suggested translation of *guan* in chapter 1. The character *guan* is composed of two radicals "bird" and "eye" (*Tao Te Ching*, p. 54).

43. Yulan, *Taoist Classic: Chuang-tzu*, p. 59.

44. Graham, *Chuang-tzu*, p. 64; Watson, *Complete Works of Chuang Tzu*, p. 51; Plato, *Protagoras* 333.

45. Graham, *Chuang-tzu*, p. 64; Watson, *Complete Works of Chuang Tzu*, p. 51.

46. David L. Hall, "To Be or Not to Be: The Postmodern Self and the *Wu*-forms of Daoism," in *Self as Person in Asian Theory and Practice*, ed. Roger T. Ames (Albany: SUNY Press, 1994), p. 224.

47. See Chen, *Tao Te Ching*, pp. 52–54.

48. See Watson, *Complete Works of Chuang Tzu*, p. 259; Graham, *Chuang-tzu*, p. 106. The complete man (Graham: "perfect man") is above the sage, who is skilled in the ways of Tian but clumsy with regard to the ways of man. The complete man is skilled in both, but he "hates Heaven and hates the heavenly in man," but above all he hates the "I" that discriminates between Heaven and humans.

49. Watson, *Complete Works of Chuang Tzu*, p. 46; Graham, *Chuang-tzu*, p. 58.

50. Watson, *Complete Works of Chuang Tzu*, p. 163.

51. Watson, *Complete Works of Chuang Tzu*, p. 46; Chan, p. 188; Graham, *Chuang-tzu*, p. 58; Fung, *History of Chinese Philosophy*, p. 52; Wu, *Butterfly as Companion*, p. 148.

52. Wu, *Butterfly as Companion*, p. 167.

53. Ibid., p. 320.

54. In the *Shanhaijing* Hungmeng's shamanic "slapping his thighs" and "hopping and dancing like a bird" is intimately connected to a typical Daoist return to *hundun*, here also called the great unity or root. See Girardot, *Myth and Meaning in Early Taoism*, pp. 110, 350 for this and other references to the issue of shamanism and Daoism.

55. Robert Eno, "Cook Ding's Dao and the Limits of Philosophy," in *Essays in Skepticism, Relativism, and Ethics in the "Zhuangzi,"* p. 138.

56. Graham, *Chuang-tzu*, p. 96; Watson, *Complete Works of Chuang Tzu*, p. 94; Fung, *History of Chinese Philosophy*, p. 109.

57. Ibid. Always wishing to tone down implications of the fully spiritual, mainline Chinese Fung has Jixian predicting with "supernatural accuracy."

58. Graham, *Chuang-tzu*, pp. 64, 135; Watson, *Complete Works of Chuang Tzu*, pp. 51, 206.

59. Watson, *Complete Works of Chuang Tzu*, p. 47; Graham, *Chuang-tzu*, p. 59.

60. Graham, *Chuang-tzu*, p. 69.

61. Watson, *Complete Works of Chuang Tzu*, p. 253.

62. *Daodejing*, chap. 55 (Chen).

63. Ibid.

64. Graham, *Chuang-tzu*, p. 68; Watson, *Complete Works of Chuang Tzu*, p. 57.

65. Parkes, "Nietzsche and Zen Master Hakuin on the Roles of Emotion and Passion," in *Emotions in Asian Thought*, p. 227.

66. Nietzsche, *Will to Power*, §691.

67. Ibid., §692.

68. Ames, "Nietzsche's 'Will to Power' and Chinese 'Virtuality' (*De*): A Comparative Study," in *Nietzsche and Asian Thought*, pp. 130–50.

69. *Portable Nietzsche*, p. 307.

70. Herbert Fingarette, *Confucius—Secular as Sacred* (New York: Harper Torchbooks, 1972), chap. 2.

71. Ames, "Nietzsche's 'Will to Power' and Chinese 'Virtuality' (*De*)," p. 133.

72. *Portable Nietzsche*, p. 199.

73. Ibid., p. 480.

74. Nietzsche, *Will to Power*, §490.

75. *Portable Nietzsche*, p. 520.

76. Ibid., p. 143.

77. Ibid., p. 176.

78. See Girardot, *Myth and Meaning in Early Taoism*, p. 189.

79. Watson, *Complete Works of Chuang Tzu*, p. 66; Graham, *Chuang-tzu*, p. 75. This must be a reference to marking off straight boundaries for fields and roads.

80. *Portable Nietzsche*, p. 406.

81. Ibid., p. 427.

82. Ibid., p. 268. Zarathustra says: "I am the enemy of the spirit of gravity" (p. 304).

83. Ibid., p. 153.

84. Ibid., p. 305.

85. Ibid., p. 306.

86. Ibid., p. 269.

87. Ibid., p. 270. In his mountain home at least having something riding on his back is seen in a postive light (p. 295).

88. Laurence Lampert, *Nietzsche's Teaching: An Interpretation of "Thus Spake Zarathustra"* (New Haven: Yale University Press, 1986), p. 165.

89. Nietzsche, *The Joyful Wisdom* in *The Complete Works of Friedrich*

Nietzsche, ed. Oscar Levy (New York: Russell & Russell, 1964), vol. 10, §341, pp. 270–71.

90. Ibid., p. 268.

91. Ibid., p. 256.

92. Ibid., p. 274.

93. Ibid., p. 175.

94. Ibid., p. 304.

95. Ibid., p. 268.

96. Parkes, "The Wandering Dance: Chuang Tzu and Zarathustra," *Philosophy East and West* 33:3 (July 1983), p. 236.

97. Nietzsche, *Will to Power*, §1040.

98. *Portable Nietzsche*, p. 438.

99. Ibid., p. 143.

100. *Daodejing*, chap. 41 (Chen). Giving the inferior person this much credit goes against the usual interpretation of the first stanza of this chapter, but I am grateful to Ivanhoe for supporting me in this reading.

101. Quoted in Griffiths, *On Being Buddha*, p. 73.

102. *Portable Nietzsche*, p. 294.

103. *Gospel of Ramakrishna* (condensed ed.), p. 279.

104. Ibid., p. 351.

105. *Portable Nietzsche*, p. 305.

106. This might after all be a proper burial for a Zoroastrian, who exposed their dead in high places so that their bones could be picked clean for later disposal.

107. Lampert, *Nietzsche's Teaching*, p. 164.

108. *Hevajra Tantra*, excerpted in *World of the Buddha*, p. 308.

109. See R. C. Zaehner, *The Teachings of the Magi* (New York: Oxford University Press, 1976), p. 134.

110. Robert E. Allinson, *Chuang-tzu for Spiritual Transformation* (Albany: SUNY Press, 1989), p. 51.

111. Ibid., p. 56.

112. Watson, *Complete Works of Chuang Tzu*, pp. 72–3; Graham, *Chuang-tzu*, pp. 79–80.

113. Parkes, "Wandering Dance," p. 246.

114. Vicki Noble, *Motherpeace* (New York: Harper, 1983), p. 25.

115. Watson, *Complete Works of Chuang Tzu*, p. 82; Graham, *Chuang-tzu*, p. 87.

116. *Book of Songs* #55 (Karlgren).

117. Graham, *Chuang-tzu*, p. 98; Watson, *Complete Works of Chuang Tzu*, p. 97.

118. *Portable Nietzsche*, p. 199.

119. Parkes, *Composing the Soul*, pp. 163–64.

120. *Nietzsche, Genealogy of Morals* 2.17.

121. Parkes, "Nietzsche and Zen Master Hakuin on the Roles of Emotion and Passion," in *Emotions in Asian Thought*, p. 217.

122. Ibid., p. 228.

123. Nietzsche, *Will to Power*, §958.

124. Ames, "Nietzsche's 'Will to Power' and Chinese 'Virtuality,'" pp. 146–47; *The Will to Power*, §567; *Beyond Good and Evil*, p. 259.

125. Graham, *Chuang-tzu*, p. 89; Watson, *Complete Works of Chuang Tzu*, p. 86.

126. Chen Guying, "Zhuang Zi and Nietzsche: Plays of Perspectives," in *Nietzsche and Asian Thought*, p. 129.

127. Nietzsche, *Joyful Wisdom,* §354, pp. 296–300.

128. Graham, *Chuang-tzu*, p. 89; Watson, *Complete Works of Chuang Tzu*, pp. 86–87.

129. See *Essays in Skepticism, Relativism, and Ethics in the "Zhuangzi,"* pp. 207–8.

130. Ivanhoe, "Zhuangzi on Skepticism, Skill, and the Ineffable Dao," p. 652 fn. 46.

131. Tu, *Confucian Thought*, p. 14

132. Graham, *Chuang-tzu*, p. 89; Watson, *Complete Works of Chuang Tzu*, p. 86.

133. Hall and Ames, *Thinking Through Confucius*, p. 96.

134. *Analects* 15:29 (Ames); *Doctrine of the Mean*, chap. 22 (Chan).

135. *Analects* 6:30.

136. *Doctrine of the Mean*, chap. 12 (Chan).

Selected Bibliography

After Patriarchy: Feminist Transformations of the World Religions, eds. Paula M. Cooey, William R. Eakin, and Jay B. McDaniel. Maryknoll, NY: Orbis Books, 1993.

Allinson, Robert E. *Chuang-tzu for Spiritual Transformation.* Albany: SUNY Press, 1989.

Ames, Roger T. "Nietzsche's 'Will to Power' and Chinese 'Virtuality (De).'" In *Nietzsche and Asian Thought,* pp. 130–50.

Ancient Indian Tradition and Mythology, eds., G. P. Bhatt and J. L. Shastri. New Delhi: Motilal Banarsidass, 1981.

Āraṇya, Swāmi Hariharānanda. *Yoga Philosophy of Patañjali.* Albany: SUNY Press, 1983.

Aśvaghosa. *The Awakening of Faith in Mahāyāna*, trans. Teitaro Suzuki. Chicago: Open Court Publishing, 1900.

Aurobindo. *The Mother.* Pondicherry, India: Sri Aurobindo Ashram, 1928.

———. *The Life Divine.* Pondicherry, India: Sri Aurobindo Ashram Trust, 1970.

———. *Śri Aurobindo Birth Centenary Library.* Pondicherry, India: Śri Aurobindo Ashram Trust, 1970.

———. *The Superman.* Pondicherry, India: Sri Aurobindo Ashram, 1991.

Bennett, Lynn. *Dangerous Wives and Sacred Sisters.* New York: Columbia University Press, 1983.

Berkson, Mark. "Language: The Guest of Reality—Zhuangzi and Derrida on Language, Reality, and Skillfulness." In *Essays in Skepticism, Relativism, and Ethics in the "Zhuangzi,"* pp. 97–126.

Bhattacharji, Sukumari. *The Indian Theogony.* Cambridge: Cambridge University Press, 1970.

Bhattacharya, N. N. *The History of the Tantric Religion.* New Delhi: Manohar Publications, 1982.

Bhuvanbhanusuri, Vijay. *The Essentials of Bhagavān Mahāvīr's Philosophy: Gaṇadharavāda*, trans. K. Ramappa. New Delhi: Motilal Banarsidass, 1989.

Biardeau, Madeleine. "Purāṇic Cosmology." In *Mythologies*, ed. Yves Bonnefoy et al., trans. Wendy Doniger et al. Chicago: University of Chicago Press, 1991, pp. 817–23.

Birdwhistell, Anne D. *Transition to Neo-Confucianism*. Palo Alto, CA: Stanford University Press, 1989.

The Book of Gradual Sayings, trans. F. L. Woodward. London: Routledge and Kegan Paul, 1982.

Boyce, Mary. *A History of Zoroastrianism.* Leiden, Netherlands: Brill, 1975.

———. *Zoroastrians.* London: Routledge & Kegan Paul, 1979.

Brown, Mackenzie C. *God as Mother: A Feminine Theology of India*. Hartford, CT: Claude Stark, 1974.

———. *The Triumph of the Goddess*. Albany: SUNY Press, 1990.

———. "Modes of Perfected Living in the *Mahābhārata* and the Purāṇas." In *Living Liberation in Hindu Thought*, pp. 157–86.

Buddhaghosa. *The Path of Purity*, trans. Pe Maung Tin. London: Luzac, 1971.

Buddha's Lions: The Lives of the Eighty-Four Siddhas, trans. and ed. James B. Robinson. Berkeley: Dharma Publishing, 1979.

Caldwell, Sarah. "Bhagavati: Ball of Fire." In *Devi: Hindu Goddesses*, eds. John Stratton Hawley and Donna W. Wulff. Berkeley: University of California Press, 1996, pp. 195–226.

Chapple, Christopher Key. *Nonviolence to Animals, Earth, and Self in Asian Traditions.* Albany: SUNY Press, 1993.

———. "Living Liberation in Sāṃkhya and Yoga." In *Living Liberation in Hindu Thought*, pp. 115–34 .

Chaudhuri, Haridas. "Sri Aurobindo's Vision of Supermanhood." *Sri Aurobindo Circle No. 1*. Bombay: Bazar Printing Press, 1944.

Chen, Ellen. *The Tao Te Ching: A New Translation and Commentary*. New York: Paragon House, 1989.

Chen, Guying. "Zhuang Zi and Nietzsche: Plays of Perspectives." In *Nietzsche and Asian Thought*, pp. 115–29.

Coburn, Thomas B. *Devī-Māhātmya: The Crystallization of the Goddess Tradition*. New Delhi: Motilal Banarsidass, 1984.

———. "Consort of None, Śakti of All: The Vision of the *Devī-Māhātmya*." In *The Divine Consort: Rādhā and the Goddess of India*. New Delhi: Motilal Banarsidass, 1984, pp. 153–65.

———. *Encountering the Goddess*. Albany: SUNY Press, 1991.

The Complete Works of Chuang Tzu, trans. Burton Watson. New York: Columbia University Press, 1968.

The Concealed Essence of the Hevajra Tantra, trans. G. W. Farrow and I. Menon. New Delhi: Motilal Banarsidas, 1992.

Coomaraswamy, A. K. "Angels and Titans: An Essay on Vedic Ontology." *Journal of the American Oriental Society* 55:5 (1935), pp. 373–419.

Cozort, Daniel. *Highest Yoga Tantra*. Ithaca, NY: Snow Lion Publications, 1986.

De Nicolas, Antonia. *Avatara: The Humanization of Philosophy Through the Bhagavad-gita*. New York: Samuel Weiser, 1979.

Dialogues of the Buddha, trans. T. W. Rhys David and C. A. Rhys David. Oxford: Oxford University Press, 1921.

The Diamond Sutra and the Sutra of Hui Neng, trans. A. F. Price and Wong Mou-Lam. Boulder, CO: Shambhala Publications, 1920.

Doniger O'Flaherty, Wendy. *Asceticism and Eroticism in the Mythology of Śiva*. Oxford: Oxford University Press, 1973.

———. *Hindu Myths*. London: Penguin Books, 1975.

———. *The Origins of Evil in Hindu Mythology.* New Delhi: Motilal Banarsidass, 1976.

———. *Women, Androgynes, and Other Mythical Beasts.* Chicago: University of Chicago Press, 1980.

———. *Tales of Sex and Violence*. Chicago: University of Chicago Press, 1985.

———. "The Scrapbook of Undeserved Salvation: The Kedārakhaṇḍa of the *Skanda Purāṇa*." In *Purāṇa Perennis*, pp. 59–81.

Dundas, Paul. *The Jains*. London: Routledge, 1992.

Eliade, Mircea. *Yoga: Freedom and Immortality.* Princeton, NJ: Princeton University Press, 2nd ed., 1969.

———. *Patanjali and Yoga,* trans. Charles L. Markmann. New York: Schocken, 1975.

Erndl, Kathleen M. *Victory to the Mother*. New York: Oxford University Press, 1993.

Essays on Skepticism, Relativism, and Ethics in the "Zhuangzi," eds. P. J. Ivanhoe and Paul Kjellberg. Albany: SUNY Press, 1995.

Feuerstein, George and Jeanine Miller. *Yoga and Beyond*. New York: Schocken, 1972.

Fingarette, Herbert. *Confucius—Secular as Sacred*. New York: Harper Torchbooks, 1972.

Founders of Constructive Postmodern Philosophy: Pierce, James, Bergson, Whitehead, and Hartshorne, ed. David R. Griffin. Albany: SUNY Press, 1993.

Frisina, Warren G. "Heaven's Partners or Nietzschean Free Spirits," *Philosophy East & West* 45:1 (January 1995), pp. 29–60.

Fung, Yu-lan. *A History of Chinese Philosophy*. Princeton, NJ: Princeton University Press, 1953.

———. *A Short History of Chinese Philosophy*. New York: Free Press, 1966.

Gablick, Suzi. "The Reenchantment of Art: Reflections on the Two Postmodernisms." In *Sacred Interconnections: Postmodern Spirituality, Political Economy, and Art*, pp. 177–92.

Gier, Nicholas F. *Wittgenstein and Phenomenology: A Comparative Study of the Later Wittgenstein, Husserl, Heidegger, and Merleau-Ponty*. Albany: SUNY Press, 1981.

———. *God, Reason, and the Evangelicals*. Lanham, MD: University Press of America, 1987.

———. "Titanism: Radical Humanism—East and West," *Dialogue and Alliance* 1:3 (Fall 1987), pp. 53–69.

———. "The Color of Sin/The Color of Skin: Ancient Color Blindness and the Philosophical Origins of Modern Racism." *Journal of Religious Thought* 46:1 (Summer-Fall 1989), pp. 221–32.

———. "Gandhi, Ahimsa, and the Self." *Gandhi Marg* 15:1 (April-June 1993), pp. 24–38.

———. "On the Deification of Confucius," *Asian Philosophy* 1:3 (1993), pp. 43–54.

———. "Hindu Titanism," *Philosophy East & West* 45:1 (January 1995), pp. 73–96.

———. "*Ahimsa*, the Self, and Postmodernism," *International Philosophical Quarterly* 35:1 (March 1995), pp. 71–86.

———. "Xunzi and the Confucian Answer to Titanism," *The Journal of Chinese Philosophy* 22:2 (June 1995), pp. 129–51.

———. "Gandhi and Mahayana Buddhism"(in Japanese), *Journal of Oriental Studies* 35:2 (1996), pp. 84–105.

———. "Jaina Superhumanism and Gnostic Titanism," *Scottish Journal of Religious Studies* 17:2 (Autumn 1996), pp. 139–58.

———. "Gandhi: Premodern, Modern, or Postmodern?" *Gandhi Marg* 17:3 (October-December 1996), pp. 261–81.

———."The Yogi and the Goddess," *International Journal of Hindu Studies* 1:2 (June 1997), pp. 265–87.

Girardon, N. J. *Myth and Meaning in Early Taoism*. Berkeley: University of California Press, 1983.

Gnoli, Gherardo. *Zoroaster's Time and Homeland*. Naples: Instituto Universitario Orientale, 1980.

The Gospel of Ramakrishna, trans. and ed. Swami Nikhilananda. New York: Ramakrishna-Vivekananda Center, 1942.

Govinda, Anagarika Lama. *Foundations of Tibetan Mysticism*. London: Rider, 1959.

Graham, A. C. *Chuang-tzu: The Inner Chapters*. London: Unwin Paperbacks, 1986.

Granet, Marcel. *The Religion of the Chinese People*. Oxford: Basil Blackwell, 1975.

Griffith, Paul. *On Being Buddha: The Classical Doctrine of Buddhahood*. Albany: SUNY Press, 1994.

Gross, Rita M. "Buddhism after Patriarchy?" In *After Patriarchy: Feminist Transformations of the World Religions*, pp. 65–86 .

Gupta, Lina. "Kālī the Savior." In *After Patriarchy: Feminist Transformations of the World Religions*, pp. 15–38.

Gupta, Som Raj. *The Word Speaks to Faustian Man*. New Delhi: Motilal Banarsidass, 1991.

Haldar, J. R. *Early Buddhist Mythology*. New Delhi: Manohar, 1977.

Hale, Wash Edward. *Asura in Early Vedic Religion*. New Delhi: Motilal Banarsidass, 1986.

Hall, David L. "To Be or Not to Be: The Postmodern Self and the *Wu*-forms of Daoism." In *Self as Person in Asian Theory and Practice*, ed. Roger T. Ames. Albany: SUNY Press, 1994, pp. 213–34.

———. and Roger T. Ames. *Thinking Through Confucius*. Albany: SUNY Press, 1987.

Handelman, Don and David D. Shulman. *God Inside and Out: Śiva's Game of Dice*. Oxford: Oxford University Press, 1997.

Howard, Angela F. *The Imagery of the Cosmological Buddha*. Leiden, Netherlands: Brill, 1986.

Hsün Tzu: Basic Writings, trans. Burton Watson. New York: Columbia University Press, 1963.

Hume, Robert E. *The Thirteen Principal Upanishads*, 2nd ed. London: Oxford University Press, Revised, 1930.

Humes, Cynthia. "Glorifying the Great Goddess or Great Woman? Hindu Women's Experience in Ritual Recitation of the *Devī-Māhātmya*." In *Women and Goddess Traditions,* eds. Karen L. King and Karen Torjesen. Philadelphia: Fortress Press, 1997, pp. 39–63.

Ivanhoe, Philip J. "Zhuangzi on Skepticism, Skill, and the Ineffable *Dao*." *Journal of the American Academy of Religion* 51:4 (Winter 1993), pp. 639–54 .

———. "Human Nature and Moral Understanding in Xunzi." *International Philosophical Quarterly* 34:2 (June 1994), pp. 167–75.

Jain, Prem Suman. "The Ethics of Jainism." In *World Religions and Global Ethics*, ed. S. Cromwell Crawford. New York: Paragon House, 1989, pp. 65–88.

Jain, Jyoti Prasad. *The Essence of Jainism*. Varanasi: Shuchita Publications, n.d.

Jaini, Padmanabh S. "On the *Sarvajñatva (Omniscience)* of Mahāvīra and the Buddha." In *Buddhist Studies in Honour of I. B. Horner,* eds. L. Cousins et al. Dordrecht, Netherlands: Reidel, 1974, pp. 71–90.

———. *The Jaina Path of Purification*. New Delhi: Motilal Banarsidass, 1979.

———. "Karma and the Problem of Rebirth in Jainism." In *Karma and Rebirth in Classical Indian Tradition,* ed. Doniger O'Flaherty. Berkeley: University of California Press, 1980, pp. 217–38.

Kalpasūtra, trans. K. C. Lalwani. New Delhi: Motilal Banarsidass, 1979.

Kaltenmark, Max. *Lao Tzu and Taoism*, trans. Roger Greaves. Stanford: Stanford University Press, 1969.

Kalupahana, David J. *Buddhist Philosophy: A Historical Analysis*. Honolulu: University of Hawaii Press, 1976.

———. *Nāgārjuna: Philosophy of the Middle Way*. Albany: SUNY Press, 1986.

———. *A History of Buddhist Philosophy: Continuities and Discontinuities.* Honolulu: University of Hawaii Press, 1992.

Katz, Nathan. *Buddhist Images of Human Perfection*. New Delhi: Motilal Banarsidass, 1980.

Keller, Catherine. "Warriors, Women, and the Nuclear Complex." In *Sacred Interconnections: Postmodern Spirituality, Political Economy, and Art*, pp. 63–82.

Kerényi, C. *Prometheus: Archetypal Image of Human Existence*, trans. Ralph Manheim. New York: Pantheon Books, 1963.

King, Richard. *Early Advaita Vedānta and Buddhism*. Albany: SUNY Press, 1995.

Kinsley, David. "Reflections on Ecological Themes in Hinduism." *Journal of Dharma* 16:3 (July-September 1991), pp. 229–45.

Klostermaier, Klaus K. "Bhakti, *Ahiṃsā,* and Ecology." *Journal of Dharma* 16:3 (July-September 1991), pp. 246–54.

Kōgaku, Arifuku. "The Problem of the Body in Nietzsche and Dogen." In *Nietzsche and Asian Thought*, pp. 214–25.

Kotturan, George. *Ahiṃsā: Gautama to Gandhi*. New Delhi: Sterling Publishers, 1973.

Kripal, Jeffrey J., *Kālī's Child*. Chicago: University of Chicago Press, 1995.

Kurtz, Stanley N. *All Mothers Are One*. New York: Columbia University Press, 1992.

LaFargue, Michael, *The Tao of the Tao Te Ching*. Albany: SUNY Press, 1992.

Lampert, Laurence. *Nietzsche's Teaching: An Interpretation of "Thus Spake Zarathustra."* New Haven: Yale University Press, 1986.

The Lankāvatāra Sūtra, trans. D. T. Suzuki. London: Routledge and Kegan Paul, 1932.

Larson, Gerald J. *Classical Sāṃkhya*. New Delhi: Motilal Banarsidass, 2nd ed., 1979.

———. "The Philosophy of Sāṃkhya." In *Encyclopedia of Indian Philosophies*, eds. Larson and R. S. Bhattacharya. New Delhi: Motilal Banarsidass, 1987, vol. 4.

The Laws of Manu, trans. Doniger O'Flaherty. New Delhi: Penguin Books, 1991.

Living Liberation in Hindu Thought, eds. Andrew O. Fort and Patricia Y. Mumme. Albany NY: SUNY Press, 1996.

Loy, David. "Zhuangzi and Nāgārjuna on the Truth of No Truth." In *Essays on Skepticism, Relativism, and Ethics in the "Zhuangzi,"* pp. 50–67.

Mabbett, Ian W. "Nāgārjuna and Deconstruction." *Philosophy East & West* 45:2 (April 1995), pp. 203–26.

Machle, Edward. *Nature and Heaven in the "Xunzi."* Albany: SUNY Press, 1993.

Magnus, Bernd. "Nietzsche's Philosophy in 1888: *The Will to Power* and the *Übermensch.*" *Journal of the History of Philosophy* 24:1 (1986), pp. 79–98.

The Mahāvastu, trans. by J. J. Jones. London: Routledge Kegan & Paul, 1976.

Maitra, S. K. *The Meeting of East and West in Sri Aurobindo's Philosophy*. Pondicherry, India: Sri Aurobindo Ashram Press, 1956.

McLelland Joseph C. *Prometheus Rebound: The Irony of Atheism*. Waterloo, Ontario: Wilfrid Laurier University Press, 1988.

Mei, W. P. "The Basis of Social, Ethical, and Spiritual Values in Chinese Philosophy." In *The Chinese Mind*, ed. Charles A. Moore. Honolulu: University of Hawaii Press, 1967, pp. 323–29.

Minor, Robert S. *An Exegetical Commentary of the "Bhagavad-gītā."* New Delhi: Heritage Publishers, 1982.

Mishra, Rammurti S. *Yoga Sutras: The Textbook of Yoga Psychology*. New York: Doubleday Anchor, 1973.

The Mother. *The Collected Works of the Mother*. Pondicherry, India: Sri Aurobindo Ashram Trust, 1979.

Muller-Ortega, Paul E. "Aspects of Jīvanmukti in the Tantric Śaivism of Kashmir." In *Living Liberation in Hindu Thought*, pp. 187–218.

Myokyo-ni. *Gentling the Bull*. London: Zen Centre, n.d.

Mythologies, eds. Yves Bonnefoy et al. and trans. Wendy Doniger et al. Chicago: University of Chicago Press, 1991.

Nature in Asian Traditions of Thought, eds. J. B. Callicott and R. T. Ames. Albany: SUNY Press, 1989.

Nelson, Lance E. "Reverence for Nature or the Irrelevance of Nature? Advaita Vedānta and Ecological Concern." *Journal of Dharma* 16:3 (July-September 1991), pp. 282–301.

———. "Living Liberation in Śaṅkara and Classical Advaita." In *Living Liberation in Hindu Thought*, pp. 17–62.

Nietzsche and Asian Thought, ed. Graham Parkes. Chicago: University of Chicago Press, 1991.

Nietzsche, Friedrich. *Thus Spake Zarathustra*. In *The Portable Nietzsche*, trans. and ed. Walter Kaufmann. New York: Viking, 1954.

———. *The Joyful Wisdom*, trans. Thomas Common. In *The Complete Works of Friedrich Nietzsche*, ed. Oscar Levy. New York: Russell & Russell, 1964, vol. 10.

———. *The Will to Power*, trans. Walter Kaufmann and R. J. Hollingdale. New York: Vintage Books, 1968.

Odin, Steven. *Process Metaphysics and Hua-Yen Buddhism*. Albany: SUNY Press, 1982.

———. *The Social Self in Zen and American Pragmatism*. Albany: SUNY Press, 1996.

O'Neil, Thomas L. *Toward the Life Divine: Sri Aurobindo's Vision*. New Delhi: Manohar, 1979.

Organ, Troy Wilson. *The Hindu Quest for the Perfection of Man*. Athens: Ohio University Press, 1970.

Panikkar, Raimondo. *The Vedic Experience*. Berkeley: University of California Press, 1977.

———. *Myth, Faith, and Hermeneutics*. New York: Paulist Press, 1979.

Parkes, Graham. "The Wandering Dance: Chuang Tzu and Zarathustra." *Philosophy East and West* 33:3 (July 1983), pp. 235–50.

———. "Human/Nature in Nietzsche and Taoism." In *Nature in Asian Traditions of Thought*, pp. 79–98.

———. *Composing the Soul: Reaches of Nietzsche's Psychology*. Chicago: University of Chicago Press, 1994.

———. "Nietzsche and Zen Master Hakuin on the Roles of Emotion and Passion." In *Emotions in Asian Thought*, eds. Roger Ames and Joel Marks. Albany: SUNY Press, 1995, pp. 213–234.

Parrinder, Geoffrey, *Avatar and Incarnation*. New York: Barnes & Noble, 1970.

Pintchman, Tracy. *The Rise of the Goddess in the Hindu Tradition*. Albany: SUNY Press, 1994.

The Platform Scripture of the Sixth Patriarch, ed. and trans. Philip B. Yampolsky. New York: Columbia University Press, 1967.

Patocka, Jan. "Titanism." In *Jan Patocka: Philosophy and Selected Writings*, ed. Erazim Kohak. Chicago: University of Chicago Press, 1989, pp. 139–44.

Potter, Karl H. *Presuppositions of India's Philosophies*. Westport, CT: Greenwood, 1963.

Purāṇa Perennis, ed. Wendy Doniger. Albany: SUNY Press, 1993.

Prem, Krishna and Madhava Ashish. *Man: The Measure of All Things*. Wheaton, IL: Theosophical Publishing House, 1969.

Questions of Milinda, trans. I. B. Horner. London: Luzac, 1969.

Ramanujan, A. K. "On Folk Mythologies and Folk Purāṇas." In *Purāṇa Perennis*, pp. 101–20.

The Sacred Books of the Hindus, ed. B. D. Basu. New York: AMS Press, 1974.

The Sacred Books of the Jainas, ed. J. L. Jaini. New York: AMS Press, 1974.

Sacred Interconnections: Postmodern Spirituality, Political Economy, and Art, ed. David R. Griffin. Albany: SUNY Press, 1990.

Said, Edward. *Orientalism.* New York: Pantheon, 1978.

Saint-Halaire, P. B. *The Future Evolution of Man.* Pondicherry, India: All India Press, 1963.

Sarkar, A. K. *Sri Aurobindo's Vision of the Supermind.* New Delhi: South Asian Publishers, 1989.

Schipper, Kristofer. *The Taoist Body*, trans. Karen C. Duval. Berkeley: University of California Press, 1993.

Schwartz, Benjamin. *The World of Thought in Ancient China.* Cambridge: Harvard University Press, 1985.

Sethna, K. D. *The Spirituality of the Future.* East Brunswick, NJ: Association of University Presses, 1981.

Shaw, Miranda. *Passionate Enlightenment: Women in Tantric Buddhism.* Princeton, NJ: Princeton University Press, 1994.

Shiva, Vandana. *Staying Alive: Women, Ecology, and Development.* London: Zed Books, 1988.

Shyrock, John K. *The Origin and Development of the State Cult of Confucius.* New York: Century, 1932.

Smith, Brian K. "Eaters, Food, and Social Hierarchy in Ancient India." *Journal of the American Academy of Religion* 58:2 (Summer 1990), pp. 177–206.

A Source Book in Chinese Philosophy, trans. and ed. Wing-tsit Chan. Princeton, NJ: Princeton University Press, 1963.

Śri Mad Devī Bhāgavatam (*Devī-Bhāgavata Purāṇa*), trans. Swami Vijnanananda. New Delhi: Manogarlal, 1921–23.

Stutley, Margaret and James Stutley. *Harper's Dictionary of Hinduism.* New York: Harper, 1977.

Sugunasiri, Suwanda H. J. "The Whole Body, Not Heart, as 'Seat of Consciousness': The Buddha's View." *Philosophy East & West* 45:3 (July 1995), pp. 409–30.

Thompson, Laurence G. *Chinese Religion: An Introduction*, 3d ed. Belmont, CA: Wadsworth, 1979.

The Tibetan Book of the Dead, trans. Francesca Fremantle and Chögyam Trungpa. Boulder, CO: Shambhala Publications, 1975.

Tiwari, J. N. *Goddess Cults in Ancient India*. New Delhi: Sundeep Prakashan, 1985.

Tsong-Karpa. *Tantra in Tibet*. London: Allen & Unwin, 1977.

Tu, Wei-ming. *Confucian Thought: Selfhood as Creative Transformation*. Albany: SUNY Press, 1985.

———. *Centrality and Commonality: An Essay on Confucian Religiousness*. Albany: SUNY Press, 1989.

Umāsvati. *Tattvārtha Sūtra* (That Which Is), trans. Nathmal Tatia. New York: HarperCollins Publishers, 1994.

Vajracchedikā Prajñāpāramitā, trans. Edward Conze. Rome: Serie Orientale Roma, 1957.

Valantasis, Richard. "Constructions of Power in Asceticism." *Journal of the American Academy of Religion* 63:4 (Summer 1995), pp. 775–821.

Vivekananda, Swami. *Speeches and Writings,* 6th ed. Madras: G. A. Natesan, 1922.

———. *The Complete Works of Swami Vivekananda*. Calcutta: Advaita Ashrama, 1970.

———. *Karma-Yoga and Bhakti-Yoga*. New York: Ramakrishna-Vivekananda Center, rev. ed., 1973.

White, John D. "God and the World from the Viewpoint of Advaita Vedānta: A Critical Assessment." *International Philosophical Quarterly* 30:2 (June 1981), pp. 185–93.

Williams, Paul. *Mahayana Buddhism: Doctrinal Foundations*. London: Routledge, 1989.

Wimalaratana, Bellanwila. "A Study of the Concept of the Mahāpurisa in Buddhist Literature and Iconography." University of Lancaster dissertation, 1990.

Wu, Kwang-ming. *The Butterfly as Companion: Meditations on the First Three Chapters of the "Chuang-tzu."* Albany: SUNY Press, 1990.

Young, John D. *Confucianism and Christianity: The First Encounter*. Hong Kong: Hong Kong University Press, 1983.

Zaehner, R. C. *Hindu Scriptures*. London: J. M. Dent & Sons, 1956.

Zimmer Heinrich. *Philosophies of India,* ed. Joseph Campbell. Cleveland: World Publishing, 1956.

Note on Supporting Center

This series is published under the auspices of the Center for Process Studies, a research organization affiliated with the Claremont School of Theology and Glaremond Graduate University. It was founded in 1973 by John B. Cobb Jr., Founding Director, and David Ray Griffin, Executive Director; Mary Elizabeth Moore and Marjorie Schocki are now also Codirectors. It encourages research and reflection on the process philosophy of Alfred North Whitehead, Charles Hartshorne, and related thinkers, and on the application and testing of this viewpoint in all areas of thought and practice. The center sponsors conferences, welcomes visiting scholars to use its library, and publishes a scholarly journal. *Process Studies*, and a newsletter, *Process Perspectives*. Located at 1325 North College, Claremond, CA 91711, it gratefully accepts (tax-deductible) contribuations to support its work.

Index

(Note: Chinese characters have been transliterated using the Pin Yin system. The Wade-Giles transliteration is given in parentheses.)